How To Avoid Making The Big Relationship Mistakes!

EXPANDED EDITION

Nigel Beckles

Cover design by Nigel Beckles, Carla Dummerauf (chickmelionbydesign) & Ismael Bennett
www.mercurylink.co.uk

Picture Back Cover: H. Spring Photography
www.hspringphotography.co.uk

Printed in the United Kingdom

ISBN: 978-0-9932426-0-1

Published by: Reflections on Relationships Publishing
Unit 201 Carton House
Kent
ME4 4PX U
United Kingdom

Tel: 01634 813 445

About The Author

Nigel Beckles is a Relationship Specialist and Online Adviser with years of experience of supporting and guiding men and women through difficult relationship issues. Supported by teams of administrators he has advised people from all over the world regarding the relationship mistakes that cause many of us a great deal of emotional distress and heartache. He is the founder of the Facebook groups *Reflections on Relationships* and *Reflections on Abusive Relationships (ROAR)* and a major contributor/administrator for the Facebook group *Narcissistic Personality Disorders Survivors (NPDS)*.

Reflections on Abusive Relationships (ROAR)

Reflections on Abusive Relationships (ROAR) – Support Group is a Relationship Abuse Survivors Network that provides information and support for people who may be going through a difficult time or in "Relationship Recovery." The Group provides useful information regarding abusive relationships and Personality Disorders as many perpetrators of abuse are often emotionally unstable but have not been officially diagnosed.

Find this group at: www.facebook.com/groups/reflectionsonabusiverelationships/

Reflections On Relationships (ROR)

Reflections on Relationships (ROR) is a very lively Facebook Group where we share opinions, experiences and information regarding relationship issues and a wide variety of other topics. We also organize regular social events where Members and friends get together to mingle, socialize and network.

Find this group at: www.facebook.com/groups/reflectionsonrelationships/

Narcissistic Personality Disorder Survivors (NPDS)

Have you ever spent years in a bad relationship trying to recapture the wonderful first few months you spent together? Have you ever found yourself getting angry or upset about your relationship without really understanding why this could be? Is your partner overly jealous and possessive? Have you ever found yourself walking on eggshells with a "Jekyll And Hyde" partner or ex-partner? Men and women with Narcissistic Personality Disorder (NPD) are often dangerous predators who devastate the lives of their victims. The Narcissistic Personality Disorder Survivors (NPDS) Group provides important information and support to members regarding NPD.

Find this group at: www.facebook.com/groups/npdsurvivors/

Over the last few years these groups have grown tremendously, currently having a combined membership of over 30,000 members. Supported by teams of administrators, Nigel provides practical online advice or support on a variety of issues to people from all over the world who find themselves experiencing problems or confusion within their relationships. He is also a contributor to the forthcoming movie/documentary *Looking for Love*, which explores relationships in the UK and is due for release in 2015.

Nigel's mission is to help others avoid the emotional distress that results from poor relationship choices and to guide people towards finding a partner for the healthy, loving relationship they deserve.

For more information please visit the website: www.relationshipmistakesbook.com or email info@relationshipmistakcsbook.com

How To Avoid Making The Big Relationship Mistakes!

CONTENTS

Acknowledgments

I wish to express my deep gratitude to the following people as this book would not have been possible without their love, kindness and support.

My mother, Shelia Beckles, for her support during some very difficult times in my life.

My brother, Nicholas Beckles, and sister-in-law, Monica Beckles, for always believing in me.

My oldest and closest friend, Josiah Oladerin. This book was written on a very old computer that had a habit of breaking down and without Josiah's generous technical support this book would not have been possible.

My cousin Claudia Rock who is always willing to support my endeavors.

Valdene Parris, a dear friend who is loyal and true.

Tony Francis, for his enduring friendship over many years.

Copyeditor Denise Roberts for her diligence and patience!

Thanks to the following Facebook Group Administrators for giving their time and expertise freely:

Reflections on Relationships (ROR)

Myke F. Wilson, Paulette White, Hutchy Bee, Elaine Spice & Basee Saka.

Reflections on Abusive Relationships (ROAR)

Susan Lawrence, Yvonne Glenn, Jam Clock, Myke F. Wilson & Bazil Stewart.

Narcissistic Personality Disorders Survivors (NPDS)

Bryan Thomas Arascain (Founder), Alice Dingham Molero-Herron, Martin Miller & Lisa Renee.

Thank you to all of our active members for sharing so many of their personal stories and experiences.

Finally, deep thanks and gratitude to my Ancestors, Spiritual Guides, Teachers and Spiritual Family for their Protection and Guidance. I salute you!

Introduction

Welcome!

Each of us experience a variety of relationships throughout our lives but it is our romantic and intimate relationships that are usually the most important to us. Many people define themselves based on whether they have a "significant other" in their lives and we all want to enjoy successful relationships. Of course, personal definitions of "success" can vary across a wide spectrum of expectations, but the fact is most of us want to share our lives with someone special. Relationships can be joyful, passionate, fulfilling and inspiring; they can also be predictable, draining, dysfunctional and heartbreaking. Our relationships can provide the greatest joys or cause the deepest sadness and heartache; intimate partnerships have the potential to assist our personal growth or badly damage us emotionally, sometimes beyond repair.

I have made some very poor relationship choices and experienced a great deal of pain, confusion and frustration due to my lack of self-awareness. Eventually, I realized my own unresolved emotional issues had compelled me to become involved with dysfunctional relationships. My personal experiences along with my keen interest in psychology made me determined to find out why I had frequently sabotaged myself while looking for someone to share my love with. This book represents over three years of research into what the top relationship experts have to say about the perils and pitfalls of falling in love. For the vast majority of people intimate relationships are a very significant aspect of their lives yet many men and women believe they have very little control or power when it comes to their romantic choices. There is wide spread misconception that each of us just "fall in love" with some believing our relationship choices are governed by destiny, astrology signs or just sheer luck.

Avoiding the big relationship mistakes is a skill not many people learn or understand. This book contains strategies that will greatly improve your chances of enjoying a satisfying, healthy relationship. The fact that you have experienced relationship failures or haven't found someone special yet doesn't mean you're destined to be alone forever! It's all about making the right choices based on a blend of practical information and intuition. This book is not a "one size fits all" approach to the very complicated subject of relationships but should be used as a best practice guide.

If you're single this book can help you to avoid many of the mistakes, pitfalls and dangerous predators lurking in the dating game.

If you're in an unhealthy relationship the guidance in this book can help you to decide to leave a relationship that is no longer working or is even abusive.

The information presented provides an opportunity to discover that you *can* take control of your relationship destiny and avoid many of the mistakes women make when they're looking for love.

CHAPTER 1:

Love Myths

"A lady's imagination is very rapid; it jumps from admiration to love, from love to matrimony in a moment." – Jane Austen, *Pride and Prejudice*

Myths and fairy tales about falling in love have been perpetuated throughout history by books, television, songs and popular movies. These factors, along with childhood experiences or conditioning, lead many people to believe in certain love myths. They form beliefs that influence the romantic expectations of both men and women who then believe their love fantasies will come true if they just meet the *right* person. Unfortunately, believing in what myths and fairy tales say about falling in love more often results in wasted years waiting around for that *right* person or, even worse, staying in a relationship that is damaging, abusive or otherwise highly dysfunctional.

Let us take a look at some of these Love Myths.

Love Myth 1: Powerful Attraction Or Sexual Chemistry Equals True Love

"Any relationship primarily built on physical attractiveness is predestined to be short lived." – Zig Ziglar, American Author, Salesman & Motivational Speaker

It's very easy to believe strong physical attraction or great sex is the same thing as being in love, especially if you have been single for a while or are feeling slightly desperate. Falling into the trap of trying to create a "relationship" after succumbing to feelings of strong sexual chemistry can happen when you try to convince yourself you "should" feel a certain way. Women often fall prone to this. Because they are more likely to believe it's wrong to have sex just for their personal pleasure they "insist" there must be some sort of romantic or emotional feelings attached to their sexual activity. Having sex can result in feelings of inherent guilt as they believe the only "right" way to sleep with a man is when they're "in love" when in reality they're really "in lust." With this mindset, the only way to emotionally justify a casual sexual liaison is to seek to make the liaison an "official" relationship with a man they have had nothing more than recreational sex with. They convince themselves they're in love so continue sleeping with him even though the overall "relationship" may have serious issues or may be nothing more than a "Friends With Benefits" arrangement. When you try to create a relationship purely on the basis of feeling strong physical attraction it's very easy to be exploited by a man who will enjoy the sex but will have nothing else to offer in terms of a committed relationship.

3

"For me, physical beauty is never the reason for attraction to anyone." – Katrina Kaif, British Actress

Strong sexual chemistry obviously indicates there is a mutual physical attraction. Of course sexual attraction and compatibility feels great but if the attraction is followed through and the sex is mind blowing it doesn't mean you're in love or even meant to be together. Once you fall into the trap of believing strong feelings of being in "lust" is the same as being in "love" there is a great risk of continuing to sleep with a man far longer than is sensible. For example, you may take a long time to recognize and accept the "relationship" lacks overall compatibility but continue to try and make it work. This process of internal emotional conflict causes varying degrees of disappointment or drama as feelings of doubt, discomfort or even guilt about continuing to have sex with a man where there is a lack of any genuine emotional connection inevitably creep up on you. After the physical passion cools down, inherent problems with the relationship usually become very obvious; it just depends on how long the self-deception lasts.

It's very important to be able to tell the difference between having great sex and falling or being in love, otherwise you can end up deceiving yourself by trying to convert a casual sexual fling into a full on relationship that doesn't exist and unlikely to become a serious partnership. Believing in this love myth can waste a great amount of time and energy; it doesn't matter how strong the attraction is or how great the sex is, if you're incompatible in other key areas the relationship will eventually fail.

Love Myth 2: Love At First Sight

"I don't believe in love at first sight but I believe in judging at first sight." – Nikhil Saluja

According to this myth you will know instantly when you have found true love and the search for "The One" is finally over. This truth will hit you like a bolt of lightning from the heavens and in a magical moment you will just *know*. The "love at first sight" myth is so engrained in popular culture it is difficult to escape the concept, especially if you're single and feeling lonely. Women who believe this myth have preconceived ideas about meeting their "perfect match" and concentrate on the positive aspects of their ideal partner. The infatuation could be based on looks, profession, what car he drives, his level of income or social status. They fall in love with the image created within their minds and create a fantasy relationship as they become obsessed with the details of "The One" and his life. This is especially true if a person is feeling lonely and desperate to meet someone special.

Reality Check!

"People who meet in airports are seventy-two percent more likely to fall for each other than people who meet anywhere else." – Jennifer E. Smith, *The Statistical Probability of Love at First Sight*

By focusing on his positive aspects it's quite possible to be blindsided or to ignore possible warning signs that could be telling you not get involved too quickly. Waiting to experience "love at first sight" can waste a great deal of your time – if you believe this myth you probably have a tendency to dismiss men who could be very compatible without ever giving them a chance. While it is important to know what kind of man you're looking for it's a question of balance and being realistic. Building a healthy relationship takes love, compatibility, commitment, hard work and *time*. Generally speaking, there are very few instant success stories in any area of life (large lottery winners being the exception!) and this is especially true of relationships. Many men and women have become involved in relationships based on this myth and made some of the biggest mistakes of their lives.

Love Myth 3: Your Every Need Will Be Fulfilled By The Perfect Partner

"In a strong relationship, you should love your companion more than you need them." – Steve Maraboli, *Life, the Truth & Being Free*

Many people who believe this myth embark on relationships consciously or subconsciously expecting a partner to fulfill their every need. This myth is based on the notion that it is their partner's responsibility to fulfill their emotional, spiritual or physical needs. Such men and women believe finding the perfect partner to share their lives with will make them feel better about themselves. However, such demands and expectations are unreasonable so the relationship ends up being a drain in terms of time and energy on the person who is supposed to be perfect in every way.

▌ Reality Check!

"For a married couple to expect perfection in each other is unrealistic." – Billy Graham, American Christian Evangelist

There is a distinct difference between what you would *like* in a partner and what you *need* from a partner. Most people have a wish list of what they would like in a partner but if your preferences and expectations are unrealistic you're just setting yourself up for failure. Placing all of the responsibility on a potential partner to fulfill your every need inevitably means there are going to be problems. Even with highly compatible couples it is impossible for each partner to totally satisfy all the needs of the other and they shouldn't have to. Expecting a partner to fulfill your every need will lead you to feel frustration, resentment and disappointment. Your partner will probably feel the same and eventually walk away as they become tired of trying to provide constant attention and reassurance.

When you look outside yourself expecting to have all of your needs fulfilled by someone else you are by definition co-dependent. Believing the "perfect partner" is the solution to all of your relationship ambitions is very unrealistic and can even entice you to become involved in unhealthy or abusive relationships. Belief in this love myth leaves both partners feeling totally disillusioned as they attempt to work out why it's not working. In reality, you should enter a relationship feeling independent, confident and fully capable of providing for your own emotional needs. If you're feeling emotionally insecure or empty on your own, being in a relationship is not going to resolve those feelings. The only person who can resolve those issues is you, with professional support if necessary.

Love Myth 4: True Love Will Conquer Everything

"Love conquers all. I heard it in a song, so it must be true." – Simon R. Green, *Ghost of a Chance*

One of the biggest love myths is the belief that loving someone enough will overcome any obstacle or problem. Those trapped by this myth believe their relationship *must* succeed and they will do everything in their power to *make* it work, believing if they just love their partner just a little bit more or stay with the relationship their partner will somehow miraculously change.

Reality Check!

"True love will triumph in the end-which may or may not be a lie, but if it is a lie, it's the most beautiful lie we have." – John Green, Author

There can be serious consequences for conducting a relationship based on this particular love myth. If you're currently in a relationship and believe loving your partner enough means there isn't an obstacle or problem that can defeat real, true, undying love, you will do everything in your power to *make* the relationship work. Believing love will conquer all regardless of the circumstances or your partner's behavior can be a very dangerous love myth to believe in.

Here are just a few examples where love will not conquer all:

- Heavy drinking or drug abuse
- Unsatisfactory sex life
- Different values, beliefs and expectations

Believing in this myth can result in failure to address serious issues, being in denial or setting yourself up to remain in a dead relationship which may be way past its "sell by date". Sadly those who believe in this myth often blame themselves when their relationships fail. They usually believe the relationship could have been saved if only they had given more love to their partner or waited a little bit longer to receive the "pay-off" from their investment of love. Authentic partnerships require commitment and work to stand a reasonable chance of success but you also need to know when a relationship has run its course. The reality is many relationships fail due to a lack of overall compatibility or other major issues, and not just because there wasn't enough love.

Love Myth 5: Only One True Love Exists That Is Your True "Soul Mate"

"I used to believe in one true soul mate, but not anymore. I believe you can have a few."
– Paul Walker, American Actor (1973-2013)

If soul mates really do exist they seem awfully hard for people to find! Despite divorce rates being around 50 percent and the enormous amount of relationship breakdowns that happen every day, you might still believe in this myth. Many people hope somewhere on planet Earth there is a unique soul mate created just for them.

Reality Check!

"The soul mate doesn't have to be a romantic relationship. Sometimes in life, you meet people when you need them, and there is an immediate connection." – Alison G. Bailey, *Present Perfect*

Seeking or waiting for your soul mate is a futile activity promoted by various forms of mainstream media. Many people go in search of the perfect and ideal partner or the mythical "soul mate" and are disappointed when their dreams are not fulfilled. Believing in this love myth can waste a great deal of time because it can greatly reduce your chances of meeting someone who could be an excellent candidate for a relationship. You can dismiss highly compatible potential partners while searching for your elusive soul mate. There is no such thing as the "perfect relationship" or the "perfect match" in the real world.

In the dating game you will meet three basic types of potential partners who will be one of the following:

- Poor matches
- Good matches
- Excellent matches

Seeking or waiting for the "perfect match" is a futile activity because the idea of the "perfect partner" or soul mate is largely a myth promoted by fairy tales or romantic books and movies. The perfect match is a very rare indeed. Men and women searching or waiting for their mythical soul mate end up being bitterly disappointed or disillusioned when their dreams are not fulfilled; they set themselves up for failure in relationships because their expectations are not realistic.

There are a number of potential pitfalls with the myth of the true soul mate. For one, if you believe your current partner is your irreplaceable soul mate and the relationship fails, you're probably going to be reluctant to explore relationship opportunities in the future because in your mind no one else is ever going to be quite good enough. If you do get into another relationship you could jeopardize it by always comparing your lost soul mate to your new partner. Alternatively, you might fool yourself into staying in a dead end relationship with a partner who isn't a suitable match or who is even emotionally or physically abusive.

The myth of the soul mate can lead to another pitfall. It takes time to establish a relationship but some people believe when they meet their soul mate everything is just going to fall into place. This is just not realistic. Every relationship involves a certain amount of compromise and this requires negotiations around various subjects or concerns. The truth is it doesn't matter how good a relationship may be it will probably go through rough patches or difficult times. Each relationship experience can teach us something new and enrich our lives in many ways but remember being highly compatible with someone does not make them your "one and only" soul mate, it just makes someone a good or excellent match. Considering a man who shares overall compatibility with you is a much more realistic approach than looking for your elusive soul mate who probably doesn't exist anyway. High compatibility combined with genuine commitment and a certain amount of compromise, trust and love provide the foundations to build a successful relationship.

Reality Not Fantasy!

"Approach each new problem not with a view to finding what you hope to find there, but to get to the truth, the realities that must be grappled with. You may not like what you find. In that case you are entitled to change it. But do not deceive yourself as to what you do find to be the facts of the situation." – Bernard Baruch, American Financier, Investor & Philanthropist

Love myths and unrealistic romantic expectations frequently get people into all types of relationship dramas which often results in massive disappointment when the fantasies fail to match reality. Women who believe in love myths can be highly susceptible (some would say gullible) to being enticed into relationships by men who are experts at weaving fantasies that closely match their dreams of the perfect romance. Becoming involved in a relationship when you are fantasy-driven is almost guaranteed to end in tears. A relationship based on the fantasies of either partner lacks any real substantial foundation because we cannot rely on fantasies in the real world. Building an authentic relationship requires a balance of being romantic and pragmatic. The idea of being practical about romance might sound dull or you may think this approach reduces any spontaneity. Blending your desires and ideals with pragmatism establishes a significant element of stability based on reality and not just pure romantic fantasy. Maintain a strong connection to reality and you and your partner will build a foundation that keeps the relationship grounded while encouraging sincere and positive growth.

Consider carefully if you believe or act on any of the above love myths. Be honest with yourself. It doesn't matter how much you or anyone else may want these myths to be true, eventually harsh realities will intrude into a world of romantic fantasy. Only by being self-aware, paying attention and being pragmatic will you be in a position to give yourself genuine opportunities to find a viable relationship in the *real* world. Leave the myths and fairytales where they belong, in books for children!

CHAPTER 2:
Relationship Failure

"Failure is simply the opportunity to begin again, this time more intelligently." – Henry Ford (1863-1947), American Industrialist and Founder of the Ford Motor Company

The natural desire of a normal, healthy human being is to love and be loved so when a relationship commitment is made it's natural to expect the emotional connection to grow and deepen over a period of time. A relationship is like a contractual agreement. Each party expects to give and receive certain things, such as love and respect. Discovering your partner cannot or will not maintain a loving emotional connection based on mutual sharing and respect can cause feelings of profound sadness, emptiness and despair. When someone feels the "contract" has been breached or not fulfilled in some way this often signals the beginning of the end.

The reality is most of us will have several intimate partners during our lifetimes and even with the very best intentions, relationships do not always succeed. The majority of men and women become romantically involved with the best intentions yet on average 50 percent of marriages fail. A tremendous amount of "common law" relationships also fail every day for a variety of reasons. Sometimes couples just grow apart. Perhaps at the beginning certain warning signs were ignored or issues which appeared manageable proved impossible to cope with and eventually took their toll.

The decline of a relationship can be a gradual process where the feelings of love and attraction slowly fade away or it suddenly becomes apparent the relationship isn't working anymore. The way it happens is often not as evident as the lack of intense feelings or attraction which no longer exists for one or both partners. Whatever the reasons, it becomes very clear the relationship is no longer viable and you or your partner have fallen out of love.

Of course we should try to make a relationship work if this appears to be a feasible option, but we also need to understand that attempting to change or control a partner in a relationship usually sets the stage for a great deal of conflict. If you recognize your feelings have changed be honest with your partner; do not go into denial or lie to yourself about how you really feel. Healthy relationships encourage each partner to be true to themselves while becoming a better person. When you choose to disconnect from your true feelings it can be very difficult to know what to do for the best. Successful, healthy relationships require both partners to compromise occasionally but constantly ignoring your own feelings and needs just to keep the peace isn't compromise; it's total capitulation. Personal integrity means being honest and saying what needs to be said, not whatever seems to be convenient. The pain at the end of a relationship can be distressing but when you're feeling deeply unhappy it's time to reevaluate any feelings of love that may remain and look at the situation objectively. The decision to end a relationship is not a sign of personal failure but a very responsible and courageous choice; it can take a great deal of courage to admit a relationship isn't working anymore with fear keeping many men and women trapped in unhealthy or deeply dysfunctional unions. There is no doubt the decision to leave a relationship can be a very difficult choice to make: on one level you may want to remain connected to your partner but feel the relationship no longer fulfills your needs and expectations or recognize with great sadness the love has simply died.

The Seven Stages Of Relationship Bereavement

"Sometimes we must get hurt in order to grow. We must fail in order to know. Sometimes our vision is clear only after our eyes are washed away with tears." – Unknown

When a relationship fails there can be deep feelings of loss and sadness over someone who was once a very important part of your life. During a relationship we become emotionally, mentally and spiritually attached to another human being so it's only natural to mourn and enter into a process of grieving. How each person deals with a break-up reflects their levels of maturity and self-awareness: while some people handle relationship failure relatively well, others can struggle with the reality of being single once again. The Seven Stages of Relationship Bereavement helps us to identify the various phases in the process. It can help you to evaluate how you're coping with a recent break-up or provide insights into how you have managed previous relationship failures.

The Seven Stages

Stage 1: Shock And Denial. The reality of the breakup hits home and you may feel numb with disbelief. In order to cope with the initial shock some people may slip into a degree of denial. This is a natural defense mechanism. At this stage you may be totally unwilling to admit the relationship is actually over, which is a very similar reaction to coping with the death of a loved one. A jilted lover may refuse to acknowledge the relationship is over and continue to call, text or arrange to "accidentally" be in the same place as their ex-partner. This type of behavior is known as stalking and is not acceptable. If someone has made it clear the relationship is over, the ex-partner should honor that and leave them alone.

Stage 2: Pain And Guilt. The initial shock begins to subside but now the emotional pain begins to take hold. This stage may be one of the more difficult to manage but absolutely necessary for proper healing to take place. Although the pain may be unbearable at times, it's important to accept the situation and deal with it in healthy ways. Immediately seeking out another relationship (being on the "rebound'), turning to drugs, alcohol or other risky behavior can be very damaging to emotional recovery and personal health. The person may also begin to feel guilt and deep sadness regarding how they may have contributed to the breakdown of the relationship.

Stage 3: Anger And Bargaining. It is perfectly natural to want the emotional pain to end quickly so trying to bargain in various ways to make the negative feelings go away can be quite prominent at this stage. Any underlying frustrations usually begin to surface during this stage and after a person experiences the sharp pain of his or her loss, they may begin to look for someone to blame. Some people can even lash out at their ex-partner or whoever they consider to be the cause of the breakup. It is important to be careful during this stage as feelings of anger and other strong emotions can cloud sound judgment so maintaining composure is vital. The rejected partner may want to ask questions to try to understand why the relationship failed or even find themselves praying for a reconciliation. Alternatively, once the anger has passed, a person may resort to tactics like groveling or making outrageous claims in order to win back their former partner. Unrealistic promises are usually made out of desperation and even if the romance is rekindled the relationship will often fail again and usually quite quickly.

Stage 4: Depression And Loneliness. Stage 4 occurs when it becomes clear any bargaining that may have been attempted will not be successful. The person may appear to give up all hope of rescuing the relationship and fall into a depression. There may be a lack of interest in eating, sleeping, socializing or participating in routine daily tasks. Some people lose focus at work while others neglect their personal appearance or even let their homes become disorganized and untidy. Although friends and family may attempt to console them this may not be entirely effective. The sadness often eventually leads to periods of quiet reflection. This is quite normal and necessary so this stage should not be rushed. Some people may take longer than others during Stage 4 as they absorb and fully acknowledge the magnitude of their loss. Coping with emotions that may still feel raw can be difficult during this stage so it's best to take it easy and seek to maintain calm and objective. Feelings of emptiness, despair and loneliness can be a major challenge but with the passage of time these emotions eventually begin to fade.

Stage 5: The Upward Turn. This stage begins the more positive side of the healing process. As the person starts to adjust to life without a significant other, they begin to feel some relief from the sadness and pain. The depression or sadness may still linger but now they develop a daily mental and emotional routine that doesn't include their ex-partner and life begins to return to normal.

Stage 6: Reconstruction. As this stage begins the person has generally begun a more functional existence and begins to focus on rebuilding his or her life. It's important to work towards redefining the self and coping more effectively in the wake of the loss of the relationship. This may involve setting personal goals such as joining a gym, starting a new hobby or interest, returning to studying or looking for a new job. Stage 6 is also a great opportunity to spend some time looking within and pursuing personal growth while integrating the lessons from the break-up. This can be a very positive phase that provides emotional reconstruction and a new direction in life.

Stage 7: Acceptance And Hope. This is the final stage of the process. The reality of the relationship breakdown has been accepted and is now part of his or her personal history. It's quite normal to still feel the sadness for the loss occasionally but now there is a positive peaceful perspective. There is optimism for each new day with the knowledge that single life can be a great adventure and represents freedom. In the final stage of grief, the dumped partner finally comes to terms with the end of the relationship and is ready to begin truly healing and moving forward with life. While being aware things will not suddenly be perfect and there might still be a few rough days ahead, acceptance that the relationship is over can be fully acknowledged.

Embrace Your Tears

"Life is full of happiness and tears; be strong and have faith." – Kareena Kapoor Khan, Indian Actress

When a relationship ends it can feel like a major part of your life has just suddenly disappeared. You can find yourself feeling empty, lonely and sad and, depending on your age and circumstances, the prospect of carrying on alone may seem quite daunting. Despite what you may have been told or believe, research strongly suggests crying is healthy and helps to clear sadness and stress. Studies indicate crying stimulates the production of certain endorphins which are natural pain killers and work to improve moods and provide human beings with positive feelings. So, generally, it appears after crying people actually feel better both physically and physiologically but feel worse when the urge to cry is suppressed. Crying can help us to cope with loss plus has the potential psychological benefit of lifting our mood. However, frequent and prolonged crying can be a sign of depression, post-traumatic stress disorder or postnatal depression.

Mental health professionals consider various states of depression following a relationship failure to be natural and a normal part of the grieving process. While psychologists have identified the different stages of grief, it's important to remember the progression from one stage to another is totally dependent on the individual. For example, after a breakup a person may find themselves feeling depressed (Stage 4) for three months while someone else may move forwards or backwards through the various stages in a matter of weeks. There are people who can handle relationship failure quite well but others can struggle with the reality of being single. Some experts claim for every year of a relationship it takes approximately a month to recover while others believe if a couple have been together for a year it can take around six months for a partner to fully recover from the split. Another factor in the grieving and recovery process is who makes the decision to leave. The person who decides to end a relationship generally recovers quite quickly when compared to a partner who has been rejected and dumped. A clear decision followed through with action usually results in feelings of empowerment but the rejected ex-partner can be left feeling powerless or inadequate in some way, so his or her recovery time may take longer. Everyone copes with relationship bereavement differently so there isn't a "one size fits all" to each stage or the overall process.

The Seven Stages of Relationship Bereavement can often be a day-by-day, week-by-week gradual process and how a person reacts to a marriage or relationship failure can depend on a variety of different factors including the following:

- Age: A teenager may experience greater emotional pain and distress compared with an adult.

- Experience: A person's first break-up may feel more intense and the emotional pain may linger for a longer period of time than subsequent break-ups.

- Character: Certain personalities adapt to change, failure and rejection better than others. Their Emotional Programming will often be a major factor that influences how they react.

- Support: When a person has a strong support network such as family or close friends the recovery process will usually be easier.

Understand that resisting any stage of the grieving process will prolong your recovery. Blaming, complaining and feelings of resentment after a relationship failure are forms of resistance that can waste a great deal of time and energy. If you have been through a break-up recently, do you keep yourself busy by blaming your former partner? Do you resent being on your own and wish things could have been different? Do you believe your emotional pain is entirely his fault? When we feel confused or rejected it can seem much easier to blame someone else for our pain believing they are responsible, but if you insist on playing the "blame game" for your relationship failures you're being fundamentally dishonest while trying to evade responsibility for your own choices, expectations and behavior. It's virtually impossible to find healing and understanding while you are busy insisting someone else is to blame for how you feel. Pursuing greater self-awareness means asking yourself questions instead of blaming someone else, questions like, "How did I attract that person into my life?", "What unresolved issues did I take into the relationship?", "What did I learn about myself?", and "What lessons can I learn from the experience?" This approach can be highly productive and certainly much better than burning up valuable emotional energy blaming someone else for everything. None of us can expect to attract a kind, loving and caring mate if we continue to insist on blaming an ex-partner for making us feel angry, bitter or sad.

"What you resist persists." – Carl Jung, Swiss Psychiatrist & Psychotherapist (1875-1961)

After a break-up it can be easy to fall into the habit of obsessing about your ex-partner and wishing things had been different but this is also a form of resistance. If you find yourself reminiscing excessively after a break-up try to monitor your thoughts and moods carefully and think about something else whenever you catch yourself pondering about anything connected to the relationship. Focusing on your ex-partner when there is no realistic prospect for reconciliation is a waste of energy and delays understanding the lessons to be learnt from the relationship and its failure. Allow the grieving process to unfold naturally and avoid putting yourself under pressure to get over a failed relationship as quickly as possible. Spend some time examining your role in any relationship dramas. Try to be honest with yourself and to accept responsibility for anything you may have done that may have been unfair or damaging to the other person. This approach provides an excellent opportunity to explore and heal any Emotional Baggage that may be sabotaging your relationship choices. Take the opportunity to embark on a journey of Self-Discovery while enjoying any platonic love and support that comes your way.

Forgiveness

"Forgiveness means letting go of the past." – Gerald Jampolsky MD, *Forgiveness: The Greatest Healer of All*

Human beings make mistakes and we must learn to forgive ourselves and others. Learning to forgive others is important for your mental, emotional and physical health because hating others simply isn't good for you! Forgiveness is a gift you give to yourself and not the person you believe has hurt you in some way.

- Forgiving doesn't mean allowing others to continue mistreating you.
- Forgiving your own mistakes and those of others is the most effective path to emotional healing.

- Forgiveness is one of the major keys to a happier emotional life and better health.
- Forgiveness provides the key to emotional liberty and peace of mind.

If you need to forgive yourself then do it now! Be honest with yourself and take full responsibility for any mistakes you may have made during the relationship. This doesn't mean blaming and shaming yourself, feeling guilty, becoming a victim of those emotions or beating yourself up. If you are struggling to forgive yourself I would suggest you have punished yourself more than enough. The truth is when you cannot forgive, accept and love yourself it can be very difficult to accept and love another human being.

Are you finding it difficult to forgive an ex-partner after a break-up? If you need to forgive someone else you should also do that now! Releasing the emotions of bitterness or hate will set you free from the past to move forward feeling more at peace with yourself. Practicing forgiveness regarding previous relationships may not be easy but will always provide great benefits for your mental and emotional wellbeing. Releasing whatever has happened in the past while firmly deciding to live in the present frees up a tremendous amount of energy that can be used to your advantage.

Letting Go of Love

"Things don't go wrong and break your heart so you can become bitter and give up. They happen to break you down and build you up so you can be all that you were intended to be." – Samuel Johnson (1709-1784), English Writer, Poet & Essayist

Letting go of a relationship can be very hard especially if you're still in love with your ex-partner or have put him on a pedestal believing he is irreplaceable. Maybe you believed the relationship was going to last forever and now think love will never feel the same way again, still clinging to the memories of all the good times shared together. If your partner died unexpectedly you may feel angry at losing the only person who has ever loved you or think falling in love with someone new would be an act of betrayal. Whatever the circumstances releasing your hopes and dreams for a previous relationship requires you to acknowledge the loss and face reality. Letting go can be difficult and sometimes we don't want to let go of a relationship due to fear.

The most common fears include:

- The fear of never being loved again
- The fear of not being able to take care of ourselves
- The fear of the unknown
- The fear of being lonely

Letting go requires facing these fears and taking charge of your own life. There is always a very clear choice to be made: continue to invest your energy in a failed relationship or motivate yourself to accept the present and plan for the future. When a relationship has run its course the best thing to do is acknowledge the fact and to let it go. There will be cases where some space and time is required before one or both partners may decide to give the union another chance, but the golden rule of truly releasing a partner is to do so without any expectations for the future. It's always better to be pragmatic rather than go through the agony of trying to hold on to a relationship that is clearly dead and merely awaiting a decent burial.

Allow yourself to cry and grieve without judgment. Crying helps to relieve deep feelings of grief after a loss and many people claim to feel better after a good cry when mourning the end of a relationship. Keeping feelings of grief and sadness locked in often results in prolonged negative moods or even prolonged episodes of depression. Resist the urge to fight your feelings of sadness, wish your ex-partner all the best and just take one day at a time. Concentrate on yourself instead of wasting time thinking about what could have been or wallowing in feelings of blame and resentment.

The hardest part about getting over a relationship can be letting go of the person as an attachment figure who you grew to rely on for validation and support. Having people in our lives we can trust is one of our most basic needs as human beings; these relationships tend to be close and intimate so the majority of people only have a few attachment-based relationships. Due to the tremendous strength of these attachment bonds, it can be difficult to let go, even if you know in your heart the relationship is over and isn't going to work. The best way to begin detaching is to replace your ex-partner with another person or other people you care about temporarily who can assume the role of a primary attachment figure. In other words, train yourself to stop relying on your ex-partner for validation by spending more time with the other people in your life who love and support you. Research shows that parents, siblings, friends, and children can all make excellent attachment figures; visit family members, arrange to catch up with old friends and remind yourself the ex-partner isn't the only person in the world you can feel close to. Eventually, the ex-partner attachment bonds will grow weaker and you'll find yourself thinking less about him. Sometimes seeing your former partner on a regular basis (for example, if you work at the same place or have children together) can make the "weaning off" process more challenging but generally the less interaction you have with an ex-partner after a break-up the quicker your emotional recovery should be.

While remaining friends with an ex-partner is quite normal, cutting communication for a minimum of 90 days immediately after a break-up is strongly recommended to support the grieving and healing process. This means zero or very limited contact by phone, text, social websites or email.

- Unfriend your ex-partner on Facebook, Twitter or any other social networking websites immediately.
- Spend time with close friends and family so you feel loved and supported.
- Make plans for the future and explore new ideas and activities such as travel, further education or a career change.

This approach provides the time and space to evaluate the break-up and your feelings much more objectively. Pay attention to your feelings and the ways you may be feeding any emotional pain. Notice how often you think about your ex-partner and how these thoughts make you feel. Monitor your thoughts as this gives you the opportunity to distract yourself before they spiral out of control or you fall into the trap of compulsively thinking about your ex-partner. Eventually the emotional pain and turmoil will fade and once you really let go of your ex-partner emotionally any feelings of bitterness or resentment will also go and you will be happy to wish him well. When this breakthrough happens you are truly ready to make plans, set goals and move forward with your life.

Another effective strategy for letting go of love is to formally release your partner in writing after a break-up. For example, you can write a letter or email about your feelings and then decide whether you are going to send it or not. Always wish your ex-partner all the best for the future; acknowledge you have both shared a certain amount of time together but now it's time to accept that particular chapter of your life is over. Say good-bye in writing, out loud and in your heart. It can be a painful emotional exercise but once a formal goodbye has been written you will probably feel much better afterwards even if you decide not to send it. Do not allow the experience of relationship failure to make you bitter in the long-term. A heart that remains open heals much faster than one that has been closed down by feelings of resentment or anger. Finally, while it is a very old cliché, time is indeed a great healer and provides valuable perspective. If you find yourself constantly struggling with overwhelming feelings of grief or loss seek professional support and advice.

Children And Relationship Failure

"Don't allow your wounds to transform you into someone you are not." – Paulo Coelho, *The Alchemist*

When there are children involved in a failed relationship no one should attempt to make them take sides or put them in the middle of any type of power struggle or custody battle, unless they are truly at risk. Name calling and petty or childish behavior is never appropriate. Seeking some kind of warped revenge can make certain parents feel empowered in the short-term but this type of behavior often causes children medium to long-term emotional damage. Responsible parents and adults never use children in the aftermath of a relationship failure. Trying to "score points" by using youngsters as ammunition can have far-reaching and unforeseen consequences. If your relationship fails and there are youngsters involved be a mature adult, maintain your self-respect, put your children first and make sure you protect them from any emotional turmoil. The most effective strategy for ending a relationship is to do it as lovingly as possible without trying to dish out blame or guilt trips. If he wants to try and find love and happiness without you let him go with love. When you give someone their freedom you also give yourself freedom and there is nothing to be gained by staying in a relationship that simply isn't working or cannot be saved.

The Way Forward

"Turn your wounds into wisdom." – Oprah Winfrey, American Talk Show Host, Actress, Producer & Philanthropist

When a relationship is over, for whatever reason, it is time to accept the situation and move on. It can be tempting to put your future on hold hoping for reconciliation but this leaves little room to handle the grieving and healing process effectively. Wishing and hoping for things to be different is not realistic or healthy and many men and women often abdicate responsibility for their own healing by refusing to let go of a relationship gracefully. A relationship failure, although often painful, can be a very valuable learning experience and how each of us manage these experiences indicate our individual levels of maturity and self-awareness. Those who are generally well-balanced, self-aware and emotionally healthy often recover relatively quickly as they understand a relationship failure is nothing to be ashamed of. A break-up can be considered as a huge disaster or part of your journey through life: it's just a matter of perspective.

While every relationship is unique and each break-up is different, the specific lessons for each of us can be very clear if we pay attention. Some people can waste too much time and energy brooding on what "went wrong" rather than taking the time to reflect and learn the lessons at hand. Instead of giving ourselves a hard time about making a "mistake" we should embrace what each relationship has the potential to teach us. When we fail to take responsibility for our part in the demise of the union this sets us up to carry any unresolved issues into the following relationship where we will probably encounter very similar issues. The end of a relationship doesn't usually feel like something to celebrate but these events can present a valuable opportunity for self-evaluation and personal growth.

A relationship failure also opens up new romantic possibilities to eventually meet someone new who may be a much better compatibility match than your previous partner. Living in the present and planning for the future means leaving the past behind once it has been properly understood and any emotional issues have been fully healed. Wanting to be in a relationship and actually being ready for one are two very different mindsets. One of the biggest mistakes many people make is rushing into the dating game when they're not mentally and emotionally prepared. They become involved "on the rebound" looking for someone to distract them from the feelings of failure, unhappiness or low self-esteem. It can be very tempting to look for a quick fix to soothe feelings of hurt and disappointment and when someone is vulnerable their personal judgment can be badly impaired. A sexual adventure, a new partner or trying to rekindle a failed relationship can all at first seem like good ideas for a quick fix to soothe feelings of unhappiness but many people are left feeling much worse when these type of liaisons inevitably fizzle out. Generally, when someone enters a new relationship without fully coming to terms with the loss of an ex-partner he or she is usually setting themselves up to fail. Always give yourself enough time to reflect and heal before deciding to date again. Then, when you feel ready to go on a few fun dates, this can help shift the focus away from the past and onto new possibilities that may have the potential to provide long-term happiness.

SunRa Pictures
PRESENTS

L**OO**KING
for
L**O**VE

A DOCUMENTARY FILM
DIRECTED BY MENELIK SHABAZZ

Are you ready for the raw truth?

Ψ ● VP

IN CINEMAS FROM 21 AUGUST 2015
(See reverse for details) www.lookingforlovefilm.com

CHAPTER 3:
Emotional Patterns And Programming

"Your past does not determine your future, what you are doing now determines your future. You are programming your destiny in this very moment." – Shola Caroline Arewa, *Opening to Spirit*

There are two major factors that usually play a huge part in a person's relationship choices: the quality of the information they possess regarding a potential partner before he or she becomes involved, and their childhood Emotional Programming (EP).

A person's Emotional Programming can be influenced by a wide variety of factors, including the type of upbringing they experience, the cultural beliefs, practices and expectations of their parents, and the community in which they live. Existentialism promotes the idea that we all have the power to recreate ourselves and external factors do not have to restrict or control our thinking patterns or beliefs. This philosophy is based on human freedom and experience, where each individual has the power to choose and shape their own destiny. Determinism is the belief that events are determined by external forces acting regardless of a person's will.

There are three theories of determinism that are generally accepted:

- **Genetic Determinism:** Your character, disposition and temperament are a result of your DNA. Whatever type of person you may be, these traits have been passed down through previous generations to you and therefore your character, personality traits, disposition and other aspects of your character are primarily inherited.

- **Environmental Determinism:** You are a product of your environment and circumstances. Something or someone in your past or current environment greatly influenced you and this now dictates your behavior and personality. Whatever it is – and *it* could be a combination of factors – it lies outside of your control and is responsible for your overall personality.

- **Psychic Determinism:** Your childhood experiences are responsible for your character, personality traits and tendencies. Your parents are primarily responsible for your upbringing and your emotional scripting is now deeply engrained and unmovable.

These various theories of determinism state we do not have any control over our ancestry, childhood or environmental factors and that it is possible a person could be influenced by a combination of all three factors.

Childhood Emotional Programming

"There is always one moment in childhood when the door opens and lets the future in." – Graham Greene (1904-1991), Author

Many researchers and psychologists estimate that during the first five to six years of a young child's life the brain absorbs a great deal of information, a bit like a sponge absorbs liquids. At a very rapid rate a young child learns how to walk, talk and coordinate his body movements. Many psychologists estimate that at age 18 approximately 95 percent of a person's thinking and behavioral patterns have been "installed" or established, which leaves about five percent of free "space." While this remaining five percent may seem a very small amount it is apparently quite capable of "rewriting" the other 95 percent of the emotional patterns and programming. This means personal change is always possible – however, the first step is for us to become aware of any programming that may be sabotaging our relationships.

Central to this is the understanding that the subconscious mind is largely responsible for a person's beliefs, attitudes and behaviors. This in turn creates our perspective on a variety of subjects and the experiences they attract into their lives. Your patterns and programming reside in your subconscious and while the mind uses both the conscious and subconscious, it's the subconscious that is the hugely dominating influence. The human brain is still the most sophisticated computer known to exist. If you think of a computer, it requires both hardware and software to function correctly. Your physical brain is the "hardware" while your subconscious is the operating system. If you have even a basic level of computer training you will understand how Emotional Baggage or damage can be likened to a "virus" corrupting the operating system or programming languages used to operate the system, like HTML, GW BASIC or DOS.

Unfortunately, there are people who are totally unaware their operating system has a "virus" that causes negative patterns of subconscious thinking and behavior. Your subconscious Emotional Programming could be motivating you to make unwise relationship choices. The truth is any negative patterns of thinking you may identify about yourself are not really you –it's just that your individual operating system has a particular virus which needs attention and healing.

The extent of the corruption of your emotional operating system may take time and effort to discover, but once you understand how your corrupted software may have been sabotaging your life you can begin to take steps to remove those malignant viruses. Subconscious beliefs and patterns of thought often influence our motivations, perceptions and self-image. Failing to address a virus or corruption within your Emotional Programming will result in repeating the same patterns and making the same mistakes. There is always an opportunity to begin a journey towards healing. You can make conscious, self-empowering decisions instead of making compulsive relationship choices motivated by unconscious Emotional Programming.

The Inner Child

"The child is in me still and sometimes not so still." – Fred Rogers, *The World According to Mister Rogers: Important Things to Remember*

Bestselling author, counselor and motivational speaker John Bradshaw coined the phrase "Inner Child" in his book *Home Coming: Reclaiming and Championing Your Inner Child.* The term refers to everything we have learned and experienced which is stored in the subconscious mind from conception until puberty.

We were all once children, and the Inner Child still lives within each of us but many adults are unaware of this! There is nothing wrong with being in touch with the positive aspects of your Inner Child, such as playfulness, joy or curiosity but a lack of awareness of the child who lives within all of us is precisely where so many behavioral, emotional and relationship difficulties stem from. You may be an adult but your Inner Child remembers very clearly all the wounds, dramas and traumas from earlier years. Abuse, neglect, being bullied or rejected can be traumatic experiences that affect the way we function as adults.

Even if you had a very good childhood there can still be a few incidents that have left their mark, it all depends on your temperament. A very sensitive child could feel deeply hurt by rejection while another with more resilience may handle the same situation well and emerge emotionally unscathed.

Many of us have inner children who have been wounded to some extent with the pain, fear, sadness and memories of every negative event and emotion still stored subconsciously. This includes everything you have ever told yourself about yourself, whether it was positive or negative. We also have various subconscious states of arrested development within, so there will be times you might act like a three-year-old and other times like a seven-year-old. It is through these emotional filters that a variety of circumstances or incidents are perceived and responded to; in certain situations you may have an intense reaction to something others consider to be relatively minor. This intense (and often inappropriate) response occurs due to the event triggering a memory within your Inner Child who then reacts out of fear.

When you observe the negative behavior of some adults who are impulsive and reckless or displaying childish petulance and temper tantrums, it is clear to see their Inner Child is acting out. For others, the Inner Child manifests as irresponsibility, the angry refusal to be an adult while blaming everyone else or demonstrating dependency, infantile neediness or abandonment fears within their relationships. When the wounded Inner Child has not been healed adults can indulge in a variety of highly negative behaviors, including self-sabotage and toxic behavior toward others.

In a relationship there may be incidents where each of you are bringing out the Inner Child in the other, which inevitably causes problems. Your partner's true emotional age will usually be revealed when certain behaviors or events trigger an emotional response that causes the hurt Inner Child to suddenly jump straight out! A husband may get home late for legitimate reasons but his wife over reacts due to childhood feelings of abandonment. A wife may be trying to be helpful and remind her husband about something but he feels unjustly criticized and becomes angry, reverting back to the child who always felt unfairly chastised when his mother pointed out his mistakes. Men and women can have a subconscious tendency to choose partners to reenact parental scenarios. These scenarios can be played out as assumed by the adult as a child, or he or she may play out a different mental script and try to recreate the scenario as they wanted it to be. The Inner Child senses who the right type of partner is to reenact their parents' actual or perceived relationship dynamics, but it doesn't understand what you truly require as an adult.

It is important to understand that there can be a big difference between your physical or chronological age and your true *psychological* or emotional age; at a psychologically level many adults are not adults all the time because their Inner Child is still dictating how they, a) select partners, and b) conduct themselves in their relationships. Are you choosing your partners using the reasoning of your actual age or your emotional 15-year-old self? Your poor relationship choices could be the teenager within you choosing your partners instead of your adult self. Many adults remain unconsciously influenced or directly controlled by their Inner Child. They believe they're in charge of their lives, but it's the emotionally wounded Inner Child who is really calling the shots.

If you had a difficult childhood you may have told yourself you have outgrown any previous hurts, fears or feelings of anger but this simply isn't true. Those emotions are very much alive within your subconscious programming, influencing your behavior and choices.

If you were brought up by a single parent your emotional age is less likely to match your physical age as there tends to be gaps and deficiencies due to the family structure. Becoming aware of the potential gap between your physical and emotional ages is key to resolving any issues from your childhood.

If you have generally experienced a lack of healthy, intimate relationships, your unhealed Inner Child could be the reason you have been sabotaging yourself. In his book John Bradshaw suggests a six-step process that can help to heal a wounded Inner Child. They are as follows:

1. Trust

To encourage your wounded Inner Child to reveal him or herself they must be able to trust that you will be supportive. The Inner Child requires any feelings of abandonment, neglect or abuse to be acknowledged. This is the first step towards healing.

2. Validation

If you have a tendency to minimize and/or rationalize the ways you may have been shamed, ignored or used by your parents, accept these things truly wounded your soul. Your parents were not necessarily bad or evil and quite likely are wounded children walking around in adult bodies themselves.

3. Shock And Anger

Shock and anger are normal emotions during any grieving process. Feelings of anger are also essential as part of the healing of the Inner Child and expressing that anger appropriately regarding any intentional or unintentional childhood experiences is natural and healthy. Acknowledgment of your parents' behavior represents the best a wounded adult child can do. Be aware you were deeply wounded emotionally or spiritually and that this has had serious consequences.

4. Sadness

The emotions of anger are followed by feelings of hurt and sadness. If you felt victimized by your parents/guardians, you must grieve that betrayal and any dreams or aspirations that may have been frustrated or destroyed. Most importantly, any unfulfilled developmental needs should also be acknowledged and grieved.

5. Remorse

When we grieve for a loved one who has died feelings of remorse are appropriate; for example, wishing you had spent more time with the deceased person. While grieving childhood wounds or even abandonment, it is important to help your wounded Inner Child to see he/she was often powerless and there was nothing that could have been done to influence or prevent whatever happened. Do not ignore or try to repress feelings of remorse regarding any negative childhood experiences.

6. Loneliness

The deepest core feelings of grief are toxic shame and loneliness. The Inner Child can feel rejected, shamed and abandoned by their parents. Feelings of worthlessness and shame often leads to feelings of deep loneliness. As the Inner Child feels deeply flawed and defective, he/she has to cover up their true selves with an adapted, false self and eventually identifies themselves with this reconstructed but false self. The true self remains isolated and alone.

This stage of loneliness is usually the most difficult stage of the grieving process for the Inner Child but as these feelings are fully embraced this helps you to create the internal space for the healing to begin. By embracing feelings of shame and loneliness, the individual begins to get in touch with their Inner Child and with the true self. This supports the process of building a relationship with the Inner Child and caring for him or her.

Situations, circumstances, experiences and relationships that remind you of past unhealed wounds do not have to act as compulsive triggers. You can assure your Inner Child that the "adult you" can keep him or her safe and take constructive action to protect that part of yourself that feels vulnerable and afraid at certain times. This doesn't mean living in the past but taking steps to understand and heal anything from your past that impacts negatively on your Inner Child. It means supporting your Inner Child so he/she feels safe; when you raise your self-awareness you may discover how to intuitively make things feel safer for the child who still lives within you.

Just because you're an adult doesn't mean you can't still be playful, silly or joyful! Staying in touch and expressing your Inner Child can bring the adult you as well as others magical moments and great happiness. Acknowledge the playfulness of your Inner Child while honoring your emotional, physical and spiritual needs. Learn to connect with your family and friends and to ask for what you need from them on an emotional level. Also, cultivate your personal boundaries and practice saying "no" when appropriate for your own emotional health and self-esteem.

Spend time alone to process your feelings while discovering and nurturing the connection with your Inner Child. Include exercise, yoga, massage, rest, regular sleep, times for relaxation and healthy nutrition and take steps to eliminate any bad habits that manifest as trying to discharge negative energy, like smoking cigarettes or drinking excessive amounts of alcohol. Practice your spirituality or religious faith and support your soul through your work or personal interests while honoring and expressing those activities that define you or bring you joy. Consider natural healing practices such as meditation or energy healing work to help clear old patterns to assist your healing. If you have experienced trauma during childhood, seriously consider consulting a professional therapist or counselor. The Twelve-step program recovery movement considers healing the Inner Child to be one of the essential stages in recovery from addiction, abuse, trauma or post-traumatic stress disorder.

Recognizing and supporting the needs of your Inner Child will improve your overall emotional and physical wellbeing and self-confidence. Your personal and professional relationships will benefit as you feel more at ease with yourself because you will be less inclined to let people or events trigger a negative response from your Inner Child.

Unresolved Childhood Emotional Issues

"What you do not master in childhood reappears in your adult lives as inappropriate responses to people, places, or things. It is these inappropriate responses that cause you discomfort. They are outgrowths of the pain and fear experienced in childhood when basic needs were not filled." – Cathryn L. Taylor, *The Inner Child Workbook*

Bradshaw claims that as children we are all egocentric. Egocentric in this context doesn't mean children are selfish or even capable of moral reasoning generally – that doesn't happen until around the age of seven or eight years old. But even at a young age there will probably still be egocentric aspects to a child's perspective. Bradshaw states that during the first three years of our childhood years each of us needs to feel admired, taken seriously and, most importantly, accepted.

A young child can interpret events egocentrically and take everything personally. For example,

- If ignored he or she feels unworthy of their parents' time or attention.
- If one or both parents are not present the child assumes it's his or her fault.
- If one or both parents are not present the child takes this personally and assumes there must be something wrong with him or her.
- When one or both parents are not present a child will often feel rejected.

Children need to feel that they will not be abandoned and they are loved and valued by their parents or guardians. When a child experiences the effects of divorce, abandonment, death or conditional love, the parental bond is broken. As adults they can feel unlovable and this often creates an inability to relate in healthy ways to themselves or toward others.

Parents and guardians should also provide "mirroring" for their babies or young children. This lets the child know someone is there for him or her who consistently reflects back their existence while providing feelings of identity and security. Psychiatrist Karen Horney identified feelings of childhood insecurity as "basic anxiety" and observed a wide range of adverse factors in a child's environment that can produce feelings of insecurity including:

- Direct or indirect domination

- Intolerance
- Erratic behavior of parents
- A lack of respect for the child's needs
- A lack of guidance
- Disapproving or disparaging parental attitudes
- A hostile atmosphere
- Too much admiration or a lack of positive encouragement
- A lack of reliable love and warmth
- Having to take sides in parental disagreements
- Too much or too little responsibility
- Over protection
- Isolation from other children
- Unfair treatment or broken promises

These childhood experiences often result in subconscious patterns of adopting negative behavior patterns from our parents where we become adults who:

- Hope our parents will love us if we are like them.
- Punish our parents by reflecting negativity back towards them.
- Punish ourselves for feeling unworthy and unlovable.

Our early experience with our parents has a profound effect on our lives, shaping our self-image, attitudes and behavior. Parents are not just role models for young children; they appear to be gods, but the reality is parents are human beings with positive and negative behavioral patterns that their children often internalize. When a parent expresses anger, impatience, contempt, indifference, neglect, or abuses the child in any way, the child assumes it's his or her fault and not the parent's responsibility. Children are not usually capable of recognizing or acknowledging the faults or abuse of their parents, but can still unconsciously imitate their parent's faults and inadequacies (behaviors, attitudes and moods) trying to be accepted. When abusive or toxic parental behavior is consistent their children often grow into adults who experience the world in very similar ways to their parents.

"We learn beliefs, and we can unlearn them. We can decide to keep or not any belief imposed on and absorbed by us, no matter the source. If any belief withholds a fulfilling life from us, we have a responsibility to give it real thought and reassessment." – Joyce Shafer, *I Don't Want to Be Your Guru, But I Have Something to Say*

Each child is born with needs that must be satisfied by their parents who should provide a constant flow of unconditional love and attention. This provides the foundation for children to become emotionally healthy and well-balanced adults.

How Parents Can Influence Your Relationship Choices

"The part of your brain that directed your search for a mate wasn't your logical, orderly new (adult) brain; it was your time locked myopic (short sighted) old (infant/child) brain. And what your old infant brain was trying to do (now in an adult body) was trying to recreate the conditions of your upbringing in order to correct them. Having received enough nurturing to survive but not enough to feel satisfied the brain was attempting to return to the scene of your original frustration so that you could resolve your unfinished business." – Author & Psychologist Harville Hendrix, *Getting the Love You Want: A Guide For Couples*

The adult you are today is a direct byproduct of the relationships observed and experienced during your childhood. Whatever you have learnt about negotiating, intimate relating, intimacy and power along with your expectations in terms of relationship fulfillment are modeled on the early relationships you witnessed as a child. The relationships we have with our parents consistently molds our beliefs about what is expected and acceptable, which has a great influence on the type of relationships we experience as adults.

Without being consciously aware of what we are doing, many of us can be attracted to partners with similar characteristics of our mothers or fathers. While it is obvious we are not our parents there can be powerful subconscious compulsion to be just like them!

In his book *Getting the Love You Want: A Guide For Couples,* psychologist Harville Hendrix describes the quest some people have for the "ideal" partner as a search for a certain blend of traits he calls the "imago." Hendrix believes each of us seeks a familiar mix of both the positive and negative characteristics with which we were raised by our parents or caretakers. Every significant detail of how we were talked to, touched, and taught along with the physical, emotional, and mental attributes of our parents is recorded by our young brains. When we become adults and interact with others, we are attracted to those who most closely match or resemble those early images within our subconscious mind. Hendrix concludes that many people are subconsciously attracted to partners who possess their parent's positive and negative traits but believes the negative traits are consistently more attractive and influential when we make our relationship choices.

You may tell yourself, "I will never marry an alcoholic like my father," but have a pattern of becoming involved with men who drink too much. A man might say to himself he will never have a relationship with a verbally abusive woman just like his mother but somehow keeps falling in love with women who are verbally abusive. Your **conscious** intention will be to find a partner who isn't like your mother or father and during the early stages of the relationship everything will seem perfect, but gradually you realize he has the main negative characteristics or behaviors of one or both of your parents. Why does this happen? Because the conscious mind is looking for one thing while the subconscious mind is looking for something else.

Many people have a tendency to play out the emotional issues of one parent and subconsciously choose partners who will play or reenact the other parent's role in the relationship. As a child you were incapable of distinguishing subtle interactions between your parents so your interpretation within your adult mind may consist of polarized relationship scenarios. Subconsciously you then play out these scenarios with your partner, for example: Mother was a "giver" while Father was a "taker" or one parent is seen as being "bad" while the other was considered to be "good." This subconscious process can be even more prevalent and have a greater impact if one of your parents were absent during your childhood and you were fed negative stories regarding the mother or father who wasn't around.

Formative Years > Influences Thinking & Beliefs > Creates Personal Patterns/ Emotional Programming = Potential to Greatly Influence Relationship Choices.

You may be a fully grown adult but could still be playing out the parental influences or interactions you observed during your childhood.

Any type of unresolved emotional business can motivate men and women to subconsciously try and resolve their unfulfilled childhood desires. Often when the primary desires of feeling loved or witnessing parents being loving toward each other are not fulfilled, a child can become an adult who constantly feels "something" is missing or incomplete. Sadly, some are driven to recreate scenarios and are unconsciously attracted to people or situations seeking to recreate their childhood experiences with the purpose of resolving those issues.

Childhood Emotional Baggage can manifest in your relationships in various ways, for example:

- If one (or both) of your parents failed to give you the love and attention you desired you could attract and become involved with someone who makes you struggle to get their love and attention or who is cold and distant.
- If you were angry with one (or both) of your parents as a child and still feel this anger you could become involved with someone who loves you but you could struggle to give them your love and attention or have a pattern of either hurting or rejecting them.
- If you have anger issues regarding your parent(s) because they hurt you in some way, you could enter relationships with the subconscious intention of wanting to hurt your partner.

These patterns of behavior represent attempts to end the sense of separation from our parents that we experienced as children when they behaved in negative ways. We can spontaneously adopt their patterns of behavior to experience feeling connected to them again, even if they are not currently involved in our lives.

If you had a difficult relationship with either or both of your parents, the only way to begin your emotional healing is to work through the issues so you can forgive them for any dysfunctional behaviors or attitudes. Sadly, many adults continue to compulsively act out negative patterns from their childhoods seeking to recreate or resolve scenarios because they want to feel loved and wanted but their behaviour causes alienation or rejection. For example, when a young boy or teenager has an emotionally difficult relationship with his mother he is more likely to have difficulties with the opposite sex in later life. If a woman has conflicts with her father the same holds true. Many people subconsciously pursue relationship experiences that recreate situations from their childhood experiences and very often it doesn't matter if those scenarios were positive or negative.

When their negative and dysfunctional behavior doesn't provide the love they crave these people end up blaming their partners. Feelings of bitterness and resentment, and being hurtful towards others and themselves often results in reinforcing feelings of remorse, guilt, and shame. These people often believe they're deeply flawed in some way and beat up on themselves emotionally.

Each person's childhood experiences greatly influences their attitudes, preferences and choices. You may be very resistant to the idea of exploring your childhood experiences believing whatever is in the past is "dead" and irrelevant but nothing dies emotionally until it has been fully processed and accepted.

Childhood Emotional Baggage can be mild, moderate or severe but there is always the opportunity to embark on a journey towards healing! You can begin making conscious, self-empowering decisions instead of compulsive relationship choices motivated by the unconscious Emotional Programming of your wounded Inner Child. If you find yourself struggling with issues from your childhood join a support group or consult a qualified therapist/counselor who has worked alongside others with similar experiences. Studying your childhood can help you to identify any wounds that require healing, help you to avoid making the same mistakes and greatly increase your chances of enjoying a happy, healthy relationship.

CHAPTER 4:

The Process of Self-Discovery (PSD)

"Know Thyself" – African Proverb

Do you really know who you are? Are you fully in touch with your feelings? How do you honestly feel about yourself? Are your actions and behavior consistent with what you say you believe? How clear are you about your personal values, standards and requirements?

The answers to these questions provide an indication of how much self-esteem, self-respect and self-awareness you currently possess. If you don't really know and love yourself (not in a conceited way but in a healthy way enjoying feelings of positive self-esteem) but insist on trying to validate your own feelings of self-worth through a partner your relationships will often be exploitative and dysfunctional. Healing any negative programming, conditioning or emotional wounds from the past are essential requirements for avoiding some of the big relationship mistakes. Many people refuse to look at themselves because it's easier and very convenient to blame ex-partners instead of spending some time alone reflecting and cultivating greater degrees of self-awareness. Searching for a new relationship too quickly after a break-up often serves as a welcomed distraction or a quick fix but just leaves old emotional wounds or negative patterns of relating misunderstood, undiscovered and unhealed. The common denominator in all of your relationships is *you*; ignoring this fact means you're probably setting yourself up for another failed relationship while repeating the same old patterns.

Self-Processing

"Most of us remain strangers to ourselves, hiding who we are, and ask other strangers, hiding who they are, to love us." – Leo Buscaglia (1924-1998), American Author & Motivational Speaker

Webster's dictionary says the word "process" means to "progress or advance" and also defines a process as "a natural phenomenon marked by gradual changes that lead toward a particular result."

Simply stated *a process* is a natural series of changes or to:

- Perform a series of operations
- Change or to preserve something
- Develop

- Clarify
- Revamp
- Simplify
- Perfect
- Refine

The word "discovery" means "the action or process of discovering or being discovered." The process or journey of Self-Discovery is an ongoing one that continues throughout our lives because the "self" is not finite or like a building with clearly defined dimensions you can explore within a certain amount of time. It's only when the journey is motivated by a genuine desire to understand deeply who you really are that it becomes clear there may be a great deal to discover.

The word "discovery" means "the action or process of discovering or being discovered" or:

- Realization
- Detection
- Uncovering
- Unearthing
- Breakthrough

As you begin the journey to learn and understand who you really are and what makes you tick, you will probably be surprised by how much more there is to discover. It is a never-ending internal journey, but the more effort you put into the quest, the greater the rewards; the more you seek to understand the deeper your discoveries will be.

During the process you will probably discover certain characteristics about yourself that you find disappointing or don't like very much; there may be aspects of yourself you feel deeply ashamed of or even feel quite disgusted by. While there may be personal revelations that make you feel very uncomfortable, looking at yourself objectively can reveal many valuable insights. Embarking on a journey of deeper understanding of yourself can begin a process of healing of any internal issues and conflicts that could be sabotaging your search for love. A thorough process of Self-Discovery requires an honest examination of yourself to understand your own behavior and actions; it's about understanding yourself in new ways and taking responsibility for your part in any past or current relationship dramas.

Consider these questions very carefully and be totally honest with yourself.

- Do you often do what is convenient instead of what you know is right or needs to be done?
- Do you frequently try to multi-task but nothing substantial gets done or is achieved?
- Are you too easily influenced by others?
- Do you lie to yourself?
- Do you lie to other people?
- Do you limit yourself by not asking for what you expect or because you are too afraid to express your needs?
- Are you prone to procrastination?

- Are you inclined to people please?
- Do you need to be right all the time?

Answering "Yes" to any of the above questions indicates you have some work to do on yourself before you should consider becoming involved in a new relationship. Looking outside for the answers while trying to figure out why your relationships keep failing is a waste of time. A new partner cannot heal any of the issues that may be subconsciously sabotaging your relationships because the answers reside in you and not with anyone else. The process of Self-Discovery begins within by exploring yourself and then being totally honest as you discover any aspects of your personality or Emotional Programming that might be damaging your prospects of maintaining a healthy partnership.

There are certain attributes, attitudes and activities that will definitely support positive personal development. These include:

- Self-awareness – requires conscious knowledge of one's own character, motives, feelings, desires and behavior obtained by a thorough process of self-examination and a willingness to look at everything in a new way.

- Self-esteem – acquiring or maintaining a high level of self-worth, self-respect, pride and confidence in yourself and your abilities.

- Self-direction – deciding who you want to be, where you are going and being under your own influence and control.

- Self-motivation – being enthusiastic, passionate and taking action without needing the influence or pressure of others.

- Self-mastery – requires self-discipline to control your feelings, being calm and confident plus the ability to identify and overcome any undesirable traits while practicing unconditional self-acceptance and being discerning.

- Self-refinement – researching and developing yourself physically, mentally and emotionally, which requires Self-Discovery and recognition, making sensible choices and experiencing the results.

- Self-expression – developing your self-expression (both verbally and by your actions) in constructive, positive and creative ways.

The purpose of embarking on the journey should be an honest, objective assessment of yourself; this is the only way you will begin to truly understand yourself and begin any healing that may be required.

Exploring yourself honestly will help you to discover if there are any issues or flaws lying dormant waiting to be triggered by certain people or circumstances. It's impossible to heal emotional damage unless you acknowledge and deal with any issues that may be sabotaging your relationships. Becoming involved without knowing yourself clearly eventually causes confusion – you will be unclear about who you are and what your honest expectations should be. The best you can hope for is that you will somehow muddle through until your unresolved issues come to the surface; any issues your new partner may have will be also added to the mix, which inevitably leads to drama! Unresolved internal issues often cause problems in relationships. Instead of considering ourselves and our behavior objectively we find it easier to blame others. The problems in our relationships may appear to be caused by outer conflicts but it's our inner conflicts that often cause the confusion and emotional turmoil.

Continuing to enter into relationships unhealed and lacking self-awareness will cause you nothing but frustration, distress and pain. It is really unfair to go into a relationship with Emotional Baggage that could have been healed before becoming involved because your partner suffers as well. When we fail to learn the lessons at hand relationships become a vicious circle where the partners change, but the dynamics essentially remain the same as we spin out of one bad relationship into another. The only way to stop the cycle is to heal any emotional wounds but first we have to acknowledge the issue and prepare to learn the lessons. We all have some work to do – none of us are perfect but we can strive to be the very best we can possibly be. The goal of PSD is not to become perfect but to support positive personal growth and development.

"Doing the same thing, expecting different results, is insanity." – Dennis Waitley, Life Transformation Teacher

Learning about yourself in new and deeper ways will provide many personal insights including:

- Deciding if your interpersonal style needs changing
- Considering if your relationship expectations are realistic
- Why you may be attracted to a certain type of partner and what motivates the attraction

Television, radio and the internet constantly advertise "quick fixes" to a wide variety of problems but these promises rarely produce any worthwhile or lasting results. We live in an era where many people expect to be offered short cuts or instant solutions to their problems but this is not a realistic approach to personal growth. Depending on a variety of factors, new insights about ourselves usually take a period of time to absorb, process and integrate.

Exploring yourself honestly requires time and discipline before any tangible results will be experienced. The more time you invest the faster the results but you have to be patient with yourself; this is often an organic process so take your time. If you learn anything new about yourself that requires attention accept that changes of any lasting benefit are not going to happen overnight.

"We mature but our emotions don't. If they are left unchecked our lives will be a series of unfinished and disappointing ventures." – Joyce Meyer, Christian Author & Speaker

You may also decide you're just fine without the need to unpack and heal any Emotional Baggage, but that doesn't mean your PSD has been a waste of time. Regular reviews of your personal expectations and goals will often prepare you for the many challenges life inevitably throws at all of us. Embarking on a journey of Self-Discovery doesn't come with any guarantees attached regarding finding the love of your life and living "happily ever after!" Understanding yourself in new ways while working on your personal development can help you to prepare for a healthy, loving relationship instead of repeating the same mistakes. PSD is a tool you can use to formulate new principles, boundaries and patterns of relating that will improve your life in many ways. The people in your life or a sudden change of circumstances always have the potential to bring unconsidered issues to the surface. When you are sincere about trying to really understand yourself you will often find yourself in situations that will test your new levels of self-awareness. Personal growth isn't always easy but there can be tremendous rewards when you begin to look at yourself objectively instead of living in blissful ignorance.

The Challenges Of PSD

"It is much more difficult to judge oneself than to judge others" – Antoine de Saint-Exupery (1900-1944), French Writer & Poet

One of the greatest challenges of PSD is being totally honest with yourself but this is absolutely necessary before you can discover if there is an aspect of yourself that requires attention or healing. You may have to dig deep and some of us will have to dig deeper than others before we can begin to make positive changes regarding how we feel and think about ourselves. If you are ready to discover yourself in new and meaningful ways and what you have read so far resonates with you, then what next? Theory is one thing while practice is something entirely different!

During the process of exploring ourselves we may discover certain aspects of our personalities that we find deeply shameful or emotionally painful. This can be quite a daunting and even frightening experience but is actually a good thing as it reveals where we have been in denial. Being in denial, sometimes referred to as "burying your head in the sand," is the refusal to acknowledge an unacceptable truth or emotion. This is usually an unconscious defense mechanism. When someone is in denial they are refusing to face and acknowledge the reality of a situation or to accept how they really feel. This strategy delays dealing with whatever needs to be dealt with and is usually adopted to protect a person from emotional pain.

Denial is always a temporary measure because suppressed feelings don't just disappear on their own: they have to be confronted and healed. When something is denied or ignored it cannot be changed or improved so refusing to acknowledge and accept the truth just means zero personal growth, as none of us can change whatever it is we refuse to recognize and acknowledge. The habit of being in denial is therefore a cruel trap: you might think you are protecting yourself from the issue but really you're sabotaging yourself. It doesn't solve anything and certainly won't help to increase your self-awareness. Ignoring issues makes it impossible to consider situations objectively so people become stuck in the past, wallowing in self-pity or repeating stories of how badly they have been treated. Many people could learn the lessons of their relationship mistakes if they were not so busy denying them. The bottom line is that if you're single and looking for a relationship you will be cheating yourself ***and*** any potential partner who comes into your life because you were too scared or too lazy to be honest with yourself.

"Until you get comfortable with being alone, you'll never know if you're choosing someone out of love or loneliness." – Mandy Hale, *The Single Woman's Sassy Survival Guide: Letting Go and Moving On*

If you have been suppressing or avoiding any issues or constantly finding other activities to distract you, then you are merely setting yourself up for more pain, distress and disappointment later on. This strategy will repeatedly fail. On the contrary, when the process of Self-Discovery is carried out thoroughly it can be a very empowering experience; undertaking the task of knowing yourself more deeply can be difficult at times but well worth the effort! There is so much to gain and nothing to lose – the work will reward you personally in many positive ways and assist you in all of your future relationships. The area of relationships is where we discover our judgments, fears, false perceptions and internal patterns regarding how we love and what we expect from love in each relationship. Once you begin to look objectively at your own insecurities, resentments, fears, anger, and motivational patterns your time alone becomes very meaningful and a highly positive learning experience. As you identify those conditioned responses motivated by your emotional patterns and programming your perspective will become much clearer. You can only relate constructively and positively with others when you truly understand yourself.

It takes courage to take an honest look at yourself but there may be aspects of yourself waiting to be discovered that have the potential to positively assist your personal growth. During a process of deep and meaningful self-evaluation you may find it necessary to dismiss certain preconceived ideas about yourself and how you relate to others. During your PSD it's important to love and accept yourself fully and not to blame yourself or beat yourself up for any past mistakes.

Very often in life there is no gain without pain; being brave enough to step outside of our comfort zones can provide us with very useful information if we are prepared to learn important lessons. Even the painful events we have in our lives can be used positively if we decide to make constructive use of those experiences. The good news is as you work through any issues, feelings of disappointment, pain and confusion you may have experienced in the past can be replaced with greater clarity and confidence. As you begin to explore yourself you may discover certain issues that need to be examined and worked through but as you continue to make progress any concerns you have about how you may be relating to yourself will be much easier to handle.

The Art Of Constructive Self-Criticism

"We don't receive wisdom; we must discover it for ourselves after a journey that no one can take for us or spare us." – Marcel Proust (1871-1922), French Novelist, Critic & Essayist

Taking an honest look at ourselves is very often easier said than done. Confronting our personal issues can feel overwhelming and lead to feelings of hopelessness and despair. While deciding to take responsibility to be honest with ourselves we may get carried away with the process, blaming ourselves and beating ourselves up mentally and emotionally. Many people believe that being extra hard on themselves will lead to dramatic self-improvement but research doesn't support this belief. Harsh self-criticism has been shown to increase the habit of procrastination while impeding the progress of personal goals. It can be very easy to lose sight of questions that are more likely to be constructive; by being specific you can avoid the trap of spiraling down into a feeling of never being able to improve the areas of your life that require improvement. If you convince yourself you are useless or incompetent in a particular area of your life it can be easy to feel that it's pointless even trying to improve.

Recognizing you have work to do on yourself can be a daunting realization: some people go into total denial or rationalize their self-discoveries, attempting to view themselves in a more positive light while ignoring the fact they have important work to do. There are some who avoid taking responsibility by blaming others or events. These strategies may make us feel better about ourselves in the short-term, but they are less likely to help us improve or avoid repeating our mistakes in the future.

Suggestions

Research shows that people who make blanket assumptions about particular aspects of themselves (e.g., "I'm just not an intelligent person") are more likely to become depressed. Constructive self-criticism involves an optimistic approach with a focus on specific areas identified as requiring improvement. Concentrate on specific behaviors that can be changed or improved while avoiding negative overall judgments.

If you have a tendency to be self-critical and blaming yourself learn to treat yourself with compassion. This approach can help to make any self-criticism increasingly manageable. Being compassionate to yourself makes it much easier to examine the areas you may be afraid to look at. For many people constructive self-criticism is seldom an easy task and there will probably be several tough challenges along the way. By approaching the process realistically you will be less likely to fall into the trap of feeling discouraged.

Instead of getting caught up in negative self-judgment it can be useful to consider how your actions affect other people. Research suggests people who pursue compassionate goals instead of goals seeking to enhance their self-image tend to have less conflict in their relationships. They also receive more support, experience less loneliness and are generally happier individuals. By focusing too much on protecting your own self-esteem, you may fail to recognize the needs of others in the process. Adopting a broader perspective can help the relationships you want to nurture while encouraging you to make amends for any mistakes that may have hurt others in the past. While it's important to spend time working on your PSD don't forget to consider the feelings of other people.

There may be situations where you totally blame yourself when there may have been situational factors that have pushed you into making a particular decision. An awareness of the power of situational factors such as peer pressure can actually help you to make better decisions. Some people believe considering external influences excessively can result in avoiding personal responsibility but when you fail to take external factors into consideration you're more likely to either ignore them or be blindsided. When you are focused on external circumstances seek to change how you manage your emotions or responses.

Try to avoid putting yourself under unnecessary pressure to be perfect because as we all know the "perfect" human being doesn't exist! Some people may appear to have it together but we all have flaws, weaknesses and negative patterns to a greater or lesser degree. Insisting on being "perfect" or seeking perfection in your relationships will set you up for a lifetime of disappointment. Constructive self-criticism requires acknowledging where you have made mistakes or identifying the areas of your life that may require improvement or healing. Each of us possess strengths and weaknesses; only by honestly exploring those weaknesses without fear or blame can we hope to enhance our personal development. Practicing compassionate self-criticism will greatly assist you during your process of Self-Discovery. Focus on the fact positive progress doesn't happen overnight and always takes time!

The Rewards Of Self-Discovery

"The mind is its own place, and in itself can make heaven of Hell, a hell of Heaven." –
John Milton (1608-1674), *Paradise Lost*

The journey within can be frightening at times but ultimately the destination is a very peaceful, positive and powerful place to be! You will probably still make a few mistakes along the way but they won't be big ones; any new mistakes certainly won't be as painful as before when you might have been stumbling blindly into relationships for all the wrong reasons. If you do make a mistake you will be less inclined to beat yourself up or feel like a victim; instead you will be able to calmly acknowledge to yourself that while you still make mistakes, no one is perfect and you are a work in progress. You will realize finding out more about who you truly are has increased your emotional value to yourself and others. With growing self-awareness and self-esteem you will be confident of entering any relationship knowing your true worth.

There are many benefits to be gained from the process of Self-Discovery, and they include the following:

- A constructive process of self-reflection
- Feeling lighter as you heal and release any Emotional Baggage that may be sabotaging your relationships
- Reduction in compulsive thinking and reactions to people and situations
- Greater objectivity; considering certain issues and circumstances in a new light
- Becoming more self-aware
- Building a better relationship with yourself
- Positive personal evolution
- Discovering self-love before trying to love someone else
- Cultivating a habit of making conscious and not compulsive relationship choices
- Adopting a realistic view of yourself and your relationships
- Adapting and applying positive new strategies to produce the relationship results you really want
- Feeling happier within yourself
- Less inclined to become involved with partners who lack overall compatibility

Engaging in the process of discovering yourself does not guarantee finding a suitable partner but will greatly improve your chances of success! For example, if you decide it's time to treat yourself to a new car and price is not an issue, are you going look for a basic model or are you going to buy a car with a high specification model which has many fantastic extras? Buying a car with lots of cool extras makes more sense because it will provide a better driving experience. It's the same principle. Are you offering a low specification version of yourself or are you a model with superior qualities that makes driving a car fun? Do you have a reputation for reliability and are the costs of your parts reasonable or are you the kind of vehicle that breaks down regularly and is high maintenance?

When you fully engage in PSD, you will eventually be justified in considering yourself a high specification human being. You will know yourself, trusting your inner guidance and be prepared to enjoy sharing and receiving love. You will be low maintenance because emotionally you trust yourself. You know your worth and the type of partner you're looking for. The compulsive behaviors that may have compelled you to make poor relationship choices can be tamed with deeper levels of self-awareness and healing. The urgency to find emotional, physical and spiritual fulfillment from a partner will no longer compel you to become involved in dead end relationships. In the process of discovering ourselves we also begin the process of creating the best version of ourselves we can be. When we decide we are ready for love and to share ourselves with someone new, the process clarifies what we are seeking, expecting and intending to experience internally and externally with others.

- If you consistently respect, honor and support yourself, you will begin to create positive expectations for yourself.
- If you accept less than what you want or expect you are sabotaging yourself.

Your next relationship might not be "the one" but by examining yourself closely it is possible to gain some valuable insights. This will help you to handle any issues that may come up with more clarity and less drama.

Conducting PSD In A Relationship

"If you cannot find peace within yourself, you will never it anywhere else." – Marvin Gaye (1939-1984), Legendary Soul Artist

For the Process of Self-Discovery to be effective and to build strong self-awareness it is usually better to spend a period of time alone without the distraction of being in a relationship. When there is a lack of relationship distractions in your life this allows you the time to clearly focus on yourself, which provides greater opportunities for healing and personal growth. It can be difficult to deal with certain personal issues when you are already in a relationship and then realize you have unresolved emotional aspects within yourself that require attention and healing.

Therapist and author of *The Divorce Doctor* Francine Kaye claims Self-Discovery is impossible outside of a relationship: "The best place to find yourself is with an imperfect partner. You can't try to find yourself through travelling, because you take yourself with you wherever you go." While I agree with Ms. Kaye that you cannot discover yourself through traveling and trying to escape from yourself, I disagree the best place to find yourself is with someone who is "imperfect." We are all a "work in progress" – it is an ongoing process and our personal development depends on our individual levels of self-awareness. It can be very difficult to begin and explore a process of Self-Discovery when you have unresolved issues, are unhappy with yourself or are in a relationship which might be dysfunctional. Of course you can discover important aspects of yourself in a relationship but a much better strategy is to cultivate healthy levels of self-awareness *before* embarking on the journey of looking for love. The goal of pursuing personal growth, greater self-awareness and being in a relationship are not mutually exclusive but being romantically involved can be a huge distraction.

Our relationships often act like a mirror reflecting or revealing unhealed aspects of ourselves that require healing. If you're carrying Emotional Baggage and lack a certain level of self-awareness there may be a tendency to project those unresolved issues onto your partner(s) while convincing yourself that any drama is totally their fault! If you have not taken the time to heal and understand yourself those issues will always return to haunt and disrupt your relationship.

When you are on your own you can concentrate on the process and sort through your inner issues and baggage. When you are in your own space, you have quality time to discover who you really are, what you really want and why you really want it. You will discover if you are being realistic or if your desires are fantasy driven. The motivation for embarking on the journey and engaging in the process should be an honest, objective assessment of yourself. You may very well discover things about yourself you do not like very much but you cannot attempt to change certain aspects of yourself unless you can first identify them clearly. This doesn't mean the process cannot be undertaken while you're romantically involved but your partner definitely needs to be understanding and supportive. Taking time out for yourself may not be easy or practical if you're actually living with someone. In this case you should talk to him candidly and arrange counselling for yourself or as a couple if he agrees. No one has the right to try and restrict your personal growth so if your partner is resistant to the idea the viability of the relationship should be considered very carefully.

If you're in a difficult relationship your primary mission should be to heal and understand yourself instead of focusing on trying save the relationship. Ultimately, you are responsible for you, so if you are looking outside of yourself for someone to take responsibility for how you feel your relationship is dysfunctional. It is selfish, unfair and unreasonable to expect a current or potential partner to manage and cope with your unresolved issues when you haven't made a genuine effort to sort them out for yourself. Ultimately, each of us should be the providers of our own personal contentment and it's always a very risky strategy to depend on a partner for your feelings of self-worth or happiness.

Defining A New Path

"When we least expect it, life sets us a challenge to test our courage and willingness to change; at such a moment, there is no point in pretending that nothing has happened or in saying that we are not yet ready. The challenge will not wait. Life does not look back. A week is more than enough time for us to decide whether or not to accept our destiny."
– Paulo Coelho, *The Devil and Miss Prym*

A very common relationship mistake many people make is seeking to have their needs satisfied by a partner or a relationship instead of focusing on building a clearer, stronger and more constructive connection with themselves.

The first step in preparing for a healthy relationship is to focus on your own personal growth while understanding clearly that change is a process not an event. It takes time to learn new strategies before we are ready to apply the knowledge for our personal benefit. There are many obstacles that can stand in the way of positive personal change; holding on to past feelings of bitterness or resentment or unconscious ingrained patterns of thinking can sabotage our relationships.

Changing your mindset and personal perspectives can present serious challenges and achieving any meaningful change will often require persistence, commitment and time. I often hear people say they just "haven't got the time" to work on themselves and my response is always the same: "There is no such thing as not having enough time to work on yourself as we are all given exactly the same 24 hours per day!" Do you believe there isn't enough time to work on your own healing and personal development? How much time do you waste watching television, on Facebook or surfing the internet for entertainment? You may tell yourself there just isn't enough time to explore, discover and heal any issues that may be sabotaging your relationships, but denying, suppressing or avoiding any emotional issues means you're probably setting yourself up for more relationship failures. The only person who can decide your priorities is you and exploring any personal issues that may be damaging to your relationship prospects is never a waste of your time – it will always be a good *investment* of your time. Before you make a commitment to a relationship you first have to make a commitment to yourself; as you gain a deeper understanding of yourself each new revelation has the potential to accelerate your personal growth.

"Knowing yourself is the beginning of wisdom." – Aristotle (384-322 BC), Greek Philosopher & Scientist

At the other extreme, trying to do everything at once will probably leave you feeling overwhelmed especially if you have more than one issue to work on. Healing emotional issues or negative thinking patterns is usually a gradual process and each of us will begin at different levels depending on our experiences and temperament. Each person's "work" also depends on their personal levels of self-awareness. We are all unique individuals so each person's healing of their emotional wounds or negative patterns of relating will be different even if two people have similar issues. The journey of Self-Discovery can feel very lonely at times but building a positive relationship with yourself over a period over time does not have to be carried out in solitude. If you find yourself struggling seek support from a trusted family member, a close friend, professional counselor/therapist or a support group. If you're in a relationship explore the possibility of working through the issues with your partner if he is willing to be supportive but ultimately you're responsible for defining your own path.

"The greatest discovery of my generation is that human beings can alter their lives by altering their attitudes of mind." – William James (1842-1910), American Philosopher & Psychologist

Defining a new path is part of the journey towards Self-Discovery with the goal of becoming the best version of yourself that you can possibly be.

During your journey you can learn how to:

- Love yourself
- Nurture yourself
- Accept yourself
- Connect with your feelings
- Connect with and modify any beliefs that do not serve you
- Cultivate and adopt new values
- Explore new personal interests
- Appreciate your own accomplishments

These practices will encourage you to love, honor and cherish yourself instead of relying on a relationship to provide a sense of self-worth or trying to fix or change your partner. The goal is to heal any underlying emotional issues and avoid embarking on relationships seeking to please, control or feel needed so you feel worthy of someone else's love.

Your self-love will not be conceited or selfish but confident and assured as you become aware of your own worth. Rather than desperately seeking a relationship or clinging to a partnership that is unhealthy and dysfunctional your new sense of self will empower you to protect your boundaries, values and standards. Instead of tolerating drama you will be prepared to walk away because you will know what serves your personal growth and what doesn't. If you find yourself in a dead-end relationship fear will not motivate you to stay; your sense of self-esteem will provide the strength to leave with your head held high instead of believing you're a failure or feeling afraid of the future.

"The truth is that our finest moments are most likely to occur when we are feeling deeply uncomfortable, unhappy, or unfulfilled. For it is only in such moments, propelled by our discomfort, that we are likely to step out of our ruts and start searching for different ways or truer answers." – M. Scott Peck (1936-2005), American Psychiatrist & Author

There are single men and women in the dating game hoping to meet someone "special" who will "discover" or "bring out" their best qualities so that everything will be perfect, but the truth is they are often waiting to be rescued from themselves. When you rely on someone else to provide your happiness you end up giving away a great deal of your own emotional independence. Believing you can build a rewarding and meaningful connection with someone without first truly connecting with yourself is a fantasy. Understanding and honoring yourself should be your very first priority before, during or after any relationship – this is the only sensible and healthy strategy. This is not about being selfish but about being practical because if you are not positively maintaining and nurturing yourself you will have very little of genuine worth to contribute to a relationship anyway. All of your relationships begin with you and the quality of the relationship you have with yourself will always be the determining factor that influences your behavior and relationship choices.

When personal growth and peace of mind and are your top priorities many of the perspectives regarding yourself and your relationships will change for the better. Accepting others just as they are without trying to change or fix them or attempting to get others to meet your needs will free up a tremendous amount of energy. Instead of wasting time trying to covertly control others you are respectful and protective of your own mental and emotional health and general wellbeing.

"The spirit of self-help is the root of all genuine growth in the individual." – Samuel Smiles (1812-1904)

Each of us can experience a turning point or an awakening during our lives and taking a hard, honest, unflinching look at your own personal history could be one of your greatest challenges. It takes great courage to fully acknowledge and accept your previous failings and mistakes. During the process you may discover aspects of yourself that have sustained emotional damage; some of your insights might even be frightening but you cannot heal what you refuse to look at. Being honest with yourself can reveal any emotional issues that may be lurking and compelling you to make unhealthy or destructive relationship choices.

Building a healthy habit of nurturing yourself will support you through any emotional turbulence that you may experience. You will find as you grow and evolve your friends will also change their attitude or leave your life to be replaced with more likeminded and supportive friends because your inner state reflects your outer reality.

"Problems do not go away. They must be worked through or else they remain, forever a barrier to the growth and development of the spirit." – M. Scott Peck (1936-2005), American Psychiatrist & Author

This process shouldn't end when you become involved in a relationship but become an on-going lifelong commitment to personal growth. The only way to understand, embrace and ultimately heal any emotional wounds is to embark on a journey of inner exploration to learn how your personal history may be influencing or even controlling your behavior and choices. This means you have to continue to evaluate yourself honestly and objectively.

Discovering and dealing with any emotional wounds or negative patterns of relating is a precious gift you give to yourself. Only after you have given yourself this gift will you be able to share it with someone else! You can only share love, peace and joy when those feelings already exist within you; a person cannot share what they do not possess. Defining a new path isn't always easy and often requires having the courage to boldly face and address issues that may be uncomfortable or even distressing, but it is only by taking the journey within that each of us can really begin to trust ourselves and our relationship choices. When we begin to work on ourselves and heal any emotional wounds, we give ourselves realistic options for finding a relationship that is healthy and loving. Always remember the most important relationship you will ever have is the one you have with yourself.

CHAPTER 5:

Learning The Lessons Of Self-Acceptance

"Before we can make friends with anyone else, we must first make friends with ourselves."
– Eleanor Roosevelt (1884-1962), American Politician & Activist

Self-Acceptance

We can all fall into the trap of comparing ourselves negatively to other people when suffering from low self-esteem or lack self-acceptance. This happens when we concentrate on our flaws believing we are lacking in some way instead of becoming proactive and putting together a strategy to heal any emotional wounds. The habit of emotionally beating yourself up because of past mistakes, not being "good enough" or entertaining constant self-criticism in your head will stifle any efforts to cultivate greater self-awareness. Self-acceptance means being honest with yourself and acknowledging any mistakes that you made in the past; it's about acknowledging and addressing any issues that require attention and accepting you're never going to be perfect, just as no one else is perfect. Considering your flaws and personal history using the correct perspective while being ready to make a genuine effort to evolve positively often requires courage and a radical shift of focus.

"When you are not happy with yourself, you cannot be happy with others." – Daryl Mitchell, American Actor

The first step to greater self-acceptance is learning to accept yourself just as you are in the present. This provides a solid emotional foundation to begin building on for the future. It's about working with yourself rather than sabotaging yourself. Albert Ellis, a renowned psychologist, described two choices: accepting ourselves conditionally (for example, when we succeed) or unconditionally (under all circumstances). Ellis said quite clearly the first choice is "deadly." If we fail the conditions we set ourselves, this can set off a pattern of negative beliefs and emotions where we think of ourselves as being a "loser" or inadequate in some way rather than accepting any failure as a normal part of life and learning from it. If someone lacks self-acceptance, they can start to worry or obsess about aspects of themselves to such a degree they believe themselves to be a totally unworthy person. This kind of mindset can lead to dwelling constantly on your "flaws" as you become trapped in a pattern of negative self-talk. This will block you from beginning your journey of positive growth and stifle any personal happiness. Perhaps when you start looking at yourself you will decide you don't have any Emotional Baggage or issues but is this really true? Complacency leads to a self-satisfied attitude that restricts personal growth. The reality is if you don't love and accept yourself enough this can often result in compromising too much, inevitably leading to difficulties in your personal relationships.

Come to terms with any image issues that may lead you into destructive choices. Stop being critical and non-accepting of potentially loving partners and open the door to a human connection. Letting yourself be controlled by your desire for perfection keeps you disconnected and empty. If you are holding on to primitive idealizations of what your partner should look like, sound like or act like, you will not move forward – change begins when you acknowledge and accept humanness in yourself and others. The very first step in building successful relationships is learning to first value who you are. Who are you? Do you like you? Are you happy and content with your own company? Until you are willing to love yourself it will be very difficult to love somebody else. For some people "self-improvement" implies there must something "wrong" that needs "fixing." But cultivating the desire to be the best version of yourself does not mean you need "fixing" – the key is to fully accept yourself while also seeking to heal any emotional issues or negative patterns of relating that may require attention. Being motivated to seek improvements without fully accepting yourself as you are now indicates a desire to improve motivated by feelings of unworthiness, guilt or of not being good enough.

Of course, you may discover certain aspects of yourself that make you unhappy or appear to need fixing but this kind of attitude and approach can damage your self-esteem. This process isn't about fixing anything: it's about accepting and healing any emotional wounds or negative patterns that may be sabotaging your relationship choices. The goal is to love and embrace yourself while learning new strategies that will help support your personal growth. Striking the right balance involves acceptance of who you are in the present moment while at the same time seeking to improve whatever aspects of yourself that may require attention and healing.

Self-Awareness

"An important part of creating a loving relationship with yourself is to acknowledge your needs and to learn to ask for what you want." – Shakti Gawain, *Living In The Light*

Self-awareness is the understanding you exist as a person who is separate from other people with your own private thoughts and emotions. Your personal levels of self-awareness will determine how you manage your life and relationships. One of the major reasons people become involved in unhappy or inappropriate relationships is due to not knowing themselves clearly. For example, someone may think they know everything that was wrong with their previous partners but be totally unaware regarding their own negative patterns and weaknesses. Lacking self-awareness means a person doesn't know who they truly are at their core. You cannot realistically hope to establish a genuine emotional connection with someone and work towards a genuine committed relationship if you don't even know who you really are. If you lack self-awareness going into a relationship, any unresolved issues will eventually surface and be reflected back to you by your partner. Alternatively, you will consciously or subconsciously project your issues onto your partner. A failure to process our "stuff" can lead to experiencing feelings of anxiety or even panic that you may find difficult to understand or explain even if your relationship is actually going well.

Poor levels of self-awareness results in reacting to other people without giving it too much thought. We cause ourselves problems by becoming involved with partners without really understanding what motivates us to be attracted to certain personality types. People who are reactive are at the mercy of other people and circumstances and are easily influenced by their environment. If you are the reactive type you will often feel helpless, believing that luck or fate is constantly leading you into unhealthy relationships.

A person who lacks self-awareness:

- Compulsively reacts to outer circumstances.
- Compulsively reacts to the behavior, actions and moods of other people.

A person who is self-aware operates from a solid foundation of clearly knowing who they are. They have learnt to trust themselves and to remain calm, which gives them the power to make better relationship choices.

- The opinions or actions of other people don't drastically influence their outlook.
- The opinions or actions of other people don't overtly affect their moods or attitude.

Understanding yourself deeply gives you the power to choose your response to any given situation and, more importantly, the wisdom to avoid potentially unhealthy relationships. It is not what happens to us that is important but how we respond and learn through our life experience. This provides the key to greater personal responsibility. When you are self-aware and proactive you will seek out alternatives, formulate strategies and decide on a course of action that will facilitate your personal growth, and this greatly improves your prospects for finding a fulfilling relationship.

Cognitive Dissonance

"Sometimes people hold a core belief that is very strong. When they are presented with evidence that works against that belief, the new evidence cannot be accepted. It would create a feeling that is extremely uncomfortable, called cognitive dissonance. And because it is so important to protect the core belief, they will rationalize, ignore and even deny anything that doesn't fit in with the core belief." – Frantz Fanon (1924-1961), *Black Skin, White Masks*

Scientific research has revealed many of the mysteries of dating, love and relationships. Cognitive dissonance is one of the most important concepts to understand and may be affecting you in your search for love much more than you realize. The term is used in modern psychology to describe the discomfort felt by a person seeking to hold or reconcile two or more conflicting beliefs, ideas, concepts, values or emotional reactions. This can result in feelings of guilt, embarrassment, anger or even surprise. It may cause people to change their beliefs to match or justify actual behavior instead of using reliable or credible information to motivate a change in behavior. Examining whether your beliefs actually match your actions and behavior can provide invaluable insights.

Understanding Cognitive Dissonance allows us to be consistent and to act with integrity; it prevents us from misleading others and causing unnecessary hurt in our relationships. If you have a cognitive dissonance pattern of thinking it can cause bitterness and resentment towards previous and potential partners as you are more likely to blame others for your relationships failures. Be honest and ask yourself how you really feel when you're romantically involved. When a relationship is going well men and women who haven't taken the time to process their "stuff" may feel vaguely uncomfortable without understanding why or experience anxiety or even feelings of panic they can't really understand or explain. Sometimes they unconsciously sabotage their relationships leaving partners feeling deeply hurt and bewildered.

Key Areas of Self-Awareness

"The only person who can pull me down is myself, and I'm not going to let myself pull me down anymore." – C. JoyBell C., Author

To develop your self-awareness, you should seek to develop an understanding of yourself in keys areas. This includes your personality traits, personal values, habits, emotions and the psychological needs that drive your behavior.

Values

Part of being self-aware means knowing and consistently focusing on your personal values, as they can be abandoned very easily if you are unhappy being single or desperate to be in a relationship. When we focus on our values, we are more likely to become involved with a partner who has similar personal standards and beliefs.

Habits

Thinking patterns create habits which are behaviors repeated routinely and often automatically. We would all like to possess positive habits that help us interact effectively with others but it's usually quite easy to identify at least a few that may cause problems in our intimate relationships.

Needs

A variety of important psychological needs drive our behaviors including a need for:

- Esteem
- Affection
- Belongingness
- Achievement
- Self-actualization
- Power and control

One of the advantages of knowing which of your needs exert the strongest influence on your own behaviors is having a clear understanding about how they affect your interpersonal relationships. For example, you probably know someone who is "status hungry," which means they are primarily attracted to potential partners who possess symbols of high status and material success. This person may be seeking a partner who matches their own levels of achievements or if they feel they are lacking in this area will look for a partner who can compensate for or even elevate their own status. It doesn't really matter if each person's needs are authentic or merely perceived, because the "need" feels real on an emotional level of perception and motivates different people in a variety of ways. When needs aren't satisfied, this often causes frustration, conflict and even emotional stress. Your aim should be to make self-awareness a habit or a pattern of thinking that replaces the autopilot part of your life that may be sabotaging your relationship choices or personal interactions.

How Higher Levels Of Self-Awareness Can Make You More Effective

Self-awareness:

- Helps you to identify and manage gaps in your personal life
- Promotes skill development
- Assists with intuitive decision-making
- Aids stress management
- Helps you to motivate yourself

With skill development, self-improvement projects normally begin with an assessment of the gap between the current situation and the desired future goal. Raising your levels of self-awareness will usually reveal a personal skills gap and having an accurate self-perception or picture helps you to decide which areas require attention, and those areas you would like to improve.

Self-awareness helps you exploit your emotional strengths and cope with any weaknesses in the short-term while you spend some time making improvements. As you become more self-aware your intuitive decision-making skills will develop naturally. In complex situations, a person who makes intuitive decisions often processes large amounts of unstructured and ambiguous information and then chooses a course of action based on their instincts or "gut feeling." People who are emotionally self-aware are equipped to understand their feelings and therefore can effectively use this knowledge to guide their decisions.

The ability to make these types of decisions can be important even when there is a lack of information, as deciding whether or not to enter into a relationship can be a complicated and emotional choice. If you don't know which behaviors to change to improve your chances of finding the kind of love you want, you can fall into feelings of despair. Developing your self-awareness is always empowering because it will reveal any negative thinking patterns which can be improved. Having a clear awareness of your psychological needs will increase your motivation by helping you to understand and seek out the kind of relationship that you really desire. When you understand "what makes you tick" you will gain valuable insights about what makes other people behave the way that they do. Once you have a sense of who you are and a vision of the person you want to become, a plan for personal development can be created. Self-awareness allows you to manage yourself more effectively and helps your intuitive decision-making process. Developing your self-awareness is a gift you give to yourself!

Increasing your self-awareness will reveal:

- How your thoughts and words impact on your emotions
- How your emotions may be subconsciously driving your behaviors
- How your hidden core beliefs affect your relationship prospects

Raising your self-awareness generally will also help you to consider important decisions calmly and efficiently. When you learn to give your mind a new interpretation you begin to see an entirely different world. With this practice we become aware of the personal stories we tell ourselves that may be highly subjective and not based on the actual facts. Growing in self-awareness gives us a real opportunity to create the life we desire and helps us to make better relationship choices. Before you can begin constructively to change certain negative patterns, beliefs or emotional issues you have to understand yourself clearly.

Cultivating Self-Awareness

Embrace Silence

With instant communications, mobile phones, laptops, radio and a zillion TV channels available 24 hours a day, many people in the modern world dislike or even fear silence. Yet silence is beneficial to your overall health and wellbeing and is the perfect medium for stimulating self-awareness. Always craving external stimulation and running away from silence is trying to evade and run away from yourself. Learning to embrace silence as a natural, peaceful and even beautiful part of your daily life is an essential on the road to cultivating self-awareness.

Learn To Meditate

Learning to meditate, even for short periods of time each day, will automatically increase your self-awareness. Basic meditation is not difficult. Regular meditation will start to bring you into contact with your subconscious; as you begin to notice and appreciate the benefits this will encourage you to practice and develop your meditation skills.

Make Better Use Of Travel Time

If you commute to and from work on public transport and can sit down during the journey, try to avoid the usual habits of reading or perhaps falling asleep. During the journey close your eyes but do not fall asleep. Other people may believe you are sleeping but don't be concerned about what they think; clear your mind of thoughts about work or other things. Try to ignore any noises or distractions and focus on quietly breathing through your nose. This type of meditation allows you to increase self-awareness as you become more focused on what is going on inside you. You will probably arrive at work or return home feeling much more refreshed and with your mind clear of the usual issues.

Do Something Different

It's very easy to go through each day, week and month on "auto pilot" without consciously thinking about how you are coping with the daily demands of life. Deliberately doing something different and changing your normal routine adds variety to your life and increases your awareness of yourself. This helps you to guard against falling into the trap of a repetitive habit-dominated existence. Breaking your routine and doing something different requires conscious decisions but is a step toward greater levels of self-awareness. Consistently exploring different activities can give you the confidence to explore your inner self, which is the essence of developing self-awareness.

Debate With & Question Yourself

Make it a habit to frequently ask what you are doing and why, not only generally, but on specific things about yourself, your life and your relationship history. By constantly debating with yourself, you will naturally increase your self-awareness. Debating and questioning yourself is best done mentally if you're in the company of other people, otherwise you will probably get some very strange looks if you start talking and debating out loud with yourself!

If you allow your days and your life to just run on autopilot you will never discover the "real you" and keep giving away your personal power and the ability to direct yourself to make positive changes. Your self-awareness and self-development will remain stagnant as you drift through life believing you have little control and limited choices. Asking yourself tough questions will encourage you to seek better ways of doing things and to make changes for the better.

Constantly cultivating a greater understanding of yourself is one of the greatest gifts you can give to yourself. There are many people who don't really look at themselves because they are scared of what they may find, but these individuals are frequently doomed to repeat the same mistakes because they have failed to raise their levels of self-awareness. As your self-awareness increases, you will begin to tap into your subconscious quite naturally instead of being constantly driven by negative habitual thought patterns, which causes so many relationship problems.

The Way Forward

"Everybody wants to be somebody; nobody wants to grow." – Johann Wolfgang von Goethe (1749-1832), Writer & Poet

Some people call it "personal power" while others refer to it as "will power" but it doesn't matter what we call it. The fact is each of us has an extraordinary amount of this power or energy at our disposal if we choose to harness it. This internal power can be focused consistently to achieve our personal goals, create the results we desire or used to control and restrain desires that may not be healthy. Effective self-awareness begins by learning to focus your attention appropriately on yourself and provides the keys to personal freedom. Before you can expect to consciously direct your life, you need to be able to consciously direct your attention. Without an appropriate and effective level of self-awareness you can waste a great deal of time and energy sabotaging yourself with subconscious patterns of behavior and poor relationship choices.

Many people just do what comes naturally for them without taking the time to check themselves out. They are doing the best they can while being unaware of how their issues impact on their lives. It's an old cliché that everyone is a "work in progress" but the truth is some people have more work to do on themselves than others. They may not even be aware they're walking around with old Emotional Baggage that consistently sabotages their personal relationships.

Everyone is at a different level of personal and emotional development, so while your task is to be the best person you can be in terms of self-awareness, don't waste energy blaming or berating others who may be farther behind on their journey. Each of us has a responsibility to investigate ourselves and make the required changes that will support our personal evolution in a positive way. A new relationship can promise romantic heaven but can easily turn into a painful personal hell if you become involved with someone when you still have unresolved emotional issues. Entering relationships treating each one like a very long and painful therapy session to try to discover and explore aspects of yourself is emotionally dishonest. It's selfish and irresponsible and has the real potential to cause serious emotional damage to others, albeit unintentional. Looking for someone to share your life with while you have unresolved issues to heal is very unfair. The best possible preparation for entering into a new relationship is to have a certain level of self-awareness while paying attention to your personal growth. This creates a solid foundation to consistently evolve into the best version of yourself that you can be while exploring the potential of a new relationship.

"What lies behind us and what lies before us are tiny matters compared to what lies within us." – Oliver Wendell Holmes, Associate Justice of the Supreme Court of the United States from 1902-1932

You can only relate constructively and positively with others when you truly understand yourself. Developing your self-awareness is the only sensible strategy for beginning to identify any negative patterns that may be affecting how you relate to other people or handle certain situations. Finding the right person for you doesn't depend on luck or fate. The higher your level of self-awareness the less drama there will be in your relationships. Meeting the right type of partner depends on your personal level of self-awareness and making sensible decisions about who you become involved with. Who you attract and become involved with in your next relationship will be a reflection of the extent of your personal self-awareness and healing. The greater your self-awareness and personal healing the less drama there will be in your relationships. Understanding yourself as much as possible doesn't necessarily increase your options for finding love but possessing a certain level of self-awareness will greatly improve your ability to make sensible decisions. Lack of self-awareness inevitably leads to poor relationship choices.

Cultivating greater self-awareness isn't going to get rid of all your negative patterns overnight or forever; there may be occasions when you slip back into your old ways of relating. This is normal and nothing to worry about. Entrenched patterns of thinking can be persistent so you will have to be vigilant and monitor your thoughts and feelings. There are rarely any short cuts or quick fixes to cultivating greater self-awareness. It takes time to integrate new insights and knowledge but the personal rewards can be tremendous.

CHAPTER 6:

Improving Self-Esteem

"High self-esteem results primarily from ones accepting complete responsibility for his or her well-being, and taking full charge of his or her life. It is rooted in unconditional acceptance despite the mistakes, defeats, failures, as an innately worthy and important being." – L.S. Barksdale, *Building Self-Esteem*

Self-Esteem And Relationships

Self-esteem is all about how you feel about yourself and how you feel about your own worth. It requires personal responsibility and unconditional acceptance of yourself regarding the aspects that are impossible to change or improve. It affects our health and our attitude towards the people in our lives generally and our intimate and romantic relationships specifically. Positive self-esteem equips us to handle many of the stresses, problems and other experiences life invariable throws at us every day. It also affects how we experience our lives and whether we find our lives generally pleasurable or miserable. High self-esteem can be a result of diverse reasons but a healthy degree of self-esteem is very important because the better we feel about ourselves and life in general, the better we perform in our lives. When you have high self-esteem the positive aspects of life are much more accessible and your ability to enjoy those aspects is greatly enhanced. Positive self-esteem is about self-love without being selfish or egotistical.

Low self-esteem varies according to each individual. It depends on what aspect of themselves they are unhappy with and the degree to which they are dissatisfied. Many of the problems experienced by people with low self-esteem can be caused by a distorted perspective regarding how they feel about themselves, which prevents them from sustaining an overall sense of wellbeing and peace of mind. When a person suffers with low self-esteem, their outlook is bleak and their life generally lacks genuine enjoyment, joy, fun, affection and, of course, love.

A person's level of self-esteem can be strongly influenced by the following:

- Gender – how someone feels about being a man or a woman
- Age – how someone feels about their age
- Body image and physical appearance – how someone feels about their external appearance
- Position in family – how someone feels about their role and status within their family

- Social status – how someone feels about their status and their possessions or achievements
- Cultural and ethnic background – how someone feels about their race or culture
- General attitude to life – how someone approaches life, positively or negatively
- General lifestyle – how someone feels about the way they live
- General health and wellbeing – how someone feels about their health. Poor health can drastically affect a person's self-esteem
- Spiritual attitude to life – how someone maintains the belief system that sustains them or how someone operates their personal values, principles and morals
- Relationships with others – how someone feels about their relationships regarding their work, family and intimate relationships

Factors that influence self-esteem are likely to include a person's temperamental makeup, individual character, upbringing and life experiences, which often impacts directly on their Emotional Programming. Each person's regular contact with family, friends and work colleagues will also influence their level of self-esteem.

Negative Consequences of Low Self-Esteem

"Emotions can be the enemy within. Be at one with your emotions and understand them. Because the body will always follow the mind." – Bruce Lee (1940-1973), Martial Artist & Actor

A person who suffers with low self-esteem issues will have a strong tendency to sacrifice their true desires and values for the sake of finding a partner, or will seek to maintain a relationship that will usually be unhealthy and dysfunctional.

When a person has low self-esteem they may not even recognize they are being abused. If someone believes they do not deserve anything positive to happen in their lives or they deserve to be treated badly, that person can remain trapped in a very unhealthy relationship. If you have found yourself in a relationship with an abusive partner more than once, you should begin your Process of Self-Discovery to understand any self-esteem issues that may be motivating your poor relationship choices.

When someone suffers from low self-esteem it has various negative consequences for their relationships including the following:

- A reluctance to express needs
- Unable to stand up for themselves
- Putting people on pedestals, admiring or deferring to them unnecessarily
- Scared to ask difficult questions or to risk any type of confrontation
- Making poor choices
- Often feeling unnecessarily grateful
- Frequently reluctant to take emotional risks if in a secure relationship
- Usually feel a need to play it safe
- May rush into relationships seeking feelings of security or validation

- May have a tendency to display inflated Egos while attempting to compensate for feelings of low self-worth
- Can be passively aggressive or excessively critical of others

If you suffer from low self-esteem, the belief you're not "good enough" will be projected onto all of your relationships, intimate or otherwise. Inevitably this results in you believing that no one is "good enough." If you believe you are lacking some type of essential quality or attribute, eventually you will believe whatever you think you are lacking will also seem to be lacking from your partner or the other people in your life. Whatever you believe at the deepest level of your subconscious will eventually be projected and attracted into your life. A person is only capable of loving a partner as much as they're capable of loving themselves.

Someone who has a pattern of losing themselves when they are involved in a relationship typically:

- Lose sight of their personal goals
- Lose sight of their personal priorities
- Lose their personal boundaries
- Lose sight of their personal values
- Lose sight of their needs or personal requirements
- Lose their personal sense of self
- Lose their personal connection with themselves completely

If you have a tendency to become romantically involved with a new partner very quickly, or to become consumed by the relationship to the extent that you feel consistently motivated to make the other person happy and obsessed with meeting all of their needs, there will be very little time left for yourself. When you lack a clear sense of self and do not know who you really are it's very easy to lose yourself in a relationship or, even worse, to be very easily manipulated. Understanding and honoring yourself should be your very first priority before, during or after any relationship because this is the only sensible strategy. If you have found yourself in an abusive relationship more than once, examine this tendency during your process of Self-Discovery to see if you can discover what type of beliefs are motivating your choices.

Low Self-Esteem And Dysfunctional Relationships

"Self-esteem is made up primarily of two things: feeling lovable and feeling capable." – Jack Canfield, American Author & Motivational Speaker

Low self-esteem in one or both partners often causes a variety of problems with the result that their relationship becomes dysfunctional. Self-esteem has a direct influence on how each person chooses a partner and how those relationships are conducted; if either partner has low self-esteem their relationship will suffer. When both partners have self-esteem issues this will usually cause major problems in the relationship. A person with low self-esteem will have a tremendous effect on their partner so it's irresponsible to underestimate the negative impact this issue can have on the healthy dynamics of a relationship. Moods and attitudes are contagious and the more time you spend with someone the greater the influence they will have on your feelings; this is especially true of our romantic relationships. If you are involved with someone who has a mostly optimistic attitude towards life their "positive vibes" will "rub off" on you, but if their attitude is mostly negative that will also affect your outlook and mood.

Low self-esteem issues are usually a result of Emotional Programming issues established during childhood. Often in life, people tend to receive what they believe they deserve. When someone suffers with low self-esteem there is a constant variation of the following self-talk or programming running through their minds:

- I do not deserve to be loved
- I do not deserve any of the good things in life
- I do not deserve happiness

If as a child you were constantly told you were not lovable this may have established a particular negative belief about yourself. You then develop a pattern of becoming what you believe and attract partners who mistreat you.

- If the belief (I am not lovable) was established during childhood you will probably continue to believe you are unlovable as an adult because you were not worthy of love as a child.
- As an adult your relationship history will likely include more than one previous partner who was unloving and emotionally distant or who had a tendency to mistreat you.
- Due to your childhood Emotional Programming you subconsciously attract toxic partners.

Low self-esteem can also be caused by something you feel you have done wrong in the past where you find it difficult to forgive yourself. If someone has been hurt and you believe it is totally your fault and responsibility, part of your Emotional Programming may have decided you do not deserve to be loved and should be punished forever. Those with low self-esteem usually view themselves negatively and constantly struggle to feel they are "good enough." A woman who is obsessed with her appearance while failing to appreciate her inner qualities, or a man who is obsessed with his achievements and external status, may have self-esteem issues even though they appear to be confident. Whenever a person is focused on their external appearances or possessions there are usually Emotional Programming corruption issues that are causing low self-esteem. The untamed Ego also plays its part. It compels those with low self-esteem to incessantly compare themselves to others, seeking ways to bolster their constantly flagging self-esteem so they can feel better, more powerful or at least equal in some way.

Lack of self-worth can be defined as low self-esteem although there are some people who cover up their low self-esteem by over compensating with massive Egos and highly egocentric behavior. Much of the behavior will usually be focused externally and can include drug or alcohol abuse, casual sex or even violence. These activities provide temporary comfort and escape from the constant feelings of "not being good enough." A variety of problems including depression, burnout, stress and many addictions all originate from issues stemming from low self-esteem. The behaviors, addictions or illnesses are not the primary causes of low self-esteem but the result of poor self-esteem.

Low self-esteem leads to self-fulfilling prophecies of despair and doom. If you believe you do not deserve anything good or you deserve to be treated badly you can stay in an unhealthy relationship where you blame yourself for your partner's unacceptable behavior or even make excuses for them. Someone with low self-esteem may not even recognize they are in an abusive relationship.

Low Self-Esteem And Abusive Relationships

"Before you allow anyone to belittle you, it's very important to understand that people with low self-esteem and low self-confidence are usually the ones that strive to belittle others." – Edmond Mbiaka, *Self-Help Writer*

Feelings of low self-esteem impacts on many people at some point in their lives causing successful, intelligent individuals to doubt their self-worth. Poor self-esteem issues can keep some men and women in a state of depression and sadness that can last a lifetime. Relationships can positively support self-esteem or destroy it. Unfortunately, those who fail to value themselves often attract or are attracted to partners who attack or undermine their self-esteem, resulting in highly abusive relationships in many cases.

Those who suffer from low self-esteem are prime candidates for emotional or mental brain washing and manipulation; once someone is trapped in an abusive relationship it can be very difficult to escape. A person who is psychologically abusive often has a conscious agenda, and part of that agenda is controlling their partner. Abusers often seek to shape their victim's reality and perception, which gradually reduces resistance to their agenda of control. An abuser will seek to do whatever possible to undermine their partner's confidence. Lacking self-esteem the abused partner believes they are indeed of little value, which further diminishes any feelings of self-worth.

The best strategy to use when dealing with any attacks on your self-esteem is to remove the source. While self-esteem can be created and rebuilt, this cannot happen effectively without leaving the abuser. This means whenever possible a clean break and NO contact with the person. It can be difficult but is absolutely essential if you are going to begin the journey of reclaiming and rebuilding yourself. Often the less contact you have with an abusive partner the weaker the desire to be in their company. Spend time with people who are trustworthy, kind and have your best interests at heart. As time passes you will find yourself growing stronger and your sense of self returning as you begin to rebuild your self-esteem. Seek professional support if you find yourself in an abusive relationship and struggling with low self-esteem issues.

The Fear of Intimacy

"Those who have never known the deep intimacy and the intense companionship of mutual love have missed the best thing that life has to give." – Bertrand Russell (1872-1970), Philosopher

Those who suffer with low self-esteem issues can experience feelings of discomfort, resistance, claustrophobia or even fear when their partner expresses or demonstrates clear feelings of love and affection. Often bundled up in this particular aspect of low self-esteem and

Emotional Baggage is a deep fear of the possible consequences of intimacy. This fear says, "If I let someone get too close to me I might get hurt!" When a person has suffered emotional pain as a result of a previous relationship or other experiences it's natural they may want to protect themselves. This results in a fear of intimacy while seeking to maintain a certain amount of emotional distance and keeping their defenses up. If your relationship history shows a consistent pattern of attracting partners who have a fear of intimacy you probably have unresolved issues of your own that require attention. If you want to have a loving relationship but fear intimacy it's time to discover what is causing your fear through inner exploration, with support if necessary.

The Way Forward

"You cannot belong to anyone else until you belong to yourself." – Pearl Bailey (1918-1990), Actress & Singer

A realistic perspective is vital for the maintenance of self-esteem. Often poor self-esteem can be caused by the habit of self-blame because of the way a person considers certain aspects of their lives. High self-esteem can be very difficult to maintain consistently but there are ways to manage how we feel about ourselves and these strategies rely on cultivating the right attitude and perspective. Here are a few pointers that can help.

Facing Reality

The ability to accept any aspect of reality regarding yourself that may be difficult or simply impossible to change.

Being Willing

Having a positive attitude regarding those aspects of yourself that may be realistically possible to change or improve.

Clear Values

Self-esteem relies on having clear values and standards so it's important to know your personal requirements and expectations. To maintain and raise your self-esteem your goals (see below) and values should consistently complement each other, which means you constantly feel good about yourself.

Setting Goals

The personal goals you set yourself are a direct reflection of your level of self-respect. When you set large but realistic goals with a plan this gives you confidence and direction and raises your self-esteem. Setting a personal goal and then breaking it down into smaller parts makes it manageable. As you complete each step your self-esteem will increase automatically. To feel good about yourself it's important to have clear goals and to be working towards achieving them because the closer you come to fulfilling your goals the better you feel about yourself. This positive attitude will naturally permeate other areas of your life.

Review Progress

You have to monitor, measure and compare your progress against your values and standards to make sure you are on track while being consistent with what you believe.

Personal Accomplishments

A great booster of self-esteem is receiving recognition for any of your achievements. When the people in your life who you respect and admire acknowledge you as a person or your accomplishments it nurtures your self-esteem.

Personal Rewards

External rewards for accomplishing your goals while being true to yourself are encouraging and fuel your enthusiasm but if your circumstances do not provide you with large tangible rewards you have to give them to yourself!

To build and nurture your self-esteem you must reward yourself, and it doesn't matter if the rewards or treats you give to yourself are big or small. The important thing is to do it. Each time you reward yourself this confirms you are a worthwhile person and encourages enthusiasm and positive self-esteem.

Personal Comparisons

This is not about making unrealistic comparisons with others or telling yourself someone else is much better than you! In any field of work or endeavor, those who are at the top of their game constantly compare themselves with other successful people. They study their colleagues or competitors' performances and then seek to match them or become better. Positive, inspiring role models can help you to build and maintain your self-esteem as you seek to emulate the personality traits and values that you admire. When someone is consistent and determined success can be a natural by-product so often the only way a person can stay motivated is to compete against themselves by continuously seeking to improve on their previous achievements.

Maintaining high self-esteem is not about being conceited or narcissistic; the fact is if you fail to positively nurture yourself you will have very little of genuine worth to contribute to a healthy relationship anyway. All of your relationships begin with you and the quality of your relationships will always be a reflection of how you are relating to yourself. Your level of self-esteem will always be a major determining factor in your relationship choices and experiences.

With high self-esteem the positive aspects of life are much more accessible and your ability to enjoy a wide range of activities is greatly enhanced. Our self-esteem affects how we experience living and whether we find our lives generally pleasurable or miserable. Possessing healthy levels of self-esteem helps us to feel good about ourselves and motivates us to be confident and loving as well as being open to receive love. Positive self-esteem is about self-love without being selfish, arrogant or egotistical and equips us to handle many of the stresses and problems that life invariable throws at us.

Self-esteem is all about how you feel about yourself. It influences your attitude, health and seriously impacts on your intimate and romantic relationships. If you believe you can build a rewarding and meaningful connection with someone else without first truly connecting with yourself and maintaining a healthy sense of self-esteem, all of your relationships will probably bring you nothing more than heartache and disappointment.

A loving relationship can greatly enrich your life, but it's not supposed to be your life! The love you have to share begins with self-love; not the negative personality traits of arrogance or extreme narcissism but a healthy and nurturing love of self. Maintaining healthy levels of self-esteem or self-worth is each individual's personal responsibility. Relying on others to feel good about yourself can leave you vulnerable to being manipulated. When someone suffers from low self-esteem their relationships will probably suffer but when both partners have healthy self-esteem the partnership will be balanced and indeed more likely to flourish.

CHAPTER 7:

Understanding And Developing Emotional Intelligence

"But the rational mind usually doesn't decide what emotions we 'should' have!" –Daniel Goleman, *Emotional Intelligence: Why It Can Matter More Than IQ*

The traditional view of having a successful and happy life relies largely on the belief that Intelligence Quotient (IQ) scores and academic achievements largely determine the destinies of children and adults. Contrary to this opinion, it's not the people with the highest IQ who become the most successful or live happiest lives but those with high levels of Emotional Intelligence (referred to as EQ or EI). Psychologists believe those who live fulfilling lives have often mastered the skill of using their Emotional Intelligence and this is absolutely essential in forming, developing, maintaining and enhancing successful careers and close personal relationships. A person with high levels of EI can be defined as someone with the ability to understand, manage and effectively express personal feelings. These people are also successful at engaging, navigating and validating the emotions of others.

Emotional Intelligence can affect the following areas of your life:

- **Mental Health.** When stress is not managed effectively it can negatively impact your mental health making you vulnerable to feelings of anxiety or even depression. A failure to understand and manage your emotions can leave you vulnerable to experiencing erratic mood swings.

- **Health.** If you find it difficult to manage your stress levels, this can result in very serious health problems. Severe stress can suppress the immune system and raise blood pressure. It increases the risk of strokes or heart attacks and speeds up the aging process.

- **Work Performance and Relationship Management.** Effective Emotional Intelligence can help you to reduce personal stress levels at work. It can also help you to develop and maintain good relationships, communicate clearly, motivate others, work well in a team, effectively manage any conflicts and succeed in your career.

- **Relationships.** The failure to form and maintain positive relationships leaves many people feeling lonely and isolated. Understanding your emotions and how to control them puts you in a much stronger position to express how you feel and to also understand how others are feeling. The ability to understand how emotions influence your choices and the decisions of others provides a healthy foundation for building healthier relationships.

Attachment styles and Emotional Intelligence are considered to be linked as childhood experiences tend to shape our expectations and the way we relate to others. If you have a pattern of becoming disconnected from others or become distant in your intimate relationships this could be due to your attachment style. While the concept of Emotional Intelligence has its critics, a vast number of psychologists believe people who struggle to maintain healthy relationships have a lower EI than those with higher levels. If you have a history of unsatisfying relationships raising your Emotional Intelligence could drastically increase the chances of interacting with others in new and positive ways, expand your options in the dating game or improve your current relationship. A failure to manage your emotions results in being at their mercy. History is littered with examples of men and women who have made very poor or even fatal decisions based on their undisciplined emotions. If you fail to manage your emotions they will dictate your choices, which can result in very unhealthy habits, situations and relationships that can be highly disappointing or even dangerous.

But what is Emotional Intelligence, and how do you know if you score high or low? Emotional Intelligence is the ability to identify, use and manage emotions in positive ways. If you have a high level you will be skilled at the following:

- **Understanding Emotions:** Comprehending emotional language while appreciating different emotions in relation to each other.
- **Perceiving Emotions:** Identifying your own emotions and detecting and understanding emotions in others. This ability makes it possible to process all other emotional information available.
- **Managing Emotions:** Regulating personal emotions within yourself and behaving in ways that influences the emotions in others.
- **Using Emotions:** Harnessing emotions to facilitate a variety of activities, such as creative thinking and problem solving. This supports adapting to any changing moods to achieve a task or goal.

The human brain processes information through our senses. When the data becomes overwhelming the body produces adrenaline while emotions become volatile and stress takes over the ability to think and act rationally. The fight or flight response can cause many to make rash decisions or freeze like a rabbit caught in the headlights of an oncoming car. The ability to make the right choices relies greatly on managing our emotions constructively. We will then find it easier to engage in effective communication, empathize with others, overcome challenges, resolve conflicts and alleviate stress.

Emotional Intelligence Test

Answer the following True or False?

- I often try to find fault in others, including my partner if I am in a relationship.
- I find it difficult to accept or admit blame.
- I find it almost impossible to see anything positive in difficult situations.
- It takes me quite a long time to recover from setbacks.
- I tend to become frustrated quickly.

- I find it difficult to read people and often miss subtle emotional cues in others, including my partner if I am in a relationship.
- I often feel some kind of enjoyment and get a "rush" when I am negative or angry.
- I often say things in the heat of the moment that I regret later on.
- I tend to respond in an aggressive manner immediately if I am criticized by others or my partner if I am in a relationship.
- I often find it difficult to say what I am feeling to others or my partner if I am in a relationship.
- I have been accused of being insensitive several times by previous partners or my current partner.
- I often feel betrayed by others.
- I often feel in a bad mood but do not understand why.

Answering "True" to five or more statements indicates you may have some work to do on developing your Emotional Intelligence. You could be limiting your chances of enjoying a healthy, rewarding relationship.

Consider what type of situations or behaviors act as triggers for negative thinking or behavior to help you to identify any recurring issues. When you have identified one or several emotional triggers, think about what causes you to react in that way. For example, are these negative emotions motivated by feelings of insecurity, fear of abandonment or a lack of being in control? If you're struggling to deal with issues that come up, a competent therapist or counselor may be able to help you understand the roots of where these feelings stem from, and learn how to respond appropriately and in healthier ways. Those with high levels of Emotional Intelligence have the ability to consistently recognize their own emotional states and to identify the emotional states of others. This means that as you address the issues that act as triggers for negative thinking or behavior you will naturally strengthen other abilities, such as:

- **Self-Awareness:** The ability to recognize your own emotions and how they affect your thoughts and behavior. You should be aware of your strengths and weaknesses while possessing self-confidence and high self-esteem.
- **Self-Management:** The ability to control impulsive feelings and behaviors while constructively managing your emotions. This supports taking the initiative when required, following through on commitments and adapting effectively to changing circumstances whenever necessary.
- **Social Awareness:** The ability to pick up on emotional cues, feel comfortable in social situations while understanding and empathizing with the emotions, desires and concerns of other people. This includes recognizing the power dynamics in groups or organizations.

There are key skills required to improve and maintain your Emotional Intelligence. Each skill builds on the other and once the first two skills have been mastered this makes it easier to practice and learn the final three skills.

The Five Foundations of Effective Emotional Intelligence (EQ) requires learning how to:

- Quickly reduce stress
- Recognize and manage your emotions
- Connect and relate to others using nonverbal communication
- Incorporate humor and play when dealing with certain challenges
- Resolve conflicts with confidence seeking win-win solutions

Developing Skills To Deal With Stress

Developing emotional awareness first requires learning how to manage stress. High levels of stress can overwhelm the mind hindering the ability to assess or read situations accurately. This can then impact negatively on your communication or inhibit your ability to understand what someone else may be saying. The ability to quickly calm yourself down and relieve stress will help you stay balanced, focused and in control of yourself. Mastering Emotional Intelligence means no matter what challenges come your way or how much potential stress the situation may contain, you remain aware of your own feelings and needs while managing yourself effectively.

Identify Your Personal Stress Response

Most of us experience stress at some time and respond to it in different ways. If your normal response to becoming stressed is to become angry or agitated learning how to effectively manage emotions is an essential. An important aspect of Emotional Intelligence and self-awareness is recognizing when you are beginning to feel stressed. Reducing stress levels requires understanding what stress feels like for you. How does your body feel when you begin to feel stressed out? Do you get a headache or does your stomach begin to feel tight or sore? Do you have difficulty breathing or suffer from feelings of anxiety? Does stress affect your regular sleeping patterns or cause you to lose your temper often? Becoming acutely aware of your physical responses to stress will help you to manage and regulate any feelings of unease or tension when they happen.

When you're feeling stressed or under pressure the most important thing to remember is to keep calm. If you begin to feel upset or angry pause, take a few slow, deep breaths and count to 10 slowly. Resist the temptation to say something you might later regret! Pausing gives you the time and mental space to consider a constructive response that can pave the way to resolving instead of escalating the problem.

- If you still feel upset after breathing deeply and mentally counting to 10 remove yourself from the situation if possible. Revisit the issue when you have calmed down.
- If you do decide to disengage go and splash some cold water on your face and then step outside for some fresh air as cooler temperatures can help to reduce anxiety levels. Avoid drinks with caffeine, which can stimulate feelings of nervousness.
- If you still feel overwhelmed or confused while outside go for a walk in the park. Surround yourself with the sights and sounds of nature if this is possible. The colors

of green and blue have a calming effect for many people. While walking take deep breaths, try to clear your mind and hopefully you will return to the issue with a new perspective.

Investigate And Discover Personal Stress Reducing Techniques

Many people find the best way to quickly reduce stress is by engaging one or more of the five senses. Each individual responds differently to sensory input, so it's important to spend some time discovering things that you find soothing or energizing. For example, a visual person may decide to relieve stress by surrounding themselves with uplifting images while someone who prefers auditory stimulation will respond positively to sound such as playing music. Behavioral or character traits can also play a role in your choice of stress-reducing techniques. Those who tend to become withdrawn or depressed often respond to stress-relieving activities that are stimulating such as aerobics, high impact work-outs or jogging. People who have a tendency freeze up will often find activities that provide both stimulation and comfort to help relieve stressful feelings. Practicing deep breathing exercises and meditation are both great stress-busting strategies. The ability to manage stress provides the foundation to feeling more comfortable responding to any strong or unpleasant emotions. Changing the way you handle stress will transform and improve how you experience and respond to your feelings.

Developing Emotional Awareness

The ability to connect with your core emotions and consistently monitor your feelings while accepting those feelings is essential for cultivating Emotional Intelligence. Understanding your emotions and how they may have influenced some of your thoughts and actions in the past can help you to avoid making similar mistakes in the future. Developing emotional awareness will also help you to understand other people in new and deeper ways. It's important to acknowledge there are people who are disconnected from their emotions, especially the powerful emotions of anger, sadness, fear and joy. This suppression or avoidance of emotions can be motivated by negative childhood experiences, where a person has conditioned themselves to shut down their feelings. Deeply engrained negative feelings can be suppressed, distorted, denied or even numbed by alcohol or drugs but cannot be removed and will always be present until the issues are healed. Those who lack emotional awareness often find themselves unable to fully understand their own motivations and needs or have difficulty communicating effectively with others.

Body Language And Nonverbal Communication

Those with a high EI generally have a greater ability to accurately perceive and assess the emotional, physical and verbal expressions of others. They are also effective communicators who make their intentions clear. Effective communicators rely on much more than just verbal skills. *What* is said is generally much less important than *how* it's said. How loud or how quickly you talk and the tone of your voice can say much more than what is actually said. Body language such as gestures, how close you stand to someone, how you sit, the position of your arms, and the amount of eye contact maintained all convey nonverbal communication. In order to hold someone's attention while building a connection and trust, it's important to be aware of your own body language. It's also essential to have the ability to accurately read and respond to any nonverbal cues other people direct at you. When you are not speaking you're still communicating nonverbally so try to be aware of what type of messages you are transmitting to others and whether what you're saying matches what you're actually feeling. For example, if you're speaking to someone clenching your teeth and looking away while insisting everything is OK, your words and body language will not match as the nonverbal communication is clearly sending the opposite message to your words.

Nonverbal messages can create a sense of interest, trust, excitement and a desire for a deeper connection, or generate fear, confusion, distrust and disinterest.

Improving Nonverbal Communication

Successful nonverbal communication depends on the ability to manage stress, recognize your own emotions and understand the signals you're sending and receiving. When communicating:

- **Focus:** If you are preoccupied with what you're going to say next, not paying attention or distracted in some other way it's likely you will miss important nonverbal cues and other subtleties during the interaction. Focus on the other person.

- **Maintain Eye Contact:** Consistent eye contact can communicate an interest in what the other person is saying, maintain conversation flow and help to measure the other person's likely response.

- **Pay Attention:** Be aware of the nonverbal cues you're sending and receiving including facial expressions, tone of voice, posture and gestures, any touching along with the timing and pace of the conversation.

People often behave or react for reasons that have more to do with them than the other person. When we avoid personalizing other people's behaviors this makes it much easier to perceive the expressions of others more objectively. Ask open-ended questions and seek clarification whenever necessary so you clearly understand the other person's position. Avoid any accusations or judgments as this will make others feel defensive and less likely to be receptive to your point of view. Compare the other person's words with their body language and behavior to monitor consistency or any mixed signals. Widening your perspective on a situation or behavior can greatly reduce the possibility of avoidable misunderstandings. In contrast, simply reacting emotionally just increases the potential for drama! There are times when it is necessary and important to set clear and firm boundaries. You have the right to set your own priorities, protect yourself against inappropriate behavior, to assertively disagree with others or to refuse a request without feeling guilty.

Using Humor To Deal With Challenges

Having a good sense of humor and enjoying laughter or being appropriately playful can help to lighten life's burdens and help us to keep things in their correct perspective. A good laugh even at ourselves reduces stress and improves our state of mind while bringing the nervous system back into balance.

- **Taking Difficulties And Hardships In Your Stride:** A good sense of humor will allow you to view any frustrations or disappointments from new perspectives. The ability to laugh even in the face of difficulties can support you in surviving annoyances, setbacks or very tough times. It will improve your general attitude.

- **Conflict Resolution:** Using gentle humor can often help you to say things that might be difficult to express without creating conflict or unnecessary drama.
- **Relax And Energize:** Playful communication relaxes the body and relieves fatigue, which will allows you to recharge effectively and therefore accomplish much more.
- **Enhancing Creativity:** Being relaxed means freeing your mind from rigid ways of thinking and this in turn supports becoming more creative or seeing situations or problems in new ways.

Developing Playful Communication

- Schedule time for regular quality playtime. The more time you spend joking around, playing and laughing the easier the habit of enjoying life becomes.
- Follow your bliss and pursue enjoyable activities that help you to discover (or rediscover) your playful nature.
- Practice having fun with outgoing people who appreciate playful banter or spend time playing with animals, babies, or young children.

Constructive Conflict Resolution

Two people cannot possibly have the same needs, opinions or expectations all the time and conflicts and disagreements are inevitable in any relationship. Constructive and healthy conflict resolution can strengthen and build trust between people. Generally, when a conflict isn't seen as being threatening or punitive, this fosters a sense of safety, freedom of expression and creativity within relationships. Effective conflict resolution that builds positive, trust-based relationships is supported by the previous four foundation skills of Emotional Intelligence. The ability to manage stress, remain emotionally present and aware, communicate constructively both verbally and nonverbally, and to use play and a sense of humor, will equip you to handle difficult or emotionally testing situations. Taken together these abilities will help to defuse a range of issues before they escalate out of control.

Resolving Conflict While Seeking To Build Trust

- **Stay Focused In The Now:** Memories and the thinking process are linked strongly to emotions; if you think of a bad or sad experience in your life these thoughts will negatively influence how you feeling in the now. Carrying around old emotional wounds and resentments cloud judgment and greatly inhibits emotional awareness and intelligence. Being focused in the present helps you to recognize the reality of a situation or experience and view it as a new learning opportunity instead of being motivated by unhealed or unresolved feelings of bitterness or resentment.
- **Choose Your Battles:** Be careful where you direct your energy. Consider what is worth making a stand on and when it might be better to walk away. Disagreements or bitter arguments can use up a great deal of time and exasperate the situation leaving you or your opponent feeling lingering resentment. Always try to resolve any disagreements in a positive way and seek win-win solutions.

- **Forgiveness:** Constantly remembering the hurtful behavior of other people means you're living in the past. Effective conflict resolution requires giving up the urge to punish others or seek revenge.

- **Know When to Quit:** It takes a minimum of two people to engage in conflict. Sometimes it's just easier to agree to disagree and take a decision to disengage if matters cannot be resolved. End conflicts that can't be resolved.

The ability to express intimate emotions effectively is essential for maintaining close personal relationships. This means sharing intimate feelings with your partner in an appropriate manner that is constructive and nourishing to the relationship, and the ability to respond positively. Psychologist Dr. John Gottman uses a term he refers to as "bidding" to describe intimate interaction within healthy relationships. Bids can be big or small and there are a huge variety of behaviors that can be a "bid." According to Gottman consistent bidding is crucial in the maintenance and development of close, personal relationships. These bids are expressions of care displaying intimate emotions between partners that create or maintain a positive connection between partners. Appreciative words and gestures convey love and care: "You're important in my life" or "I care about you" and similar phrases allows the other person to feel validated. A sincere apology can also be a bid that demonstrates remorse and respect for the other person's feelings. Body language bidding examples would be maintaining positive eye contact, hugging, smiling, and placing your arm around someone's shoulder while behavioral bidding includes empathetic listening, giving your partner a thoughtful gift or sharing any activity that creates a closer bond. Offering someone assistance or support would also be a form of behavioral bidding as it lets the other person know that you care about their wellbeing.

The Way Forward

"Your self-talk is the channel of behavior change" – Gino Norris Author, *The Stress Diaries*

There are very few short cuts when it comes to learning a new skill so a certain amount of time, discipline, perseverance and daily practice will be required to break any poor emotional response patterns that may be sabotaging your relationships. Emotional Intelligence is widely seen as an important factor in the lives of successful people living highly enjoyable lives. While Emotional Intelligence is not currently thought to change significantly over a lifetime for most people, higher levels can be developed with the right approach and a strong desire for personal growth. Significant improvements in all of your relationships are quite possible when you begin to develop and harness your Emotional Intelligence effectively.

CHAPTER 8:
Healing Emotional Baggage

"Until you make the unconscious conscious it will direct your life and you will call it fate."
– Carl Jung (1875-1961), Psychiatrist & Psychotherapist

Emotional Baggage is a common expression that generally refers to unresolved emotional issues that are detrimental to self and others. The term "baggage" is a metaphor for carrying around a heavy load of disappointments, wrongs and traumas from the past. It can also represent deep feelings of self-incrimination where you continually blame yourself for previously being too vulnerable, foolish or trusting. It doesn't necessarily require a traumatic event or any kind of abuse to create Emotional Baggage. For example, if you grew up with parents who never argued there may be unrealistic expectations regarding your intimate adult relationships. You could have an ideal (and unrealistic) picture of how a perfect relationship should be where disagreements or conflicts do not exist. Another form of Emotional Baggage is an addiction to relationship drama. Men and women who grew up in dysfunctional families often have a misguided concept of what a healthy relationship should look or feel like. Individuals who seem addicted to relationship drama often grew up in unstable emotional environments and may subconsciously try to recreate childhood scenarios to resolve unfinished business or to create situations in their relationships that feel "comfortable." This chaos and unpredictability feels "natural" and acceptable where a person believes that abuse and frequent dramas in a loving relationship are quite normal. Emotional Baggage can be created in other ways too, for example, suffering a dramatic drop in self-confidence, deep feelings of insecurity or a loss of other personal qualities we may value. It can be also caused by the loss of a significant person in our life or by the betrayal of someone we love, trust or respect. Whatever the reason the baggage often represents an emotional scar from a traumatic experience or a deep feeling of loss.

Generally, we have all experienced Emotional Baggage to varying degrees and it's likely you know at least one person who has been through some kind of severe emotional or even physical trauma during their formative years. It may have been the death of parent, a nasty divorce or even severe physical or emotional abuse. Many people have experienced something traumatic during their lifetimes but the difference is how these individuals have dealt with the trauma. When negative experiences are not processed effectively this creates Emotional Baggage. What makes a crucial difference between an emotionally healthy person and someone burdened with issues from the past is the deliberate unpacking of any baggage that may be sabotaging their relationships.

Excessive Emotional Baggage manifests itself in two ways in relationships. One is negative expectations created by *previous* negative relationship experiences. The second is a rehashing of previous problems in a current relationship where small incidents become magnified due to earlier issues which cannot be forgiven or resolved by the baggage carrier. Your perspective of the past greatly determines how you see the present and your future. Perhaps certain ex-partners mistreated you but this doesn't mean the next man will treat you badly. In the aftermath of a failed relationship it's natural to feel sad, angry or even bitter but walking around with those kinds of feelings means you're carrying baggage that could take over your life. That's why it's so important to unpack and resolve any issues from the past. Don't allow previous difficult experiences or relationships to make you cynical about finding the kind of love you would like to enjoy.

How Emotional Baggage Can Affect Your Relationships

Sabotaging Your Love Prospects

Don't make sweeping assumptions. Each new potential partner should be assessed according his own unique merits and flaws instead of being evaluated based on your previous relationship experiences. It can be very easy to miss out on a man who could be a great match by carrying Emotional Baggage into the relationship and projecting negative past relationship experiences onto someone new. Each of us are in control of our "dating destiny" and quite capable of breaking free and changing destructive dating and relationship patterns.

Attracted To Partners With Similar Or Complimentary Baggage

In the dating game people with similar baggage are often attracted to each other with disastrous results as issues are reactivated and become exposed in a variety of negative ways. The feelings of attraction can be mutual but so is the torment and resulting drama with each person blaming the other for how it appears their partner is making them feel. Their thinking and behavior are usually compulsive and damaging to others; while they may want to change and be more considerate the "demon" takes over when their Emotional Baggage is activated. Other people carrying around heavy Emotional Baggage often embark on relationships believing they need something from the other person. They can enter relationships believing they're seriously lacking in some way while hoping that their latest relationship will provide the love, validation and security they crave.

When you're not paying attention it's very easy to permit a partner to bring their baggage into the relationship. Unfortunately, the longer you stay with a partner with unresolved issues the more likely they are to dump some of their baggage on you. Dealing with someone's baggage makes you susceptible to react in ways that can activate any of your own any unresolved issues. Baggage often makes people insecure about a relationship so they end up overcompensating by being too needy or spending too much time together. They use the other person to try and compensate for their lack of self-sufficiency, self-confidence and self-respect. Matching insecurities manifest as the couple desperately cling to each other out of their own neediness, inadequacy or inferiority issues. When two people with separate sets of Emotional Baggage get together it usually equals relationship drama in one form or another. Unless they resolve their individual issues this often becomes a vicious cycle of the same type of relationships but with different partners.

Sadly their lack of self-awareness means they cannot relate to themselves but expect others to understand and accommodate behavior or outbursts that can be highly toxic. Even when an individual suspects or knows they're carrying baggage and recognize their behavior is destructive it can be difficult to stop repeating the same scenarios. When couples have matching or similar baggage one or both partners may come to realize each person has to take personal responsibility for their roles in creating pain, confusion and frustration.

Subconsciously Influencing You To Become Involved With Unkind Or Abusive Partners

Negative beliefs are generated by unresolved and unpacked Emotional Baggage. Our deeply held beliefs play a significant part in determining what we believe we deserve so if you believe you're worthless or don't deserve to be loved those are the type of partners you are likely to attract. Having a tendency to obsess about your previous relationship failures reinforces negative Emotional Programming by replaying depressing memories and feelings in your head. Obsessing about painful incidents or relationships from the past isn't healthy and is a form of self-sabotage. This will seriously hinder your ability to enjoy healthy relationships in the future.

How Emotional Baggage Impacts Negatively On Perception

Emotional Baggage stores psychological pain in the subconscious mind and when activated it appears other people are responsible for making us feel negative. Often these negative feelings are familiar but heightened emotions cloud objectivity overshadowing and dominating our experience. Men and women who feel insecure or who suffer from low self-esteem may consciously or subconsciously sabotage their relationships by engaging in behaviors that eventually drive their partners away. This reinforces and confirms their own worst fears and beliefs about themselves.

Unprocessed Negative Conditioning, Experiences or Damaged Emotional Programming = Emotional Baggage

Processed or Healed Negative Conditioning, Experiences or Damaged Emotional Programming = Healthy Relationship Experiences

The thinking processes of those carrying heavy Emotional Baggage can be very unreliable at times due to adherence to denials, distortions and convenient excuses instead of facing facts. Blaming those who identify their behavior as being irrational, unreasonable or unfair, the baggage carrier often ruthlessly attacks anyone who suggests it's their behavior or attitude that is causing a problem.

If you are carrying Emotional Baggage you will often:

- React in ways that are unconscious or unintentional and may have episodes where you're not always in control of how emotional you get.
- Suffer panic attacks creating excessive anxiety that is difficult to manage, which often results in unfairly taking out your frustrations on others.
- Feel justified in seeking revenge on those you think have treated you unfairly.

- Feel possessed, burdened or damaged in some way but struggle to understand where these emotions are coming from.
- Project your Emotional Baggage by acting out, having temper tantrums or by abusing others in a variety of ways.
- Try to make others feel guilty for any real or perceived insults or seek revenge to show the other person who's in control.
- Have urges to punish anyone who is perceived to be responsible for making you feel bad about yourself, becoming extremely unforgiving, unreasonable and vindictive.
- Experience extreme difficulty understanding or empathizing with someone else's point of view.

While some people carrying Emotional Baggage can feel threatened by different points of view, others can pretend to agree on almost everything, which results in conversations that are mostly superficial, manipulative or exploitative. Others invent disguises pretending they don't have any real issues. They present themselves as being rational, thoughtful and respectful of others or put on a show of being self-assured, gregarious and confident. The façade crumbles when someone or something activates their baggage: their subconscious minds revisits and brings to the surface a traumatic loss, setback, failure or crisis. They will then compulsively act out these repressed memories or retreat into themselves seething with intense feelings of dissatisfaction, pain or resentment. Unresolved issues can cause irrational outbursts of anger that erupt when the emotional wound is disturbed or reopened. The result is damaged relationships.

Three Steps to Unpacking Emotional Baggage

It is possible to heal unresolved issues but it takes a great deal of courage, self-awareness and a willingness to be honest.

Step 1: Be Honest With Yourself

This requires complete honesty and a willingness to dig deep into any issues with a trusted friend (not your partner if you're currently involved) or with a professional therapist/counselor. Discuss, explore and face your issues openly. For example, the issue might be a bad temper where you shout, slam doors or display even worse types of behavior. While it's obvious the temper tantrums need to be addressed the essential point is to discover what feelings or memories trigger these outbursts. Whatever the issue may be, you must be willing to be totally honest before any meaningful unpacking, progress and healing can begin.

Step 2: Stop Playing The Blame Game

It's very easy to go through life blaming other people from the past. You can blame your parents, your siblings or even an ex-partner who treated you badly, cheated on you and broke your heart.

Some people have a pattern of constantly blaming themselves. They go through their entire lives playing this destructive game. The truth is, blaming yourself or others doesn't change anything so don't engage in it. Unpacking Emotional Baggage requires you to take responsibility for your own emotions and behavior.

If you have blamed someone in your past consider how you have described their character and actions. Consider your own actions and explore areas where you may have to take some responsibility yourself. Keep in mind you may have been acting out your own issues, which may have contributed to the situation.

Step 3: Forgive

Forgiveness is an essential act for healing any emotional pain you may have experienced. Refusing to forgive means you're the person stuck with the negative feelings of anger, bitterness and revenge. It's not always easy to forgive but the truth is the act of forgiveness is a gift you give to yourself. Learning to forgive yourself is just as important as forgiving others. A person who is filled with bitterness and resentment cannot extend authentic love to others.

The Importance Of Healing The Past

"Forgiveness is not a one off decision; it is a journey and a process that takes time, determination, and persistence. Forgiveness is not forgetting; it is simply denying your pain the right to control your life." – Corallie Buchanan, *Watch Out! Godly Women on the Loose*

Many psychologists believe the difficulties some people experience in their intimate relationships are directly linked to past childhood experiences and conditioning. When a person becomes involved with someone new, dormant or suppressed memories from all of their previous programming, including any emotional damage, may be reactivated. Your past experiences are a part of your Emotional Programming and any baggage you may be carrying around isn't just going to disappear overnight or sort itself out. Unresolved issues from the past will continue to impact negatively on your present and must be healed before you can confidently look forward to the future. Each of us can only connect with our partners on whatever level our personal Emotional Programming allows us to. Only by surrendering to healing will you be able to open yourself up to the truth instead of being motivated by the illusions created by the unhealed emotional wounds.

Confronting and then healing specific issues may be difficult at times as certain patterns of thinking or entrenched beliefs can be very persistent, but with commitment, discipline and determination you can "rewrite" any negative Emotional Programming. Examining your relationship history and understanding the motivation behind certain relationship choices will empower you to make better decisions. The only way effective change can begin to happen is when you decide to identify the patterns of thinking that sabotage your relationships and then to do whatever is necessary to heal those patterns. Healing can only begin to happen when any emotional issues have been identified and resolved.

Before becoming romantically involved with anyone it makes sense to check yourself out and examine any issues that could be causing a problem. It will help you to cultivate greater self-awareness. If you do not discover, understand and heal your patterns your next relationship will bring up the very same issues that surfaced during your last relationship. That means the same patterns, the same issues and the same baggage. It also means you will continue to attract the same types of people until you have resolved your own issues and patterns. To understand why you have been entertaining inappropriate partners, you have to start look-ing at yourself and your own patterns.

You cannot keep looking outside yourself for the reason for your poor relationship choices: they reside within you. Following your heart means you can unconsciously follow your Emo-tional Programming, fantasies and hormones. If you keep doing the same old thing without even understanding why you are doing it nothing will change. Ultimately it's your respon-sibility to heal and change the patterns and habits so you can experience a different reality instead of repeating self-defeating patterns and behaviors.

Many people live with the hope of meeting someone "special" who will "discover" and "bring out" their best qualities, but really they're just waiting to be rescued – from themselves. En-tering a relationship with unresolved issues or Emotional Baggage expecting your partner to be "supportive" is unfair, unrealistic and irresponsible. You wouldn't expect to be some kind of amateur therapist for a new partner and it is very unreasonable to embark on a new relationship feeling unsure about any Emotional Baggage that may be impacting negatively on how you relate to others. Waiting for someone to rescue you from yourself is also being lazy and dishonest: why should someone else try and do something for you that you should have done for yourself? When you're relying on someone else to encourage or facilitate posi-tive change for you instead of doing it for yourself, you could be waiting for a very long time!

The Consequences Of Unhealed Emotional Issues

- A failure to identify, understand and heal your negative patterns means you're probably going to repeat the same mistakes.
- If you fail to cultivate your self-awareness your prospects for having a successful relationship will not improve.
- You will miss out on the opportunity to come face-to-face with the best version of who you can be because you are operating out of distortions rather than truth.

Walking around with unhealed Emotional Baggage leaves you susceptible to manipulation or exploitation by others with their own selfish agendas. People often complain bitterly about their past relationship choices but the truth is we each choose our relationships, they don't choose us! Talking to a trusted family member, a good friend or seeing a counselor/therapist can help you to identify, understand and heal any issues that may be affecting you and your relationship choices. If you find yourself struggling with any issues make it a priority to receive support. Once any negative patterns have been identified and healed you will be in a much better position to change the way you relate to others and make wiser and healthier relationship choices.

Becoming involved when you suspect or know you're emotionally and mentally unprepared is a recipe likely to cause a great deal of confusion, disappointment and heartache. The reality is there are many men and women who WANT a relationship but are not necessarily READY for love. You can save a potential partner and yourself a great deal of drama by not getting involved until you're relatively confident any heavy Emotional Baggage has been thoroughly unpacked, healed and dealt with properly.

However, hoping and wishing for change without a genuine effort to address your issues is a fu-tile waste of time. You also have to believe things can change otherwise it is likely they will not.

The Benefits Of Unpacking And Dealing With Emotional Baggage

"The time has come to lay that baggage down and leave behind all the struggling and striving. You can be set free as you journey forward into a balanced healthy and rewarding future." – Sue Augustine, *When Your Past Is Hurting Your Present*

Growing up in a home where you received love, encouragement, support and security from your parents is more likely to provide a positive model for conducting a successful relationship. If you didn't grow up in such an environment, it may prove harder to develop a strong bond with a partner, especially if you have unresolved Emotional Baggage. Unresolved issues represent our ghosts from the past; something happened or someone did something that needs to be understood, healed and put to rest. Nothing remains dead and buried as far as the mind is concerned so while you might try to forget and "move on" your demons may still be lurking.

Emotional Baggage can cause people to have a compulsive need to restrict or control others. Eventually this behavior feels restrictive, suffocating or confining and inevitably damages their professional and personal relationships. Unresolved Emotional Baggage can make people very toxic to be around. Control freaks, bigots and sexual or emotional predators are often motivated to behave in very damaging ways due to unhealed emotional issues. Whatever the damage is, it has been too difficult to process and resolve so has been transferred into the subconscious mind to remove it from their conscious thinking. By undertaking the process of unpacking your Emotional Baggage, you will begin to expand your self-respect and discover new perspectives, priorities, talents or passions that may have been blocked or dormant. You will also learn to tame the demons that may make you act compulsively in ways that are self-defeating and damaging to others. Another valuable outcome can be to understand how you may have kept certain aspects of yourself suppressed because you were not equipped to express yourself confidently, maturely and compassionately.

- Relating to others in healthy ways promotes mutual cooperation and provides the people with whom you interact with a feeling of independence.
- Instead of being sensitive to criticism you will be comfortable to listen to the opinions of others. This will expand your own point of view as you explore how they may see things from a different perspective.
- By effectively communicating and relating to others, they will feel understood, respected and validated. The Emotional Baggage carried into relationships often creates misunderstandings; disrespect and invalidation can make others feel small, intimidated and inferior.
- With increased self-awareness it will be easier to forgive others who may have hurt your feelings and the incident may even prompt you to ask new questions about yourself.

Tackling painful issues from the past can be difficult but there is no point ignoring issues that may still be impacting negatively on your life. "Time heals" is an old saying but this doesn't really work without engaging actively in the unpacking and healing process. Deciding to unpack our Emotional Baggage requires courage but the rewards can be tremendous.

Ultimately we can either choose to be slaves to our Emotional Baggage for the rest of our lives or choose freedom. Life always gives us a choice.

The Way Forward

"It's hard to be clear about who you are when you are carrying around a bunch of baggage from the past. I've learned to let go and move more quickly into the next place."
– Angelina Jolie, American Actress, Filmmaker & Humanitarian

All of us have various degrees of Emotional Baggage so this is nothing to feel ashamed about. Identifying and dealing with any negative patterns of relating will break the cycle of frustration, pain and sadness that may be sabotaging your choices. It is quite possible to enjoy a healthy, happy and fulfilling relationship providing you're honest with yourself and take the time to heal any issues from the past. The people who have taken the time to unpack and resolve the contents of their various "suitcases" are unburdened from carrying around baggage. They have explored their histories, what they felt about the past and reevaluated their feelings. The process of identifying and understanding certain emotional belief patterns while exploring previous experiences can serve as an amazing catalyst for valuable insights, personal growth and greater maturity.

If you have experienced a great deal of difficult, humiliating or even traumatic romantic relationships in the past it's important to protect yourself emotionally until you're truly ready to try love again. If you're currently involved and suspect you or your partner has Emotional Baggage that is negatively impacting on your relationship arrange to see a professional counselor, or therapist, or join a recognized support group.

CHAPTER 9:

Relationship Patterns

"You are the embodiment of the information you choose to accept and act upon. To change your circumstances you need to change your thinking and subsequent actions." – Adlin Sinclair, American Businessman, Motivational Speaker & Humanitarian

Many people become comfortable and complacent with second-rate, negative relationships, often being too lazy to make any real effort to investigate themselves. For many it's much easier to blame others than to take an honest look within for any possible answers regarding their relationship history and failures. Following your heart (impulses) unconsciously often means being motivated by fantasies, hormones or unresolved emotional patterns of relating. Refusing to honestly evaluate our relationship histories often results in repeating very similar interpersonal dramas with just the partners changing but the outcomes remaining the same. Looking outside yourself for answers while refusing to acknowledge that the cause could be your own negative patterns of attraction and relating means you're living in denial and sabotaging your love life. If your relationships keep failing you have to look within for the reasons, start taking responsibility and begin the process of healing any unresolved issues.

Typical Negative Relationship Pattern Scenarios

Rushing Into Relationships

The timing of significant moments of your previous relationships, like the first kiss or when a commitment was mutually agreed, can indicate a pattern of becoming involved too quickly. When there is a rush from dating into a relationship this can indicate either one or both partners being impulsive, overeager or even insecure. Stable, healthy relationships that endure the test of time usually develop gradually.

Poor Emotional Management

The beginning of a new romance can reveal a certain pattern of relating. How do you usually manage the transition from being single to being in a relationship? Some people have a pattern of beginning new relationships feeling intense infatuation, which may result in premature sex. This can lead to confusion about the status of the relationship. Strong attraction and chemistry should be a factor in a new relationship but the key is how you manage feelings of passion or lust. The way emotions are managed at the beginning often dictates whether a relationship will develop in a healthy way or establishes a dysfunctional pattern of relating.

Repeat Performances

You have been involved with several relationships that initially appeared to be full of promise but failed to deliver. Although you have been involved with different partners the relationships often begins and ends in a similar manner.

Internal or External Conflicts

Although you generally feel positive at the beginning of a relationship deep down inside you felt uncomfortable. There may be inherent feelings anxiousness, uncertainty, worry or even jealously and distress.

Physical Sensations

You may feel an uncomfortable physical response that is triggered by something your partner said or did. For example, your anxiety levels may rise, you feel your stomach tightening up or you feel generally defensive but can't really understand why.

Feelings of Loss

During each relationship you felt there was a really strong emotional connection despite there being a great deal of uncertainty, shame, humiliation, pain or suffering. After the failure of each relationship you felt a deep sense of loss and emptiness.

Obsessing

If your partner ends the relationship you tend to blame yourself for pushing him away. You then become obsessed with the idea of persuading him to be the loving, accepting person you're desperate to be with.

Vulnerability

Your sense of self-esteem often feels low or threatened. You often feel overwhelmed or very vulnerable whether you're single or in a relationship. A major factor that often creates a negative relationship pattern can be deep feelings of low self-esteem. Subconsciously you may feel unworthy, have a fear of abandonment or betrayal but really want to love someone and be loved in return. Many people blame their own imperfections for their relationship failures, which can lead to feelings of even lower low self-esteem.

Drama Junkie

Do your previous relationships have a pattern of drama? Do you have a need for constant stimulation and find it difficult to relax? When a person has been strongly programmed for drama due to their childhood experiences he or she can feel as if something is "missing" even when their lives are going well. You may be subconsciously compelled to create various problems or conflicts to regain a feeling of normality. Drama junkies often create dramas to receive attention from other people or as a distraction from their own lives. Sadly these men and women have a tendency to create dysfunctional relationships and may even cause problems deliberately to test their partner's love or loyalty. While a crisis or surviving a tough situation as a couple can, in certain circumstances, make the union feel stronger and more connected, constant drama is far from ideal for maintaining a healthy relationship or the basis for embarking on a new one. These types often feel powerless to change and fail to understand why they constantly cause themselves and their partner unnecessary problems.

Drama junkies frequently put themselves at a tremendous disadvantage when dating, often scaring away potential partners by their constant need for excessive stimulation. Those who choose to become romantically involved with these types often seem to have some kind of ongoing problem or conflict themselves that requires the drama junkies' constant attention or participation.

These kinds of underlying issues can cloud your better judgment and influence your choice of partner for all the wrong reasons. It is important to consider, identify and heal any issues that may be sabotaging your relationships by using your previous experiences to help you recognize any negative patterns of relating. Check yourself out and think objectively about how you feel or behave in your relationships.

Exercise 1: Reviewing Your Relationship History

This exercise can also help you to clarify any patterns of becoming involved with dysfunctional relationships or may reveal certain emotional issues that remain unhealed. If you suspect you have a pattern of becoming involved in unsatisfactory relationships, it's time to check yourself out.

Ask yourself the following questions:

- Am I often attracted to men who are emotionally vulnerable?
- Am I frequently attracted to partners who need to be "rescued" or cared for in some way?
- Do I often attract men who are emotionally unavailable?
- Do I rush into relationships too quickly and not pay full attention to any possible warning signs?
- Do I ignore my intuition when it is warning me to be cautious?
- Do I give myself and my trust away too easily? (In other words do you have poor boundaries?)
- How do I keep setting myself up for disappointments?
- What type of belief patterns and expectations did I inherit from my family regarding relationships?
- Do I have a pattern of becoming involved with men from broken, volatile or chaotic homes?
- Do I have any emotional issues from my childhood that remain unresolved?

Look at the questions again and consider them all very carefully. Your answers may provide valuable clues and insights that could help you to identify a negative relationship pattern.

You may know someone who consistently attracts and becomes involved with abusive partners. Unfortunately, some people act out patterns learnt in early childhood where they felt unworthy and deserving of punishment or recreate a pattern learned in the past whereby their personal concept of love and abuse are inseparably connected. They're subconsciously acting out negative patterns of relating and these men and women often decide to stay in unhealthy or even destructive relationships. Like a moth attracted to a flame, they're frequently attracted toward partners who create a dysfunctional dynamic subconsciously motivated by their childhood experiences.

Exercise 2: Reviewing Your Childhood

Conducting an honest evaluation of your relationship history also requires looking back at your childhood. Many people can be resistant to the idea of exploring their childhood experiences but it can be a very productive strategy to discover whatever is motivating your choices. An effective exercise that may help you to clarify a particular pattern is to write down the names of all your previous partners and then consider each one individually. Make a list of key words to describe each relationship. Think about what attracted you to each one. Do you have a certain type you find attractive? Are there particular physical traits that really turn you on? Write down how each relationship began listing the positive and negative aspects and experiences with each previous partner. After completing this exercise think about your childhood and write down the key words that describe your formative years and then compare the first list with the second to see if your childhood and relationship key words are similar.

For example, key words from your childhood include the following:

- Dishonesty
- Abandonment
- Betrayal

If you have described any of your relationships with similar words seriously consider whether you are recreating childhood scenarios in your adult relationships. Unconsciously relating to others on emotional "auto-pilot" can mean allowing unresolved childhood issues to greatly influence your choices and expectations. For the final stage of this exercise you should ask yourself how you would like your relationships to be different in the future and write those goals down on a separate sheet of paper or in your journal. Make sure your relationship goals are kept in a place where you can easily review them at least twice a day. This practice will help you to stay focused on the type of relationship you're looking for.

Exercise 3: Attracted To A Certain Type of Partner

A thorough appraisal of your relationship history can help you to identify if you have a tendency to become involved with certain types of men. This exercise may feel uncomfortable at times but stick with it as you may gain some valuable insights. Write down what happened in your previous relationship and how everything felt to you. Review each of your previous partners' main character traits (mostly happy, sad, moody, angry, tight with money, generous etc.), their family backgrounds and childhoods to see if there are any similarities.

Men and women often unconsciously act on their negative Emotional Programming when they're looking for a new partner and are often drawn subconsciously to partners with similar quirks or flaws that match or correspond with their own. Alternatively, men and women can deliberately or subconsciously look for certain qualities in a partner they actually lack within themselves. This often results in couples becoming involved carrying unhealed issues into the relationship, which inevitably creates a dysfunctional relating dynamic.

If you identify a pattern of becoming involved with unsatisfactory relationships it's important to understand no one is doing this to you; the problem is not outside – it's inside of you, contained in your attitudes, patterns, belief systems and expectations. When someone fails to heal any negative aspects of their Emotional Programming, there is a tendency to react compulsively with others without giving it too much thought. If you have unresolved issues this can cause you to become involved with unsuitable partners without really understanding what is motivating you to be attracted to certain types in the first place.

The Way Forward

"Those who cannot remember the past are condemned to repeat it." – George Santayana (1863-1952), Philosopher, Poet & Novelist

You may have been attracted to a particular personality type in the past but that doesn't mean you're doomed forever to make poor choices! The first step in learning how to avoid repeating a negative relationship pattern is to identify any issues that may be influencing your choices, the way you relate to others and the type of men you find attractive. Identifying any childhood experiences or conditioning that may be subconsciously compelling you to become involved in unhealthy relationships can provide important insights and help you to understand what may be motivating your beliefs and behavior.

Clearly you're not responsible for any possible negative Emotional Programming you may have received as a young child, but as an adult you're now personally accountable for addressing any issues subconsciously sabotaging your relationship choices. Your future happiness could depend on this so the stakes are very high. Taking the time to consider your relationship patterns can be challenging but a failure to tackle any emotional issues with courage means you're just setting yourself up for more relationship drama and heartache. Only when you acknowledge any issues that may be sabotaging your search for love will you be in a great position to accept and then begin the process of change and positive growth.

Attempting to consider yourself objectively is probably one of the most difficult things you will ever do. When you review your relationship history it is important to understand that being attracted to certain people is not destiny, fate or coincidence, accidental or influenced by good or bad luck. Some people prefer to rewrite their personal histories while refusing to accept any responsibility for their relationship failures. They will lie to others and themselves about what happened and how they contributed toward their relationship dramas. Honestly evaluating your romantic history will put you in the best position to discover genuine insights about yourself. Many people are very reluctant to do this but examining the past is the best way to learn important lessons and insights to prepare yourself for a brighter future.

A failure to recognize and heal unhealthy patterns of relating results in subconsciously repeating unsatisfactory, unhealthy or even destructive relationship choices. You don't have to continue repeating similar and painful relationship experiences that end up being very similar with the same disappointing results. Unpacking and dealing with any Emotional Baggage greatly reduces or even eliminates the compulsive need to continue on a merry-go-round of unnecessary drama. If you find yourself struggling to resolve a negative relationship pattern, difficult childhood memories or any other emotional issues seek professional support from a reputable therapist. It is quite possible to enjoy a healthy, happy and fulfilling successful relationship providing you're honest with yourself and determined to heal any issues from the past. Freeing yourself from negative relationship patterns can be a truly liberating and quite possibly life-changing experience.

CHAPTER 10:

Healthy Personal Boundaries

"When we fail to set boundaries and hold people accountable, we feel used and mistreated. This is why we sometimes attack who they are, which is far more hurtful than addressing a behavior or a choice." – Brené Brown, *The Gifts of Imperfection: Let Go of Who You Think You're Supposed to Be and Embrace Who You Are*

One of the biggest mistakes men and women make in the dating game is to fail to set clear personal boundaries. Your personal boundaries define how you interact with others, and how you allow others to interact with you.

Physical boundaries define who can touch us, how they can touch us and how physically close another is allowed to enter into our personal space. Those with poor or virtually non-existent boundaries are likely to touch others or allow other people to touch them inappropriately, may confuse sex with love, become sexually involved too quickly or be sexually promiscuous.

Emotional boundaries define where your feelings end and another's begins; if your boundaries are weak you will be susceptible to manipulation by guilt trips and easily convinced the negative behavior of others is really your fault. This can result in allowing yourself to be burdened with issues that in reality have absolutely nothing to do with you.

Are You A People Pleaser?

Some people have difficulty with setting personal boundaries because they don't want to say no to anyone or feel they must try to accommodate others as much as they can. This could be a sign of people pleasing.

Consider the following questions carefully to see if they apply to you:

- Do you take responsibility for your own feelings and needs while allowing others to do the same?
- Do you feel excessively responsible for the feelings and needs of others while neglecting your own?
- Do you often feel uncomfortable saying "no"?
- Are you comfortable asking for what you need?
- Do you become upset due to someone else being sad or angry?
- Do you copy the opinions of others?
- Are you emotionally overwhelmed quite easily?

- Do you give too much?
- Do you take on too much?
- Do you constantly need reassurance?
- Do you expect others to read your mind?
- Do you believe you can read the minds of others?
- Do you often anticipate the needs of others?
- Do you agree to things when you don't really want to?
- Do you take responsibility for the feelings of others?
- Do you find yourself always trying hard to please other people?

If you answered "Yes" to the majority of these questions there is a strong possibility you struggle with poor personal boundaries because you are trying too hard to please other people.

Chronic people pleasers usually lack confidence and are always putting everyone else first and themselves last. Many want to feel needed and can have co-dependency issues with their feelings of security and a self-confidence based on receiving approval from others. Some worry about what people will think of them if they say no, or are concerned about being thought of as being selfish by family members, friends or colleagues. What many don't realize is that excessive people pleasing can have serious risks. These people unknowingly put themselves under a great deal of stress by overcommitting, eventually burning out and becoming depressed or physically sick. This happens due to taking on far too much while trying to please everyone instead of setting priorities and looking after themselves.

Effective Strategies To Avoid People Pleasing

If you have identified yourself as a people pleaser there are several strategies that you can begin working on right now to change this destructive habit.

Feelings

Listen to your feelings. If you feel uncomfortable you are probably agreeing to do something you may not really want to do.

Choices

People pleasers often feel like they have to say yes when someone asks for their help. Always remember you have a choice and can also say no.

Be Selective

Make a clear decision regarding who is worth your time, energy and effort. Learn to recognize the important people in your life who you're confident would be there for you instead of agreeing with those who wouldn't return a favor.

Values

Being clear regarding your values will help tremendously when deciding whether to agree or decline a request for assistance. Decisions are not difficult (and much easier!) when you are clear about your values.

Priorities

Understanding your priorities provides the foundation to resist pleasing others and compromising yourself. Learn how to set your own priorities; this isn't being selfish, just common sense. If you give all of yourself away you won't have anything left for yourself!

Delay Your Response

If someone asks you for a favor respond by saying you will think it over. You do not have to give an immediate reply. This provides the space to consider if you want to agree to the request or to gather more information. Think about your own commitments and put those first, then ask yourself if you really have the time to do what has been asked, and if this is likely to involve any stress. Making hasty agreements can lead to regrets later on. When a person pressures you for an answer on the spot always say no. If you agree automatically your options are limited but if you refuse you leave your options open. You can always change your mind later if and when you have sufficient information.

Don't Provide Multiple Excuses

Trying to defend a decision can be tempting but is usually a mistake. The more you say increases the chances you may provide reasons why you can agree to say yes! Always say less than necessary and keep your responses as short as possible without being rude or aggressive.

Time Limits

Whenever you agree to a request set a time limit for your availability if this is appropriate.

Refuse Requests Firmly

It can feel uncomfortable or difficult to say no especially if you're inclined to be a people pleaser but the more you do it the easier it will become. Always keep in mind your own priorities and review them before agreeing to do anything for someone else.

Empathic Assertion

Let the person know that you understand their position so he/she feels validated and respected when you decline a request for a favor.

Covert Manipulation

Be aware of charmers and manipulators who use lines to hook you into a commitment such as:

- "You're really good at making cakes, would you make a cake for my child's/husband's/wife's (or any other friend or family member's) birthday?"
- "I have just bought a new .... and you're really fantastic at DIY. Can you put it together for me?"

When it comes to charm and manipulation, whatever the request, it will include the subtle subtext that says: "Nobody can do this better than you." Manipulators can be very persistent so don't be surprised if someone attempts to coerce you into doing something you do not really want to do.

Never Apologize For Saying No

Learn to say no without providing an explanation. People pleasers tend to spend a great deal of time apologizing for their decisions. Consider if you're actually responsible for the problem and be honest with yourself. If you didn't create the problem or don't have the time to become involved you're not under any obligation to help.

Don't Worry About Saying No

People pleasers often worry about the possible consequences of refusing a request but these fears are often misplaced. When you say no the person who made the request might be upset but it's also just as likely they won't be and instead will focus on who else they can approach. If a friend becomes upset at a refusal or makes a really big deal of it understand that that person wasn't really a genuine friend in the first place and move on.

Remember The Benefits Of Saying No

If you're always running around trying to help everyone else or solve their problems you will simply wear yourself out and eventually feel resentful. Constantly giving your time and energy to others without taking time out for yourself will leave you with very little or nothing to give to yourself. Putting yourself and your priorities first isn't being selfish – it's being sensible.

Recognize Your Previous Successes

Instead of recognizing and acknowledging their successes many people pleasers tend to focus on previous failures. If you keep a daily journal (highly recommended!) write down the times you dealt with a situation positively. When in doubt this can remind you of your previous good decisions and boost your confidence if you have decided to refuse a request for help. If you suspect or know you're a chronic people pleaser keep a separate journal or file with positive and praising messages from family members, friends or colleagues or anyone else. Your file can include cards, letters or emails (print off and keep) as reviewing these messages can help to boost your self-esteem.

Understand You Can't Please Everybody

People pleasers tend to want everyone to be happy but this is totally unrealistic and in the medium to long-term simply doesn't work. For those who do not learn to be assertive and say no, burning out with exhaustion is a very real danger. Understanding clearly you're not responsible for the happiness of others is a big step toward pursuing your own priorities as well as preserving your physical and mental health. Creating and maintaining healthy personal boundaries and being a people pleaser are two mindsets that are totally incompatible. Remember, setting and maintaining healthy boundaries is a skill you can learn although it can take some time before you're comfortable asserting your rights. Do not allow feelings of anxiety or low self-esteem to prevent you from taking care of yourself. Operating healthy boundaries requires a certain level of self-awareness, as well as understanding your feelings and honoring them. As you begin to accept your own positive and negative characteristics, this will help you to accept these aspects within others.

Lacking effective boundaries leaves you vulnerable to being used and abused by predators who just want to satisfy their own selfish desires. This is why women who are "easy going" often find themselves in unhealthy relationships, feeling lost and confused about what they believe about themselves. A lack of healthy personal boundaries or being too eager to please others leaves them highly vulnerable to being exploited by time wasters and Players. If you're insecure, needy or desperate to find love it can be very easy to fall into the trap of feeling frightened of being rejected if you complain about unacceptable behavior. A failure to maintain healthy boundaries will result in the average man believing he doesn't have to respect you, which is not the image you want to project. Lacking effective boundaries while allowing yourself to be strongly influenced by someone else's agenda means you're setting yourself up to be used or abused.

No matter who you are you have the right to be respected and to:

- Create your own personal boundaries that allow you to be your authentic self and to maintain healthy relationships.
- Assert your feelings and opinions. If you think your boundaries are being violated, invaded or ignored you have the right to say so.
- Take risks and to protect yourself if your boundaries are violated or ignored.
- To be yourself and not to lose your identity because of any relationship, romantic or otherwise.
- Explore your own interests and pastimes.
- Have your opinions considered fairly so others understand your boundaries and respect them.
- Listen to and respect your own feelings so you can cultivate greater self-awareness and protect yourself from potential boundary violations.

How To Recognize When Your Boundaries Are Being Violated

Three key feelings that indicate that your boundaries are being threatened or have been violated are emotional discomfort, resentment or anger. The stronger these emotions feel the higher the likelihood your boundaries are being tested or have been breached. Perhaps someone is trying to make you feel guilty or to impose their expectations, views or values onto you? Feelings of resentment usually stem from believing we are being taken advantage of or not being appreciated. Negative feelings while interacting with someone else can also be a sign you're not enforcing the appropriate boundary. Whenever you find yourself complaining or feeling these negative emotions it's likely you need to set or review a boundary.

One of the most common examples of someone crossing a personal boundary is bullying, when someone in your life is insisting you have to conform to their way of thinking and behavior, e.g. you are forced to comply with the wishes of your partner, family or group and denied the right to be yourself. In such cases the person is clearly violating your personal boundary and your right to make your own choices. Another example is lack of privacy, where you have little time or space to be yourself because you are expected to share complete details about how you feel. It feels like you have no privacy so cannot be your own person.

Common Reactions To Boundary Violations

When a person's boundaries are being constantly violated they will usually resort to some common reactions to the intrusion, for example:

- **Disassociation:** When your boundaries have been violated you go into denial and may even have difficulty noticing what happened because you are disconnected from your true feelings.

- **Defensive Mindset:** If your boundaries have been seriously breached in the past you may often be hyper vigilant to any real or perceived threat. This may lead you to constantly reject others before they have the chance to reject you as a defense mechanism.

- **Avoiding Interaction:** You intentionally avoid others so that there are very few opportunities for your boundaries to be violated. This can be a defensive strategy or caused by low self-esteem.

- **Being Shy or Aloof:** If you have been ignored or rejected by having your boundaries ignored this may cause deep feelings of insecurity.

- **Victim Mindset:** Due to low self-esteem, you meekly accept your boundaries being violated but do nothing about it except complain and develop a martyr complex.

- **Emotional Avoidance:** This is often a defense strategy motivated by being previously hurt, ignored or rejected so you build barriers to prevent your emotional or physical space being violated again.

- **Invasion:** This happens when another person is excessively eager to satisfy your needs to the extent their efforts become intrusive into your emotional and physical space. This leads to feeling overwhelmed.

If you recognize a pattern of your boundaries being breached or ignored by others, then it is time to begin thinking about creating and implementing new boundaries, behaviors and beliefs so your personal space, privacy and rights are not ignored or violated in the future. Deciding to create or improve personal boundaries can feel overwhelming at times and like any new skill, assertively communicating your new or enhanced boundaries will take practice.

Setting New Personal Boundaries

"Daring to set boundaries is about having the courage to love ourselves, even when we risk disappointing others." – Brené Brown, Scholar, Author & Public Speaker

Many people feel uncomfortable about potential confrontations that can arise from setting new personal boundaries. They certainly can cause conflicts, but taking the path of least resistance often leads to greater problems later on.

Creating and maintaining Healthy Boundaries enables you to:

- Create an appropriate emotional or physical distance between another person and yourself.
- Maintain a line to protect yourself from the negative consequences of allowing people undue access to your physical or emotional space.
- Establish and maintain a sense of wellbeing and self-respect.

Operating healthy boundaries requires a certain level of self-awareness. You need to understand your feelings and honor them. It means practicing self-discipline, acting with integrity, cooperating effectively with other people and applying rules or consequences about how you expect to be treated. Learning how to set healthy boundaries should be seriously considered as an important part of your personal development. This doesn't stop you from loving someone else but supports you in loving yourself and others in healthy and constructive ways.

To establish and maintain effective boundaries you have to identify and respect your own:

- Needs
- Feelings
- Opinions
- Rights

Values And Principles

"It's not hard to make decisions once you know what your values are." – Roy E. Disney, The Walt Disney Movie Company

Values are vital to setting new personal boundaries. If you lack clear values it can be difficult to evaluate the behavior of others towards you or a struggle to understand how to respond appropriately in certain situations. It can be very easy to become confused, lost or manipulated when you're not really sure what or how you expect to be treated. It can be difficult to know how to respond if someone is treating you badly. Working on your boundaries requires making a commitment to building a set of values that represent your core beliefs.

This means setting levels of integrity that are directly connected to what you will and will not do, or consider unacceptable. In life, we generally trust people who are predictable, where we can accurately predict what their behavior will be. In other words, we trust people who are consistent. Trust is an essential factor in any type of relationship because people know what to expect. If you want to be trusted and respected you must behave in a fashion that reflects your integrity while growing to trust, respect and value yourself.

Strongly held values do not rely on or respond to external factors or the actions or behaviors of other people. Firmly held values can help you to feel secure knowing you're unlikely to be easily influenced by what other people may be saying or doing. Creating new boundaries is much easier once you decide on your personal values and beliefs. It's always much easier to establish, upgrade and maintain your boundary priorities when you understand yourself and know what is acceptable and what isn't.

Guidelines For Creating New Boundaries

Exploring your current boundaries and setting new ones if necessary will put you in a much better position to make any required changes that may be needed in your relationships with friends, family, colleagues or a partner. You will probably find the process of creating new effective boundaries much easier when you're single as there are usually less distractions or potential conflicts. It is still possible to set new boundaries even if you are involved, but we will talk a bit more about that later.

The first step is to examine whether you have any unhealthy habits or beliefs that have allowed your boundaries to be breached in the past. Use a journal to record your thoughts and experiences, and how you feel about things that have happened. Do you recognize any of the three key feelings – discomfort, resentment or anger – that indicate your boundaries are being threatened or have been violated?

If so, take a step back mentally and emotionally. Now take an objective look at the situation. Ask yourself what it is about the interaction, the person's expectations or demand that doesn't feel right. Examine the situation or behavior of the other person, trust your feelings, decide on the boundary and then communicate your position assertively.

You will find it helpful if you first decide what kind of values reflect the type of person you want to be and write them down along with the positive personal traits you think are important. By applying a logical approach you can tackle each issue separately instead of becoming overwhelmed and trying to do too much at once. Finally, make a list of what you will do if a certain boundary is violated in the future.

Limits

It is virtually impossible to set healthy boundaries if you're unsure about your physical, emotional, mental and spiritual limits. Consider carefully what you can tolerate and accept or what makes you feel uncomfortable or stressed out as those feelings will help you to identify what your limits are. Generally, when someone acts in a way that makes you feel uncomfortable, this should serve as a red flag that they may be violating or crossing a boundary.

Put Yourself First

Learn to put yourself first. This means making yourself a priority which will strengthen the motivation to set healthy boundaries. Learning to recognize your feelings and honoring them is important as your emotions provide reliable indicators regarding what makes you happy or miserable. Putting yourself first gives you energy, peace of mind and a positive outlook. It will also support you in being more present and emotionally available in constructive and appropriate ways. This has the effect of enhancing all of your relationships, intimate and otherwise.

Your personal boundaries should be very clear and your expectations realistic. Creating new boundaries can be challenging, but the work involved will reap you many rewards. Life is a journey not a destination and mistakes will be made along the path. Develop a personal support system of people who respect your right to set boundaries while being ruthless about eliminating any toxic people from your life. Knowing and defining your boundaries, principles and values is a vital, positive step for personal growth.

Patterns Of Relating And Setting Boundaries

There are different approaches to communicating and interacting with others. These patterns determine how we relate to and experience our relationships with others. They can also affect the ability to set and maintain personal boundaries. Let us take a look at two types of relating that can get in the way of setting effective boundaries: Passive Behavior and People Pleasing.

Passive Behavior

Passive behavior is generally characterized as someone always allowing others to speak for them and to make decisions on their behalf. People behaving passively usually see themselves as victims of unfairness at the hands of other people. Making decisions can be difficult for passive types and so they often find it easier to allow others to make decisions on their behalf. A passive mindset generally indicates a negative approach to life and can leave the person feeling frustrated by their failure to act and with an engrained attitude of giving up or resignation. There can be feelings of self-pity and a constant theme of putting themselves down when challenged.

On the other hand, for some people, passive behavior can be also a very clever and effective way of manipulating others, leading many people to lose patience, decide the passive person is too draining and eventually decide to avoid contact. Others may resent the passive person, feeling that whatever they do never seems like enough.

If you tend to relate passively toward others then there are specific behaviors or areas that you may have to work on in order to build effective boundaries.

- Creating a healing environment for yourself
- Accepting personal responsibility
- Developing self-control
- Goal-setting in relationships
- Improving assertive behavior
- Handling conflict
- Overcoming any fears
- Handling any need for approval
- Dealing with insecurity
- Eliminating any passive aggressive behavior
- Eliminating any manipulation of others

- Overcoming the mindset of being a victim or martyr
- Handling guilt
- Handling the use of power and control
- Practicing forgiveness
- Becoming appropriately vulnerable

In Your Relationships With Others:

- Eliminating and healing overly dependent tendencies
- Eliminating passive aggressive behavior and game playing tendencies
- Refusing to be manipulated
- Developing a healthy detachment from others
- Building trust
- Dealing with intimacy effectively

To begin building healthy boundaries it is important to address any low self-esteem issues that may be preventing you from being assertive and looking after your own emotional well-being. Start setting your new boundaries by following the **Guidelines for Creating New Boundaries**. Again, decide on the kind of values that reflect the type of person you want to be and write a list of the positive personal qualities you think are important. Include your general personal boundaries and your relationship interaction boundaries. Certain points on each list may be similar as you identify personal priorities and how you expect to be treated. Prioritize each item on both lists so it's clear to you which issues require attention and implementation first. Follow this exercise by writing an affirmative statement for the personal boundaries you wish to improve, for example, "I will work on becoming more independent during the next four weeks," or "I will work on becoming more assertive during this month." Start with a small boundary that you feel is being violated and gradually increase this to more challenging boundaries by building on your previous successes. As you grow in confidence you will find it becomes easier to set healthy boundaries with others quite quickly.

Maintaining Your New Personal Boundaries

"'No' is a complete sentence." – Anne Lamott, American Novelist, Writer & Public Speaker

It is not enough to create boundaries, they have to be maintained and this means you have to follow through. There is absolutely no point in creating boundary rules if you are not prepared to stick to them. You have to be confident you can follow through on whatever boundaries you create. You probably know intellectually people aren't mind readers, but may still expect others to know what might hurt or upset you.

I say this because you are likely to be tested when you set new boundaries, especially by those who are used to taking you for granted. The majority of people will be willing to respect your boundaries, but some will not so be prepared to be firm about your boundaries when you suspect or recognize they're being violated. Maintaining consistent boundaries means you defining who you are and how you expect to be treated.

How each person operates their personal boundaries can be greatly influenced by the type of family structure they grew up in. In some families each person may operate independently while in others interdependency is practiced and promoted. In some cultures the privacy of each family member is acknowledged and respected while in others the lines of privacy are blurred. If you were an only child you will probably have a different style of operating your personal boundaries than someone who was required to share and negotiate space with their siblings. How you were raised and your role within the family may cause difficulties when seeking to set and maintain boundaries. This could result in ignoring your own needs while catering for others, which might feel quite normal to you.

- If you were brought up in a home without having your own space and privacy and forced to share everything, you might have issues around establishing proper boundaries.

- If you had little experience of practicing personal boundaries while growing up, you could be vulnerable to being used or exploited emotionally.

- If you had poor interactions with your parents or they were very self-absorbed, you might be used to being ignored or receiving very little attention. This kind of upbringing can result in an adult who is too eager to please others or who will compromise excessively to receive attention.

- If you had to take on greater responsibilities as a child, perhaps due to family issues and having to care for a parent or younger siblings, then you probably learned to put others first and yourself last emotionally or mentally, and carried this into adulthood.

We often carry our childhood experiences into the world as adults so a review of how these past experiences may be affecting your ability to set and maintain personal boundaries is necessary. Some people create new boundaries but don't follow through because they are scared. Some people feel selfish, guilty, or embarrassed at first because they are not used to setting boundaries. You may even experience feelings of self-doubt. There may be concerns regarding how others will respond when you set and enforce your boundaries or you might feel guilty about enforcing them, especially when it comes to those who are close to you. Some people fear their partner may become angry or even end the relationship. While people shy away from confrontations for various reasons and maintaining consistent personal boundaries can cause conflicts, if you take the path of least resistance sooner or later you will run into bigger and more intractable problems. Over the longer term other people will respect and trust you and more importantly you will grow to honor, respect and trust yourself as well.

Learning to set healthy boundaries can also feel uncomfortable, highly challenging or frightening if as a child your caretakers were physically, sexually, or emotionally abusive. Victims of abuse can learn to repress their anger or other painful emotions due to having been attacked and blamed for expressing the pain of the abuse in the past. Attempting to learn a new approach to relating as an adult may cause feelings of anxiety but it is important to work through these conditioned fears. This process of personal growth usually takes a period of time so don't begin to beat yourself up if you are not making progress with establishing new boundaries as quickly as you would like or expect.

Setting and maintaining boundaries takes courage and practice but it is a learnable skill anyone can master. It can be a balancing act at times as, particularly at first, new boundaries can be too rigid or too relaxed. When a person's boundaries are too rigid they may literally shut out many people from their lives unnecessarily, which makes for a lonely existence. Those with very tight boundaries often appear aloof and distant, fail to show any genuine emotion and avoid talking about their feelings. These people do not allow anyone to get too close, display extreme self-sufficiency and will not usually ask for help.

Assertive Behavior

"You can't talk yourself out of problems you behave yourself into." – Stephen R. Covey (1932-2012), *The 7 Habits of Highly Effective People*

Individuals with healthy boundaries are firm but flexible; they are willing to give support and accept it. They respect their own feelings, needs, opinions and rights while also respecting others, and they remain clear about their separateness. Those with healthy boundaries are comfortable in their own skin and make others feel comfortable around them. They have a strong internal sense of personal identity while respecting diversity and have empathy for others but demand to be treated with respect. Maintaining healthy boundaries means understanding you are responsible for your own happiness while others are responsible for their own. And this requires assertiveness.

Learning to be assertive supports the following:

- Dealing with personal relationships which may be difficult
- Negotiating effectively
- Handling conflict situations
- Confronting inappropriate behavior
- Feeling good about yourself

An assertive approach doesn't mean putting others down as being assertive isn't about feeling the need to win but involves having genuine respect for other people. Assertive people are capable of effective negotiation and compromises while respecting the rights of others to also be assertive.

Assertiveness is not usually considered a "traditional feminine characteristic" while men are generally assumed to be naturally assertive. Many women find being assertive difficult being concerned they may be thought of as being too masculine and aggressive, but this attitude can result in others taking advantage. Effective boundaries are a sign of self-respect and support healthy relationships.

It is important to give yourself the permission to set boundaries and to maintain them. If you would like to be more assertive begin by looking at your patterns of behavior that you think require changing. To begin this process it is important to address any low self-esteem issues that may be preventing you from being assertive and looking after your own emotional well-being. It is quite easy for some people to fall into the trap of believing they don't even deserve to have boundaries in the first place.

When your attitude is based on genuine respect for yourself and others there is the real potential for exchanging ideas, expressing feelings and sharing power. Being assertive means you can be yourself openly and directly stating what type of behavior is acceptable even though there may be a risk of being challenged or even rejected. If this happens you will not be totally devastated as your sense self-esteem is not dependent on the approval of others. Learning to set limits assertively lets others know where they stand while responding sincerely to others and coping with situations appropriately allows you to respect yourself.

When you set a new boundary be assertive, preferably without feeling or showing any anger, and use as few words as possible. Your behavior has to be consistent to establish a new boundary – clear boundaries cannot be established successfully by sending mixed messages e.g. apologizing for introducing a new boundary!

It is important to be:

- Firm
- Clear
- Respectful

Also,

- Do not apologize or try to rationalize or justify the boundary you are setting.
- Do not get into an argument about it, just set the boundary calmly, firmly, clearly and respectfully.

While you're responsible for communicating the boundary in a respectful manner you are not responsible if the other person reacts badly to the new boundary. If others become upset with you, that is their problem not yours. People who disrespect boundaries often have their own issues; if a friend ignores your boundaries he or she is not a genuine friend anyway so wish them well and move on. Always remember you can't set a firm boundary while taking take care of the other person's feelings at the same time. When you express a boundary requirement that is ignored always be prepared to follow through with a consequence for the unacceptable action or behavior.

Maintaining consistent boundaries means you have defined who you are and what is expected. When someone initially agrees to a particular boundary but then violates it, your course of action should be clear. People may not always like you but life isn't a popularity contest; you will generally command respect even if it's only of the grudging variety and as you grow to trust yourself others will trust you too. Trust is an integral part of any meaningful relationship and one of the most important foundation stones to build on to create any kind of meaningful union. Set personal boundaries. Let the people in your life know what you are and what you are not prepared to put up with. If someone's encroaching on your time or trying to cross your boundaries speak up. Be direct, honest, firm but fair.

Again, don't beat yourself up if you are not making progress as quickly as you would like or expect. If you find yourself struggling to establish or reinforce your boundaries, repeat the suggested written exercises or seek support from family members (who are not violating your boundaries), close friends, a support group or professional therapist if necessary. You should proceed at your own pace as opposed to someone telling you what to do and how to do it.

The Way Forward

"The most important distinction anyone can ever make in their life is between who they are as an individual and their connection with others." – Anné Linden, *Boundaries in Human Relationships: How to Be Separate and Connected*

Healthy personal boundaries are essential for your emotional as well as your physical well-being and the foundation for maintaining good relationships. Clear boundaries will give everyone in your life the clear message you should be respected and that you are emotionally secure. They will protect you from people who may have their own selfish agendas. Creating and maintaining new personal boundaries encourage a sense of independence while greatly improving your chances of experiencing productive relationships. This is where your personal power and influence resides; effective boundaries give you the power to limit another person's access into your world until you feel comfortable. You will know what you expect from yourself and understand what you expect from others; most important of all you know how you expect to be treated. Instead of believing others are responsible for your life or responses becoming a victim in the process, you take responsibility for your choices and behavior.

Spend sometime thinking about establishing new strategies and beliefs that will encourage you to change your behaviors and establish healthy boundaries between you and other people in the future. If you adopt the practice of setting effective boundaries as an important part of your personal growth, and make up your mind to work through the associated anxieties, it will put you in a much better position to make any required changes that may be necessary in your relationships with friends, family, colleagues or a partner.

Earlier I mentioned that you will probably find the process of creating new effective boundaries much easier when you're single. It is probably the best time to start setting new boundaries if you have found them lacking in the past as you can start as you mean to go on. The majority of men will not take a woman seriously if they believe she has poor boundaries. Becoming involved too quickly, giving a new man unrestricted access to the sexual, physical, emotional and maybe even financial areas of your life isn't very sensible. Yet, many women do this type of thing all the time and then wonder why their relationships cause them such massive problems.

Always remember: A lack of boundaries invites a lack of respect.

When you're dating or considering becoming involved in a new relationship, it's very important to express your expectations and be very clear about your boundaries. Firm boundaries will help you to avoid drifting into relationships and situations that are incompatible with your values and standards. As the relationship progresses, you can choose to gradually reveal any personal and relevant information while deciding if the man you're dating is a suitable candidate. Always remember, allowing a man into your life is quite easy; trying to get him to leave after it becomes clear you have made a mistake can be very difficult or even dangerous. Having firmly established boundaries is one of the best strategies to avoid Players and predators who will waste your valuable time or resources. Clear personal boundaries supports greater self-awareness and clarity and will boost your levels of self-confidence, which in turn will encourage better relationship choices.

Once you're in a relationship boundary issues can still be negotiated over a period of time. Yes, it's harder when you're already involved and new boundaries or personal rules will usually impact on the dynamics of the relationship, but you can still establish them. Naturally there should be fewer boundaries as the relationship progresses but agreements regarding new boundaries can be discussed and reached. You will most likely meet resistance because generally people do not like change, especially if they think there is too much change happening at once or too quickly. However, possible resistance is not an excuse for ignoring the need to create boundaries that reflect your authentic values, principles and expectations, and if you are really unhappy or perhaps even confused in your relationship, you really have very little to lose and a great deal to gain.

Sometimes people become confused about their boundaries and this can happen when they are accused of placing "conditions" on their love. You will find a great deal written about "unconditional love" in many spiritual books but:

- Unconditional love doesn't mean ignoring your own values, integrity or needs.
- Unconditional love doesn't mean accepting what you find unacceptable.

Never allow your partner or other people to send you on a guilt trip about how you expect to be treated, especially when you decide to establish new boundaries during a relationship. You cannot create boundaries for other people but you can certainly insist that your boundaries are respected.

If your partner becomes unreasonable, angry, or violent regarding any new reasonable boundaries you wish to introduce, this type of behavior represents serious warning signs, which should not be ignored. Any type of fear or abuse in a relationship is unacceptable. If you are living with your partner it may not be possible to leave immediately, especially if there are children involved, but you should seek support and advice from trusted family members, close friends, a counselor, therapist or support group. Start working on your exit strategy as soon as possible.

Never compromise or sacrifice your most important personal values and peace of mind for a relationship.

The only person who can set and maintain the standard of how you expect to be treated is you. Understanding, defining and reinforcing your own boundaries whenever necessary will greatly reduce the possibility of others taking advantage of you. Whether you're in a relationship or not, it's never too late to reevaluate your boundaries or to come up with some new ones. Effective boundaries support and enhance personal growth, a happier emotional life and healthy relationships.

CHAPTER 11:

The Science of Love (Part 1)

"Gravitation is not responsible for people falling in love." – Albert Einstein (1879-1955), Theoretical Physicist & Scientist

The most common questions people ask themselves about romantic love are:

- Why do I fall in love?
- Why do I feel unable to control my heart's desire?
- Why does love often make me feel utterly helpless and completely confused?
- Why do my emotions seem to go into overdrive?

Being passionately in love often triggers a variety of feelings for many people, which can almost feel like a kind of madness driven by a frenzy of emotions. Falling in love can alter our physical state due to biological and chemical changes within the brain.

Many people think their romantic choices are based on freewill but scientists believe a combination of chemical reactions within the brain have a massive influence on how human beings select a partner. This irresistible cocktail of chemicals can entice each of us to fall in love, sometimes when we least expect it!

The Three Stages of Love

Dr. Helen Fisher, an American anthropologist at Rutgers University, is one of the world's prominent researchers in the science of love and has defined three stages driven by a variety of hormones and chemicals.

Stage 1: Lust

Chemically, the first reaction to another person is lust, mainly driven by the sex hormones testosterone and estrogen, possessed by both men and women. These hormones enhance a person's libido and sexual yearnings, which heighten the sense of basic sexual drivers such as appearance and pheromones.

Stage 2: Attraction

This is the stage when most people feel truly love-struck and can think of little else except the person they are deeply attracted to. Scientists and researchers believe the four main neurotransmitters involved at this stage are adrenaline, norepinephrine, dopamine and serotonin.

They are like a cocktail of drugs swishing around your brain. They provide very positive emotions and are mainly responsible for those "falling in love" feelings.

Adrenaline

The initial stage of feeling attraction for someone activates your stress response, which increases the level of adrenaline within your blood stream along with a rise of cortisol. This causes sweating, increased heart rate and, sometimes, a dry feeling in the mouth.

Norepinephrine

This chemical influences the attention and reaction centers of the brain. In drastic situations, like being in love, it works alongside adrenaline to trigger the fight-or-flight response. When someone feels attracted to another person this response doesn't mean they will attack the person or run away! However, their heart rate, blood flow and energy levels will usually increase and hand palms may also become sweaty.

Dopamine

Dopamine triggers an intense rush of desire and pleasure along with increased energy and focused attention while reducing the need for food or sleep. This chemical also stimulates the brain's reward center, reinforcing the desire to see your love interest again. Helen Fisher examined the brains of new couples who were "loved up" during the early stages of their relationships and discovered they had high levels of dopamine. It is claimed dopamine can have the same effect on the brain as taking cocaine!

Cocaine and nicotine trigger many of the same feelings and reinforces the addict's cravings to continue using the drug; this is one of the factors that result in addictions. Scientists and researchers looking at the brain of a person madly in love using an MRI scanner discovered it appears very similar to an addict high on drugs. Fisher reported: "Couples often show the signs of surging dopamine: increased energy, less need for sleep or food, focused attention and exquisite delight in the smallest details of this novel relationship." Leading researcher on the psychology of love Ellen Berscheid believes new couples often idealize their partners, exaggerating their virtues while reducing, dismissing or ignoring any flaws. She also says new couples tend to acclaim and promote the potential relationship by convincing themselves the union will be closer and more special than anything they have experienced before, or when compared to the relationships of others. Ph.D. student Andreas Bartels and adviser Semir Zeki at the Imperial College of London used an fMRI (functional magnetic resonance imaging) scanner to scan the brains of people who were in love. They discovered segments of the brain related to reward and pleasure were activated while portions related to moral judgment and common sense were reduced.

Serotonin

Serotonin is also known as the "Happy Hormone" as it creates feelings of bliss. It is one of love's most important chemicals and may explain why it can be so difficult to stop thinking about your new love interest or partner. This hormone inhibits appetite, aggression, sleep, mood and sexuality. However, the levels of this hormone decreases during the attraction stage so this results in a desire for more sex.

During 1999, an important experiment by psychiatrist Dr. Donatella Marazziti at the University of Pisa, Italy, demonstrated the early "in love" Stage 2 phase really can change the way your brain functions. Marazziti, advertised for twenty couples who had been together for less than six months and believed they were madly in love. By analyzing blood samples from the new lovers, she discovered the drop of serotonin levels during the Stage 2 attraction phase were equivalent to the low serotonin levels of OCD (Obsessive-Compulsive Disorder) patients who experience anxiety and depression. With Prozac and similar drugs used to treat these conditions and increase serotonin levels, tests have indicated certain medications may numb romantic feelings in certain people. However, for this to be effective the romantic feelings cannot be very strong; if the emotions are deep those feelings can be very difficult to remove.

The similarities in serotonin levels between "lovesick" people at this stage compared with those who suffer from obsessive thoughts and compulsive behavior is not conclusive, but certainly interesting. Dr. Marazziti's findings are very similar to the obsessive component of romantic love at the beginning of a relationship that many of us have heard of and probably experienced ourselves. Research indicates this hormone can cause a chemically induced obsession, which could explain why you might find it almost impossible to stop thinking about your new partner during the early phases of a relationship. While psychopaths and murderers are known to have low levels of serotonin this doesn't mean you're likely to become a serial killer when you begin to fall in love! However, the reduction of this particular hormone during the Stage 2 attraction phase does provide a plausible explanation as to why some people feel like they're losing control when struck by Cupid's love arrows.

Stage 3: Attachment

Long-term relationships and marriages rely on forming strong bonds or attachments. Over time the lust factor and initial strong feelings of attraction begin to subside. As this begins to happen there are two other hormones introduced into the body which supports bonding and long-term relationships. These hormones help to keep couples together to have children and create families. Scientists believe this stage of a relationship is driven by two important hormones: Oxytocin and Vasopressin.

Oxytocin

Oxytocin is a powerful hormone released during a wide range of relationship-building activities including touching, hugging and childbirth. It is also released by men and women during orgasm producing feelings of heightened sexual arousal and a desire for bonding with your partner. This explains the urge for cuddling up after sex. It is believed to deepen the feelings of attachment making couples feel much closer to one another after having sex. The theory is the more sex a couple has, the deeper their bond becomes. Oxytocin reduces feelings of fear while encouraging maternal behavior, increased trust, empathy and generosity.

Diane Witt, an assistant professor of psychology in New York, discovered oxytocin aids in child-rearing. By blocking the release of oxytocin in female rats, she found they rejected their offspring, but when female rats were injected with oxytocin they would nurture their baby rats and even other young rats as if they were their own. Oxytocin is released during childbirth and appears to assist in forming a strong bond between mother and baby. This hormone is also responsible for a mother's breasts automatically releasing milk just by looking at or hearing her young baby cry.

It is generally believed the more sexual activity partners engage in the longer they stay together; obviously couples are unlikely to stay together and raise healthy children if there is a lack of bonding. Oxytocin doesn't provide all the answers about human love but there is little doubt about its powerful relationship-building and bonding effects.

Vasopressin

Vasopressin (also called anti-diuretic hormone) is another important hormone, which, like oxytocin, is released after orgasm and influences the decision to embark on the long-term commitment stage. This hormone is generally used to regulate the body's retention of water and some effects on the brain. Scientists suggest it also helps with the forming and retention of memories and strengthens bonds between sexual partners. In men it can also increase aggression against other males, which may explain why some men can be territorial regarding their partners. Scientists and researchers are still investigating the precise role and effects of vasopressin in human beings.

Dr. Helen Fisher found the three stages of lust, attraction and attachment are not necessarily mutually exclusive; they can all happen at the same time! This means a man in theory could be lusting after one woman, falling in love with another female while living with his wife and children. Scientists have broken down love as a series of chemicals being released in three stages, which doesn't seem very romantic, but science rarely is!

Is Love Addictive?

There is circuit in the brain that is responsible for feelings of happiness known as the **limbic region**. It is located deep in the brain and increases in activity whenever we're rewarded. The same system is activated by anything a person enjoys and finds pleasurable, such as sex, using drugs or even gambling. When the limbic region is stimulated researchers have discovered increased blood flow, more neurons firing and more brain activity. A significant area of this deep brain circuit runs on the hormone dopamine so anything perceived as being pleasurable tends to cause these brain cells to produce more of the hormone, which makes the neurons fire at a faster rate.

Having regular sex provides physical, psychological and even social benefits. Researchers claim the endorphins released during sex can help to clear the mind and even alleviate some symptoms of depression. Making love can leave many women feeling emotional and tearful afterwards, which is a result of heightened emotions caused by a combination of endorphins being released. Kissing before having intercourse results in better sex as the lips are packed with roughly 100 times more nerve endings than your fingertips. It stimulates a variety of brain mechanism releasing hormones that lower stress levels while boosting the moods of both men and women. This increases levels of the pleasure hormones and makes people more receptive to actually having sex. It may partly explain why having a quickie can sometimes feel less satisfying than actually taking the time to make love. The endorphin high from a surge of dopamine is an important factor in enjoying sex, especially for women.

Until recently, exactly what happens in the brain of a woman during sex and orgasm was something of a mystery to scientists but during 2011 American researchers made several interesting discoveries. Scientists at Rutgers University, New Jersey in America, used scans to monitor brain activity during orgasm and found that different parts of the brain are activated when various parts of a woman's body are sexually aroused. Thirty areas of the brain responsible for emotions such as joy, satisfaction, touch and memories were found to be activated during sex and orgasm. The scientists discovered that approximately two minutes before orgasm the brain's reward centers become active; these are the same areas activated when eating or drinking. Immediately prior to orgasm areas of the brain associated with the sensory cortex which receives "touch" signals within the brain become stimulated. The other significant part of the brain that became activated was the hypothalamus, which regulates a variety of functions including body temperature, hunger and levels of feeling tired. During the research scientists also discovered that during sexual arousal a woman increases her tolerance to pain as the female nervous system becomes numb, so her body registers sensations of pleasure while reducing any feelings of pain.

Earlier on I mentioned the work of scientists Andreas Bartels and Semir Zeki, who made a variety of important discoveries as part of their work using fMRI to measure blood oxygen levels in the brains of couples in love. They selected participants who scored highly on a scale measuring passionate love and showed them four photographs of their respective lovers and also of platonic friends of the opposite sex. Certain parts of the brain became activated when both genders were asked to look at pictures of their current partners. Brain activity increased in the areas associated with euphoria and reward but this didn't happen when the participants looked at photographs of their platonic friends of the opposite sex. However, there was less brain activity in the areas associated with distress or depression or critical thought for the couples in love. The discovery of less brain activity in relation to critical thought at the Stage 2 attraction phase may explain why many people lose the ability for logical, reasonable thinking.

Some critics claim there is a misunderstanding about how much accurate information brain scans can reveal. They say the mainstream media often provides basic interpretations of brain scans with certain areas representing a "pleasure" or "love" center but this can be very misleading. Others believe certain types of brain scan research or studies may be inconclusive and results can be overstated. Despite this, many researchers conclude falling or being in love can be a habit-forming process and there does appear to be significant similarities when comparing feelings of love and addiction.

Love Addicts

Love Addicts are men and women addicted to the feeling of being in love. They are very similar to other types of addicts who fail to realize they have an addiction! Distinguished psychoanalyst Sandor Rado described Love Addicts as having a "continuous need of supplies that give sexual satisfaction and heighten self-esteem simultaneously."

How The Addiction Begins

Often love addiction begins with feelings of attraction followed by sympathy, which results in excessively idealizing another person. The addict becomes incapable of being realistic about the prospects for a relationship and starts to create various fantasies and illusions. They convince themselves the person they have fallen in love with is definitely "The One" who has the exclusive power to deliver romantic happiness and bliss. Love addiction is often motivated by feelings that may lead to an obsessive mindset and produces an insatiable craving for another person. This obsession disrupts the addict's perception of reality and so can lead to a variety of unhealthy behaviors. The love addiction process can happen very quickly and can become a very frightening or dangerous experience for the person on the receiving end if the infatuation leads the addict to begin stalking.

The Addictive Love Relationship

Like any other addict, Love Addicts need their fix. They feel more alive with a sense of purpose while being intensely driven by deep hope and fantasy that the person of their affections will somehow complete them. Many Love Addicts are trying to fulfill an emotional need and end up becoming dependent on the intoxicating feelings of being in love. During the forming of the addiction, certain areas of the brain are activated by specific hormones within the body. While most people can manage the feelings produced during this process the Love Addict appears to have little control over their thinking or behavior. When their cravings for love remains unsatisfied this often increases the addictive mindset. Their feelings are usually very passionate and they may seek revenge if they believe they have given their love in vain.

The love addict's lack of control often stems from their childhood where they experienced an inability to give and receive affection, a lack of bonding and problems with control, which in adulthood results in self-destructive behavior and unstable long-term relationships.

Withdrawal Symptoms

With any addiction there comes an inevitable process of withdrawal symptoms. In his book, *Surviving Withdrawal: The Break Up Workbook for Love Addicts,* Jim Hall describes the various stages of love withdrawal, which can be mild, moderate or severe, as feelings of

- Abandonment
- Loss of intimacy
- Loss of enjoyment in life
- Shame
- Loneliness
- Chronic emptiness
- Depression
- Violence towards others or self-inflicted harm

These feelings or behaviors typically happen when the Love Addict believes the relationship is failing and the withdrawal symptoms can be very intense even at this stage. During the immediate aftermath of a failed relationship the Love Addict craves the perceived loving feelings of the redundant relationship just like a chronic drug user who can't get a fix. As Hall found, this obsessive craving for the "lost love" can cause extreme, unbearable emotional pain, obsessive thinking, destructive behavior towards others or self-inflicted harm. Love Addicts can receive help and support by attending counseling, therapy or support groups. The approach to treatment and recovery is similar to other addictions such as alcoholism.

Can Love Really Control You?

Love and passion can make us irrational, illogical and obsessive – for some, loving someone can turn them into a neurotic. It's no secret that someone who is madly in love will often make choices that will seem irrational or illogical, like giving priority to their new romantic interest regardless of the possible consequences for their employment, career or social network of family and friends.

In his book *Social Intelligence*, Daniel Goleman Ph.D. describes an abstract model of the brain's interpretation of events and feelings. He says the brain takes two routes when making an assessment, the "high road" and the "low road." Of course how our brains work is highly complicated and sophisticated but the abstract approach helps the concept to make sense. The high road route is slower than the low road and runs through the brain's neural systems. These systems analyze and rationalize while making sense of the world around us and the events we experience. The low road operates below our general awareness but is very fast and manages emotions such as instincts, gut feelings and our primal drives. The mix of hormones and neurotransmitters that concern the science of love operate on the low road and motivates your primal urges. Of course, commonsense, logic and individual conscience (depending on the levels of integrity) can mitigate these basic urges. For example, when you have a gut feeling but decide not to act on it, this is your high road overriding your low road thinking processes. Even by mostly using the brain's high road of logic and reasoning, there are still a variety of factors which can have a significant influence over who we may fall in love with.

A high percentage of human beings are more inclined to act on the messages from the low road brain path instead of following the reason and logic of our high road thinking process. According to Goleman, when we meet someone new the low road route of the brain takes between ninety seconds to four minutes to decide if a chemical attraction exists. This is where the science of body language and the science of love combine to provide some interesting insights into the mysteries of attraction. Non-verbal physical communication like smiling, eye contact and overall body language all play a huge part in amplifying and encouraging the initial chemical reactions that make up the "chemistry" between two people. The high road logical thinking processes can override many of these factors but the science of love combined with the science of body language does provide some interesting insights into the mysteries of attraction. Everyone's body language has a huge influence in the dating game and a variety of factors can spark the initial feelings of attraction. The brain's low road instinctive thinking along with the right chemical reactions and body language may help explain the feelings of lust at first sight!

Two popular questions when people learn about the Science of Love:

- Can you make yourself fall in love?
- Can you make someone fall in love with you?

If the initial feelings are present they can be nurtured and amplified but when there is a serious lack of chemistry nothing can help love to grow and flourish. Love cannot control you and despite the raging hormones that may have a significant impact on your brain, ultimately you do have control over your own feelings.

Is This Really Love I'm Feeling?

From a scientific perspective, love can be interpreted as a series of chemical reactions as can many of the natural functions of the human body. According to scientific research, being madly in love can cause a chemical storm of brain changes that can be compared to a major mental health crisis. Stage 2 attraction and falling in love cause a similar reaction to drug addiction and obsessive-compulsive disorder. Yet despite the confusion and pain falling in love can bring, most of us are Love Addicts to varying degrees: we know a state of being in love can be a very fulfilling and emotionally satisfying experience. The human experience of love is very similar to the human brain – both are still full of mysteries and scientists generally claim their findings are inconclusive.

While the research continues, science does warn us that it is possible to lose ourselves due to hormones and the parts of the brain which have been enhanced or suppressed when we fall in love. This can lead to a major relationship mistake when someone is attracted to and falls in love with an incompatible partner, or a person who is totally unsuitable in other ways. In this regard falling or being in love can certainly impact on your common sense if you're not careful!

CHAPTER 12:

The Science of Love (Part II): Attachment Styles

"Attachment is the great fabricator of illusions; reality can be attained only by someone who is detached." – Simone Weil (1909-1943), French Philosopher, Christian Mystic & Political Activist

Attachment is an emotional bond to another person, and attachment theory describes the dynamics of long-term relationships between human beings. The science of attachment theory says we are all biologically programmed to look for and find love. Psychologist John Bowlby is generally considered to be the first recognized attachment theorist who believed the earliest bonds formed by children with their caregivers has a tremendous impact on their adult relationships. Psychologist Mary Ainsworth expanded greatly upon Bowlby's original work during the 1970's when she devised a procedure known as the "Strange Situation Protocol." During the study Ainsworth identified three major styles or patterns that a child may have with attachment figures: securely attached; insecurely attached; and unattached.

During this study researchers observed how young children aged 12-18 months responded when they were left alone in a room for a short period of time before being reunited with their mothers. When mothers left the room some children would become distressed, cry uncontrollably or search frantically for the mother until she returned. A secure baby would start crying when his mother left the room but calm down as soon as the mother returned and would resume playing. If an insecure (anxious) baby was left by the mother the child would become distressed; when a stranger offered comfort they were rejected but when the mother came back, the child would push her away angrily still crying and try to cling to the stranger. The unattached (Avoidant) baby would not be concerned when the mother left and returned to the room but when a mother held the child he or she would usually lean away or arch their backs in a way to create distance. Tests revealed an increase in heart rate and levels of the stress hormone cortisol in the children.

Characteristics Of Secure Attachment

Securely attached children will usually show signs of distress when separated from their parent or caregiver and be happy when reunited; the child may be upset when the adult leaves but feels confident the parent will return. These children feel secure and confident they can rely on their caregivers who will provide comfort and reassurance if they are distressed or need something. When they're frightened, securely attached children seek comfort from caregivers. These children are confident their parent or caregiver will provide comfort and reassurance, so are comfortable seeking them out in times of distress or need.

Characteristics Of Ambivalent Attachment

Research suggests that ambivalent attachment is a result of poor maternal availability. These children cannot depend on their mother (or caregiver) to be there when the child is in need. Ambivalently attached children usually become very distressed when a parent leaves. This attachment affects an estimated 7-15 percent of American children.

Characteristics Of Insecure Attachment (Avoidant)

Children with an Avoidant attachment tend to avoid parents or caregivers. When offered a choice, these children will show no preference between a caregiver and a complete stranger. Children who are punished for relying on a caregiver will learn to avoid seeking help in the future. Research has suggested that this attachment style might be a result of abusive or neglectful caregivers.

Four Key Components Of Attachment

The central concept of attachment theory is that mothers who are available and responsive to their child's needs establish a greater sense of security in their children. When a child knows or senses a caregiver is dependable this creates a secure emotional base for the child to explore the world. Young children become attached to adults who are sensitive and responsive to them. From the age of around six months to two years of age the child becomes attached to the adults who consistently provide care. How a parent or caregiver responds to a child creates the patterns or styles of attachment which establishes the individual's perceptions, emotions, thoughts and expectations in that child's adult relationships.

Safe Haven: When a child feels threatened or afraid, he or she can return to the parent/carer for comfort and a feeling of safety.

Secure Base: When the child explores the world the parent/caregiver provides a secure and dependable base. When young children begin to crawl and walk exploring their world they will return to the familiar adults (attachment figures) using them as a secure base they can return to.

Proximity Maintenance: The child strives to stay near the parent/caregiver making the child feel safe.

Separation Distress: When the child is separated from the parent/caregiver, the child becomes distressed.

What happens to children who do not form secure attachments? Research suggests that failure to form secure attachments early in life can have a negative impact on behavior in later childhood and throughout adult life. Clinicians suggest that children adopted after the age of six months have a much higher risk of having attachment issues although each child's attachment style is determined by their temperament, upbringing and childhood experiences. While attachment styles displayed in adulthood are not necessarily the same as those seen in infancy, research indicates that early attachments can have a serious impact on later relationships. For example, those who are securely attached in childhood tend to have good self-esteem, strong romantic relationships and the ability to self-disclose to others. As adults, they tend to have healthy, happy and lasting relationships. Research has shown adults can behave in very similar ways to young babies in their romantic relationships.

Further studies and research have supported Ainsworth's attachment styles theory and discovered how each of us relates in our relationships is determined by which "attachment type" we are. During 1986 researchers Main and Solomon added a fourth attachment style called "disorganized-insecure attachment."

The Three Main Attachment Types/Styles

There are three main attachment types or styles, and extensive research and numerous studies have strongly indicated **these types** exist within all races and cultures. Discovering and understanding your type, your partner's type and the attachment style of any potential partners can help you to avoid making a big relationship mistake. If you're already involved this information can provide some surprising insights about your existing partner. Does he push you away or is he uncomfortable with "too much" closeness? Does he give you mixed signals? Does your relationship go through highs and lows? Are you in a Friends With Benefits arrangement by default? Knowledge is power and when you have the relevant information you're less likely to invest time and energy in a partner and a relationship that isn't going anywhere.

Securely Attached

A person with a secure attachment style is one who is comfortable with intimacy in their relationships and effective at communicating his/her needs and feelings to their partner. These types have an innate understanding that compromise in a relationship is necessary and are not concerned with minor issues. They are reliable, consistent and have a stabilizing effect on partners with less secure styles of relating. Those with a secure attachment style often have a high level of satisfaction in their relationships. They are honest and open individuals with good self-esteem. Secure types are emotionally available and their behavior encourages a comfortable atmosphere resulting in happy, stable and healthy relationships. If you're in the dating game it can be difficult to find this type but not impossible. The mistake many people make is becoming involved with partners who *pretend* to be the secure type, or becoming involved in poor relationships for all the wrong reasons.

Positive Signs (Potential) Partner Is The Secure Type
Positive Attitude Toward Relationships

Secure types believe in relationships and are prepared to begin a new one even when circumstances are not ideal. They tend to be realists who understand none of us are perfect and will put in the necessary work to make a partnership succeed. A person with the secure style of relating doesn't give up on their relationships easily even during very difficult times, and rarely dwells on small problems.

Trustworthy

Secure types are consistent, trustworthy and reliable. Personal integrity, principles and honesty are important to these types who will usually explain in advance if they can't keep a promise.

Effective Communicator

The secure type openly shares his/her feelings and opinions clearly and directly. These individuals are good communicators. Consistently open and honest they don't expect their partner to be a mind reader and don't create drama or create a scene to get attention. They are happy to agree joint plans and goals for the progression of the relationship.

Comfortable With Commitment And Intimacy

This type is comfortable with closeness, intimacy, long-term commitment and is secure within him/herself. They have positive self-esteem and are not concerned about rejection or losing their freedom. The secure type is naturally warm and loving and enjoys being intimate in their relationships. They can read their partner's emotional cues effectively and are supportive and comfortable sharing their successes, failures or problems with their partner.

Compromise And Consideration

The secure type is willing to compromise and doesn't feel threatened by valid criticism recognizing they're not perfect and everyone has their particular flaws or hang-ups. Secure partners are happy to compromise and strive to arrive at win-win, mutually beneficial agreements. Flexible regarding relationship issues, they are happy to share the decision-making process with their partner and will rarely make important decisions about the relationship by themselves. They're willing to change and respond to their partner's needs when this is reasonable and necessary. People with a secure style of relating seek their partners input before making any important decisions. They are seldom reactive or defensive and will consider their partner's point of view.

Approximately 50 percent of people are the secure type so it's not unusual to meet someone with a secure relationship style of relating. The problem is if you're single and looking for love this type is probably in a committed relationship already. They tend to take their relationships seriously and stay with their partners for a long time. In the dating game secure types usually have certain requirements when looking for a partner but are usually quite flexible regarding the type of person or relationship they would like to become involved with. A potential partner with a secure type style of relating combined with the Essential Character Traits (see the chapter on this topic) indicate a highly suitable candidate for a healthy, successful long-term relationship.

Insecurely Attached /Anxious

This type craves intimacy and is often excessively concerned with their partner or relationship; they worry their partner doesn't really want to get too close so often have negative thoughts and feelings about the relationship. Anxious types are sensitive to their partner's behavior and moods and can take unnecessary offence but are also quite effective at understanding what their partner may be feeling. Anxious types can have a healthy relationship with people with a secure attachment style but they are frequently attracted to Avoidants who make them even more anxious!

The Anxious type is usually insecure, wants to be close to their partner often and frequently worries about being rejected. They feel unhappy when they're single and not in a relationship; when they're involved they will probably play mind games to keep their partner's interest and attention. This type often struggles to express their feelings and will expect partners to "read their minds" or guess how they're feeling. Anxious types find it difficult to trust partners, often suspecting infidelity without any genuine cause. They do have the capacity for great intimacy but often waste a great deal of time and energy worrying about their partner not wanting the same level of closeness. Anxious types can become quite obsessive about their relationships and they can also overreact to their partner's behavior. These types want and need constant reassurance so expect their partners to maintain regular contact.

If they feel their partner is becoming distant or losing interest in the relationship they will begin to worry or even panic.

When this happens anxious types will typically:

- Act cold and distant if they feel neglected or ignored when their partner responds to a call, text or email.
- Be passive-aggressive in their attacks. When they meet up with a partner after feeling neglected they often try to punish their partner by ignoring them, acting in a condescending manner or by being rude.
- Threatens to end the relationship hoping their partner will increase their commitment.
- Attempt to make their partner jealous by saying someone else is interested.
- Call, text or email while they're waiting for their partner to call.
- Have trust issues. May hang around their partner's workplace in the hope of seeing him/her by "accident."

Anxious types usually have what can be fairly described as an overly-sensitive attachment system. They often withhold their feelings fearing their partner may not feel the same way or will leave feeling too much pressure. If they have the slightest suspicion their partner may be losing interest in the relationship they will persistently seek reassurances until they're satisfied the partner is not planning to leave. Anxious types tend to focus on their current relationships and usually idealize their current partner. They're also more likely to idealize previous partners when they're not in a relationship.

Unattached/Avoidant (also known as Love Avoidants)

Love Avoidant and Commitment Phobic are two terms that broadly describe the same type of man or woman who either run away from a serious commitment or has difficulty maintaining healthy, stable relationships. According to various studies, Avoidant types make up about 25 percent of society; they have the basic human need for love and attachment but tend to feel trapped or suffocated by too much intimacy. In their romantic relationships, Avoidants want to maintain their distance while keeping real intimacy and closeness to a minimum. They are usually unhappy in their relationships and often blame any resulting unhappiness on their partners. Avoidants don't usually date or become involved with their own type (other Avoidants) as two people with this style make a sustainable relationship very difficult. Avoidants also tend to end their relationships much more quickly and frequently than the other types so it's quite likely you have dated this type in the past or are even currently involved with an Avoidant.

The Avoidant type may want to experience emotional intimacy but begin to feel very uncomfortable when the relationship gets "too close" so will create and maintain distance. They are usually on high alert for any sign of their partner wanting, asking or demanding more in the relationship and will probably be very unhappy if they believe their partner is trying to control them in some way. It doesn't matter if an Avoidant is single or in a relationship, they are usually experts at keeping people at a certain emotional distance.

In their relationships Avoidants will typically:

- Not declare their love but often imply he/she has genuine feelings.
- Distance him/herself when the relationship is going well.
- Be emotionally unavailable. Avoids physical closeness and uses distancing strategies (e.g. doesn't want sex or to be with their partner in public or gives the impression he/she is not with their partner in public).
- Not truly commit to a relationship but will remain involved for long periods, sometimes for years.
- Focus on the "imperfections" of their partner (e.g. style of speech or dress).
- Seek a "perfect" fantasy partner or harbor a desire to reconcile with an ex-partner.
- Flirt overtly, which causes their partner to feel insecure.
- Become involved with dead-end relationships (e.g. with a "partner" who is married or involved with someone else).

Unattached or Avoidant types may love their partner but use these strategies to maintain their independence. Combined with other character traits they can be cold, angry, aggressive and unreliable, highly manipulative and dishonest. Ultimately these strategies sabotage any realistic prospects for a happy, healthy relationship.

The Love Addict And Avoidant Relationship Dynamic

Consciously or subconsciously Love Addicts often target and form addictive relationships with Avoidant types who are emotionally unavailable and fear being smothered by their Love Addict partners. Conversely, Avoidants are often attracted to people with poor emotional boundaries or those who have difficulties with independent thinking or suffer from low self-esteem. The Avoidant tends to shun emotional intimacy believing no one could possibly love and accept them for who they truly are. Oblivious to the early warning signs or ongoing problems, the Love Addict personality type will in many cases persevere with an Avoidant as the relationship feels so familiar. The Emotional Programming of their childhood is subconscious and compulsive and so repeated and reenacted; each dysfunctional partner is attracted to the other due to the experiences and thinking patterns created during their formative years.

These types of relationships are like an emotional roller coaster characterized by highs, deep lows and a great deal of drama! While the Love Addict chases affection the Avoidant is ducking and diving as both pretend to be in a happy and healthy relationship. There is a great deal of negativity in this kind of partnership fueled by the pretense or illusion of genuine intimacy and a genuine emotional connection. The Love Addict-Avoidant type relationship dynamic inevitably results in unhealthy interaction patterns of chaos, distance and dependency and can also become highly abusive. While this type of relationship may appear intense and dramatic, in reality it is very shallow and superficial on many levels.

Avoidant Warning Signs

It can be very easy to get caught up in an unhappy, dysfunctional relationship for a very long time if you fail to pay attention to the following warning signs.

Strict Boundaries

Avoidants create strict boundaries between themselves and their partners to ensure their space is not going to be invaded. These boundaries can take various forms including physical or emotional distance and may include keeping secrets.

Emotionally Unavailable

Avoidants are uncomfortable sharing their deepest feelings with their partners because this allows them to maintain emotional distance and their independence. Sharing their feelings would create intimacy and closeness in the relationship which is what they are consciously or subconsciously trying to avoid. It's important to understand why a partner is withholding their feelings as different types of Avoidants withhold emotions for different reasons. The Avoidant type likes to maintain distance by using emotional boundaries.

Needs "Space"

The Avoidant partner will miss his/her partner when they're apart but when they're together they want to escape! They have a basic desire for love and attachment yet can feel "trapped" and want their "space" again.

Resists Intimacy

It can at first be difficult to know if you're dating an Avoidant because he/she is usually attentive, loving and supportive at the beginning, which can lull you into a false sense of security as you assume everything is going well. However, as the dating phase progresses the Avoidant will find excuses to pull back.

Likes Casual Sex

Certain Avoidants use casual sex as a strategy to avoid genuine intimacy; this fulfils their physical needs while not having to be concerned about the feelings or emotions of the other person. Using casual sex helps them to avoid genuine intimacy.

Emotionally Selfish

Avoidants do not like to feel responsible for the happiness of their partners. They believe others should take responsibility for their own happiness so often ignore their partner's feelings. Avoidants often accuse their partners of being "needy", "over-reacting" or of being too "sensitive."

Love Fantasies

The Avoidant often idealizes an ex-partner, a previous relationship or dreams of meeting "The One." This doesn't mean they want true love but is a strategy to avoid a genuine relationship. The Avoidant idealizes an ex-partner to avoid dealing with the reality of their current relationship as they convince themselves they have either missed out on their "one true love" or the perfect partner for them is still out there "somewhere." Needless to say, this can be very confusing! It can be very painful if you're the partner on the receiving end who is always made to feel not "good enough" for the Avoidant.

Mixed Signals

Avoidants tend to be inconsistent in their relationships and can come on very strong and then suddenly pull back. They can appear to be sensitive and caring but also distant all at the same time. Partners are often left in a very confused state by the Avoidant's contradictory behavior and signals. Any agreements or promises made by the Avoidant to move the relationship forward will be broken many times.

Values Independence And Looks Down On "Neediness"

Avoidants believe in being emotionally strong and independent while disdaining what they consider to be neediness. They have little recognition of the reality of interdependence. A person with a very strong or excessive attitude towards maintaining independence in their relationships is probably the Avoidant type.

Secure types also value their independence but have a completely different mindset. They understand and appreciate the value of personal independence while acknowledging interdependence is important within a healthy relationship. Avoidants are only concerned with their personal independence and are not interested in the genuine interdependence and compromises required to make a relationship succeed. They equate intimacy with a loss of independence and are always seeking to minimize closeness, which results in an emotional disconnect with their partners.

Fear Of Commitment/Commitment Phobia

Avoidants fear being trapped by a commitment, long-term relationship or marriage. Whether they are dating or in a relationship, they maintain strict personal boundaries and are constantly on high alert just in case their space is "invaded" or suggestions are made for greater intimacy. It's important to understand this mindset is usually very rigid and highly resistant to change. They find it difficult to be realistic and to stop fantasizing about the "perfect" romance. Criticizing and pulling away when they feel trapped is easier than seeking to establish genuine emotional bonds and closeness with their partner.

In the dating game you will probably meet the Avoidant type eventually; they're often single as their relationships are usually short-term. The good news is Avoidants are not usually attracted to other Avoidants, however they can be extremely charming and gregarious so pay attention when you meet someone new. Look out for any warning signs so you can save yourself a great deal of heartache. Most people usually reveal a great deal about themselves very early on.

If you're currently involved and realize your partner is the Avoidant type seriously consider ending the relationship as it is very unlikely to improve until your partner makes a genuine commitment and seeks professional therapy and support. Both of you should be willing to work together with a reputable therapist who specializes in Avoidant issues if the relationship is to have any realistic prospects of succeeding.

Avoidant Checklist

- Sends mixed signals
- Greatly values his/her independence and seeks to maintain it
- Devalues his/her partner or previous partners
- Uses distancing strategies – emotional or physical
- Mistrustful
- Fears being taken advantage of by his/her partner
- Fails to make his/her intentions clear
- Has difficulty communicating about the relationship
- Prefers autonomy to intimacy

The Anxious-Avoidant Type

The "Anxious-Avoidant" Type represents approximately 3 to 5 percent of the population. These types are uncomfortable with a great deal of intimacy but are still concerned with the availability of their partner and the progress of the relationship. Anxious type individuals are more likely to experience jealousy while Avoidants are much less likely to do so. Anxious individuals are more likely to reveal too much about themselves too quickly while Avoidants are usually reluctant to share information or may even try to conceal things about themselves. Anxious types often make relationship commitments too quickly while Avoidants will resist making a serious commitment and will be extremely uncomfortable doing so.

Research in the field of attachment styles of relationships clearly shows avoiders and anxious types are frequently attracted to each other but amplify their respective traits; while the anxious type tries to get closer the avoider is usually attempting to create distance which results in a vicious circle and a dysfunctional relationship. Some anxious types can find the inconsistency of the avoider enticing and exciting but can end up having a very difficult relationship experience. Withdrawal by the Avoidant can make the anxious type very needy; when the Avoidant becomes more emotionally available the anxious type often becomes less demanding resulting in more independence for the Avoidant. People in this kind of partnership can tolerate the union and be "happy" despite the issues caused by two very different styles of relating. These couples can be ignorant of the negative dynamics of the relationship but may stay together for a variety of reasons.

Generally, secure types can have a broadly successful relationship with both anxious and Avoidant types. The anxious type may find the secure type predictable and even boring during the early stages of dating or a relationship but can grow to greatly appreciate the consistency the secure type provides. The downside for the secure type is they can be too tolerant or forgiving at times with the anxious and Avoidant types which can cause serious relationship problems. Overall the secure type is the best candidate for a successful relationship as they are capable of providing emotional consistency, availability and security. A couple who are both secure types is the best combination for a healthy relationship but someone who has a secure style of relating can have good partnerships with anxious and Avoidant types. This is because he or she is capable of compensating for the relating issues of the anxious and Avoidant type in the short to medium-term.

What Is Your Attachment Style?

If you're curious about your attachment style try the following Attachment Style Scale which will give you an idea of where you fit in. You can also ask your partner or potential partner to take the test! While the majority of the research I have covered focuses on the three main attachment styles – namely, secure, insecure/anxious or Avoidant – the Avoidant attachment style has been split into two categories: dismissive and fearful, to provide a clearer indication of which style may apply.

The Attachment Style Scale

Do you agree or disagree with the following statements?

I am not worried about being alone.

I am not concerned about other people accepting me.

I am comfortable when I have to depend on other people.

I am comfortable when other people choose to depend on me.

I find it relatively easy to become emotionally close to other people.

I am happy to be in a close, intimate relationship.

I am comfortable with intimacy.

I am happy to compromise in my relationships.

Individuals with a Secure Attachment Style tend to agree with the majority of these statements.

Do you agree or disagree with the following statements?

I often have negative thoughts and feelings about my relationship(s).

I often think I don't deserve to be with my partner.

114

I don't always trust my partner to be faithful.

I often think my partner might leave me.

I would like to be emotionally intimate with other people.

I would like to share more closeness or intimacy with my partner (current or previous) but he/she often seems reluctant.

I am often sensitive to my partner's behavior and moods.

I am unhappy or uncomfortable when I am not in a relationship.

I worry at times that I value other people more than they value me.

Individuals with an Insecure Attachment Style tend to agree with the majority of these statements.

Do you agree or disagree with the following statements?

I don't believe intimate, romantic relationships are that important.

I don't think intimacy and closeness are that important in a relationship.

I usually pull back and distance myself if I feel rejected by my partner.

I often hide or suppress my true feelings.

I believe I have more to contribute to my relationship than my partner (or previous partner).

I believe I have to defend myself vigorously if I think I am being criticized.

I am comfortable without close emotional relationships in my life.

I prefer not to depend on others or have others depend on me.

I have a very strong need to feel independent and self-sufficient.

I prefer not to be in a committed relationship.

Individuals with a Dismissive Attachment Style tend to agree with the majority of these statements.

Do you agree or disagree with the following statements?

I often have mixed feelings about romantic or close relationships.

I often have negative views about myself.

I often have negative views about my partner (or previous partners).

I sometimes think I don't deserve my partner.

I don't always trust the intentions of my partner.

I often suppress or hide my feelings.

I don't seek a great deal of intimacy from or with my partner and my partner complains about this occasionally or often.

I find it difficult to trust my partner completely.

I find it difficult to trust other people completely.

I often feel uncomfortable when I get too close to my partner or others.

I want to be in a close, intimate relationship with my partner.

I find it difficult to depend on my partner or others.

I worry at times I will get hurt by allowing myself to become too close to my partner or others.

Individuals with an Avoidant Attachment Style (Fearful) tend to agree with the majority of these statements.

Research shows that love can come in several different styles and many people often demonstrate their love by combining and blending two or three of the attachment styles we have explored. However, there are those who have a particular attachment style which will be dominate. Honestly review your own attachment style. Examining your relationship history may reveal some of your partners have been the Avoidant type. If you do identify a pattern, begin to work on yourself to better understand why you may be attracted to men who avoid commitment and intimacy. Seek professional support if you find yourself struggling with certain issues.

Improving Your Relationship Choices And Prospects

"You can't make decisions based on fear and the possibility of what might happen." – Michelle Obama, American Lawyer, Writer & 1st African-American First Lady of the USA

Each person's attachment style has a great influence on what happens in their relationships, including how they experience and manage a variety of behaviors and issues including love, commitment, jealousy, conflict resolution, honesty, infidelity, integrity and sexual behavior. When you're considering love and relationships always remember "love" doesn't necessarily mean the same thing to everyone. Understanding your own attachment style puts you in a much better position to decide what type of person is likely to be a suitable match, and knowing how to identify a potential partner's style can help you to avoid the mistake of becoming involved with someone who uses the avoider style of relating. If you're currently struggling in an unhappy relationship it is quite possible you're involved with a partner whose attachment style is incompatible with your own. Learning about attachment styles can help you to decide if it's worth trying to make it work or cutting your losses and leaving.

CHAPTER 13:

Being Single!

"Don't rush into any kind of relationship. Work on yourself. Feel yourself, experience yourself and love yourself. Do this first and you will soon attract that special loving other."
– Russ Von Hoelscher, Author

Single status is absolutely nothing to worry about but many women start to panic when they find themselves single and this often results in some really big relationship mistakes. Do you know anyone who absolutely hates being single? These women (and men) are usually sullen, bitter or resentful, constantly blaming their ex-partners for their previous relationship failure. They increase their own feelings of disappointment, sadness and suffering because they fail to understand that the more you resist being single, the harder it will be to enjoy being single!

Whatever you try to avoid, struggle against or resist often gains more strength as you give it more energy and attention, which means you're working against yourself. Whatever you resist emotionally will inevitably persist.

Are you resisting being single? Signs of resistance typically include the following:

- Being angry and fearful about being alone
- Wishing you were still in a relationship with your ex-partner
- Going in hot pursuit of someone new to distract yourself from the disappointment of a failed relationship

Resisting being single can leave you trapped in a cycle of emotional turmoil, anger and resentment; these feelings can quickly transform into feelings of desperation and the belief you **must** have a partner to be happy, and to feel loved and validated. However, if your energy isn't centered there is a risk any new romance could develop into an addictive relationship. Feeling happy and emotionally secure within yourself **before** becoming romantically involved again allows you to accept someone else's energy without becoming dependent on it.

The journey from resistance to surrender means:

- Giving up resisting
- Embracing surrendering
- Beginning to examine any issues
- Learning any personal lessons
- Implementing new strategies

If you're deeply unhappy with being single this can cause you to miss out on some great opportunities for valuable self-analysis. To be successfully single the first thing you have to do is make the transition from a place of resistance to a place of total surrender as this allows the healing to begin, which can lead to a very powerful process of Self-Discovery, deeper understanding and self-empowerment.

Being single presents many opportunities for personal growth.

- You have time to get to know yourself in new ways.
- You have time to conduct your inner work thoroughly.
- You have the opportunity to gain new insights about yourself and others.
- You have time to reflect on your personal patterns and what Emotional Programming you may need to heal or change.

Learning to accept and love yourself when you're single is a very important part of the process. You have to **know** how to love and accept yourself whether you're in a relationship or not. The truth is, life can be a terrific adventure when you're single! Being involved, active and interested in your own life automatically improves personal energy levels and helps to maintain a healthy mindset. Feeling good about yourself and being happy in your own skin will make you much more attractive to others. When you build a life full of meaning and satisfaction for yourself you naturally become a much more appealing person and will find it much easier to attract a new partner.

A Vision, Passion And Purpose for Your Life

Life is not happening or going to happen at some unspecified time in the future: your life is happening now! Waiting around for a relationship or believing you will only be truly complete when you meet "The One" is not only extremely naive but also a complete waste of time. The absence of a relationship doesn't mean your life should be meaningless, lacking purpose or direction. If you don't know your life purpose make discovering what it is the top priority. Find out what you really enjoy doing, what fills you with energy and passion. Investigate what fires you up because whatever it is that activity is an important part of your life purpose. Discovering your life purpose and following your passion or dreams can transform your life. It could be having a vision of what you want to achieve for yourself or to contribute to others. Whatever your purpose and passion is it should be a consistent part of your life and certainly doesn't depend on your relationship status. You will constantly find yourself feeling passionate, positive and energized when you are pursuing your life purpose!

Single Status Activities

It can be very tempting when you're single and feeling lonely to consider your single status as some kind of waiting time before you meet someone new. Whether you are recently single or have been on your own for a while, life is all about finding the right balance and having some fun. There are many constructive and self-affirming activities to pursue when you're single. These activities can be pursued whether you're single or in a relationship. Being single presents many opportunities to explore and begin practices and habits that can enhance your life and general wellbeing. For example, you can do three luxurious, pleasurable things for yourself every day. They don't have to be huge activities, just little treats you give to yourself like taking a walk in the park to be close to nature or reading inspiring or motivational books. Anything you enjoy doing that doesn't take up a great deal of time or cost a lot of money but makes you feel good can become a part of your daily routine.

Keeping A Journal

You have to understand yourself clearly before it's possible to process your experiences properly and writing a daily journal is a discipline that can lead to greater clarity. Psychologist James Pennebaker and many other researchers say that besides providing an outlet for emotional expression, keeping a personal journal can benefit physical health, physiological functioning and immune function. Keeping a journal allows you to reflect back on certain thoughts or feelings and this helps you to explore different perspectives: how you feel about something a week, month or even year later can change drastically. It can also be a vital resource for providing a certain amount of objectivity as you evaluate certain situations, how any problems were resolved and help you to monitor your personal progress. Periods of reflection can help you to discover and understand your thought processes, motivations and, even more importantly, some of your inherent fears. Your journal can feel like having a best friend who you can share your feelings with and helps you to connect with the inner wisdom that is available to all of us if we take the time to listen.

This practice helps to build the most important relationship you will ever have, which is the one you have with yourself. I have kept a personal daily journal since childhood and over the years this practice has helped me tremendously with my personal growth. You should feel totally free to record your personal thoughts and feelings without being worried that someone else might read them. Just keep your journal in safe place. Maintaining the privacy and confidentiality of your journal is absolutely essential and the only person who should have access to it is you! Writing down your thoughts daily can be a very empowering process and keeping a personal journal where you are free to explore and express your thoughts or deepest feelings is highly recommended.

Spend Regular Time With Nature

Enjoying the beauty of nature can invigorate your mind and soul. Spend quality time outdoors by walking or sitting in a park or forest, or spending time by a lake or seaside enjoying the sights and sounds. Taking a trek up a mountain or wandering around in woodland can also help you to reconnect with nature, which helps to restore a sense of inner tranquility. Taking a break from the hustle and bustle of daily life is a great way to restore your emotional, mental and spiritual balance.

Meditation

A highly effective method for gaining personal insights and greater clarity is meditation. Meditation encourages clearer thinking so this makes it easier to monitor and control any negative or distracting thoughts. Regular practice enhances a sense of happiness and contentment as the mind becomes more peaceful and worries, anxieties, fears and negative thoughts gradually subside. A peaceful mind is likely to make fewer mistakes so the natural benefits of mediation includes making better decisions while cultivating an attitude of patience and tolerance towards other people.

Mental And Emotional Benefits Of Meditation

- Increased emotional stability
- Developed intuition
- Increased ability to stay calm in stressful everyday situations
- Greater self-confidence
- Improved concentration
- Increased feelings of vitality
- Enhanced feelings of happiness
- Greater creativity
- Increased self-discipline
- Improved learning ability and memory
- Decreases restless thinking
- Reduces feelings of anxiety or worry
- Helps to combat feelings of depression
- Reduces feelings of nervousness, irritability and moodiness

Physical Benefits Of Meditation

- Increased levels of energy
- Falling asleep more easily and sleeping soundly
- Improved flow of air to the lungs
- Improved state of the immune system
- A deeper level of relaxation
- Deep rest accompanied by decreased metabolic rate and lower heart rate
- Decreased high blood pressure
- Decreased muscle tension

Spiritual Benefits Of Meditation

- Peace of mind
- Discovery of the power and consciousness beyond the Ego
- Heightened awareness of the inner self
- The ability to look within, beyond the body, mind and personality
- Discovery of one's true being
- Emotional and mental detachment
- Attaining self-realization and spiritual awakening

Many researchers and scientists recommend meditation but results depend entirely on the amount of time devoted to regular daily practice. There are many different forms of meditation so experiment to discover which form of practice resonates with you.

Exploring Your Spirituality

Exploring different spiritual concepts can be very fulfilling and when you're single there is so much more time to explore and discover new ideas or insights. There are many spiritual practices to choose from. Those who are willing to learn can discover techniques to assist in their personal and spiritual evolution. Carry out your own investigations to get an idea of what a particular practice involves and then trust your intuition to guide you toward a practice that feels right for you. Once you decide on the type of spirituality or religion that seems appealing make some enquires before you decide who you will study with. It's usually best to work with a qualified and experienced teacher who will be able to guide you. Remember, nothing is set in stone: if you begin a practice or join a religion but decide it does not meet your personal needs then try something new!

Spiritual traditions include:

- Christianity
- Judaism
- Islam
- Buddhism
- Zen
- The New Age Movement

Spiritual practices include:

- Prayer
- Contemplation
- Yoga
- Service
- Spiritual retreat
- Communing with nature

Spiritual teachings include:

- Love
- Acceptance
- Forgiveness
- Appreciation
- Non-attachment
- Understanding impermanence

Spiritual practice usually requires some discipline initially but once it becomes an established part of your daily routine the benefits can be immense. A spiritual perspective provides clarity regarding personal circumstances and life in general. To begin exploring aspects of your spirituality set your intention to start practicing, then decide a time and date to begin. The more you practice the easier it will be to stick to your routine and over a period of time you may find your personal energy levels increasing. There may also be new personal insights as you consider life from a spiritual perspective and this can encourage you to continue.

You might be thinking, "I *might* just have enough time to write a daily journal but it will be impossible to squeeze in reading books, investigating spirituality and practicing meditation into my busy schedule!" The reality is each of us are given exactly the same 24 hours a day so it's all about managing your personal priorities and being willing to explore and try new interests that can enhance your personal development. Before deciding you simply do not have enough time for these activities consider how much time you waste on highly unproductive pastimes, like watching television or using social networking sites.

Reconnecting With Family And Friends

It can be very easy to feel lonely and disconnected after a break up so a support network of friends and family who care about your wellbeing can be a tremendous asset when you are single. Life in the 21st century often feels very hectic and fast-paced, which can leave very little time to keep in touch with loved ones but being single can provide a great opportunity to reconnect. Deepening ties with family and friends can greatly enrich your life, providing practical and emotional support. Spending quality time with the important people in your life can be very rewarding while single life also presents opportunities to meet new people who might become life-long friends. So make plans to get out there and socialize! Making new friends and arranging activities with other single women can lead to sharing experiences that develop into deep friendships, plus there is always the possibility of developing meaningful platonic friendships with members of the opposite sex who may provide useful insights about men. Another great advantage of being single is it allows greater spontaneity. Relationships where a person doesn't get along with their partner's friends often leads to jealousy or conflicts about loyalty but being single allows you to be spontaneous without consulting anyone!

Traveling

Most of us dream of visiting other countries so if you can afford it seriously consider taking a trip somewhere you have never been before. It can feel scary and challenging to visit a country for the first time but travel definitely broadens the mind, exposing it to different cultures and ways of life. When you return home your perspective will probably be expanded and you will feel an amazing sense of achievement. Being single presents the perfect opportunity to travel solo or with a friend and the world is a big place with many interesting countries to explore. A big mistake many single people make especially after a difficult break up is taking an exotic trip abroad as a way of distracting themselves, trying to escape feelings of emotional pain. The truth is it doesn't matter how far you may travel physically, it's impossible to take a vacation away from yourself emotionally!

Career Freedom

Single status gives you the time and space to dedicate yourself to new career goals. Your decisions will only have an impact on you so if you're ambitious there is little to stop you. You have complete autonomy to make decisions and take action without having to consider anyone else. Whether you change jobs frequently until you find employment that provides personal satisfaction or decide to put in longer hours to move up the career ladder in your current position, you're free to pursue your career dreams.

The Time To Consider The Type of Partner You Want

Being single gives you time to work on yourself and to consider what type of man you want to be in a relationship with. Working on yourself should be one of your top priorities for at least three months. The clearer you are about the type of man you would like, the more likely you are to meet someone special. Knowing what type of man you want to be involved with can certainly help you to avoid a relationship disaster, just make sure your criteria is realistic. There are women who happily decide to live without a serious relationship or man in their lives and instead decide casual sexual liaisons suit their beliefs, philosophy and lifestyle. There is absolutely nothing wrong with two consenting adults agreeing to a Friends With Benefits arrangement and this can be a real confidence-booster. It can also be one of the most unfulfilling and catastrophic relationship choices you can make! The advantages and hazards are explored in the chapter *"Friends With Benefits: Can It Work For You?"*

Reality Check

"A willing meantime means recognizing that you are not by yourself but that you are with yourself, and you don't mind keeping company with you." – Iyanla Vanzant, *In the Meantime: Finding Yourself and the Love You Want*

Being single for a period of time isn't a rational reason to worry, but concerns about being left "on the shelf" cause some women to panic, leading to very poor relationship choices. It can be very easy to get caught up in fantasies about love and romance or to convince yourself you're ready for a new relationship when you're not. Many women can find single status difficult at times and a variety of pressures can even make a confident woman doubt herself; instead of succumbing to any fears about being single you may have work on becoming your biggest fan and grow to realize that no one but *you* can make you feel whole and complete. Practice enjoying time by yourself and learn to be emotionally self-sufficient as you learn to cultivate your self-awareness, self-esteem and self-confidence. Learning about yourself in new and deeper ways will provide many personal benefits as you discover and begin to heal any Emotional Baggage from the past and consider if you need to make any changes to your interpersonal style. Taking the time to explore within can provide valuable new insights as you develop a deeper connection with yourself. Walking around believing your happiness depends on another person leaves you open to feelings of desperation and vulnerable to being manipulated, used and abused. The truth is, if you're not a hundred percent happy being on your own you're unlikely to be happy in a relationship because sooner or later your insecurities and Emotional Baggage will come to the surface.

Are You Ready? Check Yourself Out!

You're probably *not* ready for a new relationship if you:

1. Are still in love or have romantic desires for any ex-partner.
2. Have a great deal of rage and resentment regarding an ex-partner.
3. Feel lonely, desperate or completely miserable without a partner.
4. Believe no one would seriously want to be in a relationship with you.
5. Believe whatever you have to offer a relationship is not worth a great deal.

6. Are reluctant to express your feelings to other people.

7. Often feel empty or as if there is "something missing" inside emotionally or spiritually.

8. Find it very difficult to connect with or feel any emotions.

9. Dislike yourself or suffer from low self-esteem.

10. Currently have an addiction problem.

If you can strongly relate to or identify with any of the above statements then you're definitely NOT ready to begin a new relationship.

If you identified with statements 1 and 2 your previous relationship may be causing you emotional problems. It's likely you have not healed or recovered enough to begin a new relationship.

If you identify with statements 5 and 6 you are probably emotionally blocked and will have to work on those issues thoroughly before considering embarking on a new relationship.

If you identified with statements 3, 4, 5, 8, 9 and 10 it is very likely you have issues around poor self-esteem that could leave you open to emotional abuse in your next relationship. Statement 9 indicates an extreme "needy" mindset.

There is no shame in acknowledging you're not ready for a relationship; in fact this demonstrates a level of self-awareness you should be proud of! The biggest relationship mistake people make is becoming involved with someone before they're truly prepared mentally or emotionally. If you're carrying Emotional Baggage and lack a certain level of self-awareness there will probably be a tendency to project those unresolved issues onto a partner, convincing yourself any drama is totally his fault. This cycle will repeat itself until you understand and heal any issues that may be sabotaging your relationships.

You're probably ready for a new relationship when you:

- Feel genuinely happy without a relationship.
- Are fully in touch with your own emotions.
- Can stay centered in your own energy.
- Don't feel a need to control your (potential) partner.
- Are comfortable with and have a balance between being assertive and receptive.
- Are proactive and focused on working towards your own goals.
- Can remain detached from any of your (potential) partner's problems and issues.
- Communicate effectively without blaming and manipulating.
- Don't try to use any control dramas e.g. attempting to get love, attention, approval, recognition etc. from a potential partner.

Single status gives you the time and space to reflect on your previous relationships. Most importantly it provides a great opportunity to discover and understand the one person you're definitely going to spend the rest of your life with: You! Spend some time therefore considering new strategies regarding how you relate to yourself and others before you decide to become romantically involved. If you embrace being single with enthusiasm, exploring yourself honestly while working on your personal growth, this will be more than enough to compensate for any fleeting feelings of loneliness or the lack of a relationship. There are many people desperately looking for that "special someone" to **complete** their life when they should be seeking a partner who can **enhance** their life. In the dating game a vibrant, independent woman will always be more attractive to potential partners than a female who is just waiting for a man to validate her existence.

CHAPTER 14:

Urban Myths And The Truth About (Most) Men

"I'm about to make a wild, extreme and severe relationship rule: the word 'busy' is a load of cr*p and is most often used by as*holes. The word 'busy' is the relationship Weapon of Mass Destruction. It seems like a good excuse, but in fact in every silo you uncover, all you're going to find is a man who didn't care enough to call. Remember men are never too busy to get what they want." – Greg Behrendt, American Comedian & Author

The most frequent complaint I hear from women regardless of their class, race, or socioeconomic status is: "Where are all the good men?" They tell me they're finding it very difficult to find "Mr. Right." Many women believe there is a great shortage of available men who are:

- Romantic
- Loving
- Sensitive
- Fun
- Responsible
- Confident

If you are one of them and think all the good men are taken think again! The truth is there are many decent guys out there who are single and want to be in a relationship but if you walk around believing good men are in very short supply or simply do not exist your expectations will often create your reality. There are several urban myths or stereotypes about men and their general relationship expectations that cause many women to misunderstand how the majority of men actually feel about love and intimacy. In the dating game it's very important to separate fact from fiction otherwise you can end up overlooking or even rejecting a potential partner who could be a great compatibility match. Here are the most popular urban myths about men that cause many women to misunderstand how the average man thinks and feels about himself, his life and his relationships.

Urban Myth 1: Men Are Not Emotional

Perhaps one of the biggest myths about men is we don't feel or have any great emotional depth, but studies have revealed men often experience exactly the same emotions as women – it's just that the way they express themselves is often very different. Men and women are socialized very differently during childhood and for males this often means learning to repress emotional expression. Parents talk less about feelings to their sons so during childhood they tend to be less exposed to emotionally oriented conversations and discouraged from verbally expressing their emotions. Young males are usually conditioned to be tough, fearless and to "man up" while constantly being told "big boys don't cry." They are encouraged by their parents to be "tough."

As a result boys may not learn how to handle or express their emotions well. Boys who express anger or rage when their personal possessions or status is threatened can grow into men who express their anger inappropriately. Alternatively, they may become adults who use far less words to express their feelings when speaking in public, use speech to assert their dominance in certain situations or grow into men who are emotionally repressed. Women tend to be more in touch with their emotions while for many men emotional issues are kept firmly in the background of their lives. The emotional life of a man can be just as deep, rich and complicated as any woman but due to childhood conditioning these feelings can be very difficult for men to process and understand.

Generally, men have a very different approach to managing emotions and physical intimacy when compared to women but this doesn't mean the feelings are any less for a man in an established relationship. Men are very efficient at intellectualizing and compartmentalizing their emotions; if you ask a man what he is *feeling* he will probably respond by telling you what he is *thinking!* This doesn't mean his emotions are not engaged, it's just that the way many men express themselves can leave a great deal of room for misinterpretation.

The Truth About Men

- Can have general difficulties in expressing emotions
- Tendency to exert greater control when expressing emotions
- Spend more time mulling over negative emotions
- Much less inclined to share emotions with others
- Express certain emotions with less intensity
- Use language with significantly less emotional content
- Behavior generally appears less affected by expressions of emotion
- More likely to keep negative feelings to themselves
- Inclined to express emotions that demonstrate power or control, e.g. anger, jealousy or pride

Many men are not always as confident as they pretend to be. He will usually try not to reveal any vulnerability but can often feel far more insecure than he is prepared to admit. It is also true men who work hard at trying to hide their emotions can be the very emotionally sensitive type presenting a strong but false persona to protect themselves. Some secretly fear others will judge them as being incompetent, lacking courage or simply not as manly as they should be. When things are going wrong in a man's life he can feel powerless and withdraw to reevaluate the situation, which is quite normal provided this is for a reasonable amount of time. So while women will probably want to talk about the situation immediately with her partner he will probably want to take some time out. Women often expect their partner to perform incredible emotional gymnastics: men are usually expected to be strong, solid and dependable but also emotionally open and available. These widely different expectations can cause confusion for many men who have not been generally socialized to manage or express their deeper emotions or have lacked role models to teach them how to be appropriately **strong** and **emotional.** As gender roles and rules have become less defined many men are now comfortable revealing the softer side of their personalities to their partners; of course there are still men who remain confused about how much they should really share on an emotional level and this causes a variety of relationship problems.

Strategies To Encourage Men To Manage And Express Their Emotions

Whether you're dating or in an established relationship it's important to understand how the majority of men generally feel and think. The following tips can help you to understand the male mindset and encourage a man to express himself.

Be Aware Of Male Vulnerabilities

When a man reveals his vulnerabilities and gets badly hurt he usually retreats into himself and he may go inside his emotional cave for a very long time. He may even decide not to reveal himself again at a certain emotional level. A man who has been hurt is unlikely to be persuaded, cajoled or bullied into sharing his feelings. It can take a certain amount of time, healing and rebuilding of trust before he will feel safe (and brave) enough to take the risk of revealing himself again.

Appreciation

It doesn't matter what gender we are, most of us like to feel appreciated. If you're in a happy relationship, reaffirm and validate your partner often and let him know you appreciate having him in your life. He will be very pleasantly surprised and will probably do even more to make you happy!

Developing A Creative Outlet

Does the man you're dating or in a relationship with have a creative hobby or interest? Playing a musical instrument, writing or even painting can help a man to connect with his emotions. A great deal of the world's revered music, literature and artwork have been produced by men.

Exercise

Regular exercise is a very effective activity for men to release feelings of stress, anger or rage.

Sharing Physical Activities

We're not talking about sex – there are other activities you can share together! Try doing activities like going for walks or taking bike rides together. Sharing physical activities will encourage any male defenses to come down. Avoid trying to have an in-depth emotional discussion during activities but instead allow topics or discussions to develop naturally afterwards.

Watch A Sports Movie Together

For many men the most important male relationship in their life is the one they share with their fathers. Many fathers and sons have participated in sports together and through this created a strong bond. Watching a movie with a sporting theme can therefore create a positive and relaxing atmosphere. Provided your partner enjoyed a positive relationship with his father viewing any TV show or movie that has a positive father and son theme can be beneficial. This isn't about trying to analyze his childhood but to share moments with him when he reconnects with his emotional side.

Avoid Pressuring Him After A Tough Day

If he's had a rough day, going over whatever issues he encountered isn't necessarily going to solve the problem and can be counter-productive, especially if wants to relax and chill out. Men often need more time than women to "decompress" and process their emotions so give him some space if he needs it.

Express Your Emotional Needs

Psychologist and researcher Lisa Neff Ph.D. found husbands to be as supportive and emotionally sensitive as their wives and that often problems were caused by poor timing or miscommunication. Sometimes the wife expected her husband to know what was going on in her mind without actually telling him. Neff's recommendations for married couples is for wives to let their husbands know what they require and more importantly when they want it.

Urban Myth 2: Men Don't Like To Talk

Women are usually comfortable expressing their feelings to others and establishing and maintaining close friendships. Men by contrast often have general conversations with their male peers exchanging information regarding sports, cars or the latest smart phone. Men will share their relationship hopes and aspirations with other men but will be careful how they express themselves. They are more likely to discuss the practical aspects of what they expect from a woman.

In the dating game, if a man shows he is interested you have to be careful not to misread the signals. Ask lots of questions! A man may show an interest but he could just be after sex. The way how he communicates and his actions will provide clues to his true intentions. Whether dating or in a relationship face-to-face discussions can often feel strained or competitive for both men and women. For couples, discussing issues sitting side-by-side instead of face-to-face can be a better approach and more productive; encouraging a man to express his emotions gradually can help him to open up if he starts with small declarations of feeling sad or scared. Men generally consider having sex as a form of communication as they tend to express their emotions and affection physically rather than verbally; he is also more likely to open up and express himself after making love with his partner so it can make sense for a woman to relate to her partner sexually in certain situations, for example if he is worried about something or stressed out. I am not suggesting a woman should have sex to encourage her man to communicate but it is important to understand how the minds of many men work.

Urban Myth 3: Men Scared Of Intelligent, Successful Women

There are men who are scared of intelligent and successful women but a man who runs away from a relationship in fear of these positive attributes isn't a suitable candidate for a serious relationship anyway!

Men and women have very different basic requirements; men want to feel needed, while women want to feel wanted. If a man comes to the conclusion that he won't be able to fulfill his traditional role of being the provider or will be merely an accessory in a woman's life he is going to be very reluctant to take the dating phase any further. If he is already involved but is hindered in his need to function as a man he will probably feel severely emasculated and no amount of money or high-end lifestyle is going to make him feel any better about himself. Of course there will be men who stay just because of the comfortable lifestyle but deep down they will not be happy and eventually are going to cheat. A successful woman can have a great career and earn substantially more than her partner but has to understand clearly that the male Ego can be very fragile and has to be handled with care. Emotionally secure men do not avoid successful women because they feel intimidated, however, they're not prepared to have a relationship with a woman who makes them feel emasculated.

Urban Myth 4: Men Want To Control Their Relationships

There are still traditional or expected roles for men in many cultures and societies. A man is supposed to be:

- The significant bread winner
- Main protector of his family
- Head of the household
- The final arbiter of all the major decisions

Many women believe all men want to fulfill the above roles within their relationships and of course there are men who do! There are men who believe this is what "real" men should be doing in their relationships, but contrary to this popular urban myth the majority of modern men are not looking for a woman they can dominate and control; they're looking for a woman to share a genuine partnership with.

Urban Myth 5: Men Are Scared Of Commitment

The fact is it takes longer for a man to truly commit to a relationship. Of course there are some men who are Commitment Phobic, but that doesn't mean most or all men are afraid of commitment, it just means it takes us longer to make a decision. When you're dating a guy you like your expectations and timescales have to be realistic or you will come across as being needy or desperate and probably scare him off or create some type of unnecessary drama. What scares men away from considering getting seriously involved is making the wrong decision. Men usually take the logical approach not the largely emotional criteria women use to choose a partner. It can take a man time to decide if the chemistry is right and if you're both compatible in the right areas but once a genuine decision has been made he will probably follow through. Men don't like to be pressured and nagged into making a commitment and prefer to "get there" naturally and on his own timeline and terms.

Of course this can be frustrating for a woman who may be desperate for a relationship commitment but complaining, applying pressure or issuing ultimatums will usually be counterproductive. Healthy relationships grow organically so the sensible strategy is to go with the flow. Allow the dating to develop naturally over the reasonable period of time it takes to discover if there is any real potential for a loving union.

The Type Of Woman A Genuine Man Is Looking For

A survey published during August 2011 found that more than half of men are strongly attracted to a potential partner after the first meeting, with one fifth of men claiming to fall in love at first sight and almost three-quarters saying they had fallen in love within three dates. Approximately 3,000 men and women aged between 16 and 86 were surveyed as part of the work commissioned for the launch of the novel *The Way We Were* by Elizabeth Nobles. Surprisingly, the findings seemed to contradict the popular belief that only women fall in love quickly. Experts have claimed the results probably reveal the different criteria men and women generally use to choose a partner.

The main conclusions were:

- Men tend to tick more superficial boxes, for example appearance, which strongly influenced deciding whether they were "in love."
- Women were likely to weigh up the pros and cons of becoming involved before making a decision to proceed and take matters further.
- Women appear to take much longer before deciding to give their hearts away and become emotionally involved.
- Only one in ten women said they had experienced love at first sight and the majority of women surveyed said they waited until at least the sixth date before deciding if the relationship was worth pursuing.

"Women are better at reading social situations and are more likely to ask more questions of themselves after meeting someone, like is he going to make me feel secure and will he be a good father to my children. They are cannier than men at making a lifetime choice."
– Professor Alexander Gordon, Chartered Psychologist & Member of the British Psychological Society

It's important to understand that a man's opinion regarding female attractiveness is highly subjective. Most men are not looking for a beauty queen but tend to be attracted to a particular type. They often have a certain expectation regarding a woman's appearance. When deciding whether a woman is worth pursuing for a serious relationship men generally use a blend of factors which include physical or sexual attraction and appealing personality traits. Men rarely ask a woman on a date if they don't feel some kind of physical attraction or are curious to find out more about her or a combination of both. The bottom line is provided a woman meets a man's personal minimum appearance requirements he will probably be happy to pursue her to explore the possibilities of having a relationship.

Men who are seriously looking for love will usually be seeking the following qualities in a partner:

- Loyalty
- Kindness
- Positive attitude
- Caring
- Loving
- Sense of humor
- Supportive
- Appreciative of his efforts
- Understands men!

The majority of single men want to be in a relationship with a woman they can love, trust and respect; they also want a woman their families and friends respect because whoever a man chooses as his partner will be a reflection of his personal judgment and standards. Despite what your friends, family and the mainstream media may tell you, there are decent single men out there looking for a stable, loving relationship and very willing to make a commitment to the right woman.

CHAPTER 15:

The Seven Essential Character Traits

"The key to choosing the right partner is to look for a person with good character not simply a good personality." – Barbara De Angelis, TV Personality, Personal Growth Adviser & Author of *Are You The One For Me?*

People write lists before they go shopping for one simple reason: they want to go home with all of the items they want or need! It might sound obvious, but the best way to avoid making a big relationship mistake is to be clear about what type of personal qualities you're looking for in a partner. If you don't even know what your requirements are, it can be very easy to drift into a relationship disaster that gives you nothing but disappointment and distress.

A common mistake many women make in the dating game is to focus on physical appearance and appealing personality traits instead of concentrating on a man's *character*. He might be funny and make you laugh, have a magnetic personality or pursue interests you find fascinating; you may even share similar views on a variety of subjects. All of this can make a man appear very appealing, but these things will not give you an accurate measure of his character. Depending solely on a few attractive but superficial personality traits cannot provide enough reliable information to assess a man's overall character, temperament and compatibility. The majority of people strive to make a favorable impression when they meet someone new and some men can have a very slick personality but the main reason their presentation can be impressive is usually due to lots of practice. By closely examining a potential partner's character you can begin to understand his motivations and intentions instead of relying on luck or fate, hoping the relationship will work out for the best. To maximize your chances of finding the right kind of partner there are **7 Essential Character Traits (ECTs)** that should be on your "shopping list" when considering becoming involved with someone new. Each ECT quality a potential partner lacks increases the risk he will not be a suitable candidate for a constructive, healthy and loving relationship.

The 7 Essential Character Traits (ECT)

- Emotional Openness And Availability
- Positive Mindset
- High Self-Esteem
- Integrity
- A Responsible And Mature Attitude

- A Commitment To Self-Discovery And Personal Growth
- Kindness

Before becoming too deeply involved you need to discover a potential partner's values, beliefs and his capacity to be a kind and loving partner. Investigating a potential partner's true character will reveal how he treats others and, more importantly, how he is likely to treat *you*.

ECT #1: Emotional Openness And Availability

"Connecting with those you know love, like and appreciate you restores the spirit and gives you energy to keep moving forward in this life." – Deborah Day, *Be Happy Now!*

The emotional availability of each person determines if their relationships will be healthy and positive or frustrating and dysfunctional. When you enter into a relationship, it's quite natural to expect the union to grow and become deeper over a period of time but if you become involved with a man who refuses to maintain a consistent emotional connection, this will inevitably cause frustration and distress. You may even begin to question your own ability to love as your efforts to connect lovingly with your partner are rejected. Some women ignore very obvious warnings signs that their partner is not emotionally available.

A man is not ready to be in a relationship when he is:

- Emotionally repressed
- Emotionally closed down
- Confused about *how* he feels
- Lacking emotional awareness
- Unwilling or unable to share his feelings
- Constantly struggling to show affection and appreciation

These are serious warning signs so pay attention when you're dating someone new. Remember, if you identify these types of problems they existed before you met him and you're not supposed to try and fix him! Any man who struggles to identify and share his feelings is simply not ready for a serious relationship. Period. The capacity to be emotionally available and open is a very important quality and a key ECT to look for.

You should only consider a potential partner who is:

- Emotionally available, open and accessible
- Fully in touch with his feelings
- Communicative and willing to share what he is feeling
- Understands how to express those feelings in an appropriate way
- Truthful
- Receptive to your personal opinions, feelings and emotions

The only sensible strategy to discovering his attitude regarding his emotional openness and availability is to ask questions. He could give you answers that *sound* good so look out for any contradictions that may suggest he is not being entirely truthful. Pay close attention to his answers and how you *feel* about his responses.

Emotional Openness And Availability - Suggested Questions:

- Have you had difficulties expressing certain feelings in the past and has this improved or changed significantly?
- Do you still have difficulty expressing your feelings? What type of feelings do you find difficult to talk about?
- If there are certain feelings you still have difficulty expressing or feel uncomfortable revealing, where do you think that comes from?
- How do you feel after you have shared your thoughts and emotions?
- How do you feel about expressing your feelings to the people in your life that you care about?
- If you had problems expressing yourself in the past do you think this had a negative impact on your previous relationships?
- What do you think your previous partners would say regarding your levels of emotional availability and openness?
- What are your parents like? How did they express themselves during your childhood?

All of these questions are important, but the last one could be vital because emotionally unavailable parents frequently raise children who become adults with issues connected to repressing or understanding their own emotions. Men who find it difficult to share their true feelings usually fail to show their love and appreciation. Finding yourself in a relationship where you're constantly starved of emotional nourishment, support and mutual understanding can be a very painful experience and a total waste of time.

- A partner who withholds love and affection or has difficulty expressing himself on an emotional level will always make you feel his love has to be "worked" for or you have to be worthy to be in his life – definitely not a good situation to be in!
- A partner who makes you feel his love is somehow limited, evasive or difficult to share can result in you consciously or subconsciously wanting to prove to him or yourself you actually deserve his love.

Emotional availability and openness is a very important ECT because when a man struggles to understand his own emotions or finds it difficult to express his feelings the challenges that are inevitable in every relationship will be very difficult resolve. When a partner in a relationship fails to communicate and lacks the capacity to provide the emotional intimacy every relationship requires he probably has unresolved emotional issues, and these will inevitably surface in behaviors that can be highly frustrating or destructive. A relationship can only succeed with a partner who is capable of consistently showing their love and appreciation. A man who struggles to express and share his feelings will always find it difficult to contribute positively to any relationship until he learns how to open up, express himself and to be emotionally receptive. Men who are emotionally available will be open and willing to accept a woman into their hearts and lives. Successful relationships always depend on emotional openness, availability and honest communication by both partners so don't sell yourself short by settling for less.

ECT # 2: A Positive Mindset

"What is the difference between an obstacle and an opportunity? Our attitude toward it. Every opportunity has a difficulty, and every difficulty has an opportunity." – J. Sidlow Baxter (1903-1999), Pastor, Theologian & Author

Whether you are aware of it or not, your family and friends are constantly influencing your thoughts, actions and goals. We can all be extremely susceptible and very much influenced by the moods, emotions and mindsets of the people we spend the majority of our time with. When you pay attention to the life of someone who has a negative attitude, they always seem to attract some type of "bad luck!" Their lives are frequently littered with a long list of broken relationships, featuring ongoing dramas and emotional turbulence. Most of us pick up "vibes" from other people and places at times, but make the mistake of dismissing these feelings believing they are caused by an over active imagination. If you spend a great amount of time with people whose lives are a mess, your life is likely to become unstable and messy, too.

People who are negative typically:

- Find it difficult to trust other people
- Resist or ignore possible solutions
- Focus primarily on the problem
- Behave in a reactive rather than proactive way
- Are reluctant to resolve issues due to being overwhelmed by worry or fear
- Consider the future with a pessimistic or cynical attitude

Most of us like to be helpful, we also like to feel intelligent so when someone approaches us for advice we usually do our best to help. However, we have to be careful that the urge to help others isn't being motivated by our Ego's need to feel important instead of being purely altruistic in seeking to be of assistance. When someone seems sad or even distressed it's natural to feel sympathy but it can be very easy to become involved in a relationship that starts off with just trying to help out. You meet a new guy and believe he is basically a "good" person who has just been "unlucky," taken advantage of or perhaps confused about how to resolve his particular "problem." Everyone deserves sympathy or compassion in certain circumstances but when you meet a man who appears interested in you but has problems or seems unhappy with his life don't be tempted get involved. If he seems to be swamped with problems do not naively assume you can rescue him and fix his problems. This type isn't really interested in any practical solutions and his problems can just be a tactic to keep you interested and engaged. Once he has your attention and if you become his partner, you will probably be tempted into trying to solve them. The frustrating part will be when you come up with the most sensible, practical and "doable" solutions to his problem and he finds an excuse not to follow your advice. In addition, his negative moods will eventually affect *your* moods and you too will begin to attract problems or "bad luck" into your own life. Some people will never be happy no matter how supportive you may be and a partner with a negative attitude will eventually infect you with his pessimistic outlook. If you insist on associating with negative or problem-focused people or worse, become involved with a partner who has this type of mindset, eventually *you* will become negative and problem-focused.

People who are positive are typically:

- Consistent and optimistic in attitude
- Proactive
- Able to view obstacles, adversities and challenges as opportunities to learn and grow
- Focused on solutions
- Believers that destiny and reality can be created according to their personal vision

When you associate with positive people who have stable lives this will encourage you to manage your own life effectively and help you to maintain an optimistic attitude. Spending your time with those who exude infectious enthusiasm will influence you to become more enthusiastic and adventurous too! Stay alert by constantly measuring your personal levels of maturity, responsibility and self-awareness by paying attention to who you're hanging out with. The bottom line is if you're serious about finding a great relationship, you have to be vigilant regarding who you spend your time with!

The best way to find out if a potential or current partner has a positive attitude towards life is to ask the right questions.

Checking Out A Positive Attitude - Suggested Questions:

- What type of difficult situation has he dealt with recently?
- How does he feel when situations in his life go wrong or he is faced with a challenge?
- What important lessons has he learnt from any painful personal experiences?
- What is his personal philosophy regarding life in general and has it changed due to his experiences?
- Does he think whatever happens situations usually have the potential for a positive outcome? *Ask for reasons that support his answers.*
- How does he see most people – does he think they are fundamentally good or essentially bad?
- How would he explain the current state of world affairs to a child or his children if he has any?

Listen to his answers and always trust your feelings or observations; for example, if he constantly complains about his life or other people then he isn't a suitable candidate for a serious relationship. Becoming involved with a man who has low self-esteem or a fearful, negative attitude will eventually drain you mentally and emotionally. This ECT is very important and you should carefully consider if a potential partner possesses a generally negative attitude. It will always be much easier to build and maintain a rewarding relationship with a man who is broadly positive about himself, his life and his personal goals. For a relationship to have a realistic chance of success, both partners should generally have a positive attitude; it's impossible for love and mutual respect to grow when there is constant negativity as this fatally undermines any prospects for success.

ECT # 3: High Self-Esteem

"Everything that happens to you is a reflection of what you believe about yourself. We cannot outperform our level of self-esteem. We cannot draw to ourselves more than we think we are worth." – Iyanla Vanzant, Inspirational Speaker, Author, Life Coach & TV Personality

Having a consistent optimistic attitude is a very important component of maintaining high self-esteem. The most important relationship you will ever have is the one you have with yourself and each of us can only love another human being as much as we are capable of loving ourselves. Our subconscious beliefs dictate how we feel about ourselves and these beliefs will be projected into all of our relationships. When someone has unresolved emotional issues those feelings will eventually surface and be projected onto their partner and the other people in their life. **Positive or high self-esteem is a mindset.**

People with positive or high self-esteem typically:

- Have a positive and realistic view of themselves
- Protect personal boundaries by setting appropriate limits
- Make good decisions using a balance of intellect and intuition
- Have meaningful and reciprocated relationships
- Maintain appropriate emotional connections with others
- Make sure personal relationships are clearly defined
- Are emotionally available
- Are truthful and honest
- Trust their intellect and their intuition
- Are not judgmental of others

People with healthy self-esteem are not remotely threatened or concerned with the achievements, appearance or possessions of other people. Those who suffer with low self-esteem will usually view themselves negatively and have not learnt to accept themselves. They also spend a great deal of time constantly comparing themselves unfavorably to others, and will lack pride in themselves or beat themselves up for not being "good enough." In extreme cases they will believe life is generally very unfair and is out to get them! It can be difficult to spot someone with low self-esteem issues because while some will lack pride in themselves others try to over compensate by having a big Ego. The behaviors of a person with low self-esteem can include drug or alcohol abuse, casual sex or even violence, which provide temporary comfort and escape from the negative thoughts and feelings they have about themselves. Depression, stress, burnout and other various conditions and addictions all originate from issues stemming from low self-esteem. The activities and addictions are not primary *causes* of low self-esteem but the *result* of poor self-esteem.

Low Self-Esteem Warning Signs:

- Poor boundaries
- Ignores or belittles any advice
- Constantly seeks advice

140

- Frequently problem-focused
- Usually expects the worse to happen

Men and women with low self-esteem often believe they don't deserve to have a relationship so will use problems as an excuse to connect with someone. The type of "love" they offer is usually motivated by a need to bolster feelings of inadequacy and many "fall in love" just to try to feel better about themselves. Those who suffer with low self-esteem often need constant reassurance due to their deep feelings of insecurity and lack of self-worth. They can be desperate to be loved and prove themselves "worthy" of love, but the "love" on offer is twisted and deficient; at first a partner with low self-esteem can make you feel needed or special for rescuing him and even may be grateful for making him feel worthy of being loved, but constantly having to boost his low self-esteem will be very hard work. He may love you, but if he doesn't value, appreciate and love himself the relationship will become extremely draining.

High Self-Esteem Indicators

Low esteem is often the root cause of procrastination and low confidence with a fear of failure being so terrifying for some sufferers they simply refuse to try anything new, resist change and avoid taking risks.

Individuals with high self-esteem are confident in their abilities and not overwhelmed by the idea of taking chances, seeking new opportunities or being proactive. They are always seeking to stretch and grow beyond their personal comfort zone trying new and different things, which gives their lives excitement and meaning. A person who sets a goal and pursues it is taking a risk; there are no guarantees of success but taking action demonstrates self-confidence and high self-esteem. These people are naturally motivated to give their love from a secure emotional foundation because they feel good about themselves. Those with positive self-esteem know who they are while being proactive to improve and evolve to become the best version of themselves they can be. When a person respects themselves their personal boundaries are secure; he or she will not tolerate abuse or allow themselves to be manipulated or taken advantage of by others. How you allow others to treat you is a direct reflection of your own levels of self-esteem; if you permit others to treat you badly this clearly indicates low self-esteem issues but when you're assertive and have high self-esteem, you will not tolerate any type of emotional or physical abuse.

High self-esteem means *the more you love yourself the less you will allow others to mistreat you.* Those with high self-esteem are assured, confident and assertive but not arrogant. Self-awareness and self-respect greatly enhances personal authority. These attributes provide effective internal guidance and dictate how a person treats themselves. The more self-respect a man or woman has the better they will treat themselves both emotionally and physically. They make looking after themselves a priority and this is a reliable indicator regarding how they will treat a romantic partner and the other people in their lives.

Checking Out Positive Self-Esteem - Suggested Questions:
- What makes him feel proud regarding himself?
- What makes him feel proud regarding his achievements?
- What does he think are his most important achievements?

Pay close attention to the responses you receive to the above questions. If he struggles to respond, this indicates he probably believes he hasn't done anything to be proud of or suffers from low-self-esteem.

Further questions:

- Does he have any unhealthy lifestyle habits? Which habit does he consider to be the worse one? Does he have a plan of action to address any unhealthy habits?
- What kind of risks has he dared to take during his life?
- Has he taken any risks recently?
- When was the last time he took a risk?
- Has he tolerated any type of mistreatment or emotional abuse during any previous relationships?
- If yes, why does he think he tolerated this abuse?
- Does he think he would tolerate abuse now or in the future?
- Does he believe he's generally decisive or does he have a tendency to procrastinate?
- How does he demonstrate he respects and cares for himself?
- Does he give himself treats? What kind of special treats or pampering does he give to himself?

The old saying "talk is cheap" is very true. Is your potential or current partner a good talker but doesn't back up his words with actions? Does he always seem to have a problem? How does he treat himself? During the dating or honeymoon phase of a relationship many women make the mistake of concentrating solely on how a man treats them while completely ignoring obvious warning signs that indicate low self-esteem. Observe a potential partner's attitude and how he looks after himself as these factors can provide important clues regarding his levels of self-esteem. Pay attention and consider whether he has a habit of giving his ideas or problems a lot of lip service but isn't very proactive. There's nothing wrong with being cautious, exercising due diligence while considering a situation thoroughly, but a man with a strong aversion to making decisions, taking action or taking calculated risks may have self-esteem issues. When you begin to date someone new seriously ask yourself if you would feel proud to have him as your partner. If you're currently involved ask yourself if you're proud of your man and what he represents; this doesn't mean you should attack him for being indecisive or weak but to explore why he may suffer from low esteem and to discover if there are steps that can support his personal development.

There are very few dramas, "blame games" and point-scoring in a relationship when both partners have high self-esteem and a positive attitude. Mutual high self-esteem provides part of a solid foundation for greater cooperation, and makes any conflict resolutions much easier, which creates a healthy, loving relationship. A couple who share their love feeling confident and secure within themselves naturally benefit both partners as the interaction is more likely to be positive and balanced. When you're serious about finding the love you deserve, look for a partner who has high self-esteem, self-respect, pride and confidence in himself. Just remember there is a huge difference between having pride or confidence and being conceited and big-headed!

ECT # 4: Integrity

"There can be no friendship without confidence, and no confidence without integrity." – Samuel Johnson (1709-1784), Poet Essayist, & Literary Critic

We all lie occasionally and you're lying if you claim you don't! Sometimes we tell "white lies" to avoid hurting someone's feelings or for other altruistic reasons. People who are economical with the truth or who have a habit of consistently telling "white lies" may have decided the best way to get what they want is to be dishonest or to lie to avoid uncomfortable confrontations. There is a big difference between being truthful and being honest. The truth can change over time, even in a fleeting moment because the truth is about facts and facts can change constantly. For example, you may have a certain amount of money in your bank account today and *today that amount is a fact*; the money in your account could be more or less tomorrow but the amount in your bank account today is a fact. Truth is about demonstrable, empirical facts, but facts can often be subject to change. Being **honest** is about how you're feeling at any given time, but of course how you feel can also change! When you're being honest with someone it means being open and clear about your feelings at that moment in time. A person of integrity is honest with others and themselves; they do not deceive themselves, deceive others or fail to acknowledge the reality of a situation.

For example, I have a friend called Tyrone (not his real name) who lived with his partner. During a conversation we shared he said he was unhappy because his partner had been complaining about his habit of putting his cell phone on silent/vibrate mode when he was at home. Tyrone didn't think these complaints were justified but I also know his partner so asked him why he thought she was suspicious. He explained that a few months previously he didn't go home and told his partner he had stayed out overnight at a friend's place because he was tired. I don't know where he spent that night or who with, but it was obvious to me that by not going home and without an acceptable explanation he clearly displayed a lack of integrity. In addition, Tyrone having his cell phone on silent/vibrate mode was fueling the suspicion he had been unfaithful and his integrity was being questioned. The reason his partner was giving him a hard time was hardly rocket science!

There is a big difference between being private, the right to privacy and keeping secrets. Individual private matters include personal ideas or beliefs, like how the world operates politically, practically, economically or spiritually. A belief in an afterlife or of intelligent life existing on other planets would also be considered subjects that are private. Each of us has the right to our own private beliefs, personal fantasies, daydreams or goals which we can decide to share or keep to ourselves. Revealing our private beliefs allows others a certain level of insight into our individual character and some people hide certain beliefs fearing others may judge them harshly.

However, keeping secrets is not compatible with conducting a relationship with integrity, undermines trust and is seldom beneficial in the long-term. Secrets always have the potential to devastate a relationship; when the truth is revealed the lies told to cover up secrets inevitably have serious consequences. Secrets and lies always make it extremely difficult to make a genuine emotional connection and the person keeping secrets uses up a great deal of energy that could be directed at maintaining the relationship.

Checking Out Personal Integrity - Suggested Questions:

You need to ask questions to find out about someone's levels of honesty and integrity.

- What type of activities and behavior does he believe are unacceptable?
- Is stealing money, goods or supplies from work acceptable?
- How does he feel about cheating others for money or scamming? Is this acceptable in certain circumstances?
- Has he lied to his family, friends or colleagues in the past? When does he think this is justified?

Checking Out Relationship Integrity - Suggested Questions:

- What type of behavior does he think is unacceptable in a relationship and why does he believe they are wrong?
- Does he think cheating on a partner is okay if he's unhappy?
- Are there things he would lie about in a relationship, for example, if he was having an affair, unhappy with his partner's appearance or just generally unhappy with the relationship?
- Does he think his previous partners consider him to be a person of integrity? If you asked his previous partners their views, what does he think they would say?
- Has he ever experienced an act of betrayal during a relationship or been lied to? How did that make him feel and what happened as a result?
- Has he ever lied in a relationship? What was the aftermath of his betrayal, lies or deceit?

It's important to discover if he thinks keeping secrets is acceptable or believes in being honest and open. If he admits to lying or betraying any of his previous partners you should ask follow up questions to find out why this happened; make it a priority to find out if he is likely to behave that way again. The eyes are described as the windows of the soul for a reason so pay attention to his eye reactions, general demeanor and body language during and after your questions. To avoid the mistake of getting caught up in a web of deceit you have to be curious and very skeptical before you become too involved. Listen to your intuition, refuse to be taken in too easily and always remember that anything that sounds too good is probably an exaggeration! Predators in the dating game lie all the time to make themselves look desirable and to get quick, easy sex. If a man is evasive, withholds information or you suspect he likes to play mind games, just walk away.

Will you be able to truly rely on and trust him?

You should never have to interrogate your partner to find out what he is thinking or feeling and he shouldn't be hiding certain aspects of his personality or his life from you either. A man who is honest and open will be willing to share his truth and all of himself within a relationship. Living with a partner who lacks integrity can cause heavy feelings of insecurity and doubt especially when there are shared financial commitments. Uncertainty about what is happening or could happen will leave you constantly on edge never feeling confident he can keep his promises or whether he is telling the truth. Those who habitually use dishonesty or manipulation often believe they must be in total control and "win" at any cost so the feelings of others are considered to be merely "collateral damage." A man who lies constantly to his partner simply doesn't understand what love is no matter how many excuses or apologies he may offer. Psychopaths and other toxic personality types can lie very easily and a partner who lies routinely will be extremely difficult to connect with on an emotional level. Chronic or pathological liars always cause major difficulties in their relationships; besides being emotionally unavailable they are totally untrustworthy using mind games to target and lower their partner's self-esteem.

A man who constantly lies to his family, friends and associates or feels it's perfectly reasonable to use deception, deflection, half-truths or blatant lies to gain an advantage should be avoided at all costs. A healthy relationship cannot grow or survive without trust, honesty and integrity; when these essential elements are missing it doesn't matter what else is happening in the relationship because feelings of insecurity will dominate your thinking and eventually wear down your self-esteem. Lacking trust in your partner means never being able to relax into the relationship as you're always left wondering exactly what's going on or spending time trying to catch him out and looking for clues to prove he's lying. Over time, deception destroys intimacy, and without intimacy couples cannot enjoy true or lasting love. Eventually feelings of tension and resentment will cause you to withdraw emotionally and then physically as the relationship dies a slow death.

If you are aware that your partner often lies to others and you accept this type of behavior you may find yourself covering up for him or even lying on his behalf to keep the relationship intact.

Those who practice integrity consistently demonstrate honesty and their "word is their bond." How he treats other people will provide important clues regarding how he is likely to treat you so keep an eye on how he interacts with others. Healthy relationships are built on honesty and truth because these are the building blocks that provide predictability, reliability and a strong feeling of security. Integrity naturally builds confidence because it encourages trust; if you want to avoid drama, distress and disappointment look for a partner with high integrity who is honest and open about expressing himself. Wait until you're confident he is genuine, trustworthy and honest before making any kind of firm relationship commitments.

ECT # 5: A Responsible And Mature Attitude

"When a man blames others for his failures, it is a good idea to credit others with his successes." – Howard W. Newton, Author

Response-ability is our ability to respond to circumstances appropriately. There will be times when we fail to consciously choose our responses but instead react compulsively and then blame others for our reaction. Blaming others is often a tactic to try to avoid taking personal responsibility but we are all accountable for our own emotions and behavior. All of us face challenges or experience setbacks but there are some people whose lives are constantly chaotic and unstable and this is often caused by a failure to take responsibility. Those who refuse to take responsibility are stuck in an "arrested development" mindset so they resist becoming "real" adults. Failing to take responsibility leaves many men and women living a life of endless procrastination, at the mercy of the decisions of others or being constantly buffeted by circumstances. Very few irresponsible people actually achieve anything of value or substance in their lives. Responsibility and commitment involves personal choices about where our attention and energy will be focused. Once a responsibility has been accepted and a commitment made part of being a responsible adult requires us to make decisions and follow through on our commitments. Being responsible does not always guarantee success as nothing in life is certain, but taking responsibility provides a greater chance of succeeding and enhances feelings of self-respect.

If you have a tendency to try to rescue others it's likely you're susceptible to becoming involved with an irresponsible and immature type of man. Of course we should help others when this is appropriate but providing indefinite support can encourage others to avoid taking responsibility for their own lives. A man who is great fun to be with and has a great sense of humor might seem attractive but if he lacks maturity and has an irresponsible attitude towards life he is not ready for a serious relationship no matter how much he makes you laugh! A relationship with someone who constantly evades responsibility and lacks maturity will always be very frustrating where you're manipulated into providing most if not all of the emotional input. How does this happen? A man who is emotionally immature will suddenly withdraw completely without any explanation and will not share his feelings, leaving his partner feeling very confused. He will find it very difficult to process his emotions and struggle to discuss his feelings with his partner or those closest to him; in extreme cases he may turn to alcohol or drugs seeking to numb feelings of failure and low self-esteem, or simply try to avoid the burden of taking responsibility. These men fail to understand this behavior cuts them off from valuable support that could be of great assistance and can cause their partners great distress. Men who are emotionally mature respond to a personal crisis in a totally different way; he may withdraw for a short period of time to think things through but will re-engage his partner or those closest to him relatively quickly to avoid damaging his relationships. He knows honesty is the best policy and understands it is a sign of strength, not weakness, so expresses himself and strives to keep the lines of communication open. A mature and responsible man respects his partner and doesn't expect her to be a mind reader. He isn't scared to show his feelings if he is going through a difficult time.

Checking Out Responsibility & Maturity – Suggested Questions:

The Basic 4

1. Does he earn enough to support himself and to be independent?
2. Can he cook and feed himself?
3. Can he look after himself?
4. Is he capable of keeping where he lives reasonably clean and tidy?

These questions may seem very basic and even funny but you might be very surprised at the amount of fully grown men who can't maintain their basic day-to-day living!

Further Questions Regarding Responsibility:

- When he borrows from others does he return their belongings? Does he return the items in a good condition?
- Would his friends describe him as being responsible, irresponsible or "average?"
- Is he sensitive and considerate regarding the feelings of others?
- Where does he think he fails in meeting any of his promises and commitments?

146

- What is his time keeping like? Does he think it's important to be on time?

- In the past, has he ever been sacked from a job? If yes, what was the reason?

- In the past has he ever quit a job without having alternative employment? If yes, what was the reason?

- Does he think he can be irresponsible in certain areas such as his health or finances?

- In his previous relationships does he think he was usually more looked after or was he the more proactive and dominate partner in assuming the role of looking after his partner(s)?

- What does he think his previous partners would say about his attitude towards responsibility?

How a person lives their life is a very reliable indicator of their general attitude and behavior towards responsibility so pay attention to how a potential partner lives his life. Being a mature adult requires each of us to be responsible and to accept we are all accountable for our decisions and actions. Being responsible means being prepared to deal with any consequences that may arise from a failure to handle or meet those responsibilities and commitments. A man with a responsible and mature attitude will *consistently practice* being responsible by keeping his commitments and promises; he will clearly demonstrate this not only by what he may say, but also with his actions. Being responsible builds a foundation of trust in all of your relationships, intimate or otherwise. Our outer world reflects the inner world of our psyche; when we're responsible and trustworthy we tend to attract people into our lives who are also dependable, supportive, trustworthy, and truthful. Maintaining a committed relationship requires both partners to have a mature, adult attitude towards life and each other.

ECT # 6: A Commitment To Self-Discovery And Personal Growth

"Life isn't about finding yourself. Life is about creating yourself." – George Bernard Shaw (1856-1950), Playwright

Whether you're single or in a relationship pursuing personal growth should be an ongoing priority in your life. A commitment to personal growth enhances each of us and encourages constructive interactions in all of our relationships. When you're interested in finding a partner for a serious relationship, look for a man who has a genuine commitment to personal growth and self-improvement. If you meet a man with a "know it all" attitude who doesn't understand the value of pursuing personal growth and honest introspection, you can safely assume he thinks he's already perfect and has all the answers. There are people who refuse to acknowledge they need to work on themselves and live a life of denial, which is usually a delay tactic to avoid facing inconvenient or uncomfortable facts about themselves. This is a short-term coping mechanism as issues don't just disappear. Before any goal of self-improvement can be effective we have to be honest and practice self-acceptance of the negative and positive aspects of ourselves. Refusing to acknowledge and accept the truth about your feelings results in zero personal growth; no one can change what they refuse to recognize and acknowledge. It is unrealistic to expect a relationship to work with a partner who is stagnant mentally, emotionally and spiritually when you have made a commitment to personal growth. A man who is resistant to working on himself or the relationship will only create situations that result in poor communication and a lack of cooperation. This type of partner will constantly react to circumstances without trying to evaluate what the appropriate response should be leaving you to sort out problems he has created. A man who refuses to acknowledge the importance of pursuing personal growth and self-improvement will struggle to contribute positively to any of his relationships.

Ask questions to discover what he's actually *doing* about his personal development. Greater self-awareness doesn't happen by just reading up on a few principles and finding them interesting or even intriguing; theories and concepts have to be put into practice to be effective. If he is saying all the right things and has read several books about self-development this doesn't mean he actually believes in pursuing personal growth or is *actively* doing anything! Actively pursuing means being proactive in seeking a greater understanding of yourself; he doesn't have to know everything about personal development but should at least demonstrate a willingness to learn and grow. The desire to seek personal growth not only reflects a level of humility but also maturity, which indicates the ability to compromise and negotiate when any relationship issues or conflicts arise.

A Commitment To Self-Discovery & Personal Growth - Suggested Questions:

- What lessons has he learnt from his previous relationships and how would he behave differently in the future?
- Would any complaints about him by his previous partners be justified and would he agree or disagree with their opinions?
- Has he ever used any external resources to try and resolve any relationship issues in the past such as researching online articles, books, counseling or talking to friends and family? Did any of these help to resolve the problem?
- What does he think his greatest weaknesses are? What does he believe caused these weaknesses?
- What emotional lessons has he learnt and have those lessons changed him in anyway?
- Are there any areas of himself he is currently working on improving? Are there any aspects of himself he intends to improve over the next three years? Are there any aspects of himself he would like to change, greatly reduce, control or eliminate?
- What personal qualities is he keen to develop and improve?

If you become involved with a partner who doesn't believe in personal growth this can prevent the relationship from evolving in a healthy manner. You will face major problems if he is actually aware of any unresolved Emotional Baggage but refuses to acknowledge these issues. Once you have invested emotionally in a relationship it can be difficult to disengage so make it your mission to find out his attitude towards personal growth *before* you get too deeply involved. If he isn't interested in evolving beyond his current outlook, concepts or beliefs it is not for you or others to judge or try to change his mind. We each have our personal journey to make in our own time and if he isn't interested in improving himself that isn't your problem, so don't waste time trying to persuade him to change. Simply acknowledge he lacks one of the ECTs you're looking for in a partner and move on.

If, however, he is receptive to the concept of personal growth or actively pursuing self-development then this is a man you should consider seriously for a relationship. Before you become too excited there are a few points that require your attention: he should be able to discuss his personal growth, explain his progress over a period of time, be able to describe his progress in particular areas and have specific goals for improvement. His opinions and behavior should demonstrate he is taking responsibility for his personal development. A man who is committed to personal growth is serious about becoming the best version of himself he can be, not just for selfish motives but also for his partner and the people he shares his life with. Men with this type of mindset are usually very keen to contribute positively to their relationships; many issues can be dealt with productively and resolved amicably with a partner who is interested in learning and growing. When both partners are committed to personal growth and willing to learn the many lessons intimate relationships provide, this greatly reduces the potential for point scoring and power struggles and instead increases opportunities for deeper levels of mutual understanding, loving cooperation and compassion. Sharing a mutual interest and commitment towards personal growth provides a solid foundation for a productive, healthy relationship.

ECT # 7: Kindness

"Kindness in words creates confidence. Kindness in thinking creates profoundness. Kindness in giving creates love." – Lao Tzu, Chinese Philosopher

In the Bible, the Greek word for kindness in Galatians 5:22 is *"chrestotes."* *Chrestos* has various meanings, one of which is "having integrity in relationship to others" and another, "kindness is useful." It is assumed the word "kind" was adapted by ancient Germanic culture and meant "nature" or the "natural order" or how "one would treat their kin." Other meanings also included "kind-heartedness" or being "warm-hearted" and, most importantly, the "innate character" of a person.

A kind person is thoughtful and naturally:

- Gentle
- Warm-hearted
- Emotionally generous
- Courteous
- Considerate
- Attentive
- Caring
- Helpful

Kindness is not just about good deeds but includes a certain attitude and habit that stems from high self-esteem motivated by compassion and respect for other people, as opposed to being self-obsessed. It can be very easy to overlook or underestimate the importance and power of kindness. Some women believe men who show kindness are weak, but kindness, like honesty, will only be found in a person with a strong character and positive values. A partner who is kind and thoughtful is a tremendous asset in a relationship and acts of kindness are actually good for you too!

- Kindness to others stimulates positive health. Various studies have shown being kind and acts of kindness enhance or improve health.

- Being genuinely thoughtful and showing we value and think of the needs of others greatly improves our relationships. Thoughtfulness validates the people in our lives. Feeling validated is very important for the majority of people.

- Expressing gratitude promotes beneficial states of health. Studies have indicated the benefits include psychological, social, and physical health improvements.

Showing kindness automatically makes you feel better about yourself and as you lead by example this encourages the people in your life to be kind to others. When a person is loving and kind people enjoy sharing their company, especially the people they are closest to. A man who is considerate and thoughtful will be careful not to harm or inconvenience others. He will treat people with respect, which means he is more likely to treat *you* with respect as well. Seeking a partner who is loving and kind should be a top priority when you're interested in finding a suitable man for a serious relationship; men with a "treat her mean to keep her keen" attitude should always be avoided!

❙ Reality Check!

"Character is like a tree and reputation like a shadow. The shadow is what we think of it; the tree is the real thing." – Abraham Lincoln (1809-1865), Former US President

A combination of these 7 Essential Character Traits indicates a potential partner with a good character and the type of man who can be considered for a serious relationship. Men (and women) with these traits usually enjoy positive interpersonal relationships that helps to maintain their mental, emotional and physical health. Many people make the mistake of failing to really think about what type of qualities they would like in a partner and just drift into one unsatisfying, dysfunctional relationship after another, attracted by superficial physical attributes or particular personality traits. It's always much better to make informed choices rather than just to cross your fingers and hope for the best! When you use the 7 Essential Character Traits as your check list this will give you a huge advantage in the dating game. Take your time when you meet a new man and get to know him properly. Discuss and explore his character so you can make an informed decision before embarking on a serious relationship.

Already Involved

If you're already involved, consider whether your partner has these 7 ECTs as this information can provide valuable information about the state of your relationship. Asking the suggested questions can reveal important information and attitudes about your partner you may have been previously unaware of. A lack of one or more of the ECTs may cause you to reconsider the viability of the relationship, and although this can be painful at first, ultimately it is a positive thing. Examining your partner's character can help you to negotiate changes of attitude or behavior you're unhappy with and then agree with your partner on an appropriate course of action to try to improve the relationship. We are all capable of change so do not rush into making any decisions to leave unless you are very unhappy. If you still have serious concerns about the lack of a particular ECT after a period of time (say two to three months) then it would be sensible to consider ending the relationship. Whether you're dating and looking for a serious relationship or currently involved, asking the right questions can save you a great deal of time and unnecessary heartache.

CHAPTER 16:

Looking for Love Strategies

"Finding your partner online was once regarded as a bit of a novelty, but this survey suggests it has become a common if not dominant way of meeting new partners, particularly if you are between 40 and 70 years old." – Dr. Bernie Hoga, Research Fellow, Oxford Internet Institute

The following Looking For Love strategies can be very effective. Everyone is different so consider what may suit you and do not be afraid to step outside your comfort zone!

Online Dating

For those looking for love in the past there were a variety of ways to try and meet someone special. You would go along to nightclubs and social events, use personal classified adverts in newspapers or ask family or friends to introduce you to someone they considered a good match. Times have changed tremendously over a relatively short period of time, and the internet has given the world online dating. There used to be a stigma attached to the idea of trying to find a potential partner online but this method of trying to meet someone special has become widely accepted. According to estimates by Metaflakes, a company that reviews online dating agencies, more than nine million adults in the UK go online each year to find a partner and now a third of all new relationships start online. Research indicates that one in five people marry someone they have met on the internet and more mature men and women over the age of 40 choose to use dating sites after being single for a period of time. Regardless of your personal opinion, the fact is the dating game is a numbers game and your chances of meeting someone special will increase dramatically if you try online dating. One of the greatest advantages of looking for love online is you don't even have to leave your home to begin searching for a date!

"Internet dating is the fastest, most efficient way to gather a pool of qualified candidates. It could take you a lifetime to do the investigation that the computer comes up with in seconds." – Judsen Culbreth, *The Boomer's Guide to Online Dating*

A number of online dating sites provide Psychometric Testing to identify and match compatible partners. Such dating sites include *match.com, datingdirect.com* and *eharmony.co.uk*, which each offer a service that promises to match couples by using scientific methods. A thorough psychometric test questionnaire consists of approximately 200 detailed questions that measure each person's values, general attitude, personality traits, attitude to relationships, interests in life and emotional make-up. The data is then scientifically analyzed to reveal how the subject interprets certain situations, makes decisions and responds to problems.

This creates a psychological profile to better match people looking for love with potential partners with their personality type and interests.

Psychometric testing to match couples for compatibility appears to increase the opportunities for meeting someone who matches your specific criteria and preferences. For example, if you wanted to meet someone who likes to be organized, enjoys outdoor activities and believes in traditional family values, psychometric profiling could be very effective for refining the search and matching process. While psychometric testing appears to increase the chances of meeting someone with a high compatibility match this isn't an infallible or foolproof system. Conducting research and knowing the type of answers to provide can produce a profile that is not accurate or which can even be highly misleading. This type of testing certainly can't tell you if there will be any genuine chemistry with a potential partner but is worth considering to discover if there are mutually shared interests.

"Psychometric assessment allows us to take the pool of all potential partners, narrow it down and introduce only those you're highly compatible with." – Dr Gian Gonzaga, Senior Research Scientist at eharmony.co.uk.

Dating websites market their services offering you the chance to find love at a price. One of the major hazards of using these services is they can give their members an air of legitimacy and the assumption can be made that everyone has been checked out. Another major pitfall is having to rely on someone you have never met to be telling the truth about themselves. Some people will add highly flattering photos of themselves taken in their younger years to their profiles that can be very different to how they actually look now. First impressions are very important and being discovered to be dishonest at the very first meeting does not inspire confidence; if a person can lie about something obvious like their physical appearance or age, it's quite likely they will lie about other things too! If you are thinking of trying online dating honesty is always the best policy. Avoid lying about your age, appearance or any other general information on your profile page. It won't matter how well the first meeting or date goes, the fact you were not honest will not be forgotten quickly or easily. It's also important to make sure you're being realistic about the kind of person you would like to meet. During 2012, psychologists from Rochester University in the US warned that dating websites were making people increasingly judgmental. Professor Harry Reis argued that skimming over numerous profiles can promote a "shopping mentality" resulting in people becoming excessively fussy while forming unrealistic expectations. Some people can spend weeks or even months emailing potential partners before meeting up.

Online Dating Scammers

"Scammers create a fake profile on dating sites and build up an intense relationship with their victim, grooming them before testing the waters to see if they can make some money out of the 'relationship'." – Professor Monica Whitty of Leicester University

The internet provides a very effective method for meeting new people but it's also a great cover for scammers who use dating websites or social media sites such as Facebook to look for victims. A survey by YouGov (UK) interviewed 2,028 victims of internet dating fraud and the results revealed men were just as likely to be targeted as women. Lesbians and gays were also targeted by criminals seeking to exploit those who are looking for love on dating websites.

Scammers use dating websites to find victims to "groom" in a fashion similar to that used by pedophiles seeking children to abuse sexually. These predators create attractive fake profiles, pretend to be genuine about wanting a relationship and then scam money from their victims over a period of time. Professor Monica Whitty of Leicester University says the first step is usually a test to see if the victim will give them money. Often the excuse is some kind of emergency situation or they may even send a small gift as a token of their "affection" to sucker the victim in. This hooks the target into an imaginary relationship as the con artist begins asking for more expensive gifts or money. These criminals know exactly what to say to those who are desperate for love and some victims can be so blinded by their desperation for a relationship they can be deceived for a very long time. Sadly there are also victims who are in very serious denial about what is actually happening and may even find it difficult to end contact with a scammer even after they discover their "lover" has been lying.

"One woman had been a victim three times – all on different occasions – and lost between £50,000 and £60,000. When she was told what had happened to her, she couldn't understand why she was being called a victim." – Professor Monica Whitty, Leicester University

During January 2011 it was reported that a 47-year-old divorced mother of three living in the UK had given £80,000 to her online "boyfriend." The man turned out to be part of a gang of Nigerian scam artists who were pretending to be a handsome American soldier on a dating website. The woman was scammed into taking out loans and credit cards, and borrowing money from family and friends. Several months after the police told her she had been the victim of a scam her house had to be sold to repay the debts she had built up pursuing the romantic fantasy. In a newspaper interview she said: "Aside from losing the money I feel like I've lost the love of my life. I know he wasn't real, but the feelings were real to me and that's very difficult to come to terms with. Hundreds of other women must be getting conned right now." This woman was clearly lonely and desperate for a relationship which made her an easy prey for the predator scammers. She gave over a substantial amount of money to a man she had never met because she wanted to believe the illusion of having found true love instead of using her common sense. When someone is feeling deeply desperate they are far more likely to make very poor love choices, find themselves in unfulfilling relationships or just end up being used and abused.

Avoiding The Scammers

These predators use a variety of stories and whatever you're told will be designed to push your emotional buttons to persuade you to part with your money, so read all profiles carefully. If a man claims to be in the military service consider if any photos on his profile or sent to you are actually genuine. Pay attention to the standard of his grammar and the syntax of his emails or online chat. Is the background information he has provided about himself consistent with his communication style? Is his online communication style consistent with English being his first language? If you are communicating with a man online who asks lots of questions but seems vague or evasive about providing basic details regarding himself this should be considered as a major red flag. Fraudsters often use fake US or UK military ranks and obtain photographs from the internet so before you become too engaged in any communication, check if his uniform and background can be identified and verified. A scammer who claims to be military personnel will often use excuses like he is on "operations" or on "active service" and at some stage may say he needs a cash amount in order to be "released" from his duties to come and see you, or needs the money to pay for the flight. The fraudster will probably ask for a cash payment to be made via Western Union, MoneyGram or another money transfer company in a name that's different to the one he uses with you. If he asks for the funds to be transferred directly into a legitimate bank account this is where the fraudster's contacts help to collect the money. As soon as the funds are paid in it will be immediately withdrawn.

If he does not claim to be in the military but appears interested in meeting up make sure his employment details such as his telephone number or email address are genuine, and insist on seeing some type of ID to verify his story. People are usually quite easy to find at their job even if you only want one of his colleagues to confirm he actually works there. A man who appears reluctant to provide his employer's details should make you very suspicious. Make sure his home address is genuine by checking the freely available public records for yourself to see if he is registered at a particular address. Fraudsters often trawl the internet for addresses to use and can obtain enough information to convince someone they actually live at an address so checking an address in and of itself is not foolproof but it does provide a level of protection. When a man insists on maintaining contact only via the internet, is difficult to speak to directly or his address details appear to be unreliable, these should all be considered very serious warning signs.

Is it wise to hand over a large amount of money to someone you've met for the very first time in a wine bar or nightclub? Does it seem sensible to send substantial amounts of money to a man you have never met to pay for an airline ticket or anything else? The answers to these questions are obvious and yet thousands of love-hungry women all over the world fall for these scams every day! Never send money to a person you don't know and have never met; if a man really wants to meet you then he will find a way to make it happen and pay for his own travel! Laws do not currently exist in the USA or UK that hold online dating website companies liable for any financial or physical harm experienced by their members. Most reputable dating websites operate strict controls and "vet" their members but experienced fraudsters are very resourceful and frequently bypass vetting procedures. Looking for love online can be extremely hazardous with heartless predators seeking out new victims everyday so use your common sense, always trust your intuition and pay attention. If you have any doubts about a man who has contacted you via a dating website you can also talk to a friend or a family member to get advice on whether it is sensible to proceed.

Facebook And Dating

Fraudsters don't just use online dating websites to find their victims; they also operate on social networking sites such as Facebook, LinkedIn or Twitter. This technology has also introduced a new set of rules into the dating game encouraging some women (and men) to become amateur detectives seeking out information about potential or actual partners online. They can spend hours trying to find out if he or she is a suitable person to consider dating, continue dating or stay in a current relationship with, but the problem with this approach is the information provided on Facebook profiles may not be reliable!

Some people create fake personal profiles on social networking sites or dating websites by using another person's pictures and/or fake personal information. They are referred to as "Catfish" and can waste a great deal of your time. They often trick other people into falling in love and in some cases those who are desperate enough can "date" someone online for months or even years without actually meeting the person. Episodes of the MTV Show "Catfish" (this television series featuring true stories can be viewed on YouTube) provides many examples of people using fake dating profiles and the hurt they cause to others. Always remember, Facebook gives everyone the opportunity to become their own online publicist and the ability to create powerful and sometimes highly misleading profiles.

Taking control of your own image and being selective about what type of information is shared on your profile gives you and everyone else a great deal of power over how you are perceived online. Receiving inbox messages and "Friend Requests" from men might flatter your Ego and make you feel attractive in the short-term but this can be a dangerous strategy. You should keep in mind that updating your Facebook profile with alluring or sexually provocative photos can attract the wrong type of attention. Think carefully about what type of pictures you include on your profile or online photo albums to avoid setting yourself up as a target. Whether you're single, dating or in a relationship never use information from a profile to assume you know what another person is thinking or doing. Facebook can give you a useful snapshot of a person but it can never provide the complete story about someone's personality. There is nothing wrong with arranging a date via Facebook or any other social networking websites but always pay attention and use your common sense!

Online Dating Mistakes

Internet dating is becoming increasingly popular and is a very effective method of meeting someone new. However, women looking for love online should avoid making the following mistakes with their dating website profiles.

Including Too Much Information On Your Profile

There is a balance to be struck between offering too much information and not enough. Supply details about what you like to do, such as your hobbies, interests and preferred activities. This will provide the opportunity for a potential date to see if they have a shared interest with you, which can result in a response to your profile. When men can see what you enjoy doing, they are more likely to explore your profile further and make contact. Including phrases like, "I have so much love to give!" is a major mistake. It will scare potential partners away as you will be seen as desperate. Describe your personality and interests, instead of focusing on your desire for a relationship. If you have posted your profile to a dating website, it's obvious you're interested in meeting someone new to explore the potential for a relationship. Share what you enjoy doing and the things that make you passionate or even excited – which will be far more appealing and will create intrigue and curiosity about you. From a man's point of view, there is little point in making contact with a woman if he doesn't know if she shares the same interests – and even less if she actually doesn't have any interests of her own. Men generally have interests or hobbies they can pursue by themselves or with other male friends. A man who believes a woman doesn't have interests of her own will probably assume she expects him to devote a substantial amount of his time to her and the dating process. That's a big turn-off for the average guy.

To obtain the right type of responses from men who are likely to be compatible with you, your profile information has to be specific. A woman who doesn't explain her likes, interests and preferred activities will usually come across as being hard work and not very appealing. When a woman is unclear about what she likes or her interests, this can be interpreted by a man as being indecisive or even desperate; she could even be waiting for a man to make her life "special" or complete. A lack of information on your profile can also suggest a woman who may be "high maintenance," as her life appears to be quite empty. Avoid divulging too much information, for example what type of car you drive, or details about your home address or financial situation. Be careful how you describe yourself on your dating profile. Do not pronounce yourself "easy going," "fun," "easily pleased" or "happy-go-lucky," especially all in the same sentence! Those types of phrases can be a green light to predators and scammers, who will probably consider you vulnerable and very easy to exploit financially. It's important to be confident that anyone you make contact with online is genuine and not a fraudster or internet sexual predator. Dating websites provide an introduction service for a fee and, while you're required to provide some personal information, this doesn't mean revealing everything about yourself! If you decide to use dating websites, it's very important to ensure your personal information is protected. Do not include your cell/mobile or landline number or your actual address and *never* share any of your financial information, such as your bank account details. Once you connect with someone you find interesting, there will be plenty of time to share your personal information, if you're comfortable to do so.

Unrealistic Relationship Expectations

Stating your relationship expectations can make many men reluctant to respond to a dating website profile. It's obvious you're interested in meeting someone new – otherwise you wouldn't have your profile on a dating website in the first place! To the average guy looking at a dating website profile, statements like, "Seeking a serious relationship" can be interpreted as being demanding. Men who are in a committed relationship still like a certain amount of freedom to pursue their own interests or to hang out with friends. If a potential partner suspects he is likely to be smothered or restricted unreasonably, he will not be keen to make contact. Include information regarding what you enjoy about life, instead of explaining your relationship expectations. Don't jump to conclusions or rush into anything if a man makes contact: it usually takes a certain amount of time to get to know someone and begin to feel comfortable. The best strategy is to take one step at a time, allowing any dates and possible relationship to evolve naturally, at their own pace.

Failure To Identify Fake Or Exaggerated Profiles

"Online dating is just as murky and full of lemons as finding a used car in the classifieds. Once you learn the lingo, it's easier to spot the models with high mileage and no warranty."
– Laurie Perry, *Crazy Aunt Purl's Home Is Where the Wine Is*

Before you actually begin using dating websites, contacting or responding to men, carry out some research and learn how to read profiles properly, so you're not fooled by some of the tricks people use online. Anyone can create a dating site profile, so you can't always take what you read and see at face value.

Best Practice Guidelines:

- If you begin to receive contact from website members soon after posting your profile, wait at least three days before responding, and in that time read their profiles very carefully.

- If you're uncertain about making contact or responding to someone online, you can always ask a trusted friend to look at the profile and give you an objective opinion.

- If possible, use Skype or a similar service, so you can see and speak to a potential date online before deciding to meet them.

There are men and women who will embellish or blatantly exaggerate their details to try to increase the number of responses they receive. Take some time to study different profiles, as this will help you to filter out the time-wasters, Players, sexual predators or scammers. Anyone who sounds too good to be true is probably misrepresenting themselves – so, if you decide to proceed, do so with extreme caution.

Failure to Block Potential Psychos

Learn to develop a low tolerance level for anyone who begins to badger or harass you online. Being a person who is well-mannered and respectful, or trying not to hurt someone else's feelings, is admirable, but not at the cost of your own emotional health. There is absolutely no point in risking your personal safety because you're too tolerant or easy-going or because you failed to identify any warning signs. If someone starts to make inappropriate, lewd or threatening comments, or becomes abusive, it's very likely he will be unpleasant when you meet up with him in the real world. Delete or block him immediately and move on to explore other dating options. Trust your intuition and use your commonsense. By being cautious and paying attention, you can learn to spot the red flags that can save you a great deal of stress and could even save your life!

Unrealistic Salary Or Career Expectations

Most women value security and would like to meet a successful man with a fantastic career and income. Concentrating purely on a guy's level of income is a mercenary strategy for a potential relationship and will severely restrict your options (just because a man earns good money doesn't make him a nice person and certainly doesn't mean you are going to be compatible). Many women's profiles state unreasonable salary range expectations in their search criteria. Most women would like a partner who is successful, but a good salary or high-flying career doesn't automatically make a man a perfect choice. Men who earn considerably more than the average salary are usually not stupid and are fully aware that there are predatory women who are only interested in men with a high financial status and the lifestyle to match.

If you state that a potential partner should earn at least a certain amount or have a "professional" career, the men viewing your profile will assume (correctly) that you don't want a man, you want his money! By specifying on your profile that you will only consider dating a man with a certain financial status, you will give many men the impression you're a gold-digger. The fact is, there are men who will lie on their profiles and claim to earn more than they actually do, to attract women; alternatively, others will downplay what they actually earn, to avoid meeting and becoming involved with predatory women. For genuine men who are financially secure, this strategy filters out predatory women who are just after a man for his money. Of course, a successful man can offer material stability and financial security in a relationship; these are not unreasonable aspirations – but it's a mistake to include preferred income, profession or financial status on a dating website profile. Money can provide material possessions and status, but it can't buy or guarantee happiness and love. During the dating process, information regarding career, salary and ambitions will be revealed over time. By insisting on meeting someone based purely on their financial or career status, you will be restricting your options and running the very real risk of missing out on meeting someone special. Don't make the mistake of having unrealistic criteria for meeting someone new, motivated by a materialistic mindset.

Online Dating Best Practice

A carefully considered, well-structured and informative personal profile will usually produce favorable responses online from potential partners with average or even high compatibility. Don't be disheartened if your profile doesn't generate a large number of responses at first: just continue to "tweak" it and adjust certain key elements, until you're happy with it. Also, remember, quantity doesn't equal quality; it's better to have four or five quality men contacting you during a month and showing an interest, than 40 or 50 guys, the majority of whom could be losers or even psychos. After meeting someone with potential, it can be very tempting to maintain a relationship status of "single," "available" or "active" on your dating profile, trying to keep your options open. Your Ego often receives a great boost when you have people still checking out your profile, showing an interest and leaving requests to meet up. Being distracted by other possibilities is not a good idea so, when you connect with someone promising online, give yourself time to explore the possibilities for a genuine relationship.

Dating websites can be great fun and present huge opportunities for meeting new men, but there are potential pitfalls, traps and dangers when you're looking for love online. It's not much fun when you end up being ripped off, involved with a stalker or much worse. If your expectations are too high and are not realistic, you are setting yourself up for frustration and disappointment. There are many success stories of people finding love via dating websites but, if you decide to start looking for love online, take good care and use your commonsense. Being proactive and becoming involved in social activities is still one of the best ways of meeting new people. There is no point in just sitting at home and hoping that Mr. Right is going to magically appear at your front door!

Rotation Dating

Rori Raye introduced the term "circular dating" in her book *Have the Relationship You Want*. I prefer the term rotation dating but it doesn't really matter what we call it, the point is this strategy is very effective for women who want to succeed in the dating game. Rotation dating means dating (not having sex with) at least three men at the same time; some women feel uncomfortable with this approach and make the mistake of dating a man exclusively after only a very short period of time while expecting him to do the same. This isn't a realistic strategy or mindset. The fact is men and women are different; men enjoy the challenge and the chase but the reality is a woman doesn't get caught unless she wants a man to catch her! Men often pursue more than one woman at a time and there is nothing wrong with women dating men on rotation. A single female in the dating game should put herself in a position where she can choose from a variety of options. With this system, invitations to go out on dates are accepted on a "whoever calls first" basis without giving any preference to a particular guy you may like or prioritizing dates with men who might offer to take you to the best dating locations or activities. Always accept the first offer and don't hang around waiting for a man you may be interested in to make dating plans. The rotation dating strategy allows a woman to keep her options open. One of the great advantages of this approach is it can prevent a woman from investing her time and emotional energy in a man until he has made his intentions clear. If there have only been a couple of dates he's probably dating other women so there is no point in putting all of your eggs in one basket.

Rotational Dating Keeps Men Interested

Rotational dating isn't always about seeing several men simultaneously; having men as friends to socialize with is a good idea and you may even gain some valuable insights into how some guys think! In between dates accept offers from friends or family to go out or do something as well (see Being Too Available). Keeping busy doesn't always mean having a date but you should always have a lively schedule. Never change your plans and do let men know you have a life and value your time. If he wants to spend time with you he has to give you notice and plan ahead. Men usually find a woman with an independent attitude intriguing and a challenge and will consider a woman who is not readily available as being more attractive and valuable. A woman who is in charge of her own happiness will always be considered favorably as a potential partner. Most men are conditioned to accept a woman will automatically change or rearrange plans to spend time with them and the woman who doesn't will certainly get a man's attention. Instead of focusing on one man feeling unsure about whether he is serious you keep your options open.

Rotation Dating Filters Out Time Wasters

In the dating game there will be men who occasionally appear and then disappear from your life. You might connect with someone on a dating website and exchange a few messages or emails and then he goes quiet for a couple of weeks. Perhaps you went on a few dates with a man and then he vanished without making any contact, then out of the blue he contacts you again to see how you're doing or what you've been up. What he is really doing is testing to see what your response will be. Don't assume he's just a busy man; it's quite possible he is rotation dating and seeing other women. If you decide to see him again after his brief disappearing act it's better not to have any expectations but to consider him as one of the men on your dating rotation cycle. Enjoy yourself but remember you're dating and not in a relationship; ask appropriate questions to find out more about him. If you like him but feel unsure about his intentions mirror his level of interest. It's possible he might begin to take you seriously as a potential partner but don't allow yourself to get caught up in any romantic fantasies.

Actions speak louder than words. Being always available at someone else's convenience is always a bad move. Rotation dating can be an effective filtering strategy – if you meet a guy you really like but he isn't that interested this method of dating can keep you busy and distracted so you don't waste too much time thinking about him. It also filters out men who are not suitable potential partners and can help to attract the ones who are worth your time. Most emotionally healthy men don't like to feel they're being rushed or pressured into a relationship. This is when they disappear. It's easier to disappear than to deal with unrealistic demands or expectations or to be held responsible for how a woman may feel.

Dating Websites And Rotation Dating

The rotational dating strategy can be used if you decide to use dating websites. You might connect with someone online and arrange to meet for a date. If the first date goes well there aren't any guarantees he will consider you to be serious relationship material or even want to see you again so it's best to keep your options open. If a man wants to see you again accept the invitation if you like him; continue to communicate with and meet other men instead of assuming a couple of enjoyable dates means you have met "The One." Some women de-activate their website dating account after a couple of good dates with one guy assuming, expecting or hoping for the dating process to lead to something more. A common mistake women make is to begin acting as if a relationship has already been agreed and established much too quickly.

Should You Be Honest About Your Rotation Dating?

It's quite reasonable for a man to wonder if you're dating other men. Dating doesn't involve any type of commitment so neither party has any obligation to explain their dating habits or strategies. Some women think they're being deceitful by "withholding" information but this is misguided; sensible people don't share personal information with someone they hardly know. Information is volunteered or offered on a need to know basis and a man doesn't need to know whether you're dating other guys. I suggest a "didn't ask, don't tell" policy – in other words don't volunteer the information but if a man asks if you're dating other men be honest.

If you are asked the question there are two possible responses:

- 'Yes. I date other guys. I haven't met anyone who wants to date exclusively."
- 'Yes. I date other guys. How do you feel about that?" Listen carefully to his response. If he reacts negatively, he is probably not emotionally mature enough for a relationship, in which case you can cut your losses and move on.

When the man you're dating hasn't suggested dating exclusively there isn't anything to feel guilty about. If he wants to date exclusively then have the conversation, consider if his intentions are genuine and decide if dating exclusively is really what you want to do. If the dating phase is going to progress to "exclusive status" there will be a conversation about this eventually. Unless you're asked the question directly it's usually better to leave the subject of dating strategies alone during the early stages.

However, you should be honest and upfront about your expectations at the appropriate time during the dating phase.

- If you want to take the dating process to the next level let him know.
- If you're dating with the intention of getting married let him know.
- If you don't want to ever get married, let him know.

Of course telling a man you're dating that you do see other men can work to your advantage and can motivate a guy to secure a relationship with you if he is genuinely interested in you and believes there is competition. Everyone is different so you will have to decide which approach feels comfortable for you.

Conclusion

Rotational Dating Can:

- Help you to consider your options.
- Help you to focus on the type of man you want.
- Help you to raise your self-esteem through receiving positive attention.
- Help you to clarify any personal issues that may be negatively impacting on your relationship prospects and choices.
- Help you to build your confidence.
- Help to filter out time wasters.
- Prevent wasting time trying to figure out if a guy is serious or not.

Many women make the mistake of dropping their rotational dating strategy after just a few successful dates with one man. The reality is the majority of men are not going to stop dating other women after dating one woman on a few occasions. Men in the dating game don't put all their eggs in one basket and neither should you! Investing all of your time and energy into a new man you're dating isn't a smart strategy. Keep dating other guys until you meet someone who meets your standards and requirements. Never invest into a man more than he is investing in you. *Rotational dating helps you to keep your options open and provides opportunities for dating until you meet someone with whom it is worth exploring the possibilities of a worthwhile relationship.*

Speed Dating

The first speed dating event reportedly took place in the US during late 1998 at Peet's Café in Beverley Hills. By the year 2000 it had become very popular. Speed dating is now also popular in the UK, Canada and many other countries. Supporters claim speed dating saves time as most people quickly decide if they're interested or romantically compatible. To determine whether speed dating is a viable option for meeting a potential partner, it's important to understand the basics of this method of dating.

How Speed Dating Works

Men and women are rotated to meet potential partners over a series of brief "dates" which last between three and eight minutes. At the end of each interval a signal is given for the participants to move on to the next date. Personal details and contact information are not traded during speed dating to reduce any pressure to reject or accept a person. When the event has finished participants submit a list to the organizers of the people they would like see again along with their contact information, which is only given to both people if there is a match. Speed dating events often require attendees to register in advance but some organizers will accept a few walk-ins if they want a good balance of men and women. Some event planners use waiting lists to try and get an equal number of men and women while others try to create a fun or party atmosphere and just aim to have an approximate gender balance. Many events

161

specify a certain age range for those who wish to attend; certain organizers may use a slightly older range for men. Many event organizers offer niche speed dating with exclusive events for specific groups or demographics including ethnic groups, graduates, gays and lesbians, younger women looking for mature men, Cougars or for people who have a particular religious belief, such as speed dating for Christians.

Scientific Research

A research team at the University of Pennsylvania studied several speed dating events in 2005 and found the majority of people made their choices within the first three seconds of meeting. Personal preferences and habits such as previous marriages, religion or smoking habits were of less significance than expected. A study in Edinburgh, Scotland, in 2006 found that 22 percent of the men and 45 percent of the women at a speed dating event decided within the first 30 seconds whether someone was a good match or not. The study also discovered that when couples discussed movies there were fewer successful matches, while talking about travel resulted in a higher percentage of positive matches. Another study in 2011 at the University of Edinburgh, conducted by psychologist Alison P. Lenton and University of Essex economist Marco Francesconi, analyzed over 3,700 dating decisions from 84 speed dating events. They found when participants varied in attributes such as age, height, occupation and educational background, there were fewer matches or dating requests. This was found to be the case particularly when attendees were presented with a high number of prospects. Where the characteristics of the daters varied significantly the majority of participants didn't actually follow up on any of their matches.

Selectivity, Age And Height Preference

According to a variety of studies on speed dating events, women are more selective than men. For example, one study reported that the average woman was chosen by 49 percent of the men and the average man was chosen by 34 percent of the women. Recent studies suggest participants base their selections on which gender remains seated and which is rotating. A new study indicated that when men were seated and the women rotated, the men were usually more selective. The University of Essex conducted a study in 2006 which found the most important determining factor for a man regarding a woman was her age. Age was less of a determining issue for women but was still a highly significant factor. This study also found that a man's height was very important to the average woman; for every inch in height a man lacked, this reduced his desirability at the rate of 5 percent per inch!

Advantages Of Speed Dating

Speed dating does have several obvious advantages when compared to meeting someone at a nightclub, party or bar including:

- Events are designed for singles.
- Events are usually a safe way to meet someone for the first time and held in public places by the organizers.
- Venues are selected and organized so it's quiet enough for people to communicate easily.

- People who attend usually feel more comfortable.
- The majority of those who attend an event are there with the intent to meet someone new.
- Often those attending have been previously grouped into compatible age ranges or personal preferences.
- Structured interaction removes the need to introduce yourself.
- It's time-efficient.
- The potential for rejection is minimal; and if one of your choices isn't interested there hasn't been a great deal invested in terms of your time, effort or emotions.
- Women are able to attend in groups, which they prefer.

The majority of speed dating events match participants at random so it's quite possible to meet different types of men. The restricted time limit makes sure a participant isn't stuck with someone who clearly isn't their type for too long and prevents participants from monopolizing a particular person's time. If you don't really like the person, you can avoid feeling obligated to spend time on a date where you feel uncomfortable or trying to find an excuse to leave. The duration of the "date" is very short so this potential problem is easily avoided. With speed dating people tend not to feel pressured to select or reject someone; the actual matching happens after the event and participants must wait a day or two for feedback and their results. You don't have to contact a particular participant again unless you want to, although you must remember this works both ways: you may meet someone you like who may not be that keen on you!

Disadvantages Of Speed Dating

- A few minutes in someone's company is definitely not enough time to make a reasonable assessment or get to know someone.
- It can be difficult to get all of your best qualities across to the other person in the short time you have and first impressions can often be permanent.
- While some people are naturally confident others can be anxious taking longer than the allotted time to warm up to their prospect.
- Attraction at a speed dating session is often based on physical characteristics. Research indicates there is usually more emphasis on physical appearance rather than positive personality traits such as kindness, integrity or high self-esteem.
- You could overlook or reject someone with great compatibility who initially may not seem like potential partner material.
- When you participate in a speed dating event, you have absolutely no control over who you're selected to meet so it's possible you won't find anyone interesting. These type of events generally last for two hours or more so you could feel attending was a waste of your time.
- Random matching removes a variety of body language flirting cues like eye contact which are used in other scenarios to show interest or attract a potential partner before talking to them.

Strategies For Attending Speed Dating Events

The most important point to remember when attending a speed dating event is to have a plan of action.

- Plan the type of questions you intend to ask potential matches before attending any type of speed dating event. Avoid talking about yourself too much. Be polite and show interest in the other person even if they're not your type. Three to eight minutes isn't a long time to be courteous and pay attention to whatever he (or she) has to say.

- Speed dating is all about first impressions so if you attend an event make an effort to look presentable.

- Make sure you complete the speed dating score card as the event progresses or you might lose track of someone you really want to meet again.

- Arrive early or on time for the event. This will give you time to observe the venue and, more importantly, the participants, and perhaps begin marking potential partners before the rotations begin.

- Be yourself!

- Speed dating moves quickly so a little flirting can help. If you like someone let them know without being excessive.

- Be careful how much you drink! Having a glass of wine to calm any nerves is acceptable but do not consume too much alcohol at these types of events. Getting tipsy or drunk is not going to leave a very good first impression.

- Speed dating is meant to be a fun. Don't put pressure on yourself to find the love of your life.

- Keep yourself safe by letting a friend or family member know where you're going. Don't give out your home address and be careful on your way home.

You could also consider Online Speed Dating where users meet online for audio, video or text messaging. A major advantage is users can go on "dates" while sitting at home or by using an internet enabled mobile phone.

Of course the big disadvantage with this is people don't actually meet each other during the speed "date" but they can still get an idea or a feel for the other person. Speed dating can be a fun way to meet several potential partners in one evening. It's safe, relatively inexpensive and convenient. There are several advantages that make speed dating a viable option for meeting potential partners or just making new friends.

The Way Forward

"You can learn new things at any time in your life if you're willing to be a beginner. If you actually learn to like being a beginner, the whole world opens up to you." – Barbara Sher, Author

Make sure you take sensible precautions but don't be afraid of trying different strategies to connect with a potential partner. If you would like to meet someone new be proactive instead of waiting for Mr. Right to magically appear in your life!

CHAPTER 17:

Dating

"You know, the man of my dreams might walk round the corner tomorrow. I'm older and wiser and I think I'd make a great girlfriend. I live in the realm of romantic possibility." – Stevie Nicks, American Singer/Songwriter

A survey was published during August 2011, commissioned for the launch of Elizabeth Noble's novel, *The Way We Were,* about childhood sweethearts who reappeared in each other's lives many years later. They surveyed 3,000 men and women in equal numbers aged between the ages of 16 to 86 with some surprising results! The survey found that more than 50 percent of men were strongly attracted to a potential partner after the first meeting, one fifth of men claimed to fall in love at first sight and almost three-quarters had fallen in love within having three dates. The findings seem to contradict the popular belief that only women fall in love quickly. Certain experts have claimed the results probably revealed the differences in perspectives between the sexes of what falling in love means to them while highlighting the different criteria men and women generally use to choose a partner. Of those surveyed men and women both agreed their very first and true love was the longest and hardest relationship to get over. A quarter of those surveyed said they felt they would never fully recover from the heartbreak of losing their first love.

Professor Alexander Gordon, a chartered psychologist and member of the British Psychological Society, said the findings were interesting and the gender differences regarding how men and women pursued love appeared to be very different.

The findings included:

- Men tended to tick more superficial boxes, for example appearances, which strongly influenced them in deciding whether they were "in love".
- Women were likely to weigh up the pros and cons of becoming involved before making a decision to proceed and take matters further.
- Women appear to take much longer before deciding to give their hearts away and become emotionally involved.
- One in ten women said they had experienced love at first sight and the majority of women surveyed said they waited until at least the sixth date before deciding if the relationship was worth pursuing.

"Women are better at reading social situations and are more likely to ask more questions of themselves after meeting someone, like is he going to make me feel secure and will he be a good father to my children. They are cannier than men at making a lifetime choice."
– Professor Alexander Gordon, a chartered psychologist and member of the British Psychological Society

Dating Signals Quiz

Actions speak louder than words! It's important to understand your body language so you know what kind of signals you are sending out in the dating game.

Try the following quiz to discover what type of signals your body language is sending out.

1. You decide to try online dating and see someone's profile that looks interesting and attractive. What kind of message would you send?
   A. Ask to meet up because you would love to know what their skin smells like.
   B. Ask about their interesting travel experiences mentioned in their profile.
   C. Send a detailed introduction about yourself.
   D. Hope they make contact with you.

2. How often do you make eye contact with strangers?
   A. As often as possible.
   B. Fairly regularly.
   C. All the time!
   D. As little as possible.

3. How would you respond to an attractive stranger staring at you during a social event?
   A. Hold their gaze.
   B. Smile and then look away.
   C. Go over and start a conversation.
   D. Avoid eye contact.

4. How would you find someone to talk to at a party where you hardly knew anyone?
   A. Look for someone attractive and make eye contact.
   B. Stay in the kitchen as this is often the best place to start random conversations.
   C. Circulate trying to find someone who looks friendly.
   D. Hope someone will approach you.

5. It's your first date with someone new and you think they are really hot! What are your hands doing?
   A. Touching their thigh.
   B. Touching their arm sometimes when they say something funny.
   C. Touching your face or stroking your head.
   D. Making full contact for example sitting really close or on their lap.

6. During the conversation you lean towards them. Why are you moving closer?

   A. Because you find your date sexually alluring.

   B. Subconscious reaction because you feel there is a connection.

   C. Conscious decision to move closer as this makes the conversation feel more intimate and you know this strategy works.

   D. No choice because the venue is crowded.

7. The first date has been good. What type of personal information do you share with this person?

   A. What you find most physically attractive about them.

   B. You give them your personal phone number.

   C. You tell them how many children you hope to have and your favorite names for babies.

   D. You keep it basic and just give them your name.

8. The first date is over and it was full of conversation and even flirty. You decide you would like to see them again. As you part company, do you:

   A. Invite them back for a coffee at your place.

   B. Give them a quick kiss and your mobile number, and then go home alone feel pleased with yourself.

   C. Complain about how a previous date gave you a wrong number or other unhappy stories about your dating mistakes.

   D. Thank them for their time and go home.

9. It's the day after your date and it's lunchtime but you haven't received a phone or text. Do you:

   A. Call and offer them a booty call.

   B. Text to say how much you enjoyed the date.

   C. Ring and tell them about your horrible journey to work and to ask if they have any plans that evening.

   D. Do nothing and wait for them to call you.

10. Two months after that first date you are still seeing each other. You are out together one evening and an attractive stranger smiles flirtatiously at you? Do you:

   A. Flirt back and when your date is not looking pass the stranger your phone number.

   B. Acknowledge their smile by smiling back and then kiss your date to show you are already involved.

   C. Make it clear you are with your date but glance over occasionally because you feel flattered.

   D. Ignore them.

Check Your Score!

Mostly A's: You Send Out X-rated Signals

Showing someone that you are interested and find them attractive is a good strategy but your strong sexual vibe and approach could scare someone away or worse, if you're a woman, give the impression that you are willing to be sexually intimate too soon in the dating process. You should think about how your behavior could be sending out the wrong signals and try to curb your tendency to touch or stroke a potential partner during the early phases of seeing someone new.

Mostly B's: You Send Out The Right Signals

Your body language conveys positive self-esteem, high self-confidence, approachability and the correct level of interest. While you are not afraid to let someone know you find them attractive your approach does not come across as being needy or excessively sexual. This combination is very effective and not easy to learn so if this approach comes naturally to you this puts you ahead in the search to find someone special.

Mostly C's: You Send Out Needy or Desperate Signals

When someone is seen as needy or even desperate this is a massive turn off for the majority of people. Being friendly is a good thing and as they say it is "nice to be nice" but someone who is clearly needy will eventually become irritating and eventually annoying. You will either be considered desperate, high maintenance or a potential stalker. Trying to be liked by everyone you meet is a recipe for a dating disaster. Striking the right balance between being too available and being somewhat elusive can be difficult to execute. It is certainly not about using mind games but keeping a potential partner engaged and interested during the dating phase; there is nothing wrong with keeping someone new intrigued.

Mostly D's: You Send Out "Stay Away" Signals

While being too friendly can be a mistake, so is appearing cold, aloof or uninterested when you are interacting with others. If you are serious about finding love you're not doing yourself any favors in the dating game. You could be very shy, suffering from low self-esteem or subconsciously projecting a certain type of persona to discourage potential partners from approaching you. Some mystery and intrigue when you are dating someone new is advisable but coming across as being emotionally unavailable or generally unsociable will destroy any realistic prospects of finding a great relationship.

Rejection Anxieties And The Attachment Factor

"Most fears of rejection rest on the desire for approval from other people. Don't base your self-esteem on their opinions." – Harvey Mackay, American Author & Businessman

When a person has a poor self-image they may constantly worry about what others may think of them and the fear of rejection can cause a great deal of anxiety. Being overly dependent on others for your feelings of happiness and contentment means you are actively undermining your confidence, which automatically increases any fears of rejection. Self-esteem eventually becomes extremely fragile when a sense of self-worth depends on the opinions of others. Constantly thinking about how unhappy you are without a partner or believing you're not good enough to attract the right kind of partner will often create a self-fulfilling prophecy. The fear of rejection keeps some people trapped inside feelings of loneliness and desperation and while this can affect many of us to varying degrees, some suffer intense fears of rejection for long periods in their lives. Being scared of rejection is quite natural and conquering this fear can help you to positively expand many areas your life. Learning to manage these kinds of fears can help you to increase your relationship options in a variety of ways.

The most effective strategy for controlling fears of rejection is not to become overly attached too early in the dating process. The greater the emotional attachment factor, the more anxiety you're likely to feel about the possibility of losing that person. Resist fantasizing about the relationship and projecting too far into the future, and avoid having sex too quickly. There are different levels of intimacy and the amount of time spent together sharing communication, intimacy, commitment, mutual assistance and a variety of other factors influences the level a relationship operates on. When you meet someone new there shouldn't be a great deal of emotional attachment. For example, you might think he is attractive, or has a great sense of humor but there won't be any deep feelings of attachment. It may seem obvious to say rejection shouldn't be an issue when you're dating and hardly know him but it is for many women. The fact that you may spend some time dating a man where there is a lack of chemistry doesn't mean you've wasted your time; it does mean that particular dating process achieved its maximum level of connection and it wasn't viable to continue.

The best ways to control any fears of rejection is to avoid:

- Having unrealistic expectations
- Becoming overly attached to someone too quickly

The more you want to be wanted the more the feelings of anxiety will increase and the greater the fear of rejection will be. If you believe there is only one "special" person on Earth who can make you happy this will create anxiety if he decides he doesn't want you. When you believe there are a variety of men in the world who you're compatible with this automatically decreases any feelings of anxiety and removes the fear of being rejected by someone you may consider to be your only option. Believing there is only one special person who is just "right" for you is to seriously restrict your options.

Many men and women believe certain gender stereotypes, for example:

- The general stereotypes men have about women includes they want a man who is extremely handsome and charming with a great career and lots of money.
- The general stereotypes women have about men is they want a partner who looks like a super model but can keep home and bake and cook like a top chef.

Think about any stereotypes you have that may prevent you from approaching others or from being yourself and then make a list. Consider ways you may try to make a good impression based on the stereotypes about men you believe. For example, you may try to be funny or humorous all the time when you're on a date believing this is what most men are looking for but that's not really you. Trying to make a "good" impression while failing to be who you really are is always a big mistake; you're also misleading the person and underestimating what he may think of you.

There are three main reasons you could be rejected as a suitable partner:

- Lack of chemistry
- Lack of physical attraction
- Lack of compatibility

You're less likely to be rejected by a potential partner who shares similar values and beliefs. Before going on a date remind yourself of your own:

- Personal values, such as honesty and integrity
- Personal philosophy on life
- Family values
- Religious or spiritual beliefs
- Material values
- Education values

After a date that you think has gone well there is nothing to stop you sending a text or email saying you had a great time and would like to meet up again. Of course, you could be rejected because a potential partner doesn't think you're his type, but it's also true that he might not be your type either! If he doesn't seem interested in pursuing a relationship after a few dates or makes this clear, ask for feedback. Find out why he doesn't find you attractive or doesn't want to get to know more about you.

The golden rule about rejection is not to take it personally; a thumbs down in the dating game can knock your confidence but it can also save you a great deal of time!

Making The First Move

"Life shrinks or expands in proportion to one's courage." – Anaïs Nin (1903-1977), French Author

In *"The Rules"* by Ellen Fein and Sherrie Schneider, one of the primary rules they advocate is a woman should not approach a man first. I think this advice is flawed. Whether a man approaches a woman or not is not the issue: ***how*** the approach is made and ***what*** happens soon afterwards is what makes the difference. I have spoken to women who are struggling to make a man fully commit and with husbands who are ambivalent about their marriage. It's often the case many of these women approached their partner first but the woman making the first move hasn't caused the problem; often she had sex with her partner too quickly so he now lacks respect for her. There can often be a fine balance between maintaining healthy boundaries and appearing unapproachable, aloof or even arrogant. When you meet someone who may have potential, be polite, pay attention but don't rush into anything and certainly don't believe everything you're told! Looking approachable and friendly can encourage a man to approach you but let's be realistic; how is a man supposed to know if a woman is interested? Men can have very fragile Egos and no one likes rejection.

This is the 21st century and generally there are more single women than men. If a woman is going to hang around waiting for a man to make the first move, she could be waiting for a very long time. Women can start a conversation and even flirt with a guy within certain sensible limits. This doesn't mean a man is going to automatically assume the woman is easy or just after sex; however, a woman who approaches a man and then has sex with him soon afterwards is unlikely to be considered a serious candidate for a proper relationship. A woman can start a conversation with a man or even suggest going on a date without compromising her dignity or self-respect. Whether a woman makes the first move or not is not the big issue; it's the way she conducts herself afterwards. Everyone is intrigued by this mystery in the dating game; just because a woman makes the first move doesn't mean she has to be too eager or readily available during the early stages of the dating process. Approaching, meeting and talking to people or showing a subtle interest means taking risks, but if you focus solely on their evaluation or approval of you, you're going to feel anxious and helpless.

When you show a man you're interested consider it to be a gift, invitation or a compliment. For example, at the end of a date which you've enjoyed say, "I really enjoyed talking and spending time with you and would really like it if we could do it again." If he rejects the gift, accept that it's his right and certainly not the end of the world. You know the gift was given without conditions and any rejection cannot damage your sense of self-esteem. In fact it is a gift on two levels; you have given the other person a compliment because you found them attractive enough to give the invitation and you offered them the gift of your time. Even if the gift or invitation of your time is rejected you can still feel good about offering the compliment of finding that person interesting enough or attractive enough to spend some time with. This is a very effective and efficient way to give an invitation. If the other person doesn't feel the same way it's not a big deal – in fact it saves you time and increases the chances of meeting someone who is a better match.

Dating Negotiations

"In life you don't get what you deserve, you get what you Negotiate." – Krishna Sagar, Author

There can be some confusion about what the word "dating" actually means and the definition of what it involves can vary according to a couple's culture or country. Some people will say they're dating when conducting a relationship but have not made a commitment to get engaged or married. In the UK men and women often say they're "seeing someone" or "going out together" which can mean they're just getting to know the other person or actually in a relationship. I define dating as spending time getting to know someone without any sex involved or until there is a mutual decision or agreement to engage in an exclusive relationship. It's quite acceptable to date more than one man at a time using this definition if you're comfortable adopting this approach, which allows you to explore your options.

Research indicates that men initiate dating negotiations about four times as often as women, while 20 percent of women never negotiate. More men than women claim they are happier in their relationships and it's possible that the application of effective negotiation techniques are responsible. Although many women like men to anticipate their needs we are not mind readers! There is an art to negotiating in the dating game and if you're scared to ask for what you want, a man isn't going to know your standards and expectations.

Set Your Boundaries

Before you get involved in the dating game you need to be very clear about the following:

- What are your priorities?
- What is important to you?
- What are you prepared to compromise on?

The easiest way to sabotage yourself in a dating negotiation is to not be clear about your boundaries. Knowing clearly what you are prepared to compromise on and what may be unacceptable is absolutely essential before any dating negotiation. Like a good lawyer structuring a defense, you need to frame your argument first. Begin with the end in mind so that you are clear on what your goals are and you won't be enticed into an agreement that may cause bitter regret once you're involved.

What do you want?

- Romance
- Fun
- Security
- Wealth and power
- Privacy and commitment

We are all different, with different needs so it makes sense to negotiate for what you want, but your **first priority** should always be to be yourself. You can negotiate your personal interests or pastimes to a degree but not your core values such as personal standards, requirements, integrity or spiritual beliefs. For example, agreeing to give up your religious or spiritual beliefs should be non-negotiable. Before embarking on the dating game make sure you have a strong sense of self and don't be scared to express what you're looking for in a partner.

Going Dutch Dating

Men and women have different views about going Dutch on a date. It's not as straight forward as you might think and depends on a variety of factors, including what country you live in. The tradition in many Western societies is for a man to pay for a date in full to show he has a romantic interest while hoping or expecting something to develop. In the United States it's widely accepted the man pays the bill; while in most of Europe and Australia the practice of splitting the bill is often practiced. In Germany, Canada and Australia sharing the cost of a date is normal practice where both people have a similar financial status. The tradition of men always paying for a dinner date is considered old fashioned and dating couples generally take turns paying a bill or divide it. Young women in many urban areas tend to decline a man's offer to pay or will often insist on paying for the following date. Some women object or can even be offended by a man offering to pay for the date so men often have to make a judgment call on a date by date basis. While what is expected can vary according to the country and culture, dating is still viewed by many as being steeped in the tradition of a man pursuing and wooing a woman.

Who Asked Who For A Date?

It is widely accepted that the person who asked should at least offer to pay the total bill. Asking someone on a date means you are assuming the role of host (or hostess) just as if you had invited a potential partner to your home for a meal; you wouldn't ask for half of the cost for the ingredients!

What Type Of Date Is It?

There is a big difference between two friends hanging out and going on an official date. Men and women can make a variety of assumptions when it can be a lot easier to ask and clarify before meeting up. Before going on a first date the general rule is for a woman to decide to allow the man pay. It may seem old fashioned but there are still men who believe in paying for a date and insisting on going Dutch can send the message you're not interested in him romantically and just want to be friends. The status of the activity should be understood by both parties to avoid awkward moments when it's time to pay. Whether to go Dutch or not can depend on the type of date it will be with the factors of location, time and probably cost taken into consideration. On a casual date a woman can offer to split the bill or take turns buying the drinks. When a man asks a woman out for a standard dinner date she can offer to go Dutch but it's courteous to allow the man to pay without making a fuss. If he has pushed the boat out with a high end romantic dinner followed by a night club or late drinks a woman can sincerely offer to go Dutch. If he insists on paying the bill in full gracefully accept with the intention of covering the costs of the next date – it's not worth the hassle of making a big deal out of who is paying.

Whatever your views on going Dutch, you should know after the first date if you're interested in seeing him again for date number two. Agreeing or even insisting on going Dutch can depend on your levels of integrity and if you want to see him again. If you decide a second date isn't viable it's fair to politely offer to pay your half of the bill; this can be a subtle way of letting him know you're not interested in seeing him again, at least not romantically. When a woman pays her own way it can convey the message to back off without being direct or rude. If a woman decides to go Dutch on the first date because she isn't interested in seeing him again romantically this puts her in a good position to refuse any further meetings with a clear conscience.

Repeat Dates

When there are a series of dates and a relationship seems to be developing a good general rule is a woman should offer to pay by the third date. With many women now being as financially independent as men, certain guys naturally expect a degree of equality in the dating game. While they're happy to pay for the early dates these men often appreciate a woman offering to treat them as well! A woman can assert her independence while allowing a man to show his interest and good manners but it can be a delicate balancing act at times. These situations have the potential to result in awkward or even embarrassing conversations, but if you don't feel comfortable discussing sharing the costs of dating this will not bode well for any future relationship as conversations about finances will eventually come up.

Reality Check!

"If you kiss on the first date and it's not right, then there will be no second date. Sometimes it's better to hold out and not kiss for a long time. I am a strong believer in kissing being very intimate, and the minute you kiss, the floodgates open for everything else." – Jennifer Lopez, American Actress, Author & Singer

Most men want to show a woman a good time and make her feel special but there are some men who will spend generously on a date but will be looking for a return on their "investment" relatively quickly. If you identify this type it can be tempting to let him wine and dine you knowing what he's after but this strategy can backfire badly. Maintaining your integrity will help you avoid any bad feelings or drama; if you're not interested walk away regardless of how much money a man is prepared to pay for a date. Some women are hardcore traditionalists when it comes to dating and will always insist a man foots the bill for the first date and every date thereafter. These women want to know a man will spend money on them and any subsequent relationship and are often perceived as materialistic gold diggers. Gender roles have become very flexible in the 21st century and can be adapted for various situations providing both parties discuss their expectations and share a mutual understanding.

Ultimately, it's your choice whether you choose to go Dutch or allow the man to foot the bill for the first date. Many women still believe a guy should always bear the cost of a date, especially the first one and for them this is prudent requirement in the dating game. Allowing the average man into your life without expecting him to make any effort means you're setting your standards too low and he will probably take you for granted if you become involved. If you're asked out to dinner on a first date and he suggests going Dutch that really should be the last date. Many relationship experts agree men should pay for the initial dates if only to give him the opportunity to show off his gallantry and good manners, which are qualities most women appreciate!

Understanding And Exploring Chemistry

"Let me tell you, you either have chemistry or you don't, and you better have it, or it's like kissing some relative. What I'm saying is, chemistry is a place to start, not an end point." – Deb Caletti, *The Secret Life of Prince Charming*

When you meet someone new there may be an initial attraction or "spark" that encourages you to explore the possibilities and find out if there is genuine chemistry. The only way to discover whether there is genuine chemistry is to be yourself – a potential partner can't really get to know the real you if you're pretending to be someone else! It is virtually impossible to discover if you share genuine chemistry with someone by being false or withholding parts of your personality because you're worried your date might not like you. Trying to rush chemistry or trying to fake it is also a big mistake regardless of how attractive a potential partner may be. A few dates with a new man probably isn't going to provide enough information to decide if there is the potential to share any genuine chemistry. Sharing your opinions and thoughts on issues that are important to you over a period of time will usually reveal if there is a greater potential for chemistry and compatibility. Developing a good rapport is essential for exploring if any genuine chemistry exists.

Definitions of "Chemistry" include:

- A romantic or sexual spark between two people
- An unconscious decision influenced by a complex blend of factors or criteria
- A combination of love, lust or infatuation
- A desire to be involved intimately with someone

Genuine chemistry can be difficult to define, especially if you have never shared that special feeling with someone else before. It can be recognized almost immediately or intuitively but two people can often decide if they share negative or positive chemistry relatively quickly. Many people define chemistry as a strong feeling of connection that feels good and as though they're just meant to be with their partner. There is often a comfortable feeling of being very at ease with each other along with a powerful sexual, physical, mental and emotional attraction. This will be built on a foundation of two people sharing similar values, beliefs, goals or even habits!

Types Of Chemistry

There are various types of relationship chemistry including:

- Emotional chemistry
- Romantic chemistry
- Sexual chemistry

There are lots of different opinions regarding relationship chemistry. Some believe it is possible to create chemistry artificially but that it is better when it is spontaneous while others believe it either exists between two people or it doesn't. Alternative views claim chemistry is a process that builds, eventually creating a type of chemical bonding instead of just happening instantly. Mutually shared chemistry during the dating game is generally considered to be the catalyst for pursuing a relationship with someone. It is often the deciding factor between whether a relationship becomes romantic or remains platonic.

Topics and conversations about general issues can reveal if you both share mutual interests that may provide opportunities for bonding. When you're exploring potential chemistry, serious topics can be discussed but should be kept to a minimum. Avoid heavy topics during the early dating stage as this helps a potential partner to associate being with you as having a good time. When a couple share a similar sense of humor this is usually a good indicator of good chemistry; laughter and humor make most people feel at ease so cracking a few jokes can remove any tension during a date providing your humor is not considered offensive! Several research studies have indicated that people who meet in exciting or even dangerous situations often find each other more attractive. Although it could be considered as a type of manipulation, some experts recommend that men take women on dates that will get their adrenaline flowing such as theme park roller coaster rides or going to watch a horror movie. There is a very practical reason for this advice: the subconscious mind associates the excitement, danger and rush of adrenaline with the person you share the experience with. This adrenaline rush feels good but can be mistaken for feelings of physical attraction so if you go on a date which involves some kind of exciting activity and suddenly find the man attractive, it's probably your increased adrenaline levels causing the effect!

Various studies have concluded that the majority of successful and satisfying partnerships and marriages are often the result of couples being good friends before they decided to become involved romantically, so if you are looking for a serious lasting relationship, becoming friends first greatly improves your chances of a lasting union. This is not really a big surprise because couples who were friends before they became romantically involved have already established a stable foundation to build their relationship on. Two people can know each other as friends for several months or years and then actually realize they have loved each other all along but failed to recognize the potential for a successful relationship.

What actually creates chemistry and makes it work often varies enormously when comparing different couples but a shared sense of humor, a good rapport and dates that have an element of excitement can be a positive beginning to help you to discover or increase chemistry, providing the initial spark is there.

Sexual Chemistry

Two very important considerations for many women who are dating are:

- *When* to have sex for the first time
- *If* the timing is appropriate

When you're dating a new man and feel a strong sexual attraction you might indulge in many fantasies as your imagination wanders but the only way to discover if you're a "good match" sexually is by having sex with him! It always makes sense to "try before you buy" to discover if you're both sexually compatible, but don't make the common mistake of being so overwhelmed by physical attraction or sexual chemistry that you abandon commonsense. Women should exercise their freedom to explore their sexuality while understanding the average guy is less likely to take a woman seriously if he believes she has had sex with him too quickly.

Powerful feelings of mutual chemistry and attraction lay the foundation for many successful relationships but it can also influence men and women to act impulsively resulting in poor decisions. Blindly pursuing romantic or sexual chemistry can influence people to ignore obvious warning signs or entice them into embarking on unsuitable relationships with partners who lack overall compatibility. Becoming involved solely on the basis of sexual or physical attraction and resonance (the resonance creates the chemistry) you might have great fun for a while but it's unlikely to result in a fulfilling relationship. Experiencing powerful sexual chemistry doesn't mean you have finally met your "soul mate" and will be going off into the sunset to live happily ever after. When you *do* feel physical attraction and sexual chemistry, it's also important to consider other important areas of key compatibility and adopt a holistic approach regarding really getting to know another human being. Successful relationships are built on the solid foundations of mental, emotional and physical compatibility along with strong sexual chemistry.

Attraction and sexual chemistry can grow over time but a seed or spark often has to be present at the very beginning. It's quite possible to meet someone new and not to feel an instant attraction or fail to sense any kind of sexual chemistry. This doesn't mean you should immediately dismiss someone as a potential candidate for a relationship; over time he may "grow on you" and the attraction could increase during the dating process as more of his character and personality are gradually revealed. Rushing to judgment about someone because you do not feel an instant spark of sexual chemistry or physical attraction can lead you to overlook a partner with great potential! You could discover over a period of time that you resonate with a potential partner in the other important areas of compatibility, which in turn could make him more attractive sexually so take your time, and always follow your instincts. Sexual chemistry and attraction are two very important components of any relationship. If it isn't there at the beginning this doesn't mean it won't happen. However, if it fails to establish itself over a reasonable period of time then you need to seriously consider if the relationship is viable.

Discovering His Mindset

"I'm so an all-or-nothing person in dating, always. I'm big on not wasting time. And so, yeah, if something's not working, it's time to not hold people back." – Ginnifer Goodwin, American Actress

We have explored several topics so far and now it's time to look at the ways you can really begin to understand a potential partner's mindset and what his intentions are likely to be.

Perhaps you have been dating a guy for a while and believe he could be "The One" but feel unsure about how to proceed. Asking him the right questions can help you decide. Ask questions to help you discover important information about his history, personal circumstances, character flaws, habits and any potential problems that may not be unacceptable to you. It just isn't sensible to make hasty decisions when you're lacking such important information! Clearly there are men in the dating game who are very economical with the truth and who are just after sex but asking questions is always the first sensible step to seeking the information you need to determine your next move. If a man shows an interest and you're ready to explore the potential of having a relationship with him find out if he is single. While this may seem obvious many women make the big mistake of making assumptions instead of asking pertinent questions. For example, a man may claim to be single (which might be the truth), but your follow up question should be: "You say you're single but are you *sleeping* with anyone else?" Clarify whether he is having sex with or emotionally involved with another woman as soon as possible. He might not be honest but it's much better to ask rather than just jumping to conclusions.

Asking the Right Questions - Part 1: First Things

So asking the right questions can help you to discover how a potential partner thinks about the important areas of his life. Your questions should be designed to discover what type of man he is emotionally and professionally. These questions can be asked directly or indirectly but asking direct questions during the early stages of the dating process is usually not productive. This approach can make a man feel uncomfortable or could even scare him away.

If your approach is too direct it will often put a man on the defensive and make him clam up. Besides making him feel defensive, you will probably give him the impression you're stern, nosey, bossy or even desperate. It's usually much better to use the subtle but more effective ***indirect approach*** as this tends to make people less guarded in their responses. Indirect questions will usually be about his family, friends, background or work asked in a causal manner during a date. A good indirect question would be: "Where do you see yourself in your professional and personal life three years from now?" It's a general question, but his answers could provide valuable information regarding his mindset and help you to avoid unnecessary problems and heartache later on.

If you have asked all the right questions within the first three months you should know his:

- Personal and professional goals
- Financial background and goals
- Values, morals, principles and ethics
- Relationship history
- Why his previous relationship(s) failed
- What he has learnt from his previous relationships
- His attitude regarding relationships, love, communication and commitment
- Life experiences and important lessons he has learnt
- Quality of family relationships
- Family's background
- Religious or spiritual beliefs or practices
- Attitude regarding personal growth
- Activities around personal growth
- His attitude toward personal health, diet and maintaining fitness
- Any history of addiction

Men generally like to talk about who they are, what they have achieved or hope to accomplish so getting a man to talk about himself shouldn't be a problem. Once a rapport has been established by using indirect questions, gentle direct open ended questions (e.g. questions that begin with what, where, who, how, where and when) can be used to obtain further information. It's important not to ignore or dismiss any concerns you may have about his responses otherwise you could be setting yourself up for major difficulties later on.

Asking The Right Questions - Part 2: Relationship History

The relationship history of a person can often be a reliable indicator of their character. A man with a long list of failed relationships or numerous children for different women suggests an individual with serious commitment issues who is very unlikely to change. Asking questions regarding a potential partner's relationship history is vital. Be alert if you discover:

- His relationship history indicates he has left several relationships for reasons that do not appear realistic or reasonable; or,
- He insists on blaming all previous relationship failures on his previous partners (a big warning sign!).

If he is reluctant or refuses to take responsibility for *any* of his previous relationship failures this will usually indicate those relationships failed due to *his* behavior or issues. This should be considered as a very serious warning sign; a man (or woman) who doesn't take responsibility for at least some of their past mistakes is probably trying to reinvent their romantic history to make themselves look better or a prospective "good catch." He could also be trying to present himself as being the victim and this could be true, but if there appears to be a pattern of being victimized this could also be a clue regarding possible low self-esteem. Whatever way you look at it, if you are presented with a "perfect" relationship history by a potential partner this should immediately raise your suspicions. These types are unlikely to change and you should proceed with extreme caution.

Asking The Right Questions - Part 3: Life Goals

What are his short-term goals?

Short-term goals are goals usually considered to be planned within the next two to four years.

- Does he have a plan?
- Is he working on his plan?
- Where is he in the actual process?
- What is he doing **now** that will positively contribute to attaining his goals?

If he cannot answer these questions to your satisfaction he is probably wasting your time.

What are his medium-term goals?

Medium-term goals are usually those considered to be planned for the next five to 10 years. If he has no short-term goals then obviously there will be no plans to progress in the medium-term or next five to 10 years of his life. He is a very poor prospect for a serious relationship.

What are his long-term goals?

Long-term goals are usually plans for the next 10 years and beyond. Men like to impress women and will talk about what they are doing and plan to do next. A man who lacks long-term plans for himself clearly hasn't got any short or medium goals to pursue as stepping stones toward his ultimate ambitions. If his thinking is extremely short-term for himself he isn't going to have any long-term plans for the woman he's dating.

Once he describes his plans, think about whether they sound feasible and if you can see yourself supporting him and his goals. This approach can decide whether he is a suitable candidate for a serious relationship. Pay close attention to his views on committed relationships, marriage and raising a family; if his goals do not include seeking a partner for a stable relationship he is probably not thinking about you in that role either but this is a good thing because it lets you know where he's at! Discovering a man's mindset puts you in a much stronger position to make informed decisions. There isn't any point in dating a man who doesn't want what you're looking for or staying in a relationship that is way past its sell by date. Adopting a strategy of asking pertinent questions at the right time can help you to avoid some of the biggest relationship mistakes women make every day.

Act Like A Friend, Work Like A Spy

The dating game can be tough so if you're serious about finding a suitable partner you will need to exploit certain opportunities to obtain important information, which may include questioning his family and friends. The idea of acting like a friend while working like a spy may seem contrary to your principles or personal codes of conduct. *However, the truth is it may be necessary to act like a spy in certain situations to obtain valuable information that could save you a great deal of time, disappointment and heartache.*

It is also true that we naturally do this anyway when getting to know someone new, it's just that we are not always conscious of what we are doing. This is how it works: You decide to continue dating a particular guy and after a period of time he begins to introduce you to his friends and perhaps even some of his family members. These occasions present a variety of opportunities to conduct further research concerning his integrity and character.

When you are presented with such opportunities, always remain relaxed and friendly as it is the most effective approach for obtaining important information when you are interacting with others. You should feel free to ask questions about him – in fact, his friends and family will probably expect you to as a sign of your interest in getting to know the man you're dating. You might be on a serious mission to obtain information but you don't have to be pushy so avoid using questions that are too obvious or probing. You also want people to be comfortable with you. Ask indirect questions which tend not to raise suspicions of prying and remember to talk to people about what they find interesting, too. Be approachable and encourage people to talk about themselves as this approach builds a connection and those who consider you non-threatening and friendly may reveal useful information that you haven't even asked for. You should always appear to be engaging in friendly conversation and not on a spying mission, even if you are! Having a reputation for being too nosey or pushy will seriously undermine your information gathering efforts so be very careful.

Finally, be observant. How does he interact and talk to others? Does he appear to have a good relationship with his friends and family members? Listening to what they say to him as well as about him can reveal plenty, including whether certain things he has told you about himself, his work and past relationships were actually true, exaggerated or lies. It is always better to find out as much as possible about a potential partner *before* investing emotionally.

General Dating Guidelines

Be Yourself!

If you're spending time with people pretending to be something you're not, it's time to stop! Trying to impress others while negating who you truly are means you're setting yourself up to become extremely dependent upon the opinion of others. This in turn increases the fear of rejection. Pretending to be someone or something you're not is a waste of time and energy because eventually you will be exposed and rejected anyway. You might be scared others will not like you but by being yourself this efficiently filters out those who are not really compatible with you anyway. If you insist on pretending (lying) to be someone else no one gets the chance to discover the real you, and the bottom line is you can't please everybody: there will always be people who don't like you for whatever reason, so get over it!

Practice being assertive and expressing your true inner feelings and thoughts. When you present the real you at the beginning of any interaction or relationship, this will automatically attract or repel people at a much higher rate. Most people find honesty, high self-esteem and self-confidence appealing as opposed to fake attributes put on to impress others. Seek out people who can positively contribute to your overall happiness and support you in being the person you want to be. By being authentic you are more likely to have friends who value you; being yourself also increases the chances of meeting a man who is compatible.

Confidence

A research study at the University of Oregon had single women evaluate their conversations with single men. The men who didn't date often underestimated how much the women liked them, while the men who dated frequently overestimated how much they were liked. The men who overestimated how well they were liked were confident and would go and ask the women for a date, while the ones who underestimated themselves wouldn't. The mindsets of each group of men became a self-fulfilling prophecy and it often works the same way for women. If you have low self-esteem and self-confidence regarding how you are perceived by the opposite sex you're probably underestimating yourself. You're therefore likely to be restricting yourself socially due to your reluctance to approach other people. By focusing on external outcomes that are beyond your immediate control, you put your emotional health at risk as those inevitable feelings of being anxious and helpless creep into your consciousness. When you're feeling confident you are more likely to interact with more people, which in turn means more opportunities for meeting someone with real potential for a serious relationship.

It's not always a case of waiting to be approached or letting a man know you're interested – your female friends might know of a single man who could be the perfect match so let them know you're available for a new relationship! Approaching, meeting, and talking to people means taking a risk but if you focus solely on their evaluation or approval you're going to feel anxiety and helplessness. It's a fact of life you're going to meet men and women who are not going to like you and that's okay.

Be Alert

You could meet a potential partner anywhere at any time or day but you will probably miss the opportunity if you are constantly wired up to your smart phone Player or walking along in a world of your own. Practice engaging with those around you when you're out and about. This strategy could lead to a date and remember fortune favors the bold so be alert and sociable; make eye contact and start conversations.

Smile And Be Approachable

Smile and be friendly. A warm smile makes you much easier to approach and will make others feel much more comfortable in your company. You're far more likely to be seen and approached if you're wearing a warm, open expression instead of a frown. People who always look miserable or who are always frowning are a turn off.

Look Your Best

Always be groomed and well-dressed. Of course this is not always possible but you should make an effort even if you are only dressed casually. You never know when you might bump into someone interesting and if you feel positive and confident about how you look you will automatically become more attractive because confidence is a very desirable personality trait.

Look After Yourself

People with a positive attitude and lifestyle are far more attractive to others. Eating a balanced diet and making time for regular exercise will keep you in optimum health and, contrary to what the mass media keeps telling us, being healthy and attractive does not mean you have to look like a stick insect! Looking and being healthy, a positive outlook, the way you carry yourself and your general outlook will make you more desirable.

Be Independent

Do not become fixated on finding a partner. Being desperate is highly unattractive and people can sense when someone is desperate. When you are feeling lonely and desperate you are much more likely to make poor love choices and end up in unfulfilling relationships. Maintain your standards and look for the kind of relationship that you know you deserve instead of settling for second best or whoever happens to be available. You know you're in deep trouble when you sleep with someone just to avoid your own company! Independence is far more attractive than desperation so you're better off embracing being single instead of frantically throwing all your energies into finding love. People are drawn to others who make things happen for themselves so discover a new hobby, begin writing that book, start training for a marathon, learn to meditate, try learning a new language or start reading inspirational books – whatever takes your fancy. The more independent you are, the more skills, talents and hobbies you have, the more interesting and attractive men will generally find you!

Be Sociable

This is the bottom line: You're not going to meet or attract a suitable candidate for a relationship sat at home watching television under your duvet. You have to get out there into the big wide world and meet new people so accept every social invitation you receive. Make the most of each occasion by really putting yourself out there and mingling. Making new acquaintances and reconnecting with old friends will enable you to cast your social net as widely as possible and increase the chances of meeting "The One."

Keep The Faith

The dating game can feel very frustrating at times and you will probably encounter a few Players and timewasters before you meet a man worth exploring relationship options with. It may be frustrating at times but don't give up hope; your next date could turn out to be with the perfect man for you. The most effective way to meet the type of partner you're looking for is to maintain a positive, happy mindset. Work on becoming the type of person you're hoping to meet and you could be pleasantly surprised!

Be Sensible

Whenever you are meeting someone new make sure the venue or location is a place you are familiar with. Tell your friends or a family member where you going and take your mobile phone with you. Remember, the dating game isn't a race to find a partner! Take your time and explore different strategies to maximize your options.

Whatever strategies you may decide to pursue the bottom line is, if you want to meet someone new for a serious relationship, you have to put in the time. There are many successful, available women who would really like to be involved with a loving, fulfilling relationship but trap themselves into believing they just haven't got the time to get into the dating game. The reality is meeting someone special doesn't always "just happen" as often portrayed in the movies. If you're serious about meeting someone to share your life with you have to make the effort.

CHAPTER 18:

Major Dating Mistakes

"When you really don't like a guy, they're all over you, and as soon as you act like you like them, they're no longer interested." – Beyonce Knowles, American Singer

There is no doubt the dating game can be tough, especially if you are not prepared, so here is a comprehensive summary of the most common dating mistakes and how to avoid them!

First Date At Your Place

Keeping yourself safe is paramount, particularly in online dating. Do not under ANY circumstances agree to meet a man at your home on the first date. Always meet at a public venue and let someone know where you're going and what time you expect to be home. You can arrange to text or call a friend when you get home.

A sensible date can be meeting up for a coffee. There are several advantages to this strategy: it is unlikely there will be any alcohol available; you will be in public with other people nearby if there are any problems; and, if you're unhappy with how the date is going you can terminate it and make a quick, polite exit. You can also figure out his attitude towards money and dating. If he offers to pay the tab or asks to go Dutch that won't tell you a great deal about his personality but it will provide an indication of his "dating rules" and preferences, which can be useful to know if you decide to meet up again. If you have recently broken up from a relationship do not discuss your ex-partner, talk about anything negative or spend the time complaining about your bad relationship experiences.

You might feel comfortable after the first date and be happy to see him again but any further dates in the early stages should be at public venues. If you decide to get together in private it is always better to go over to his place than invite him over to yours. This approach has several advantages: you can confirm where he lives and just as importantly *how* he lives. People tend to relax in their own homes so you may discover aspects of his personality that you missed previously. If you decide he's not your type after spending some time alone with him it's a lot easier to make your excuses and leave than having him at your place and trying to get rid of him. In the event you just decide you've had enough of the date for the night it's better to have the option of leaving as opposed to asking him to leave. Always have several dates before inviting a man to your home. Wait until you feel relatively comfortable in his company and confident you can trust him.

Being Fantasy Driven

If you catch yourself fantasizing about a fairy tale wedding before the third date, you need to slow down! During the dating stages and the first three to six months of a relationship, the hormone Oxytocin is likely to be activated as a normal part of the bonding process along with a sense of wellbeing and euphoria. This hormone encourages the feeling of "falling in love" and can also interfere with the ability to think clearly. For this reason it is prudent to slow yourself down and to avoid creating romantic illusions about the man you're dating. Falling into this trap is to set yourself up with unrealistic expectations, which can lead to deep disappointment or even depression if the relationship fails.

A second major fantasy trap is where women become obsessed with not wanting to settle for what they consider to be "second best," which of course is their prerogative, but you have to be realistic. This is fuelled by the influence of the mainstream media which constantly bombards us with images of handsome men or beautiful women. These images feed into each person's narcissistic tendencies to a greater or lesser degree as we all like to feel attractive, especially when it concerns the opposite sex. However, being on a quest to find the "perfect" partner may cause you to overlook or undervalue a man who could be very compatible.

People often complain about the lack of available and decent potential partners but this is a myth. The reality is many of the images we see on TV, in celebrity magazines and in the movies are the exceptions, not the rule! Most of us are average with regular features so if you're only considering potential partners who are very physically attractive and look fantastic all the time you're living in a fantasy world.

"I want a man who's kind and understanding. Is that too much to ask of a millionaire."
– Zsa Zsa Gabor, Actress

If you **do** insist on looking for a partner who is very attractive physically you also have to be realistic about your own looks. Men and women who are attractive tend to know it so are more likely to attract or seek out a partner who is comparable in the looks department. Of course there are those who are very good looking but also conceited, arrogant and shallow with very low levels of personal integrity. If you're the type who insists on a great looking partner then make sure you're not fooling yourself about your own appearance! Put in the necessary work to enhance and maintain yourself physically, emotionally and mentally.

Becoming caught up in these three fantasy driven mindsets can cause you to ignore perfectly good candidates for a meaningful relationship. There is a balance to be struck between knowing your requirements and the type of man you're looking for and being sure your criteria is realistic. If you're in the dating game and meet someone new don't automatically make assumptions and dismiss him out of hand. Judging too quickly or having unrealistic expectations can result in missing out on someone who could be highly compatible for a lasting relationship. Spend some time considering the kind of attributes you would like in a man in addition to the 7 Essential Character Traits described earlier. Write down your requirements. Be honest with yourself ensuring your desires and expectations are reasonable.

Mind Games

People usually play mind games to manipulate a person or situation with the objective of gaining an advantage or obtaining something they wouldn't normally get by being honest.

Those who manipulate want to be in control but this doesn't mean that the motivation behind the manipulation always has to be negative. We all use manipulation strategies to varying degrees, for example withholding privileges from a teenager who fails to obey his or her parents' rules. When dealing with adults most of us do so with ethics, politeness and integrity, which involves a fair exchange, but ruthless manipulators lack integrity, sympathy or empathy. At some level men and women fear rejection and some will play mind games to protect their Egos. Manipulation may provide short-term advantages but most people usually figure out they're being played sooner or later. This form of manipulation ultimately doesn't lead to creating healthy relationships and damages others unnecessarily. Having the courage to be yourself while using your common sense will provide genuine relationship opportunities; playing games with the feelings of others is dishonest and demonstrates a serious lack of integrity. Appearing aloof and detached can make you feel safe but may give the impression you think you're better than others and turn prospective partners off. The most effective strategy in the dating game is just to be yourself and to use your common sense, although it can be difficult to strike the right balance between indicating an interest and maintaining your dignity and composure.

Always remember there are various types of Players and predators in the dating game and one of the very basic manipulation techniques they often use is telling a woman what she wants to hear. Pay attention to a man's approach, general behavior and comments; do not allow yourself to be taken in by slick but shallow presentation or expect a man to read your mind. Avoid playing any mind games and make sure you communicate and express yourself clearly.

The Job Interview Date

The number one complaint I hear from men who are dating is that they feel they're sitting in a job interview instead of being on a date. There are women who have a huge checklist of things they want to know immediately and quiz their date as though it's a job interview for an executive position in a large corporation – this is not sensible. A woman who bombards a man with numerous questions is unlikely to be dating that guy for any great length of time! It is natural to want to know as much as possible about someone you're dating including information about his past romantic relationships, his tastes, experiences, career, and hobbies. If you ask too many questions within a short period of time this can backfire and you will probably be seen as nosey, intrusive or too pushy. It is always sensible to ask pertinent questions early on in the dating process before you become too involved or attached but there should always be a balance; being patient and restrained is usually the best strategy. Trying to discover his entire life story during the first or second date is going to make a man very uncomfortable. Asking a man "How many children would you like?" on the first or second date is definitely a big mistake!

Dating someone new should be about relaxing and having fun while you obtain important information so don't be afraid to ask questions. Spend time getting to know him and ask general questions. Dating can be unpredictable but it's important to remember you can avoid many of the mistakes by asking the right questions and paying attention.

Questions on a first date or early during the dating phase can feel awkward but are vital for discovering the values, beliefs and mindset of a potential partner.

It's important to find out:

- If there are any areas of incompatibility that will be impossible to reconcile.
- If there is any chemistry or a connection.

Here is a selection of questions that can reveal important information. They will help you to avoid treating a date like you're interviewing him for a job while at the same time enabling you to find out what you need to know. It's much better to slip your questions in during the conversation.

Is He Dating Anyone Else?

One of the most important questions to ask a man. Rotation dating (dating more than one person at a time) is becoming increasingly popular so if you want to date exclusively the answer to this question can help you to decide if you want to continue dating him. If you're uncomfortable with his response you can decide not to see him again unless he is happy to date exclusively.

Type Of Day

What type of day have you had? This question can help to clarify if your date generally has a positive or negative attitude. In addition, if your date has experienced a rough day you can take this into consideration if his mood seems to be subdued or agitated.

Friends

What are your friends like? A good indirect question that can reveal a great deal about the type of friends your date hangs out with. Remember, the friends and family of potential partners are going to have an influence on his relationships.

Employment

Do you enjoy your work? Does he see his employment as vocational or as a job to pay the bills? If he is ambitious and keen to climb the ladder of success this can have implications for his relationships.

Health

Do you work out? How do you feel about personal fitness? What do you like to eat? Do you smoke or take drugs? It's important to gather this information especially if you have strong views on these topics.

Living Arrangements

Who do you live with? This is important! For example, if he is still living with an ex-partner or estranged wife this is something you need to know.

Religion/Spirituality

What do you believe in? It's important to find out if your date has any strong religious or spiritual beliefs so you can avoid any major disagreements later on.

Holidays/Vacations

What type of vacations do you like? Holidays can be a contentious topic especially if one person prefers a longer vacation while the other likes short breaks.

Pets

Do you like pets? Do you prefer cats or dogs? If you are not an animal lover and your date is that could be a major problem.

TV Shows He Enjoys

This will tell you about his preferences, if he tends to reflect on experiences and can clearly articulate his thoughts.

Free Time Activity

What do you do in your free time? This question can provide some insight into his interests and preferences. If he doesn't have any free time this could indicate a tendency to be too involved with work or other issues that are consuming his time.

Interests And Passions

What do you find interesting? Is there anything you're really passionate about? A person's interests can provide clues as to what kind of person they are.

Family

Do you get on with your family? This can help you to be aware of any family dramas or issues with his family or if there appears to be a great deal of family conflict.

These questions can help you to discover what type of man you are dating to determine whether he is worth seriously considering as a potential partner .

Trying To Impress

Trying to be something you're not or acting in ways you think will convince a date to pursue a relationship is a waste of time and doesn't allow you to reveal your true personality. Trying too hard to dazzle or to impress by pretending to be someone you're not is covert manipulation. Misrepresentations and using mind games can often backfire in spectacular fashion later on so don't set out to impress a man or dazzle him, just be yourself. The more you listen the more you will learn. Maintain conversation flow but don't dominate the discussion; let him talk about himself, which most men are quite happy to do! Constantly trying to impress your date will inevitably make you feel nervous and tense so relax and have a good time but do try to be observant.

Pretending To Be Dumb

There are women who hide their intelligence believing that men find a woman with a sharp intellect intimidating. Any man who fears an intelligent woman is not a suitable candidate for a serious relationship. Period. Well-adjusted men admire and respect intelligent women and a man considering starting a family will want the woman who has his children to be smart, not stupid!

Dressing Inappropriately

How we dress sends out a message and this is particularly true for single women in the dating game. A woman doesn't want to give the impression she is overtly sexual to a man she has just started to date. Always consider carefully the image you want to project whether you're going on a date or just socializing. Dressing in a sexually provocative way will usually get an instant response from most men but if you do then expect to be treated like a sex object. Meeting a potential partner who will take you seriously depends on a man respecting and admiring you from the very beginning.

Lack Of Common Courtesy

When you go on a date make sure you're punctual and arrive on time. Keeping someone waiting by being late shows a lack of courtesy, is rude and certainly not appealing. The only acceptable reason for being late is a genuine emergency. No one likes to feel ignored so give your date your full attention; do not take phone calls or accept or send texts during any date. The best thing to do with your mobile phone is to turn it off! You cannot afford to be distracted when you are on a date as the objective is to spend time getting to know someone new. Dates also present an ideal opportunity to observe and gather information that could be very important in helping to decide if you want to take things any further.

Lacking Femininity

It may sound very old fashioned but men don't like a woman who acts like a man and who comes across as being dominant, masculine or aggressive. There are women who believe this kind of attitude helps them to protect themselves. It can be a part of a defense mechanism engrained into their personalities but either way they are usually sabotaging themselves. The majority of men are attracted to women who have a feminine persona; the "I'm a strong woman and can manage on my own" attitude is a massive turnoff for men regardless of race or culture. In the dating game or an established relationship it's important for a woman to allow a man to retain his sense of masculinity and avoid threatening his pride. The woman who tries to subjugate the male Ego and its inherent drive to feel masculine and needed usually won't keep a partner for very long. Men involved with an excessively dominant woman are likely to cheat eventually. If they stay it's because it's convenient in some way.

Ungrateful And Unappreciative Attitude

Contrary to popular belief if a man likes you he will actually give some serious thought to planning a date and this may cause him stress or anxiety. It takes confidence to ask a woman on a date, and a certain amount of consideration to make sure the venue or activity is acceptable. Even if you didn't have an absolutely wonderful time with him saying "Thank you" acknowledges that his efforts have been appreciated. It shows you have a certain amount of class. Please note however, particularly during the early dating phase, showing your appreciation does not extend to having sex with him afterwards!

Excessive Alcohol

It can be very tempting to have a drink during a date to calm your nerves but don't make the mistake of over doing it. On the first date or even after several meetings, drinking too much to steady the nerves can lead to disaster! A date with someone who is drunk is not a charming, alluring or a pleasant experience. Whether you're meeting a man you have connected with online or elsewhere always avoid alcohol when you're dating someone new. It doesn't matter where the date is, always resist the temptation of having a drink to "relax." You need to pay attention and avoid dulling your senses. If you really need to have a drink, limit it to just one. If the dating develops into a relationship then the restricted alcohol rule can be gradually relaxed. Alcohol generally clouds sound judgment and makes human beings less inhibited; if you drink excessively you could put yourself at risk of being sexually assaulted.

Sharing Too Much Information Prematurely

In the dating game, sharing too much information too quickly can make a woman sound desperate and even neurotic. The mission is not to tell him everything about you and your current problems; the objective is to find out about what makes him tick. The more you talk, the less time you're spending observing and paying attention. Honesty is the best policy but this doesn't mean telling someone your life story on the first date! Have the courage to reveal who you are in stages but exercise sensible caution until you become comfortable and gain confidence in the man you're dating. When a woman expresses her thoughts and feelings she is telling a man how to understand her so he understands her preferences, but she is also revealing her thinking patterns. Men enjoy a mystery and a challenge; a woman who becomes predictable too quickly will dull a man's interest. So, avoid sharing too much personal information early in the dating process and do not introduce him to your friends and family until a relationship has been agreed and established. When a man takes a woman seriously he wants to show her off so it's always better to wait and see if he invites you to meet *his* family and friends first before you introduce him to the important people in your life.

Discussing Previous Relationships

Sharing too much information about your ex-partner or your relationship history during the early dating stages can be a major mistake. If you have recently split up with your previous partner or are still hurting you could sound very bitter or even angry. Complaining about how badly you were treated or let down will be a big turn off. Sharing horror stories about any previous partners are what friends are for… it's not what you talk about on your first date! There will be a time when it may be appropriate to share information about your relationship history but during the early dating stages you should really be concentrating on what he has to say. Why did his previous relationships fail? How much responsibility does he accept for his previous relationship failures? How does he feel about his previous relationships or ex-partner? Getting to know a man's relationship history and character can help you to avoid becoming involved with someone unsuitable. If you ask the right questions early during the dating process important information can be discovered before you get in too deep.

Excessive Phone Calls

You had a great date and think he's a great match but afterwards your excitement begins to fade waiting for him to call. You have probably heard advice regarding how women shouldn't pursue a man as well as the opposing opinion of how a woman should go after what she wants, and now you feel confused! After a successful date there is nothing wrong with calling a man or sending a text or email saying you had a great time and would like to meet up again. However, you should also avoid making too much contact. Generally from a male perspective too many phone calls and texts can make a woman look needy or desperate so it's sensible to resist the urge to call him constantly or to send several text messages in one day. A basic rule is the new man you're dating should be calling you more than you're picking up the phone to call him. Allow him to call and make plans for getting together. If you're expecting him to call at a certain time and he doesn't, wait for at least an hour before calling him. When you do call him make sure it's for a good reason and not just to say "hello" or to see how his day is going, and end the call before the conversation dries up. If you want to test his level of interest avoid calling him every day. Avoid texting too often, early in the morning or when you think he has just got home from work. You might think it's nice to text and ask "how was your day" but your average guy is probably going to read more into it. You never want to be perceived as a burden or a "chore" by a man. You want to be the mysterious new woman he wants to learn more about and get to know on a personal level.

The reality is there isn't a strict "one size fits all" formula that will work for every dating scenario. Getting to know someone new has its own unique dynamic with each person and situation being different so the pace and style of communication will vary accordingly. If a man is genuinely interested he will communicate consistently and won't be playing games and if he decides to pursue you this will be based on a variety of factors including how attracted he feels and what he thinks about you.

Being Too Available And Accommodating

A big mistake many women make during the dating phase or at the beginning of a relationship is trying to please a man by agreeing to everything too easily. They make premature compromises regarding their own personal preferences and tastes which can also result in alienating her family, friends or people in her social network. Always saying "yes" and agreeing to accommodate a new man is a bad move, especially if plans with friends or family are frequently broken. This can lead to isolation if he is the possessive type or a control freak, and you will play right into his hands. Even if he is an average type of guy, establishing this type of pattern often leads to problems as the relationship progresses; he becomes conditioned to getting his own way all the time which will cause a problem when the woman begins to assert herself. He might believe he has been tricked or misled so he could be lulled into a relationship with somebody who pretended to be someone she wasn't. This can result in resentment, conflict and eventual relationship failure.

Generally men like to pursue women and a woman who is too available doesn't present a challenge or stimulate a guy's genuine interest. He may put some initial effort into the pursuit early in the game if there is a possibility of some quick and easy sex, but once he gets it he will be looking elsewhere. Many women do not realize they are in control of their own destiny when it comes to dating and relationships. Men, often being goal and achievement orientated, usually love a challenge. We often like to compete and pursue objectives and it is a reality of human nature that both men and women usually want what they can't have. When you make yourself too available this sends a signal that can be interpreted as being clingy, needy or desperate. Just because you're dating someone new doesn't mean dropping your other friends, hobbies or activities. Maintain your friendships and make sure you don't suddenly ignore your friends just because there is a new man in your life. Having a busy, interesting life makes a person a much more attractive prospect for a relationship.

Never cancel meeting up with friends or other plans for a man you're interested in. Once you have made plans stick to them, you can always reschedule with the guy if he asks to see you but you have already made other plans. Do not accept last minute "spontaneous" dates during the early dating phase. You need to demonstrate you have a life of your own with friends and interests. When you accept invitations at short notice (e.g. the same evening or the following day) this sends a signal that says your life is empty and you have nothing important to do – and even if you do have something scheduled you're prepared to change your plans to see him. Players usually have more than one woman in their "harem" and will use a woman as a back-up plan if she allows it. If a man has fast, easy access to a woman he will often treat her accordingly so make sure he treats you like a priority and not an after-thought. When he wants to see you at the weekend have a deadline day for when you will accept a request. For example, Thursday could be your deadline day; if he calls wanting to make plans for the weekend on a Thursday do not accept whether you're busy or not. Well-adjusted men like women who have a life of their own; a man who believes he is solely responsible for keeping you happy and entertained all the time will be nervous about becoming too involved. A woman has to find a sensible balance between being too available or appearing very elusive or uninterested; this balance can be difficult to achieve but it's important not to make the mistake of being too accessible.

Premature And Excessive Public Displays Of Affection

The majority of women are affectionate by nature but forcing public displays of affection can make men very uncomfortable, especially in the early stages of the dating process or at the beginning of the relationship. It's important for a woman to understand when displaying affection or intimacy is appropriate; trying to kiss and cuddle your new man in front of his male friends will probably make him feel uncomfortable and even when the relationship is established being overly affectionate at the wrong time can cause problems. Learn your partner's preferences about when it's acceptable to steal a kiss or reach for his hand because doing so inappropriately can scare a new or potential partner away. Allow a man to make the first move so you can observe his comfort levels regarding public displays of affection; as you spend more time together his style will usually become apparent, which will give you confidence to instigate showing affection in public. Holding hands and kissing in public should come naturally as the relationship progresses. A woman has to be careful about declaring her love too quickly as she can be perceived as being clingy, needy or desperate. Men generally enjoy their freedom and independence so the early dating stages should be casual; the more pressure a man thinks he's under the more likely this will scare him away.

Acting Jealous, Needy Or Desperate

Coming across as being too needy, desperate or clingy will usually be a big red flag for men. Unfortunately, many women don't realize this is how they're behaving or perceived. Don't visit a man at home or his place of work unannounced as this sends a signal that you're needy, desperate or a potential stalker. Men generally avoid women who are jealous, pushy or possessive. Never make a decision to embark on a relationship motivated by desperation or lower your relationship expectations due to pressure from family or friends.

Discussing Commitment Prematurely

There is a common myth that men are generally afraid of commitment; this isn't true. What most men prefer is to take some time getting to know a woman; what they don't like is feeling pressured or rushed into making a commitment. Asking him about his general life goals and relationship preferences should be acceptable but the first weeks or couple of months should be devoted to getting to know each other without any pressure about major relationship expectations. Raising the subject of his intentions regarding your "future together" too soon in the dating process or within the first few months of a relationship can be a mistake. Trying to force issues or plan for a joint future too quickly is usually counterproductive during the early stages.

Mothering

The majority of women are hardwired to be nurturing but a man doesn't want to be treated like a toddler. If you start feeding him food while you're sharing a meal or insist on constantly telling him to be careful during the dating process he will probably find this very annoying! Avoid telling a man to "take care" or to "be safe." Women are generally nurturers by nature but telling a guy to constantly "be careful" will sound like you're trying to be his mother. For example, telling a man to make sure he wears his seat belt, not to drive too fast, apply sunscreen and so forth will usually be interpreted as mothering. Men like to be men and to be seen as being manly – we like to maintain a certain image of being the male of the species. A man is very unlikely to continue to date a woman or stay in a relationship if she constantly makes him feel like a five-year-old who doesn't know what he's doing.

Settling For Whoever Is Available

There are women who will settle for a man just because they're available. Usually it's the desperate types who are fed up of sitting on the dusty singles shelf or perhaps their biological clock is ticking and they want a traditional family unit. In some cases there is pressure from family members to get married or at least have a steady partner or the subtle pressure comes from friends who are already settled in stable relationships where there is a feeling of being "left behind." Sometimes a woman will settle for a man because he is "available" and her friends and family thinks he is a relatively nice guy or even a great catch. So despite not being in love or even feeling a real emotional connection she agrees to a relationship hoping it will work out while overlooking the important factors that are essential to give the union any reasonable future prospects.

There is no such thing as the perfect relationship; that's a myth created by romantic novels and Hollywood. Once you have been together for a while you will gradually become more aware of the things about him you do not like. He probably hasn't changed anything about himself but the fact is a woman or man in love will always be prepared to compromise or overlook certain character traits that might be irritating or even annoying. These "faults" become more apparent as the relationship progresses because likely you were not really in love with him in the first place. This eventually results in deep resentment and feelings of being trapped in an unhappy relationship with a man who might be suitable as a friend but nothing more. The partnership lacks that magic spark, certain chemistry or you simply don't feel any genuine love. A woman might even try and force herself to love him but this can never succeed no matter how "nice" a guy he may be.

When it gets to the stage where she realizes it will be impossible to love him she also knows she's caught in a dilemma: stay in a loveless mediocre, failing relationship or break his heart and walk away. If he's in love with her either way he'll eventually end up feeling inadequate and rejected so it's a lose-lose situation for both partners. This type of relationship is probably doomed from the start and even if the woman leaves to pursue true love she will probably feel bad about hurting a decent guy unnecessarily; the break-up and aftermath can be very messy.

Sacrificing Yourself For A Relationship

Having a "people pleaser mindset" usually helps to make a relationship easy going in the short-term but is ultimately a very poor medium or long-term strategy for a healthy partnership. The self-sacrificing type who always puts their partner or other people first often suffers from low self-esteem. Being upfront about your needs while respecting your partner's requirements and expectations helps to build a strong connection. Mutual understanding and respect where each person believes their views are properly considered and taken seriously creates an effective strategy for establishing balance and harmony in a healthy relationship.

Valuing yourself enough to be honest about your standards and requirements is the key to establishing clearly what you find acceptable. A healthy relationship is one between two equals, both giving and receiving in reciprocal fashion. Playing the martyr and believing if you sacrifice enough this will win a man's love or sympathy isn't likely to succeed. Eventually you will become frustrated and resentful which inevitably surfaces in some kind of conflict or drama, and this is always a major turn-off. Valuing yourself enough to respect your own needs as well as the other person's provides a foundation to establish balance and harmony within a healthy relationship.

Being A Doormat

Men respect women that respect themselves. Maintain healthy boundaries and standards while asserting and expressing yourself clearly. Don't start acting like you're in a relationship when you're only dating. Don't start sacrificing your own needs and become totally accommodating; this is a big mistake in a relationship and even a bigger one when you're only dating! While you might be overflowing with love, compassion and kindness those qualities have to be revealed slowly until you are relatively confident he is worthy of these gifts. If you put it all on a plate too quickly your average guy will enjoy the perks and move on when he gets bored. Unless you are aware and have the ability to directly communicate your needs you're setting yourself up to be used, abused and misunderstood. Having a doormat mindset puts you at a very obvious and serious disadvantage.

A Lack Of Assertiveness

There is a big difference between being assertive or self-confident and being self-righteous. Assertiveness doesn't mean being demanding or bossing people around; it does mean communicating clearly, directly and tactfully with respect for others. Practicing being assertive is an essential skill when you are seeking to have your needs respected and fulfilled while the ability to be clear when communicating is vital for maintaining healthy relationships. Failing to be assertive will put you at a serious disadvantage that can be very difficult to recover from, especially if you failed to make clear your expectations at the very beginning. Communication issues indicate there will be inevitable conflicts and major problems in the relationship – it's just a question of when they happen.

Dismissing Potential Partners Too Quickly

There is a balance to be struck between knowing your requirements and the type of man you're looking for and being sure your criteria is realistic. If you're in the dating game and meet someone new don't automatically make assumptions and dismiss him out of hand. Judging too quickly or having unrealistic expectations can result in missing out on someone who could be highly compatible and who could even be "The One." Some women can become obsessed with not wanting to settle for what they consider to be "second best" which is understandable, but you have to be realistic.

Single Mother Dating

If you're a single mother there isn't really an optimum time for introducing your children to a new partner but you should be cautious. As a general rule you should avoid introducing a new man to your children until you are confident the dating phase is going to develop into a relationship. You should explore his attitude towards children, especially if he has a child or children of his own. While youngsters can be resilient it is not healthy for a child or children to have serial "uncles." There was a story I heard about a mother who had an argument with her teenage son. The following morning she woke up to find a note attached to her bedroom door; it was a list of every "uncle" her teenager had witnessed spending the night with his mother. You cannot expect your children to respect you if you allow a variety of different men into their lives only to then disappear. It's unfair on them and can be also dangerous as studies show step-parents are more likely to abuse children in their care.

In the dating game some women hide the fact they have children – this is a very bad idea. From a man's point of view if you have hidden the fact you have children what else have you lied about? Honesty is always the best policy.

The Ms. Independent Mindset

These days many single women are employed and support themselves. To survive the economic realities of life women have to be independently minded for a variety of reasons just as men have to be. A woman who has been single for a long time handling her own life while perhaps fulfilling certain traditional male roles like decorating or taking out the household rubbish can find it difficult to adjust when a new man enters her life. It isn't easy for some women to just turn off the Ms. Independent mindset but if they don't they're often sabotaging themselves. When a decent man with genuine intentions comes along a woman needs to learn to adjust and gradually reduce that mindset if she doesn't want to go back to being single. Generally, men like to feel manly and be treated like men; a man who feels constantly disrespected or belittled for any reason by a woman isn't going to tolerate this kind of treatment for very long. The male Ego can be a fragile thing and when a man with any self-respect feels he is not needed or appreciated this is perceived as an attack on his masculinity. I know of several long-term relationships or marriages where the woman earns significantly more than her partner but these women are intelligent enough to allow their men to retain their sense of male pride. These women make sure their men feel needed and appreciated and their relationships have been very successful.

There is a big difference between being assertive and aggressive or demanding. A woman who insists on acting like this will usually be a huge turn off for the typical man. A woman who constantly undermines her partner's efforts, achievements or status isn't going to be with him for very long unless he is staying due to financial or other reasons that have nothing to do with being in love. Women who insist on being Ms. Independent while demanding or dictating how a relationship operates without compromising will usually end up being single again or cheated on. Intelligent, genuine men are attracted to women who have self-respect, clear values and standards, women who manage their lives effectively. Men appreciate women who have a certain degree of control and direction over their lives and are emotionally stable. Most of all men appreciate being treated like men while being allowed to fulfill their traditional masculine role as much as possible. "Men are from Mars, Women are from Venus" may be an old cliché but it's very true! Men have different priorities and motivations than women – not better, just different; but those gender differences can be a tremendous asset with the right partner.

Rushing Into A "Relationship"

According to the dating book *The Rules*, men fall in love quickly. Being a man myself and having spoken to a great deal of men over the years I don't believe this generalization; men often fall in *lust* very quickly, which is a very different thing! A woman being pursued by a man might think he has "fallen in love" because he uses lots of public displays of affection to try and convince her he is genuinely interested. She might be enjoying the attention or could even be desperate and deceiving herself, but men don't usually fall in love quickly because we are often quite logical in our approach to love and romance. Understand this: when a man is constantly calling you and wants to meet up several times a week it doesn't necessarily mean he has fallen madly in love. He might wine, dine and romance you but that doesn't mean he's in love. Acting as if you're an established couple while you're only in the dating phase is a huge mistake. Preparing and sharing a romantic meal occasionally is acceptable but don't start doing his laundry or cooking him meals on a regular basis. Men generally don't like feeling pressured into a relationship and like to take their time. When you meet someone new and like him, pace yourself instead of rushing into an "instant" relationship. During the first six weeks limit dates to no more than once or twice a week and keep your phone calls brief; it's always better to take time with a man when you're getting to know him. Never rush into a relationship and always remember that taking your time doesn't mean you're wasting your time.

Premature Unprotected Sex

In these liberated times of sexual equality some women want to "act like a man" and have sex on the first date or at the earliest opportunity. Becoming caught up in a whirlwind romance and having sex too quickly usually results in the "romance" just fizzling out; this is especially true if the man is a seasoned Player who has accomplished his mission (sex) and quickly moves on. Even if he isn't a Player, a woman who sleeps with a man too quickly is unlikely to be considered suitable for a serious, long-term relationship. Receiving a man's attention means absolutely nothing if you do not also have his respect. In the dating game **always begin with the end in mind**; if you want to be respected and desired it is usually better to avoid becoming physically intimate too quickly.

This means asking questions, which might feel awkward or embarrassing for you and even for the man you're dating, but it's better to discuss sexual matters openly. Many people like sex to be a spontaneous act and prefer to "go with the flow" believing that asking too many potentially embarrassing questions will take the fun out of having sex and makes it all too "predictable."

There can be serious consequences for deciding to have some "fun" and failing to ask sensible questions:

- You fail to discuss, agree and practice safe sex options and subsequently test positive for HIV.
- You fail to discuss, agree and practice safe sex options and your partner gives you gonorrhea, herpes or some other type of STD.
- You fail to discuss, agree and practice birth control options and end up with an unwanted pregnancy.
- You fail ask enough questions and find out your partner is sleeping with someone else and get your heart broken.
- You realize you feel alone or used while you are lying next to the person you just had sex with.
- You are too trusting and allow yourself to be too susceptible by having sex with someone and then realize that was all they were ever after in the first place.

These scenarios do not sound like very much "fun" because they are not! Being sexually spontaneous, having sexual fun and having sex purely to satisfy lustful urges can have devastating consequences that involve enormous amounts of distress, pain, heartache, humiliation and even premature death. Sexual intimacy with another human being is a wonderful experience but you have to be levelheaded if you intend to avoid potentially unpleasant or even dangerous outcomes.

You need to:

- Find out as much as possible about your partner's sexual history.
- Discuss sexually transmitted diseases.
- Find out if he has been tested for AIDs. If he hasn't ask him to take a test as soon as possible. If you have not been tested arrange to do so.
- Discover if he likes to practice any potentially hazardous sexual activities (e.g. anal sex).

It can be awkward or embarrassing conversation but your potential partner's sexual history needs to be discussed. STDs are on the rise generally but especially among those who are 40 or over; he may not have a condition as serious as HIV/AIDS, but gonorrhea is still very unpleasant while genital herpes is recurring and incurable. If you have any doubts about your own sexual health make sure you have yourself checked out as women can carry certain infections without knowing due to the lack of obvious symptoms. Becoming pregnant is always a possibility when indulging in sexual activity so birth control methods should also be discussed. If the system of contraception does not require condoms (e.g. birth control pills, cap, diaphragm etc.) you should still both agree to use condoms in order to practice safe sex. A failure to ask sensible questions about sex and agreeing how sexual relations will be conducted can result in finding yourself in a variety of difficult or distressing situations and could even mean you're gambling with your life.

In the dating game there are predators who are just after quick and easy sex. Men generally don't take women who have sex too easily very seriously; while guys often want *sexual intimacy* the woman who agrees to have sex too quickly will often try to persuade a man to share *emotional intimacy*. If a man you're dating suggests having sex or implies it's "time" this doesn't mean he necessarily wants to sleep with you but could be just testing to see if you will give it up without too much resistance. Most guys like a challenge and will respect a woman who respects herself. If you have sex with a guy too quickly expect to be dumped sooner or later. Rushing into sex with a man hoping it will develop into a relationship is not going to work and you're leaving yourself wide open to be used as a sexual toy. Most men are hardwired for sexual encounters without emotional content while women are generally very different. If you have a habit of rushing into relationships or becoming sexually intimate too quickly there are probably underlying issues motivating this type of behavior. It's usually going to be a lot easier for a woman to stop dating a man if she hasn't had sex with him. This allows her to walk away with her self-respect intact. Having sex often involves a woman engaging her emotions at some level so being prudent about sexual activity can provide effective emotional protection.

When a woman decides to have sex quickly that's her choice but she shouldn't expect to be taken seriously or considered suitable for a long-term relationship. It might sound old fashioned but being respected and alluring is still one of the most effective strategies to employ in the dating game. When a man has genuine intentions instead of just being interested in getting between the sheets, he will wait. Take time getting to know a man properly before deciding to sleep with him; it's important to establish respect and an emotional connection before any sexual activity takes place. You may discover while being sexually attracted to him you don't really like him very much as a person!

CHAPTER 19:

Dating Warning Signs

"When someone shows you who they are, believe them the first time." – Maya Angelou (1928-2014), Author, Poet & Actress

Probably the biggest mistake men and women can make when seeking to meet someone new is to ignore or overlook obvious warning signs while dating. This can be a very easy trap to fall into if you're desperate to be in a relationship – or have had too much to drink! When you're looking for love it's quite possible to meet a variety of potential candidates for a relationship and the ability to identify certain warning signs can save you a great deal of time, disappointment or even distress.

Potential warning signs are missed by:

- Denying obvious warning signs
- Reducing the importance of obvious warning signs
- Making excuses for the other person

Potential Alcoholic

Many people have the stereotypical view that a person who is an alcoholic gets drunk every day, only lives to drink and is a social outcast who has lost everything. A person can also be a binge drinker and yet still have a problem, while others will go out with the sole intention to "get wasted." This type of behavior can be encouraged by some peer groups and can be easily observed in many Western cities on a Friday or Saturday evening. Enjoying a few drinks responsibly at the weekend is quite acceptable but someone who needs to have a drink *every* evening indicates alcohol has become a way of life. This is a person who probably needs alcohol to function. Someone who needs a drink every night can be fairly described as an alcoholic just the same as someone who needs to drink all day long. You will often hear people say they just need a drink to "settle their nerves" or will claim they're generally a "social drinker." Some people will rationalize their drinking by saying they just stick to "light" drinks like wine or beer but if they are drinking everyday they have a problem; it's just a question of *how much* of a problem.

When you meet someone new or go on a date with a person for the first time pay attention to their alcohol intake. How much does he drink? Does he drink to excess? Does he use hard drugs? People often use excess alcohol and other addictive drugs to try and escape their negative emotions and fears, or even themselves. They want to be numb emotionally so they will not have to feel and deal with their issues. Alcohol dependency often causes huge problems in relationships so if you suspect a man you're dating drinks too much it's sensible to walk away sooner rather than later. Do not deny the warning sign and compromise yourself to accommodate his drinking habits, which could indicate an addiction to alcohol. If you are already in a relationship and you have been ignoring your partner's excessive drinking the issue has to be confronted. He has to agree to seek help and be serious about giving up alcohol or you have to seriously consider leaving the relationship.

Illegal Or Prescription Drugs

Those who use illegal drugs or abuse prescription drugs can become physically dependent over a relatively short period of time.

Illicit drugs are expensive and dangerous with addictions to drugs such as heroin and cocaine often having severe consequences for addicts damaging their

- Intimate and family relationships
- Professional relationships
- Finances
- Health

Smoking marijuana is now considered to be socially acceptable by many people with some claiming they enjoy medicinal benefits or relief from certain illnesses. Despite its wide spread use the consistent use of marijuana also has dangers. There are many different varieties of this drug and the stronger enhanced "skunk" types are many times stronger than the natural herb as it is cultivated by using additional chemicals. The consistent smoking of marijuana, and especially of "skunk," can have long-term effects on a person. It can make them paranoid, forgetful, lethargic, mentally lackluster and emotionally insensitive. The constant use of illegal drugs can accelerate a person's decline into oblivion. In many cases addicts destroy their lives and severely damage the people who love them.

The reality is anyone with an alcohol or drug addiction problem isn't ready to be in a relationship. He may promise to change and even display a genuine willingness to resolve these issues but it's usually a mistake to become involved with a man when there are clear and obvious warning signs. Jumping to conclusions can be counterproductive but make sure you pay attention to patterns of behavior and use your common sense. If you identify a pattern (a minimum of two incidents that are the same or very similar) don't ignore it! Make sure you address the issue immediately and don't waste time trying to fix him. If you suspect the man you're dating has any kind of addiction problem and he isn't prepared to acknowledge and discuss any possible solution you should walk away without looking back. When a man is in denial it doesn't matter how much "potential" you think he may have. The myth that "love conquers all" is just that – a myth. This advice may seem harsh as women generally are nurturers by nature but addictions and destructive patterns of behavior are usually caused by emotional issues that you will be poorly equipped to deal with. While it is possible for anyone to change, any meaningful transformation is very unlikely without the assistance of a support group or therapy.

If you are already in a relationship and you know your partner is using drugs or clearly has a drug problem then the issue has to be confronted. He has to agree to get help to quit or you need to get out of the relationship ***now!***

Disrespects The Women In His Family

The majority of men grew up with a mother and may also have sisters, aunties and nieces. If he lacks respect for the female members of his family he will eventually disrespect you. Pay attention to how he speaks about or treats the other women in his family and don't be deceived by his chat up lines or how nice he may appear to be.

Poor Relationships With Friends And Family

How a man treats his family members, parents, friends and siblings will usually be a reliable indicator of his general personality. When someone's life appears to be full of broken friendships, betrayals and difficult or dysfunctional relationships, you should see this as a very clear red flag. If he avoids discussing details regarding his family background or has very little contact with them this may indicate concealed resentment, anger or rage concerning family members and his negative emotions will eventually be directed at you. Do not become involved unless you're prepared to be the next person on his list of failed relationships.

Disrespectful And Demeaning

When a man doesn't respect your ideas, opinions or choices this is a clear warning sign not to become involved. Relationships require compromise and being with a bully who undermines your confidence will stunt your growth and end in tears.

Possessive And Controlling

Controlling or possessive behavior is a clear warning sign you're dating a man who is probably a physical or emotional abuser. He may try to convince you there is nothing to be concerned about and he is just confident, outgoing or very assertive but don't be fooled. Also pay attention if a man is too quiet or intense and always trust your instincts.

Difficulty Maintaining Regular Employment

It's common and perfectly acceptable to experience short-term periods of unemployment especially in the current economic climate. A freelancer is likely to have periods when there is little or no work. However, if he has a constant pattern of being hired and fired, alarm bells should start ringing loud and clear.

The inability to hold down a job could be a warning sign of

- A problem with authority
- Bad time-keeping skills
- A poor work ethic
- A poor attitude
- General laziness

Any of these warning signs can indicate an inherent instability or an irresponsible attitude toward managing his life. These types often have a pattern of looking for someone to bail them out when they hit their next financial problem or crisis and there are no prizes for guessing who that will be if you become involved!

Has A Pattern Of Giving Up

When someone has a pattern of quitting on things like their career, relationships, education, or any other major responsibilities they will probably lack staying power for a long-term relationship. Sometimes in life it's wise to know when to quit or to walk away but a pattern of giving up should be a major cause for concern.

A Lack Of Personal Goals

Sharing goals and planning ahead is the key to a stable and satisfying relationship. The majority of people enter relationships with an idea of what they want so both partners should set mutually agreed goals for the relationship. You should also pay attention to his personal goals; if he doesn't have any medium to long-term goals for himself then it's unlikely he hasn't seriously considered being in a committed relationship.

Enjoys Making Jokes About Other People

Most people say they would like their partner to have a good sense of humor and the ability to make someone laugh during the dating process can be a powerful aphrodisiac. However, it's not very funny when the jokes are demeaning, belittling or cruel and always at the expense of others. Making nasty and spiteful jokes about people to impress others is actually a sign of low self-esteem, toxic behavior and demonstrates a clear lack of respect. If you decide to ignore this warning sign and laugh along just remember it will not be too long before the jokes will probably be about you, and when that happens it won't seem very funny.

Constantly Complains About His Ex-Partner

You have a few dates and you notice he has a habit of complaining, blaming or being disrespectful about his ex-partner or even a few of his previous partners. Constantly attacking another person who isn't present to defend themselves says a great deal about his character and demonstrates a lack of integrity. One of the hallmarks of maturity is taking responsibility and admitting our mistakes instead of constantly blaming others. Anyone who constantly holds on to bitterness and resentment will make a relationship a miserable experience. When it's clear your date still feels raw about his previous relationship it's not a wise strategy to embark on a new one. A man who is constantly living in the past and holding on to feelings of resentment clearly has unresolved issues and should be avoided. If he has a habit of blaming his ex-partners it's only a matter of time before he will start complaining about you.

Refuses To Take Responsibility

If you notice during conversations your date believes all of his previous relationship failures were someone else's fault, pay attention! Those who constantly blame others often have a victim mindset and look for someone else to blame for their failures. A tendency to try and avoid taking responsibility also indicates a serious lack of maturity. If he has a child or children from a previous relationship find out if he maintains contact and pays support. A man should take responsibility for his children irrespective of what type of relationship he has with the child's mother. An irresponsible father is not a good prospect for any type of serious relationship.

Selfish

Kindness is not about how much money a man may spend on a date, it's about a person's mindset and attitude. If you're dating a man who is inconsiderate or selfish towards others he will eventually be unkind to you so be prepared to walk away. There is nothing wrong with having a prudent approach to finances but there can be a thin line between being careful with money and the type who is a tight-fisted miser.

Poor Time Keeping

A man who is always late and doesn't bother to call to say he is running behind is being disrespectful and unreliable. If he fails to turn up for the first date without a very good reason, cut your losses and refuse to rearrange another meeting with him.

Claims His Marriage Or Relationship Isn't Working/Is A Living Arrangement For Financial Convenience

It's a fact of life that married men look for naive single women to date and have sex with. When a man is prepared to betray his wife he will probably cheat on you as well. Whatever promises he may make, it's very unlikely he is going to leave his wife for you so don't waste your time with a cheater.

Keeps You Guessing

Small, thoughtful gestures can be reassuring and builds confidence. If he gives you vague responses regarding his activities or whereabouts most of the time and you're constantly wondering what he is doing your trust will begin to fail. Successful relationships rely on effective communication so if you constantly feel insecure this should be considered as a very serious warning sign.

Prefers To Be With His Friends

While young boys and teenagers like to hang out together a man who is always spending time with his friends is obviously not that interested in his partner or the relationship. It's quite normal for healthy, heterosexual men to occasionally spend time with their male friends, but if you begin to feel you're competing for his attention or suspect you're being taken for granted it's time to tackle the issue. Ask questions to discover why he spends so much time with his friends and give him an opportunity to explain himself. Discuss events or activities you could both share and enjoy together, but if it becomes obvious he just wants to spend time with you at his convenience it's time to let go and move on. There are men who can talk a great game but ultimately actions speak louder than words. Pay attention to what he does, not what he may say.

▌Reality Check!

"It's a date, not a duty" – Johnnie Dent Jr., Author

Cultivate the habit of paying attention to any behavior or red flags that make you feel uncomfortable. This can save you a lot of wasted time and heartache!

CHAPTER 20:

Commitment Anxieties

"Don't be reckless with other people's hearts, and don't put up with people that are reckless with yours." – Kurt Vonnegut, Jr. (1922-2007), Novelist

Making a commitment to another person can be scary but it's perfectly normal for men and women to feel that way during the early stages of a new relationship. After all, considering and deciding on commitments brings up a lot of our own issues, and as we grow closer to someone and reveal more of ourselves the risk of being hurt or rejected inevitably increases. Creating and maintaining an enduring emotional connection includes a great deal of soul searching, honesty and trust as each person reveals their emotional vulnerability. As the relationship progresses and a couple grow closer they share deeper levels of intimacy and various anxieties and self-doubts may come to the surface.

If you are at the stage of a relationship where you are looking for commitment and he is resisting, then ask yourself the following questions:

- Do you tend to ignore any obvious warning signs or rush into relationships too quickly?
- Are your expectations for a further commitment at this stage of the relationship reasonable?
- At the beginning of the relationship, were there any difficult circumstances surrounding your partner that could make him reluctant to commit?
- When you got together was he still recovering from a previous relationship?
- Is he under any type of financial pressure that might prevent him from being comfortable with making a further commitment?
- Does he have any commitment fears or anxieties?

These fears will often surface when serious relationship commitments are being considered or discussed and represent a challenge that needs to be dealt with courageously. It can take great courage for a person to totally reveal themselves so if you're dating a man who seems reluctant to commit he may be experiencing anxieties that need to be discussed. Dealing with these fears and concerns with a partner who is well-intentioned will indicate his state of emotional maturity.

Typical Commitment Fears

The Fear Of Choosing The Wrong Person

The fear of choosing the wrong person can cause considerable anxiety. There are many factors to be considered before a final decision can be reached regarding whether it is prudent to take "the plunge." Is this person really "The One?" What's going to happen if I meet someone who feels more compatible? Getting "cold feet" before making a commitment is not unusual but you have to know the difference between feeling naturally apprehensive about making a commitment and a clear warning from your intuition. If you have been dating a man for a while who seems reluctant to make a commitment he may be concerned you're not the right woman for him. His concerns or fears may grow after you have been in a relationship for a period of time or you begin to raise the possibility of getting married.

The Fear Of The Future

Many people think that making a relationship commitment means they're making a promise about how they will feel about their partner in the future. No one can make a commitment regarding how long their relationship will actually continue. The only realistic commitment anyone can make to a relationship is in the now! A relationship commitment can only be a promise made to love our partner and respect ourselves rather than the amount of time love will last. Ask if any fears about the future are preventing him from making a commitment as you need to clarify why he cannot give you the emotional security you seek. If his explanation is not satisfactory you will have to consider if the relationship is viable.

The Fear Of Being Like His Parents

Many people feel that the commitment of being married means settling down to a monotonous routine, a lack of fun and spontaneity, reduced sex life and a general loss of freedom. There are many different ideas and concepts regarding what a serious relationship commitment is supposed to be and the most obvious example each of us gravitate toward and try to emulate is the model presented by our parents. When parental examples are negative or dysfunctional this can create anxieties about repeating the same mistakes. If he grew up in a home where his parental models were poor there may be concerns about ending up in a bad relationship. He should confront any of these types of fears and redefine his expectations regarding what a picture of a happy, normal and committed relationship should be. Discuss any fears he may have to see if there is a reasonable way forward.

The Fear Of Being Hurt Again

Experience is a great teacher but its lessons can often feel very harsh. This is especially so when it comes to falling in love. The fear of being hurt after a difficult or painful relationship or marriage failure can make many of us frightened to trust someone new and try love again. Sometimes these memories loom larger than anything else, even if there were some good times in the relationship. Discuss his relationship history to discover if any previous hurts may be holding him back from making a commitment.

These questions should be discussed and explored to help you discover his mindset. When a woman is desperate for a commitment or eager to take the relationship to the next level she may pressure her partner into making premature promises when he isn't ready. This is immature, manipulative and definitely not the right thing to do. It can be tempting to issue threats to end the relationship or to present an ultimatum when feelings of frustration about the lack of commitment begin to surface. There can be occasions where issuing a relationship ultimatum is appropriate and necessary to shake up a complacent partner or a man who is taking you for granted, but they should be used wisely and not too often. Most importantly, you have to be prepared to back up any ultimatums with consequences for non-compliance. If you make an ultimatum but fail to follow through your bluff will have been called and your position severely weakened. The bottom line is you have to be prepared to back up your words with action and walk away or for the possibility he may end the relationship. The only sensible approach is to engage in an honest discussion to see if it's possible to take the relationship forward. Be honest with yourself and make sure you're not pressuring him into making a premature and inappropriate commitment.

A commitment to take a relationship to the next level has to be mutually agreed. There is no point trying to use underhanded tactics like nagging, emotional blackmail or guilt trips when you're looking for a relationship commitment. Your partner will probably feel manipulated into agreeing to take the relationship to the next level, especially if he thinks your demands for a further commitment are premature. You may "win" in the short-term and get a grudging commitment but it won't be genuine, he will feel resentment and blame you when things start to go wrong.

However, there are times when you will need to take a no-nonsense approach to his resistance to making a commitment. Commitment fears feel very real and while sympathy may be appropriate don't accept any of the following possible reasons as an excuse.

Is Your Partner A Commitment Phobic/Love Avoidant Or Just Scared?

While negotiating with a partner who is experiencing common commitment fears can be difficult, dealing with someone with serious issues will be highly challenging. A partner who has Commitment Phobic issues is more likely to overcome his fears than a man who is a Love Avoidant, as those types of issues often go much deeper and can be very challenging to resolve. Whatever the case, being with a partner who has commitment issues and conflicts will use up a tremendous amount of emotional energy and ultimately can result in wasting a huge amount of time. A person who generally displays an unrealistic attitude to life with intense periods of indecision often has unresolved issues regarding making commitments. Be prepared for a great deal of frustration; while you're trying to get closer he will be doing the exact opposite by creating obstacles designed to sabotage any positive growth. A man who is pressured into making a relationship commitment he does not want will probably feel trapped and this can only lead to serious relationship conflicts.

You need to clarify:

- How long does your partner feel he needs to be ready for a further commitment?
- Is he willing to work on being ready for a further commitment?
- What is he prepared to do to take your partnership to the next level?

Conversations of this kind have the real potential to turn into confrontations if he insists on being evasive. Remaining in a relationship without knowing where it is going when you clearly know what you want will inevitably cause resentment tension and frustration.

A man who appears reluctant to provide a basic level of commitment within three months isn't interested in having a serious relationship and is probably just after sex. Successful relationships require a genuine commitment from both partners, and a direction. It's important to know what your partner is doing to resolve any commitment issues and vague or evasive responses should not be accepted.

If he has commitment issues but is serious about the relationship then he should be willing to work through them by:

- Researching commitment issues
- Going to a support group
- Attending therapy/counseling
- Discussing his fears with friends who are married or in long-term relationships

You can support your partner but it's his responsibility to resolve any issues that are holding him back from moving the relationship forward. Allowing him time to work through any issues is reasonable but this cannot be indefinite. A man with deep commitment issues will not be interested in resolving any challenges or problems. For the Commitment Phobic/Love Avoidant types making a genuine effort to maintain or improve the relationship is *exactly the same thing as making a commitment*.

If he is unable or unwilling to resolve his issues and make a firm commitment within a reasonable timescale you basically have a two choices:

1. Accept you're involved with a Friends With Benefits arrangement and continue to see him
2. Walk away

Trying to understand his issues and how he feels believing this will provide an opportunity for him to eventually change his mind is a very common mistake. This approach eventually leads to resentment and conflicts within the relationship because people with deep commitment issues often don't want to change. If he is unable or unwilling to provide the emotional security you seek it's time to seriously consider why you're wasting your time because the reality is his conflicts are not going to just disappear. Trying to persuade a man to commit to a relationship when he has this type of Emotional Baggage is a bad idea and staying with him is even worse! Each relationship carries a certain amount of risk and once a deep emotional investment has been made it can be very difficult to walk away with nothing much to show except feelings of frustration, resentment and bitter disappointment. This is why it's always better to be as upfront as soon as possible regarding your relationship goals; whatever age a woman may be, if she wants a long-term commitment this should be made clear as it can be very easy to drift into an unfulfilling or even dysfunctional relationship. Falling in love can be a fantastic experience but it doesn't make any sense to just give your heart away. You are responsible for your personal choices so do not allow a man to waste your time if you're looking for a committed relationship and he isn't.

The Foundations Of A Successful Relationship

Many people are looking for someone special to share their lives with but they often overlook the main components required on which to build a loving and fulfilling relationship. There are a variety of factors required for a successful relationship but four which are absolutely essential.

Know Yourself

Many people make the mistake of looking for love before discovering who they truly are. It is an absolute waste of time becoming involved with a relationship if you're not ready. If you don't truly know and love yourself first then seeking to share your life with another human being is not only being unrealistic but also very unfair. When a person carries unresolved issues into a love affair those issues inevitably come to the surface during the relationship causing drama.

Develop A Friendship

When you share a healthy friendship with your partner a successful relationship becomes a great deal easier to accomplish. If you want to build something genuine do not overlook the importance of being friends first with a potential partner. Sharing a genuine friendship means being able to enjoy that person for who they are and not necessarily what they can give you. Friendship creates a great foundation for a happy and loving relationship. If he isn't the type of person you can be great friends with it's a waste of time trying to build and share a successful relationship.

Communication

One of the fundamental building blocks for any healthy relationship is effective communication. A relationship lacking communication is more likely to have major misunderstandings and less likely to be successful. Healthy communication minimizes the chances of issues festering and not being properly addressed; if you can't talk to your partner then it's a waste of time being together.

Honesty

A relationship that begins on a foundation of lying is very likely to fail due to more lies. Untruths eventually catch up with one or both partners sooner or later and creates an unhealthy environment of doubt and mistrust that inevitably spreads like a disease, infecting the relationship with even more negativity. Many people fail to be a hundred percent honest. While no one can claim to be perfect it is always best to be honest with your partner and, more importantly, yourself. Ignoring the truth or living in denial is usually a set up for living a lie.

The Way Forward

"If we commit ourselves to one person for life, this is not, as many people think, a rejection of freedom; rather, it demands the courage to move into all the risks of freedom, and the risk of love which is permanent; into that love which is not possession but participation."
– Madeleine L'Engle (1918-2007), Author

Relationships can be very challenging and even highly compatible couples have to work at them. A truly committed relationship requires a deep desire to love, respect and validate your partner in a union where each person consistently supports and encourages the other. A commitment to the right partner offers many wonderful gifts including sharing love, joy and deep contentment along with many important lessons and mutually life affirming experiences. Making a commitment to a relationship is always a risk but the rewards can be truly tremendous.

CHAPTER 21:

Relationships - Commitment Progression And Agreements

"Without commitment, you cannot have depth in anything, whether it's a relationship, a business or a hobby." – Neil Strauss, *The Game: Penetrating the Secret Society of Pickup Artists*

Many women enter relationships with the hope of getting married and secretly hold dreams of a fairy tale wedding. The problem is not all men want to get married; some just want to stay in the relationship enjoying the benefits and will stay in it as long as there isn't any great pressure from his partner for marriage. Men who witnessed unhealthy or even violent parental relationships as a child can develop a very negative attitude regarding marriage. A man can also be resistant to marriage if he believes he is receiving all the "wife benefits" already and will not see any reason to make a more binding commitment. This type of man will still enjoy the companionship a relationship provides but avoid any discussions about marriage. There are also men who will delay making a marriage commitment to simply keep his options open to have sex with other women. They actually find it easier to cheat when they're in a relationship but not married; these men also know there is a great deal more to lose if a married man is caught cheating and his wife files for divorce.

Sadly for many women their partner may be resistant to marriage simply because he doesn't love her. This can be a very bitter pill to swallow but the reality is there are men who just stay with a woman simply for convenience. A man can care for a woman but that doesn't mean he is in love with her; what she provides is just enough to encourage him to stay in the relationship but not enough for him to seriously consider proposing marriage. Her partner isn't actively investing but often does the bare minimum to keep the relationship going. This can cause a woman to doubt herself and wonder what she is doing wrong why her partner will not commit to marriage. She may assume she is not doing enough and go into constant overdrive trying to "fix" the relationship. She tries everything and sacrifices a great deal hoping her partner will finally realize she is worthy to be his wife, but this is just a vicious cycle. Eventually her self-esteem begins to suffer, which can lead to insecurity, clinginess and, in extreme cases, depression.

In this way women can fall into the trap of trying to prove they are wife material investing a great deal of time, energy and love into a relationship without receiving a fair exchange. If you want to be married and your partner isn't interested there will be various cat-and-mouse games as you try to make him agree to marriage while he does everything in his power to avoid this happening. This constant tension has the potential to damage and even destroy a

213

relationship as each partner has different goals in life. Marriage isn't for everybody but if you want to get married it is pointless being with a man who doesn't value marriage the same way you do. A successful relationship requires two people holding the same values and wanting the same things out of life. A woman who truly wants marriage with a partner who doesn't is wasting her time and it's always better to leave than compromise deeply held desires or beliefs.

Therefore, when you're seriously considering embarking on a relationship there are two essential questions to ask yourself:

- Are you clear about your own values, requirements and expectations?
- Are you clear about what you expect from a relationship regarding commitment?

Planning for Commitment - Realistic Timescales

Phase 1 Commitment Agreements: The Beginning

New Relationship: 0-3 months

During the dating phase of a relationship the "rules of engagement" are established as both people get to know each other. Commitment agreements will be required to move the dating phase toward a relationship status. Generally there should be a mutual agreement to be emotionally and sexually exclusive within the first few months.

Key Questions

If you have asked all the right questions during the first three months you should know:

- The reasons why his previous relationships failed
- What he has learnt from his previous relationships
- His relationship history
- His sexual history
- His ethics and morals
- His personal career or professional goals
- Financial background
- Financial goals
- How he feels about personal growth
- His activities around personal growth
- Religious or spiritual beliefs or practices
- His attitude towards personal health, diet and maintaining fitness
- Any history of addiction

It's important not to dismiss or ignore any concerns or you could be setting yourself up for difficulties later on. You should be confident he is a decent person with the personality attributes that are important to you and doesn't have any significant Emotional Baggage or any major external compatibility hazards. There should be a mutual agreement the relationship is exclusive and neither partner will pursue any other person emotionally or sexually. These are fundamental components which represent the first level of commitment as each person agrees to devote their time, focus and energy to the relationship and give it a high priority. A man who appears reluctant to provide this basic level of commitment within three months isn't interested in having a serious relationship and is probably just after sex. If you're happy to be involved in a Friends With Benefits arrangement continue to see him but if you want more cut your losses and look for a man who wants a committed relationship.

Phase 2 Commitment Agreements: Taking The Relationship Forward

Exploring Relationship Potential: 3-6 months

This is often a crucial period for a new relationship. Having invested a considerable amount of time and emotional energy you should be confident he doesn't have any serious toxic flaws and that he has the 7 Essential Character Traits.

Review the Relationship Objectively

- Are there any compatibility hazards impacting negatively on the relationship? These should be discussed and agreements reached regarding how the issue will be dealt with. If there are serious issues which cannot be resolved the relationship probably isn't viable.
- Does he have any toxic flaws which he is not willing to address? Any unresolved issues means the relationship isn't viable and you're probably putting yourself at emotional or physical risk.
- Are you confident you're not involved in the type of relationship that is probably doomed to fail? Review the chapter *"Relationships Probably Doomed To Fail"* and be honest with yourself to avoid disappointment and heartbreak.

Do not ignore any problems hoping they will sort themselves out. Certain issues or agendas are not always obvious during Phase 1. If you have serious concerns your partner is unable or unwilling to address it's sensible to terminate the relationship at this stage. As couples begin to know each other areas of compatibility, values, beliefs and habits are explored at deeper levels. If the relationship progresses positively each person grows more comfortable, confident and emotionally secure as they gradually share aspects of themselves.

This phase should lead to the next level of commitment decision where both partners mutually agree and acknowledge Phase 2 Agreements.

Phase 2 Agreements

- The relationship is important and deserves to be pursued to discover if it has the potential to succeed.
- Both partners agree to nurture the relationship by continuing to communicate honestly, and they make a commitment to understand each other.
- Each partner agrees to work on themselves as necessary to ensure they're both making a positive contribution to the relationship and its continued growth.

During this phase agreeing further relationship commitments is crucial. Many women assume these commitments just "happen" automatically or take it for granted there is some sort of implied understanding. The easiest way to waste time and have your heart broken is to discover a relationship isn't going anywhere and doesn't have a future. If you have not discussed and agreed this level of commitment with your partner after being in a relationship for six months or more you're probably wasting your time.

Phase 3 Commitment Agreements: Laying Strong Foundations

Established Relationship: 6-12 Months Plus

This level of commitment sets the medium to long-term goals for the relationship where further foundations are put in place to strengthen the partnership. This level is where the couple formulates a strategy to take the union forward in a positive direction although the final level of commitment may not have been acknowledged and agreed. During this stage foundations for the relationship have been established and a mutual commitment agreed to make a genuine effort to build a lasting relationship. However, the timing of Phase 3 agreements can vary depending on a variety of factors which have to be taken into consideration such as:

- External circumstances that may impact on the relationship
- The age, attitudes and expectations of the people involved

Every relationship is different so will develop in its own unique way. For example, young females usually experience less "time pressure" so may delay making a serious relationship commitment while a mature woman might be looking for a serious level of commitment within a couple of years. Mature partners with greater experience often know what they expect from their relationships so they may agree to a higher level of commitment quite quickly. Generally, the younger a person is the more time he or she should take before deciding to make this level of commitment.

If you're considering making a Phase 3 Commitment, ask yourself the following questions:

- Would I consider having a child with this person? Even if you're not interested in having (more) children this question can help you to clarify your feelings about making a long-term commitment.
- Do I want to spend the rest of my life with him if he remains the same and never changes? This question can help you to clarify if your partner has any issues you're unhappy with.

Relationships are ready for a Phase 3 Commitment when:

- The relationship is generally happy, healthy and functioning positively and each person generally feels appreciated, loved and respected the majority of the time.
- Both partners are happy and very confident they have found the right person and each desires a shared future and is not tempted to check out anyone else for a possible relationship.

At this stage it should be mutually agreed to work together to deal with any unresolved issues as a priority. This agreement will support and encourage the positive growth of the relationship as both partners commit to deal with any current or new issues that may arise. If you are happy with your partner and the relationship it's time to discuss Phase 3 agreements.

Phase 3 Commitment Agreements

During the discussion it should be acknowledged and mutually agreed to spend your future together and to make a *public* commitment, which means beginning to make *serious plans* to do one or a combination of the following:

- Become engaged
- Live together
- Get married

These plans should be based on the SMART system of goal-setting. Whatever age a woman may be, if she wants a long-term commitment this should be discussed *within the first year of the relationship*. When there hasn't been a discussion regarding overall commitment goals there is the potential for the relationship to just drift along. This can lead to frustration and feelings of frustration eventually cause drama!

SMART goals are:

- **Specific**
- **Measurable**
- **Achievable**
- **Realistic**
- **Timely**

For example, if the goal is to be a married woman the plan should be:

Specific – The goal is to be married.

Measurable – There is a timescale for certain events to happen so you can measure and see whether the plan is on track e.g. wedding invitations sent out, church booked, honeymoon destination selected and so forth.

Achievable – The goal to be married is attainable within an agreed budget.

Realistic – The wedding plans are realistic within a mutually agreed timeframe.

Timely – The date (deadline) when the wedding will happen.

Phase 4 Commitment Agreements: Lifetime Commitment

Similar to Phase 3, the timing of Phase 4 agreements can vary depending on a variety of factors. All previous levels of commitment should have been negotiated and agreed before you arrive at this stage. Any major issues that have the potential to sabotage the relationship should have been successfully resolved before considering this level of commitment. Both partners should have an unshakable belief their relationship can survive any adverse circumstances or major challenges. Sharing complete trust and belief in each other provides solid support that will enhance the relationship's ability toward positive growth. Each partner should also be very clear about what will constitute a "deal-breaker" for the other e.g. infidelity, physical or emotional abuse, and have deep respect for each other. For some people this level of commitment can feel full of obligations and responsibilities; if this depth of commitment feels too heavy or scary you're probably not ready for this step. Alternatively, there may be unresolved issues causing you concerns which are making you feel apprehensive. When embarking on this level of commitment both partners should be feeling highly optimistic and excited about continuing the relationship. A lifetime commitment provides the kind of union where each person can experience greater love and deeper intimacy.

Phase 4 Commitment Agreements

The ultimate commitment a couple can make to each other is a lifetime commitment. A serious relationship commitment can take various forms with some couples deciding to have a traditional wedding or civil ceremony. Whatever a couple decides, the ceremony normally represents a formal, legal and public declaration of the love shared between two people. If you want to get married set the date within 18 months of becoming engaged as research shows waiting any longer reduces the likelihood of marriage.

Both partners agree to:

- Protect, nurture and cherish the relationship
- A mutual agreement that any further commitments will be designed to enhance the relationship
- Committing to spending the rest of their lives together

Marriage is a commitment that should always be considered very carefully!

Are you ready to get married? If you're seriously thinking about making the ultimate relationship commitment, ask yourself:

- How do I feel about the institution of marriage?
- Why do I want to marry my partner?
- Do I feel as if I am married to my partner already?

Agreeing to get married should be a confirmation and a declaration of the love shared between two people. The decision to get married is agreed privately but is also a commitment made in public which legally (and religiously where relevant) confirms a couple's commitment to each other. If there is a lack of mutual love, understanding and respect before a marriage these essential qualities are not going to magically appear in the relationship after the wedding. Wedding rings and marriage certificates are merely symbols; these documents and objects cannot make a relationship work or hold two people together. Some couples get married believing it will make the relationship "better" or automatically heal and solve any serious inherent flaws within the partnership. Getting married hoping this will miraculously transform a strained or volatile relationship into a match made in heaven is very misguided. Relationships inevitably magnify each partner's unresolved issues and any major underlying tensions, flaws or instability eventually come to the surface. Rushing into a marriage hoping it will solve any existing problems within a relationship means you're signing up for heartache and disappointment. Never rush into a marriage and when you are ready set a time limit of at least six months engagement prior to the actual wedding. This gives you and your partner more time to consider and decide if getting married is really what you both want to do.

Wedding Finances And Marriage

Marriage is a legal and financial contract, as well as a social and/or spiritual union. Those who believe that love and money have nothing to do with each other are being naive. If you are unfortunate enough to go through a divorce you will discover the financial consequences can be very severe. Many married couples struggle financially early in the marriage due to exhausting their savings or taking on too much debt to pay for their wedding day. Money can't fix a hasty marriage entered into for the wrong reasons, but bad money habits can destroy the potential of enjoying a healthy one. Always be totally open and honest about your financial habits and history, including your credit reports, taxes, debts, assets, child/spousal support obligations/income, etc. Never hide money from your partner or use financial information as a weapon to punish or ridicule your mate's past financial mistakes. Avoid the common mistake of focusing on which partner may be bringing in the most income; concentrate on financial planning as a team, eliminating debt and increasing total household net worth. All income should be treated as partnership income regardless of who is the major income generator. Agree a budget, discuss it monthly and manage it together. Make financial decisions jointly, even if one or the other partner actually spends the money, handles savings, and pays the bills. Spending or withholding money to hurt or punish your partner will always cause resentment and unnecessary drama. Agree to set financial goals as a couple; placing individual wants above jointly agreed upon objectives is a mistake that can destroy a marriage.

The Way Forward

"A good marriage is different to a happy marriage." – Debra Winger, American Actress

Successful marriages require a constant reaffirming of the original commitment the couple made to each other when they took their vows. This means consistently sharing love, respect and joy and understanding successful marriages are built on a foundation of honest communication, trust and mutual respect.

A successful marriage requires certain ongoing agreements to maintain:

- A consistent mental, emotional and spiritual harmony within the union
- A constant process of mutual participation
- A constant process of renewal

Marriage is a mindset and if you enter a marriage with the wrong attitude it is probably doomed even before the vows have been exchanged. A genuine commitment to a marriage is reflected by how lovingly and consistently each partner treats the other. A couple may decide not to get married but choose to live together instead but this doesn't mean they're any less committed to each other. Each relationship model has distinct advantages and disadvantages which need to be considered carefully before deciding which approach suits the beliefs and aspirations of each partner.

Living Together

In the 21st century there is very little social stigma regarding couples living together. Divorce rates prove beyond any reasonable doubt marriage isn't for everyone. They also prove that being married doesn't guarantee a relationship is going to last "forever." Living together provides a personal lifestyle choice, represents a higher level of commitment and an excellent opportunity to explore the relationship further.

Advantages

- You may discover sides of your partner's personality you didn't know about.
- You are exposed to the best and the worst of your partner's personality traits.
- Living with someone requires compromises which you may not be prepared to make depending on the circumstances.
- When you live with someone you have to share control and power.
- Your partner may be great on a part time basis but you could discover you are not suitable or compatible living together.
- You may enjoy being in a relationship with your partner but discover you absolutely hate living with him.
- Living with a partner is the best way to discover if you share overall compatibility for a healthy relationship.

Living with your partner results in discovering aspects of his personality you may not have been aware of: the good, the bad and sometimes the ugly. None of us are perfect but there may be aspects of your partner's personal habits and behaviors that you may discover and find totally unacceptable. Whatever attracted you to your partner initially may not be enough to sustain the relationship once you experience living together. When you live with someone you discover if you share overall compatibility or whether this is limited to a few key areas. For example, decisions have to be taken regarding a variety of household issues such as finances which provide many important insights concerning how your partner handles sharing power, control and responsibility. Living together may also expose negative or toxic behaviors which are damaging and it's much better to find out about these types of issues as soon as possible, especially if marriage has been discussed. A healthy relationship requires both partners to be able to compromise and work in harmony while each retains and maintains their individual and unique personalities.

Couples who decide to live together are usually demonstrating a certain level of commitment to each other and may be willing to explore the possibility of being married if the arrangement works well. If you cannot live with your partner before marriage due to religious or other beliefs this may place you at significant disadvantage. The only way to find out if you can maintain a healthy relationship is by living together; cohabitating with a partner for a period of time before making a final decision to get married can be a very sensible strategy. If you're not sure if you want to get married, then review the situation again in six months before deciding to live with your partner; if you decide you *would* like to be married he needs to know as soon as possible! If you decide to live with your partner and want to get married make sure the wedding date is set within two years. If your partner doesn't want to get married within that time he doesn't want to get married full stop. It is always better to clarify his views on marriage before agreeing to live together if that is what you ultimately want.

Disadvantages

The reasons couples decide to live together can vary. Some people consciously decide to live together to rebel against the institution of marriage while other couples just "drift into" cohabiting. A lack of finances can influence the decision of some couples to live together as getting married can be very expensive; others may decide to live together as it appears to be the best available option but not really what one or both partners really wants for the relationship. The decision to live with a partner is usually quite exciting as this announces a new chapter in the relationship with two lives joining together. Living together announces privately and publicly an agreement to take the relationship to a serious level of commitment. While there is often great optimism this decision can also create a false sense of security; deciding to live together doesn't necessarily support the positive growth of a relationship, especially when the decision has been rushed into.

Many women assume living with their partner will automatically lead to marriage but research suggests living together for too long is less likely to result in a stable, committed relationship regardless of age or income. Cohabiting relationships can be fragile and pose an increased risk of failure when compared *to* marriages; and when these couples decide to get married, the longer they have lived together prior to the wedding the higher the risk of divorce.

Studies have indicated:

- Living together for a long time can inhibit a further commitment towards marriage – potentially a major source of conflict if a woman wants to be married.
- Men and women who live together are more likely to be unfaithful than couples who are married.
- Partners who cohabitate tend to have more health problems than married couples because those who cohabit tend to tolerate more negative behaviors such as smoking, alcohol and substance abuse.
- Partners who live together are more likely to suffer from periods of depression.
- Unmarried women who live with their partners are often at a higher risk of domestic violence.

A 2012 study titled *Re-examining the Case for Marriage: Union Formation and Changes in Well-Being*, led by Kelly Musick, associate professor of policy analysis and management at Cornell's College of Human Ecology, found married couples enjoyed relatively few advantages compared to partners living together. Musick and co-author sociologist Larry Bumpass tracked almost 3,000 single men and women to discover when each person began a relationship or married. Over the 20-year period almost 900 participants married or started a romantic relationship with a partner. They were asked to assess their overall health including self-esteem, any issues with depression, and the strength of their social ties with family and close friends. Generally the researchers found marriage and cohabitation both increased overall wellbeing. They also found those who began living with a romantic partner experienced higher levels of happiness and lower levels of stress and depression compared to participants who remained single. Participants who were married reported greater health benefits than those who cohabited together but whether married or living together, this led to reduced contact with family and friends over an extended period of time when compared to being single.

The study noted that in recent years the number of people opting for cohabitation before or instead of marriage has increased significantly with cohabiting partners tending to be happier while experiencing greater self-esteem. The researchers found for some individuals living together can mean less commitment, avoiding unwanted obligations plus more

221

flexibility, independence and personal growth. Musick and Bumpass said marriage has been considered an important social institution for many decades but concluded that while the experiences of married and cohabiting couples had become increasingly similar, being married may still attract greater social status in Western countries.

There are millions of happy cohabiting couples who are fully committed to their relationships and raising healthy, well-adjusted children. Provided both partners are happy with the arrangement there isn't any need to conform to the opinions of others; deciding to live together is fundamentally a lifestyle choice. Whether you're living together or married you need to have mutual integrity, honesty, willingness and openness in order to build and sustain a successful relationship.

CHAPTER 22:
Compatibility Hazards

"What counts in making a happy marriage is not so much how compatible you are but how you deal with incompatibility." – Leo Tolstoy (1828-1910), Russian Novelist, Essayist, Playwright & Philosopher

Understanding Compatibility

When you begin to date someone new there is usually an exchange of experiences and opinions which can provide important clues regarding compatibility. You begin to assess whether he likes the same things and shares the same views on certain topics. You will find similarities and differences but these differences do not necessarily indicate pursuing the relationship is a waste of time. Every couple experiences disagreements but the key to resolving differences is to seek a solution both partners can accept. If there is an inability to compromise compatibility issues can begin to surface leading to major conflicts.

Two people can have different tastes, styles and world views yet still enjoy a successful relationship. Often each person finds the stark differences in their partner intriguing; they appreciate the different personality traits and often stay together because they complement each other. For example, a normally shy person feeds off their more gregarious partner and vice versa so each partner find aspects they are missing within themselves in the other person, which makes the relationship mutually supportive and helps it to thrive. The key to success with this type of relationship is each partner respecting the views and opinions of the other. It usually takes several dates before discovering if you have met someone who is really compatible with you so take your time instead of committing to a relationship too quickly. While unresolved emotional problems can cause you to create difficult and unhealthy relationships, becoming romantically involved with a man who has a compatibility hazard can present huge challenges that may be impossible to resolve. These hazards are not usually obvious and may be dismissed or ignored at the beginning but eventually surface after the relationship has been established.

The Long Distance Relationship

"Distance makes the heart grow fonder." – Thomas Haynes Bayly (1797-1839), English Poet, Songwriter & Dramatist

Many relationships have begun this way and succeeded but there can be a variety of potential hazards. Long distance relationships can be romantic and exciting as you countdown to the next meeting and this encourages couples to indulge in fantasies about meeting each other again. The distance also creates the illusion of a relationship, which may not be as promising as it appears on the surface and allows each partner to avoid certain realities.

This is how it works: when your partner is not readily available, both of you are probably filled with emotion and desire which encourages you both to fantasize about the next meeting. Waiting to hear his voice on the phone makes the calls between each meeting exciting and passionate. The time together will always be limited so this usually increases the longing for the next meeting and intensifies the sexual desire. The limited time together places an emphasis on having a good time (and great sex) and it's all very intense and great fun while the goodbyes are usually sad and emotional. The romance and distance easily entices many couples into a dramatic fantasy where the focus is on the next meeting and seeing your lover again. This type of relationship can be highly romantic but is also a high risk strategy as the separation can encourage a great deal of unrealistic expectations and love myths to be played out mentally by one or both partners.

The long distance relationship can also create a distraction from asking yourself the really important questions such as what is this guy *really* like as a person. Spending short periods of time together you always try your best hoping to encourage the relationship to grow. Each person is usually on their best behavior, which creates an artificial interaction that results in only the positive aspects of each personality being revealed. Of course you want to believe you know all about your partner; the relationship is bursting with potential and promise but the reality is you won't really know anything substantial about him.

If a decision is made to move closer to each other or even to live together, aspects of his true character may be gradually revealed. When you begin to spend decent amounts of time together you may suddenly discover behaviors, habits and attitudes that are extremely irritating, annoying or frustrating, which can lead to serious disagreements.

You may discover things about him that cause great concern or are simply unacceptable; by this time you may be in over your head emotionally before realizing that the relationship has major compatibility issues. A lack of spending consistent time with a partner delays discovering his true personality and it is very difficult to know how someone reacts under normal circumstances or under pressure when you don't really know him. The lack of time spent together can often delay the discovery of possible compatibility issues, some of which may be impossible to resolve. A "match made in heaven" can swiftly transform into the relationship from hell.

▌ Reality Check!

"Maintaining a long-distance relationship requires a lot of discipline. The loneliness that they experience is a formidable force to be reckoned with, and not everyone can withstand it. A physical entity is always more powerful than a voice distorted by static, more so when they encounter problems and want to share them with their partner in real time. In such cases, they usually turn to a third party, and that's when the relationships fall apart like a house of cards." – Alexis Lawrence, Author of *O.U.R. Café.*

Various studies have shown that long distance partners tend to excessively idealize each other or view each other in unrealistically positive terms. It's usually much easier to hold on to an idealized view of a partner when you're not with them for significant amounts of time. At the beginning a long distance relationship might feel great and they can be a lot of fun but despite the initial excitement and euphoria, these relationships often have a tendency of becoming little more than sexual arrangements or Friend With Benefits agreements.

The only way to discover if the relationship has a viable future is for each person to be authentic and true to themselves while pursuing normal activities together. You have to be honest at all times and avoid suppressing certain aspects of your personality instead of just enjoying the positive elements of a long distance relationship. Effective and honest communication is the key to dealing with any conflicts as they happen. An important element in any relationship is the *intentions* of both partners: if you're being strung along for convenient sex obviously it's better to find out sooner rather than later. A long distance relationship doesn't mean it has to be a part time romance or love affair but you have to be realistic and avoid getting caught up in a romantic fantasy.

There are no shortcuts to getting to know someone properly. The key to building a solid foundation for any relationship is to spend consistent, quality time with your partner. Think very carefully before embarking on a long distance relationship and pay attention to the potential pitfalls if you decide to get involved. There are inherent constraints that restrict the natural growth and development of a long distance relationship because these types of relationships are by definition limited. This type of relationship isn't doomed to fail; there have been many successful partnerships that began as long distant liaisons.

Commitment Phobics And Long Distance Relationships

There was a period of several years when I was a classic Commitment Phobic and preferred long distance relationships as they allowed me to:

- Maintain distance and keep my own emotional "space"
- Enjoy sex without making a firm commitment as I didn't want a serious relationship
- Enjoy the best of both worlds: I had a "relationship" but also had my space
- Indulge in fantasies of romantic love without feeling pressured
- Only see my partner when I wanted to
- Freedom to see other women so I could keep my "options" open
- End the relationship without too much hassle as I was not deeply involved emotionally

For a Commitment Phobic man, the long distance relationship meets two very important requirements; due to the distance he feels less threatened and there is always the option to end it if the woman begins to expect or demand more.

Men with commitment conflicts can be very attentive, highly seductive and romantic but this is often motivated by the fact that any real potential for a genuine relationship is limited. The distance provides a built-in "buffer zone" that allows either partner to indulge deeply in thoughts and feelings of romantic fantasy.

Already Involved

When a woman is just looking for some fun and good sex a long distance relationship can be the perfect arrangement but if you want a serious relationship it can be a very high-risk strategy. This is especially true when you're unclear about your partner's intentions regarding taking the relationship forward. There are women who have drifted along for years in these types of relationships believing they have invested too much time to walk away and yet feeling desperately unhappy as their partner will not make a commitment.

Being involved in this type of scenario can excessively prolong the honeymoon period if it is not managed properly. This is caused by a failure to set specific relationship goals. If your partner is not interested in spending quality time with you and avoids genuine intimacy, love and commitment it's time to face facts. End it and look for a partner who is emotionally, mentally and physically available and wants a genuine, committed relationship. A long distance relationship can waste a great deal of your time, energy and love if you get caught up in a romantic fantasy. If you're in this type of relationship and decide to spend serious time together be prepared for a period of transition and learning.

Different Ethnic Or Cultural Backgrounds

"When people rely on surface appearances and false racial stereotypes, rather than in-depth knowledge of others at the level of the heart, mind and spirit, their ability to assess and understand people accurately is compromised." – James A. Forbes, Christian Author

Multicultural communities are established and widely accepted in many Western countries with various races or cultures working and living together in urban areas. In many of these cities where there are large amounts of people from different ethnic, social and financial backgrounds, it is no longer unusual to see people of different races in relationships and going about their daily lives, with interracial relationships being the highest in Britain. According to the UK National Census published in 2012 there were more couples involved in interracial relationships than in any other country in Europe with bi-racial or mixed raced individuals representing the largest ethnic group. While interracial relationships are more widely accepted than ever before dating outside your own race can still be problematical. When a couple decides to have an intimate relationship across the racial divide there is the potential for various dilemmas and complexities to be dealt with.

Interracial Relationships In America

In America the Pew Research Center Report of 2008 used the US Census Bureau 2008 American Community Survey to produce a study which found:

- A record 14.6 percent of all new marriages in the United States in 2008 were between spouses of a different race or ethnicity from one another.
- Of all the newlyweds who got married in America during 2008, 9 percent of whites, 16 percent of blacks, and 31 percent of Asians, married someone whose race or ethnicity was different from their own.
- 22 percent of all black men who became married in 2008 married outside their race.

- 9 percent of black female newlyweds married outside their race.
- 40 percent of Asian female newlyweds married outside their race.
- 20 percent of Asian male newlyweds married outside their race.
- Interracial marriages more than doubled in America between 1980 (6.7 percent) and 2008 (14.6 percent).

It is important to note interracial relationships and marriages are not necessarily intercultural and different races can share the same cultural perspectives and background. Despite great progress being made over the last several decades racism still exists while discussions regarding issues of racial or cultural beliefs can make some people feel very uncomfortable or even defensive.

Marital Instability Among Interracial Couples

A study published by the Education Resources Information Center and led by Jenifer L. Bratter and Rosalind B. King in 2008 examined whether interracial relationships were more likely to end in divorce. They used the 2002 National Survey of Family Growth (Cycle VI) and compared the likelihood of divorce for interracial couples to that of same-race couples. The study found interracial couples have higher rates of divorce; this was especially prevalent for interracial couples who married during the late 1980s. The study concluded that black male/white female and white female/Asian male marriages were more likely to end in divorce than white married couples. The study also found marriages between white males/ non-white females and between Hispanics/non-Hispanic persons had a similar or lower risk of ending in divorce than white/white marriages.

Different Communication Styles

Individuals are often unaware of how their culture influences their opinions and behaviors or make negative assumptions about different cultures. For example, communication styles vary widely within and across different cultures meaning certain words or phrases are used in different ways. Body language such as facial expressions and gestures or different degrees of assertiveness can also cause cultural misunderstandings. For example, some White Americans typically consider raised voices as a sign of trouble or a fight, while some Black, Jewish or Italian American people often consider loud voices as a sign of friends merely having a lively conversation. While some White Americans may become alarmed by a loud discussion, individuals from a different cultural or ethnic racial group could easily interpret raised voices as being quite normal. It is possible for different cultural communication styles to cause misunderstandings and problems within interracial relationships.

Different Decision Making Styles

The roles men and women expect to play in any decision-making process can vary widely according to their culture. An individual's expectations about their roles in influencing decisions may be motivated by their cultural frame of reference.

Different Attitudes Toward Disclosure

There are different cultural attitudes towards disclosure of events in relationships, too. In some cultures it is not considered acceptable or appropriate to be open regarding emotions, for example revealing the possible reasons behind a disagreement or conflict, a misunderstanding, seeking or revealing private thoughts or personal information. Individuals from cultures other than European can be reluctant to reveal their inner most thoughts so asking questions that may seem quite normal to some can be considered intrusive to another.

Different Attitudes Toward Conflicts

Certain cultures view conflict as a positive while others consider it something to be avoided. In European culture face-to-face meetings are often recommended to work through issues while in many Eastern countries, open conflict can be seen as embarrassing or demeaning. A different approach that deals with disagreements quietly is often preferred.

Different Approaches In Completing Tasks

When two people are working together on a task, their respective cultures may have differences regarding how the goal should be accomplished. An alternative approach doesn't mean a partner from a different cultural background is more or less committed to achieving the task or doesn't value the relationship, but it does mean he or she may approach the matter influenced by their cultural background. For example, in group situations, Asian and Hispanic cultures tend to attach more value to developing relationships at the beginning of a shared project with more emphasis on task completion towards the end. European-Americans tend to focus immediately on the task at hand, and let relationships develop as they work towards completing the task at hand.

Different Approaches To Learning Or Knowing

European cultures tend to prefer gathering information by cognitive methods, such as counting and measuring and usually consider these means to be more valid than other ways of learning. African cultures tend to have a preference for affective ways of knowing such as rhythm and symbolic imagery. There are differences among cultural groups regarding how an individual learns new ideas or concepts, or researching how to resolve a problem. Some may want to do internet or library research to identify possible solutions or understand a problem while others may prefer to talk to people who have experienced similar challenges.

External Pressures

External factors may cause problems, pressure and disagreements; different cultural views can result in different moral, ethical and value perspectives as to what is considered acceptable regarding individual, family and societal expectations. Couples in interracial relationships and marriages often have to deal with issues partners of the same the race are not exposed to. Major factors which can impact on interracial relationships is the attitudes of the couples' respective family, friends and the wider community. Families and friends can be hostile, resistant or even refuse to accept someone due to their race. Many black men have shared their experiences with me describing the hostility not only from white people but also their own families or friends who dislike the fact they're in relationships with a white woman.

Potential Problems With Family Or Friends

- Your immediate family or friends may be strongly opposed to the relationship or let you know quietly they disapprove of you being involved with a man from another race or culture.
- His immediate family and friends may not accept you or the relationship; they may consider you as unsuitable and unacceptable.
- Your family and friends or his family and friends may be concerned about the possibility of there being mixed race/bi-racial children.

The issue of racism from external sources has been widely reported as causing conflict within inter-racial relationships. Great pressure can be brought to bear by family or friends who may threaten to snub or actually exclude you from their lives. According to a variety of research studies many interracial couples have also reported disagreements regarding how their children are raised or which religion they should adopt. Children of mixed racial parentage may also face challenges such as establishing a clear cultural identity or perspective. Young adults who are bi-racial in the 21st century appear to be generally proud of their dual heritage but for some there can be a tendency to over-compensate one side of their racial identity. For example, adopting an extremely White persona or deeply embracing Black culture by becoming Dreads, Rastafarians or being extremely militant concerning Black issues.

"In 1967, only 4% of Americans approved of interracial marriage, yet the Supreme Court dismissed the desire of 96% of Americans who did not support it in order to preserve the rights of the minority." – Kathy Baldock, *Walking the Bridgeless Canyon: Repairing the Breach Between the Church and the LGBT Community*

Individuals from a variety of races claim to be "color blind" and to embrace Martin Luther King's philosophy of judging a person by "the content of the character and not the color of their skin." The real truth about an individual's personal beliefs are not revealed by making politically correct or socially acceptable statements but when they're challenged with the reality of their child, family member or close friend embarking on a relationship with someone from a different race. We can all benefit from examining our personal beliefs, philosophies and values occasionally but this should be motivated by a desire for personal growth, not by pursuing a relationship that feels different or exciting while having serious reservations. Ethnic and cultural backgrounds can greatly influence education opportunities, life experiences, beliefs and value systems. Personal beliefs, perspectives and values greatly influence:

- Religious and spiritual views
- Political views
- Health habits
- Levels of self-esteem
- Personal goals (and how you choose them)
- Ethics
- Life expectations

- How your children are raised
- How you treat others
- How you treat yourself
- Attitude to those who are less fortunate
- How and where you spend your money

The quality of the basic connections and similarities between two people impacts on the prospects for any potential relationship. This dimension of each relationship covers many aspects including social skills, communication style, intellectual compatibility and interpersonal styles of relating. Important issues associated with family background are holiday customs, family rules, finances, domestic responsibilities, and raising children. A relationship where a couple has vastly different beliefs, perspectives and values will often produce very different expectations. Like all couples, partners don't have to agree on everything or to have been through similar experiences, but where there are significant differences this increases the potential for tensions, disagreements and conflicts.

Cultural and racial differences may cause various compatibility issues. If you're involved in an interracial relationship or with a man from a different culture it's important to try and see the world from his perspective. Ask yourself how your partner's culture may be shaping his attitudes and behaviors but remember there is a big difference between reasonable compromises and suppressing or ignoring your personal values and beliefs. Trying too hard while constantly capitulating to keep the peace will inevitably lead to feelings of resentment and bitterness. Practicing sensible compromises and respect is the only way to prevent tensions and conflicts escalating to the point where the relationship tears itself apart.

Make sure you're not motivated by parental rebellion and choosing to date men who are the complete opposite of what your parents or family expect. People engaged in these types of relationships are often angry with their parents or attempting to define themselves as a way to establish a sense of independence. Deciding to date men exclusively within your own race is a personal decision or you may choose to provide "equal opportunities" for any man you find attractive. Choosing a partner from a different ethnic or cultural background is a personal choice but you should be very clear regarding your motivation. The relationship can be based on the allure of being with someone completely different in so many ways. Seeing a man from a different racial background may feel very exciting, liberating, edgy or even exotic and you may be intrigued by his accent, cultural differences or other factors. This can feel highly stimulating during the early stages but if you know deep down there is a certain point you can't go beyond in dating a man from another race you're being emotionally dishonest. Convincing yourself you are happy when you have serious doubts is a dangerous form of denial as any repressed feelings will come to the surface eventually.

- If you suspect the attraction is based on trying to prove a point take some time out to consider the implications of pursuing the relationship. It's much better to concede your principles may not be as pure and uncompromising as you would like to believe before the relationship becomes too serious. You may not approve of your own judgments about other races, but it's very important to accept those views and to be honest with yourself.
- If you feel unsure about your long-term preferences regarding a partner's race don't judge yourself harshly.

- If you decide your preference is to be with a man of the same race or from a similar culture or social class as your own, this is nothing to be ashamed of.

Trying to accept a partner from a different race when you're uncomfortable with the idea will only cause conflict when the relationship is established. Discovering you have concerns about his race will probably leave him feeling hurt, bitter and probably angry when your true feelings emerge.

White Men, Interracial Relationships And The Plantation Mindset

I have been employed by a Local Government department for sixteen years during which time I became a trade union representative. There was a White senior manager whose ex-wife was Black and he had a history of only having relationships with Black women he met in the workplace. This man always loudly proclaimed he could not be a racist as he was only attracted to Black women and had mixed race children from his failed marriage. Yet when I attended disciplinary proceedings representing Black members of staff, I observed the decisions he took were always supportive of his White colleagues even when they were clearly in the wrong. This manager was particularly consistent at unfairly targeting and punishing male Black members of staff while protesting when challenged that he could not possibly be motivated by racism.

These types of White men believe in the plantation system used during the years of slavery where Black men were forced to be subjugated and "know their place" while the women were used as sexual objects to be used and abused. I am not opposed to interracial relationships but in my experience Black women and women of color should exercise caution regarding becoming involved with a White man until they're confident he is genuine when it comes to matters of race. The White man with the plantation mindset desires and accepts a Black woman as his partner but will often be suspicious or even hostile towards her Black male friends or members of her extended family. Strong-minded and intelligent Black men can be seen as a threat even to White men who may claim to have very liberal views. The reality for Black people and other races living in Western societies is while overt racism is generally rejected and not considered to be "politically correct" covert racism is very alive and in some areas thriving. The plantation mindset exists in the 21st century and it is extremely naive for a Black woman or women of color looking for love to assume otherwise.

Black Women And The "Shortage" Of Eligible Black Men

For Black women in the dating game there can be additional challenges to navigate which can result in deep feelings of frustration. Law professor Ralph Richard Banks' book *Is Marriage for White People? How the African American Marriage Decline Affects Everyone*, published in 2011, explores the apparent "man shortage" among the Black middle-class community. Banks claims some Black women feel bitter as they cannot find a decent Black man to marry and his views have caused controversy regarding the stereotyping of Black females. The phrase "marriage squeeze" refers to the social phenomenon and perceived "plight" of some Black American females who believe the most eligible and desirable Black men are marrying outside their race. These women believe high caliber Black men are deserting their race leaving very limited choices for Black women who would prefer to settle down with a decent Black man. This is a very common complaint I have heard expressed by Black women in various relationship debates, seminars and online forums.

Several sociologists have stated that the desire for Black women to marry within their race may be motivated by racial loyalty while White men may be reluctant to become involved with a Black woman due to the possibility of being shunned socially. This has been quite common for White male/Black female couples in the past but there has been changes in attitudes over the last several decades. According the 2011 UK Census approximately 50 percent of Black men are likely to date or marry women from a different ethnic background. I don't think there is one specific reason why Black men become involved with interracial relationships. I have several Black male friends who either married outside their race or who exclusively date women from other races. My conclusion is, like most people, these men are mainly attracted to women they like and for them a woman's race is inconsequential although it should be noted there are Black men who will consciously or subconsciously date or marry outside their race seeking to escape their feelings of racial inferiority.

Reality Check!

"Some white people hate black people, and some white people love black people, some black people hate white people, and some black people love white people. So you see it's not an issue of Black and White, it's an issue of Lovers and Haters." – Eden Ahbez (1908-1995), American Musician

A couple may have different ethnic or cultural backgrounds and quite different life experiences, but this doesn't necessarily mean the relationship is doomed to fail. It could be argued they often require more love, compromise and flexibility to succeed but there have been many successful inter-racial relationships and marriages. Differences in ethnic or cultural backgrounds can certainly enrich each partner's life when they embrace certain aspects of their respective cultures. The only sensible strategy for embarking on *any* relationship is to ask questions to discover the values and beliefs of a potential partner during the dating phase. Despite feelings of mutual attraction your potential partner's culture, habits and life-style may differ so greatly from your own that those differences could be insurmountable. It is important to know how you really feel about being involved long-term with a man from a different race. If you have any doubts it's much better all round to be honest with yourself and others sooner rather than later. If you decide to become involved with a man from another race make sure your approach is pragmatic as well as romantic and be realistic about the possible challenges ahead. The inherent compatibility hazards may not be apparent until you have begun to develop feelings for your partner or fallen deeply in love.

There are times when opposites attract but sharing similar values, interests and beliefs will usually provide a better chance of building a successful partnership. Sharing mutual cultural reference points such as beliefs, tastes and lifestyles supports natural cohesion and effortless familiarity. Generally, there are fewer areas of potential conflict and sharing similar values provides a strong foundation for a healthy relationship.

Differences In Religious And Spiritual Beliefs

"Responsibility and respect of others and their religious beliefs are also part of freedom."
– Horst Koehler, German Statesman

Individuals who hold deep religious beliefs are usually taught a particular religion during childhood. Religious indoctrination at a very young age is often powerful and provides the foundation for adult belief systems and values that shape a particular world view. A child who has been brought up in a religious home is unlikely to abandon their faith during adulthood and can be very resistant to even considering alternative concepts about life, death and spirituality. Having deeply held religious beliefs is an important part of life for many people and shapes their perspectives. Religious beliefs are not usually discussed during the dating phase as couples are often too busy having a good time getting to know each other but conflicting beliefs regarding religion and spirituality can cause unexpected compatibility hazards with disagreements causing tremendous resentment and frustration.

It can be beneficial to explore your beliefs regarding religion and spirituality providing this is something you're not pressured into but a personal choice to explore another aspect of human existence. It is important not to allow another person to control your views; failing to take the time to consider and define your own personal beliefs may leave you susceptible to being influenced by someone else's. Allowing another person to strongly influence your beliefs means giving someone else permission to define your perspective. For example, if you become involved with a man who holds strong opinions regarding his religion, you may accept his views during the early stages of the relationship but then decide to explore your own religious or spiritual "truth." Each individual has the absolute human right to decide what they believe for themselves but choosing a different belief system than your partner will often cause major disagreements.

Exploring Religion And Spirituality

We live in a diverse world where many different beliefs compete to be heard or to dominate. There are people who don't believe in any type of spirituality, religion or the paranormal or existence of God and others who believe in various spirits, angels, astrology, numerology, alternative dimensions or paranormal activity. There are others who believe in their personal interpretation of God but who are not involved with any type of religious organization; they rarely attend a church, mosque or synagogue but have a flexible approach within their belief system. A person may choose to demonstrate their beliefs and values through their behavior and attitudes instead of being a slave to religious rules and doctrines. You may decide religious or spiritual practice doesn't interest you and it's absolutely your personal right to make that choice.

In the dating game it is always sensible to discover a potential partner's views on religion, spirituality and children. The majority of men and women have clear opinions regarding how children should be raised and when a relationship becomes serious the possibility of marriage and children will probably be discussed.

Suggested Questions

- Does he believe parents have the right to indoctrinate their children with a particular religion and to limit a child's horizons of knowledge?
- Do parents have the right to bring up their children in an atmosphere of strict religious dogma?
- Should parents have the right to insist their children strictly follow their faith?
- If a child grows up and rebels or abandons the faith, should the parents and religious community reject their son or daughter?

When a person has strong religious or spiritual beliefs this will be a great influence on their views regarding how their children should be raised. If there is significant difference in religious or spiritual beliefs this can result in very serious disagreements when the relationship has already been established. If you hope to have children it is vital to share your personal views and expectations regarding how they will be raised concerning their religious or spiritual beliefs.

Finding out what a potential partner's religious or spiritual beliefs are may not seem like a big deal during the dating phase but this issue can cause major problems. The simple way to avoid this potential compatibility hazard is to raise the subject during the early stages of dating someone new. Discovering the religious and spiritual beliefs of a man you're dating is important so make it a rule to ask questions about his and be open and honest about your own. There are some people who will try to avoid discussing religious or spiritual issues when they are dating or early in the relationship to prevent any possible conflicts. Alternatively, they may evade the subject in an attempt to create the illusion there is more compatibility than actually exists. These matters can be discussed generally and his responses will provide valuable clues as to whether there could be any potential conflicts. Don't assume raising the topic of religious or spiritual beliefs will lead a man to think you're too serious or are trying to pressure him into making a commitment. Any reluctance or delay discussing the subject can lead to major problems; hiding or avoiding the truth regarding your spiritual beliefs can be a major mistake if significant differences are discovered later on. The relationship could be doomed no matter how much love a couple may share resulting in a very distressing and painful experience.

Already Involved

"God has no religion." – Mahatma Gandhi (1869-1948), Leader of Indian Independence Movement

The question, "Can a couple with different religious backgrounds work?" comes up quite regularly in my relationship forums. It's obvious if you're a hardcore atheist and become involved with a man who is deeply religious there will be major disagreements. These conflicts have the potential to tear the partnership apart as a couple experiences deep conflicts regarding different belief systems, traditions and attitudes. What you believe about God, how you pray, which holidays you celebrate and which books you believe to be sacred are just a few of the components that will support your spiritual belief system. Religion or spirituality and how this is expressed represents an important part of life for many people and you may find yourself struggling to connect with your partner. Attempting to resolve this compatibility hazard without support can be difficult and a great deal of commitment and compromise may be required. A flexible attitude by both partners will be required to avoid serious conflicts even if the differences are not very severe. A couple in these circumstances may discover areas of compatible beliefs and compromise may be possible even where there are different belief systems. A compromise may be possible if there is a mutual belief in "God" even though there is a difference of opinion concerning who or what "God" is. A relationship can work where a person isn't a strict follower of a particular religion but does have a belief in "God", a Higher Power or follows a particular spiritual practice while their partner may have a strong religious faith. A couple committed to the relationship can conduct research regarding mixed denomination partnerships or seek advice and support from their respective religious spiritual advisors or support groups. Interfaith relationships and marriages can succeed when there is willingness to compromise and a tolerance for different religious and belief systems.

▌Reality Check!

"You are here to evolve and make your consciousness high. You are here to dance, sing and celebrate life. You are here to help others to make their life happy. We are here not to compete, but to learn, evolve and excel. We are not here to make divisions in the name of prophets and religions. We are here to encompass the world with love and light." – Amit Ray, *Nonviolence: The Transforming Power*

The reality is a person with deep religious beliefs is likely to be intransigent if a workable compromise cannot be achieved, and if so the relationship simply isn't viable. Leaving a relationship due to this compatibility hazard is a small price to pay for your emotional, mental and spiritual freedom along with your peace of mind. Never allow a partner to pressure you into following a particular religion or belief; it's very important to follow your own conscience, inner guidance and personal path wherever it may take you.

Significant Difference In Age

"The fact of the matter is that young men lack skill and experience and are very likely to approach a girl as though she were a sack of wheat. It is the old man—suave, debonair, maturely charming—who knows exactly what to do and how to do it, and is therefore better at it." – Isaac Asimov, *The Sensuous Dirty Old Man*

Whether you are single or not right now, it's quite possible you may become involved with a man who is significantly older or younger during your lifetime. Attitudes regarding relationships and significant age differences often change as we get older; an age difference of five years probably seems huge during our teenage years but by our mid-twenties doesn't seem like such a big deal. It is socially acceptable for a 17-year-old girl to have a boyfriend who is several years older or for a man in his forties or fifties to marry a woman who is considerably younger. Studies across all cultures and nations have shown a consistent trend for men to seek and have younger partners which can be an uncomfortable reality for a woman over the age of 45 who is looking for a new partner. Men of a similar age usually have a certain criteria and will often consider a younger age range although it could be argued women who are aged 40 and older are probably more sexually mature than younger females. A survey during 2012 found eight out of 10 women over 50 believed they were not considered seriously for any kind of relationship by men of a comparable age. Research by dating website *Match.com* revealed being a divorced mature woman in the dating game can be complicated, causing great anxiety especially if she is a single parent. Trying to meet men in bars and clubs can feel like a young person's game where mature women often feel they're competing to meet a potential partner. Men using traditional dating websites often refuse to consider mature women of a comparable age preferring to seek out younger females instead.

This can affect women above a certain age where they may become:

- Desperate, believing time is running out to find love
- Prone to falling in love too quickly if they meet someone new
- Overly cautious or cynical about relationships
- Crushed, suffering from low self-esteem and so decide to give up on finding love again

However, a growing number of mature women are redefining their criteria of what constitutes an acceptable man, which is influencing the type of relationship choices they make. In the past a woman could rarely support herself so looked for a man to be the provider which often meant choosing a man who was older, financially established or advanced in his career and so capable of supporting a wife and any children. More women than ever before are now financially independent and making very different choices compared to previous generations. There are greater numbers of dynamic and intelligent women employed in high-powered positions or running their own businesses, earning their own money and enjoying greater independence. There has been a tremendous shift in attitudes over the last several decades with women enjoying much greater freedom to choose who they become romantically involved with. A divorced woman with children isn't necessarily looking for a new husband and may seriously consider the option of dating a younger man. Author and sex therapist Jacqueline Hellyer believes the increase of female economic power is an essential factor in this shift of attitude. With many also deciding to delay having children and higher divorce rates there has been a steady change in the expectations of women living in Western societies. According to certain studies women choosing partners who are ten years younger or more has risen by 25 percent. The fact is women and men are fitter and living longer and with the average age of divorce rising (41 for women and 43 for men) there are more confident and experienced women at their sexual peak who are looking for love.

The Rise Of The Cougar

"When it comes to age, it's all about the quality of the preservation," – Donna McDonald, *Dating a Cougar*

In the past men have often been admired and praised for having a much younger partner while mature women who prefer younger men have often attracted disapproval or even open hostility. It's clear an increasing number of mature women are dating younger men and these women are often referred to as "Cougars" after the predatory puma or "big cat" of the same name. An early example of a Cougar was portrayed in the groundbreaking movie *The Graduate (1967)* in which the middle-aged Mrs. Robinson seduces her daughter's boyfriend, Benjamin Braddock.

236

There are a variety of definitions and perceptions regarding what qualifies a woman as being a Cougar. They include the following:

- Primarily attracted to and has sex with men who are significantly younger.

- A mature woman who is sexually experienced.

- An older or more mature woman who frequents clubs, venues, bars, beaches, etc. to seek out younger men for sex or a relationship.

- Aged 35 plus who "hunts" for much younger and energetic males and who looks after herself and probably does not look her true age.

- Attractive woman in her 30's or 40's who is looking for a relationship or casual sex now she is single and available. If she is just interested in sex she will be direct about what she wants.

- Mature woman in her sexual prime who prefers to be the "hunter" rather than be the "prey." She enjoys role reversal and often seeks partners who are usually under the age of 25.

- A woman aged between 30 and 50 years old who enjoys the sexual adventures of younger men.

- A mature woman who dislikes being in a committed relationships or could even be Commitment Phobic/Love Avoidant, who has multiple sleeping partners; usually interested in men under the age of 25.

- Mature women who sleep with different men within the same group of friends or acquaintances.

- Attractive women aged between 40 and 50 tired of men in the same age range because they have let themselves go physically or they find them boring. They know what they want and are not shy or afraid to go after it.

- A woman considered to be mutton dressed up as lamb.

- A woman with class and sex appeal.

The most generally accepted definition of a Cougar is a woman who is 40 or older who only pursues men who are significantly younger. Others believe a woman can be considered a Cougar at 35 years old, but at this age her partners or sexual conquests would have to be 25 or younger.

There is very little stigma attached to a woman being the significantly older partner in the 21st century with an increasing number of famous women with younger partners including Demi Moore, Joan Collins, Susan Sarandon and Naomi Watts. These and other high profile examples give older women the confidence to explore relationships with significantly younger men who are also interested in becoming involved with a Cougar. During 2007 Julia Macmillan set up the successful toyboywarehouse.com dating website and claims younger men are keen to meet older women, with 70 percent of the members being male. Men and women of any age can join but can only search for potential partners who are women at least one year older. Macmillan believes these and other assumptions or myths can hold many women back from pursuing a relationship with a man who may be significantly younger. She states her mission is to help mature women find love by doing what many men do and her website is a sexy, fun, intelligent dating community. Macmillan claims the most successful age gap relationships are between 10 to 15 years difference with many successful matches being made on her website.

Cougar critics claim there are risks for older women becoming involved with significantly younger men including the following:

- A younger man may be looking for sex with an older woman to fulfill his sexual fantasies rather than seeking a serious, committed relationship.
- Young men may prey on older women seeing them as desperate and willing to put up with poor treatment just to have a man in their life.
- Men may have a tendency to see an older woman as a sex teacher but not serious long-term partner.
- A younger man may be motivated by money wanting to be looked after financially.
- He may operate as a Gigolo with several women supporting him.
- A younger man may be actively seeking out "Sugar Mommas" intending to scam as many women as possible out of their money.

Cougar critics also claim some women receive a huge Ego boost by proving they are still attractive to younger men who are still in their sexual prime, while others disapprove believing an older woman shouldn't seek to be with a younger man. There are urban myths which claim Cougars typically prey on younger men who are almost young enough to be their sons, so a woman who is 40 or older would generally pursue or be attracted to men in their 20s, while women in their fifties would "prey" on men in their 30s. Other critics accuse Cougars of being predators who are more interested in sexual conquests and not concerned about securing a stable relationship.

However, Cougars do enjoy two advantages:

- They have more freedom to decide to become involved with a younger man who makes them feel good and compliments them instead of seeking a partner to provide security or support their lifestyles.
- A mature woman seeking a younger partner for a committed relationship is usually more interested in his character than what he does for a living or his financial status.

Not every woman who is in a relationship with a younger man planned it that way. Through a variety of circumstances some women become accidental Cougars who are surprised to find themselves involved with a younger man. There is absolutely nothing wrong with having a relationship with a man who may be younger if it feels right and makes you happy. However, whether a woman falls into the "official" Cougar age range or not, it's important to understand there can be serious compatibility hazards when there is a significant age gap between couples.

Older Partner In Relationship

Impatience

When there is a significant age difference both partners are experiencing two very different phases of life so may have very diverse perspectives according to their levels of experience. The older partner can struggle with the younger person's lack of maturity or life experience.

The older person in the relationship may become impatient with their younger partner. This can result in feelings of:

- Annoyance
- Frustration
- Anger

Feelings of frustration can be a persistent problem because the older person has the maturity and experience their younger mate lacks and the bigger the age gap the more likely it is there are going to be problems for the older partner. A mature person is naturally going to be more confident and possess capabilities or life experiences the younger partner will lack; as a result the older partner may develop a tendency to monitor the younger person to ensure any previous mistakes made by the mature partner during their lifetime are not repeated. It can also become very tedious continuing to witness a younger partner repeating mistakes that appear obvious or avoidable.

It is true that the younger partner will probably be immature and lack life experience but that is not their fault and just the way it is. Generally, the older we are the more experience we gain. We grow to understand that not every apparent "crisis" is actually a disaster so can often be more relaxed about certain matters while those who are younger may worry or begin to panic. It may be difficult for the older person in a relationship to watch as their partner struggles to deal with issues he or she has already been through and dealt with successfully.

The greater the age differences the more likely there are going to problems for the older partner so understanding the potential hazards at the beginning can help a couple to negotiate constructively, and this can give the relationship a better chance of succeeding.

Older Partner Acts Like A Parent

When someone is significantly older than their partner they may have the tendency to act like a parent resulting in him or her acting:

- Protective
- Guiding
- Patronizing

The mature individual has the benefit of greater experience so it's natural for the older person to try and protect and guide their younger partner to help him or her avoid mistakes and pitfalls. The older partner may find it very difficult to resist directing or advising; the intentions may be sincere and motivated by just trying to provide guidance and protection, but the younger partner may become resentful and angry. This can lead to accusations of interfering, undermining and belittling or preventing the younger partner from learning from his or her own experiences and mistakes. When the older partner constantly treats their younger partner like a child it can be very destructive to the dynamics of the relationship. The younger partner can end up feeling disrespected because their credibility and judgment is always being questioned and can respond just like any other healthy rebellious teenager! Any relationship with a great deal of parent-child interaction will be plagued with tension.

Conversely, when a person is seeking a partner to act out the role of a "parent" they usually become overly dependent and irresponsible. This often places an unreasonable burden on the older partner as he or she is forced into a role they do not want to play, especially if they have already raised their own child or children. Resentment can build over having a type of hybrid "step-child" as a partner who can be irresponsible, unreasonable or demanding.

Older Partner Is More Financially Successful

Tempted To Control

The older partner may be tempted to control their partner because they hold more of the financial power in the relationship. There is an old saying: "He, who pays the piper, calls the tune."

- The older partner usually enjoys greater financial stability and resources.
- The person who controls the finances makes the financial decisions regarding how and where money is spent.

Most of us strive for financial stability and security and these issues usually become even more important as we grow older. Mature, established individuals are more likely to be quite comfortable or even successful financially. This may cause tensions when there is a significant age difference, as the older partner possesses more financial power and influence within the relationship.

When a partner is significantly older and has greater financial resources, experience and success it can be very easy to take full control of the relationship. For the older partner this could be a gradual subconscious process or a conscious decision taken at the very beginning of the relationship. However it happens, they're probably going to be tempted to take control and make all of the major decisions while rarely consulting with their younger partner. They may also begin to feel resentful about being the main provider, which tends to happen when the older partner is a woman.

The younger partner may feel not having an equal say in any financial decisions is very unfair (especially if a couple are living together), which can cause feelings of antagonism, resentment and bitterness.

Tempted To Compromise: Older Partner

The older partner in a relationship may be tempted to compromise or sacrifice their friends, interests or activities to appear more compatible with a younger partner. Dating someone much younger can be a great adventure, but before you decide to embark on a serious relationship ask yourself:

- Am I trying to recapture my lost youth?

- Would I trust him in terms of his judgment and experience?
- Can I trust him not to trade me in for a younger model?
- Is my Ego motivating me to prove I can attract and keep a younger man?
- Am I actually learning anything from my younger partner?
- Does he/would he make me feel proud?
- Do I respect him for who he really is?
- Will it be a relationship based on genuine love and integrity or just lust, an Ego boost and mutual convenience?

We have all seen middle-aged adults making fools of themselves while pretending to be younger than their years! It can be a huge mistake compromising too much trying to accommodate a younger partner especially if you reduce your standard of living to fit in with a younger partner's lifestyle and activities. Men and women who compromise too much for a younger partner often end up feeling resistant and resentful. It is always best practice to explore your motivations and to be honest with yourself before compromising excessively.

Younger Partner Treats Older Partner Like A Parent

Unresolved Emotional Baggage can also be a factor where childhood issues subconsciously compel individuals to seek out older partners who act like a parental figure. A significantly younger partner may be motivated by a mindset that encourages a childlike attitude toward adult relationships. The younger partner may reconstruct previous childhood scenarios while reliving the child-parent dynamic within their relationships. While the younger partner is acting like a child or teenager, the older partner may actually be encouraging an arrested development mindset by assuming a pseudo parental role of authority within the relationship.

- In such cases, the major decisions are taken without the younger partner providing any substantial input or opinion.
- He or she constantly relies on their older partner for guidance and advice, which is an abdication of responsibility.

When a partner is significantly younger it can be tempting to conclude, either consciously or subconsciously, that their partner is "superior" because he or she is more experienced, successful and/or financially secure. The younger partner may be too eager to defer or reluctant to express their opinions fearing they will be overruled, dismissed or even ridiculed. When a younger partner considers their opinions inconsequential and lacks confidence they will usually ignore or suppress their own desires and feelings. This can result in unhealthy behaviors and attitudes such as:

- Avoid challenging the older partner's opinions
- Accept undeserved criticism
- Accept advice and "guidance" without questioning
- Instead of trusting their own judgment the younger partner merely follows instructions

This type of partnership dynamic is severely unbalanced, especially when the older partner uses the advantages of superior age difference, experience and financial status to exert and maintain control over the relationship. The younger person may still feel intimidated and controlled by the superior knowledge, experience and financial status even if their partner is trying to be fair. The younger partner may become rebellious or angry as the relationship feels like the relationship with their actual parents and previously repressed childhood attitudes and behaviors begin to emerge. These type of issues eventually create tensions and conflicts often causing the relationship to fail, leaving both people hurt.

This kind of relationship dynamic can also result in the younger adult constantly compromising themselves while placing their partner "on a pedestal" instead of considering them realistically. If you're the significantly younger partner in a relationship and suspect you are compromising excessively, ask yourself the following questions:

- Does my partner treat me as an equal?
- Does my relationship feel equitable and fair?
- Does my partner show me respect?
- Does my partner consult me regarding important decisions?

When you are the younger partner and feel insignificant it's easy to feel subjugated and give away your power, missing opportunities for personal growth in the process. Instead of tackling your own life challenges and learning from the experiences you can begin to rely on a partner to avoid difficult situations and to provide excessive support. If you're currently the younger partner in a relationship, take some time to consider and explore how you feel about your answers to the above questions.

▌ Reality Check!

"He said he thought I was about twenty. Which is still too young. But not running-from-the-law young." – Kirsten Reed, Author

At their very basic level these type of relationships can be about the need to be looked after or the desire to be in control. The ages of each partner will often be a major factor; a relationship between a 35-year-old with a partner who is 15 years younger is likely to have more problems due to the difference in life experience, maturity and expectations. The 20-year-old is more likely to want to socialize and have fun and have different interests while the older partner has probably been there, done that and got the tee-shirt – or several! A relationship with a 65-year-old with a 50-year-old partner will probably have fewer issues and hazards because as we become older, any differences in age become less apparent due to shared maturity and life experience. The age difference has less of an impact as the relationship evolves and each person grows older. A six to 10-year-age gap between partners is usually tolerable but a difference of over 10 years can be risky. A significant age difference can cause a great deal of unhappiness, tension and resentment within a relationship due to underlying areas of incompatibility.

A large age gap can cause serious conflicts and the bigger the difference in age the greater the potential for major problems will be. Middle-aged or mature men with much younger women often consider their partners as a vindication of their sexual prowess and masculinity. With younger men or so called "toy boys" they're often seeking a sexually experienced older woman instead of trying to prove something to their peers or the wider world. A woman with a younger partner is less likely to take it very seriously and while the relationship may be a great Ego boost, she probably won't expect it to last.

When the younger partner is a woman in the relationship she is probably going to emerge with several advantages:

- An older man will often be considered to be a mentor providing guidance, information, knowledge, contacts and opportunities.
- She can enjoy the security provided by a partner who is likely to be more successful, financially established or even wealthy.
- She will be usually looked after financially while she is developing her personality and talents.
- Can leave the relationship while still being relatively young or attractive.

After a period of time the woman grows confidence and experience so the mentor role of the older man becomes redundant. The guidance and protection her partner provided is no longer required so one of the usual primary motivations for becoming involved expires and the relationship ends. Every relationship possesses its very own unique dynamics and a big age difference doesn't mean a relationship is automatically doomed. It can succeed when both partners avoid succumbing to dysfunctional patterns of relating and both are committed to a fair and equitable relationship. One of the crucial factors will be sharing strong compatibility in the key relationship areas. When both partners enter the relationship with genuine intentions, honesty and self-awareness the relationship can succeed.

Regardless of age anyone looking for a serious relationship should be seeking a partner who is:

- Mentally, emotionally and physically compatible
- Shares similar relationship goals, values and beliefs

While having a relationship with a much older person has its challenges, it is also true a significant age difference can encourage mutual growth, love, understanding and appreciation which can expand each partner's character, awareness and personal growth.

If both partners decide the relationship is going to be long-term and are determined to make it work, serious thought has to be given to the future. The reality of having to look after a partner who is considerably older who may become infirm or sick can be a daunting prospect and a deal breaker. For the older partner these relationships can be exciting, fun and improve self-esteem in the short-term, but the longer the relationship continues the more likely the difference in age is going to become an issue. If you're the older partner in an age gap relationship understand these type of relationships are often transitional so are very unlikely to last. A significant age gap has great potential to produce conflicts. The inherent issues and disadvantages can be too great to overcome for the majority of couples. Many people believe "opposites attract" but the opposite can also be true. These relationships can also be difficult and often fail under the pressure of the huge differences or the reality of everyday life. There are certain romantic partnerships that are doomed to fail from the beginning according to many psychologists and incompatibility is a major factor in many relationship failures.

Toxic Ex-Partner

"Your basic extended family today includes your ex-husband or -wife, your ex's new mate, your new mate, possibly your new mate's ex and any new mate that your new mate's ex has acquired." – Delia Ephron, Author

One of the most difficult compatibility hazards to deal with isn't always obvious until you become deeply involved. A toxic ex-partner of the man you become involved with can cause severe problems and create havoc in your relationship. There are men and women who will refuse to accept a relationship is over and will be extremely upset when they realize their ex-partner has found happiness with someone else. Opening shots in these particular types of vendetta are not always fired immediately; the passive-aggressive behavior, harassment and psychological warfare may not begin until it becomes clear your partner is moving on with his life and serious about building a relationship with you.

Men and women who refuse to accept and respect their ex-partner has moved on typically:

- Refuse to acknowledge your relationship
- Fail to respect your privacy
- Try to cause problems between you and your partner
- Attempt to use up great amounts of your partner's energy and time
- Refuse to respect certain boundaries despite being your partners ex
- Make themselves sexually available to your partner
- Turn any children from the previous relationship against you or your partner
- Threaten or punish your partner by using the children to blackmail him e.g. severely limiting or stopping visitation
- Threaten or punish your partner by seeking increased child or spousal support

Before he became involved with you he may have been still recovering from the previous relationship for a variety of reasons or perhaps he was dumped and still feels he has something to "prove" to his ex. In my experience, the partner rejected in a relationship usually feels far worse than the person who makes the decision to end it. This can leave someone feeling rejected, hurt and not "good enough" or lacking full emotional closure.

- If it's clear there is still some kind of emotional connection then he hasn't made it clear there is no chance of any kind of reconciliation with this ex.
- If he has made it clear he is with you and there isn't any possibility of a reconciliation but his ex-partner refuses to accept this, she could be mentally unbalanced so prepare for some serious "bunny boiling" antics and psychological warfare.

Before jumping to conclusions about why his ex-partner is toxic, you need to find out why she is seeking to disrupt or destroy your relationship. Does she want him back? Is she jealous her ex-partner has moved on with his life? Could it be the behavior is a direct result of your partner being in denial or is he actually encouraging her to behave in ways that are causing problems? If your partner felt abandoned as a child (or was actually abandoned) by his parents there could be emotional issues where he subconsciously disrupts his relationships by refusing to totally release his ex-partner emotionally. He could have emotional issues if during childhood one of his parents abandoned the other. A failure to make his position crystal clear about his previous relationship being over may indicate he may be deliberately giving her hope of reconciliation. He might be concerned or scared of hurting his ex-partner, especially if he still cares about her, but if he is more concerned about his partner's feelings than yours, clearly his priorities are badly wrong.

An ex-partner, lover or wife sabotaging your relationship will make you feel:

- Angry when your partner appears to be giving a higher priority to his ex-partner's feelings than to your own.
- Angry when your partner doesn't understand how you feel while accusing you of being insecure or jealous.
- Frustrated and impatient when he constantly makes excuses for his ex-partner.
- Resentful when your partner excludes you from certain areas of his life that include his ex-partner (such as collecting or returning children for visitation) because he wants to "avoid any problems."
- Insecure and suspicious when you begin to think it's quite possible your partner is using his ex-partner as a tactic to avoid making a genuine commitment to your relationship.
- Worried or scared when you know the toxic behavior is clearly escalating but your partner dismisses it saying it's not a "big deal" or he will "sort it out", even though you know he won't.

In extreme cases men and women with personality disorders can be obsessed with destroying the lives of others and commit terrible acts. Ignoring toxic behavior or being in denial could even be dangerous and any reluctance on his part to establish clear boundaries will probably encourage her interference or any toxic behavior.

▎ Reality Check!

"Some people don't realize what they have until it's gone, but that does not always mean they are supposed to get it back." – Stephan Labossiere, Certified Relationship Coach, Speaker & Author

Paying attention to any red flags and asking pertinent questions during the dating phase may reveal whether or not he has any "unfinished business" with an ex-partner. Questioning a man about his relationship history doesn't guarantee he is going to tell you the complete truth; he could be worried about telling you about a toxic ex-partner because he doesn't want to scare you off. There could also be concerns you may judge him harshly for being involved with a woman who may be emotionally unstable.

Already Involved

"No matter how angry his ex-wife is, or how frustrated or hurt you are, don't involve your husband's kids in the problems." – Laurie Pawlik-Kienler, Relationship Coach

Do not ignore the warning signs and refuse to accept any excuses your partner may offer regarding his ex-partner's behavior. Where there are issues due to serious disruption and sabotage caused by the ex-partner, it's your partner's responsibility to deal with the problem. Don't wait for the problem to solve itself because it won't so discuss the matter with him and make your concerns very clear.

- If your partner has not established clear boundaries he is just as responsible for his ex-partner's behavior.
- When your partner has established clear boundaries the tactics of his ex-partner will be nullified no matter how toxic she may be.

If your partner is serious about the relationship he will do whatever necessary to resolve the problems his toxic ex-partner is causing. He needs to establish and stick to clearly defined boundaries regarding his ex-partner and if the problems persist a "no contact" rule has to be introduced for a while, even if there are children involved. It shouldn't be difficult for your partner to see his children without interacting with the ex-partner providing the child or children are not very young (generally under six years old). Providing any children can be safely collected and returned without him having to come in prolonged or direct contact with his ex-partner he should agree to this if he values his relationship with you. The bottom line is he cannot be committed to his past, present and future all at the same time. If he allows his ex-partner to interfere in your relationship this will be a constant distraction mentally and emotionally. If he has not severed the emotional bonds he cannot truly be in a relationship with you or anyone else.

If your partner is allowing his ex-partner to undermine your relationship and makes it clear he is not prepared to take action explain how you feel and give him an ultimatum. Explain that the situation is unacceptable and you will only remain in the relationship if he establishes clear boundaries with his previous partner. It will probably hurt to end it but the emotional costs will be very much higher if you decide to stay hoping that things will get better. If your partner will not support you things will only get worse. In this type of relationship dynamic, it's also important to look at yourself and consider if you are being unreasonable. If you suspect you have jealousy issues due to your partner just having a friendly and appropriate relationship with his ex-partner which is not causing unreasonable disruption, you need to be honest with yourself and make arrangements to tackle the issue. Seriously consider attending counseling or therapy either on your own or with your partner. Whatever you decide to do, understand doing nothing is not a realistic option.

See the section on strategies, tactics and behaviors used by toxic in-laws as many will be very similar to those employed by a toxic ex-partners.

Stepchildren From Hell!

"It takes a strong man to accept somebody else's children and step up to the plate another man left on the table...." – Ray Johnson, Actor

A child or children from a previous relationship can present tremendous challenges if they have issues with a parent's new relationship. They can seriously disrupt or threaten the harmony and progress of a relationship. A child's toxic behavior is often motivated by emotional pain, distress or fear, which has the real potential to turn into rebellion and deep anger. While their parent may be excited about being with you in the new relationship this doesn't necessarily make the situation any easier for a youngster to manage. A step-parent is likely to be on the receiving end of a certain amount of displaced anger and while your partner's child may not be hitting out at you directly, it can often feel that way.

Children who have lived through witnessing their parents' relationship fail can feel:

- Rejected by the parent who left, especially if there has been little or no further contact.
- Frightened of being abandoned and hurt again.
- Ignored as a result of having their needs overlooked during the breakup.

Children and teenagers can feel ignored or unimportant when a parent has not discussed embarking on a relationship with someone new and a stranger is suddenly introduced as a part of their lives. When a child has been abandoned by a parent and has had little or no contact there will probably be feelings of resentment along with a combination of volatile emotions. The child may reject a step-parent fearing they will eventually be abandoned again and children with emotional issues due to divorce or parental separation can be very disturbed. There can be a range of behaviors when a child is trying to deal with certain thoughts or emotions but lacks the maturity to process these feelings effectively.

Even if a child doesn't have any severe emotional issues he or she can have an agenda including:

- Trying to keep the remaining parent (your partner) as their exclusive "property."
- Attempting to frighten off any potential partners.
- Taking every opportunity to try and make your relationship as difficult as possible.

A child or teenager acting in this way may also be hoping their parents get back together, which is not likely to happen when there is a new partner involved in a parent's life. Intense, unexpressed emotions can manifest in rebellious or angry outbursts against their parent's partner. When your new partner has a child (or children) you may be reluctant to intervene and offer advice feeling you have no right to question or discipline someone else's child. Couples can make the mistake of being too lenient with their children/stepchildren or choose to ignore serious issues that need to be urgently addressed. This can happen when a parent feels guilty about splitting up with their previous partner; the guilt motivates a parent to use "kid gloves" while failing to assert proper parental authority as they fear upsetting the child any further, especially if the previous relationship ended badly.

Feelings of guilt can make a parent resistant to establishing clear boundaries for a child even when it's very obvious this is exactly what the child requires. Alternatively, they can hope their child will stop the toxic behavior or it will just burn itself out and disappear. Dealing with your concerns can be very frustrating if you're ignored, disrespected or dismissed when you're trying your very best and know you haven't done anything wrong!

Becoming involved with a partner who has children can cause serious compatibility problems leaving you feeling:

- Your partner's child lacks discipline, boundaries and gets away with too much.
- Defensive because your partner believes valid observations are unwarranted criticism.
- Unsupported because your partner always backs up his children.
- Dreading constant arguments and avoiding any "awkward" conversations.

I have been involved in relationships where I believed my partner's children were rude or undisciplined and my relationship history includes walking away due to disagreements over how the children were being raised or disciplined. I understand how difficult it can be to express your opinions about someone else's children and disputes of this nature can destroy a relationship.

▌ Reality Check!

"Step parents are not around to replace a biological parent, rather to augment a child's life experience." – Azriel Johnson, Author

In the dating game you are probably going to meet a guy who has children so don't be afraid to ask questions. Pay attention to the answers. If you're in the early stages of dating someone with children don't ignore or dismiss any concerns. Approach the subject sensitively but be upfront; a partner in denial about certain aspects of his children's attitude or behavior or who refuses to discuss any issues is not serious relationship material. Deciding to stay with him without addressing any obvious issues will be a decision you are probably going to bitterly regret. Procrastinating leaves the problem to grow unchecked which will make it much harder to sort out later on. A parent with a resentful or difficult child who assumes they will eventually "settle down" or just has to "accept" the new relationship, situation and arrangements is being irresponsible and very unfair.

When a child is exhibiting toxic behavior or is out of control this usually causes too many issues and has the real potential to eventually seriously damage a relationship. A partner who fails to understand how to be an effective parent with rude or emotionally dysfunctional children isn't an effective parent. Toxic stepchildren create conflict and confusion and will give you major grief or emotional stress. Eventually the relationship will begin to feel like a struggle especially when it's obvious the child is deliberately trying to destroy the relationship and he fails to provide very little or zero support. Observe how he interacts with his child during the dating stage whenever possible and discuss any concerns you may have, but if he is resistant to your opinions or is in denial it's better to just walk away.

Already Involved

"The beggarly question of parentage-what is it, after all? What does it matter, when you come to think of it, whether a child is yours by blood or not? All the little ones of our time are collectively the children of us adults of the time, and entitled to our general care." – Thomas Hardy (1840-1928), English Novelist & Poet

If you and your partner have a child or children from a previous relationship there will probably be certain challenges to negotiate. For example, the children may resist changes while you or your partner may become frustrated when the new family unit fails to function as expected. While you as parents are likely to be excited about getting together and making a commitment to the relationship, the children will probably be feeling uncertain and concerned. They may be worried about how the changes will affect the relationship with their natural parent or concerned about living with new step-siblings who they do not know or may not like.

Laying Solid Foundations For The Future

When you have been through a difficult split or divorce, it can be tempting to rush into a new relationship or remarriage without planning ahead or laying solid foundations. It's better to take things slowly to give everyone involved the opportunity to get used to each other and the new arrangements.

- **Don't rush changes.** When a couple waits two years or more after a divorce to remarry they have a higher success rate. Making too many drastic changes too quickly is usually counterproductive.

- **Don't expect to fall in love with your partner's children quickly.** Love and affection takes time to develop and grow.

- **Limit your expectations.** You may invest a great deal of time, energy, love and affection into your partner's child but this may not be returned immediately.

- **Insist on respect.** Insist everyone involved is treated with respect.

- **Refuse ultimatums.** There may be situations with the children or your partner where you feel you have to choose between them. Always say you love both of them and want your partner and your or his child in your life.

- **Make parenting agreements.** Agree with your partner how you intend to parent together. Make any necessary adjustments to your parenting styles *before* you live together or get married. This will pave the way for a smoother transition and the children are less likely to feel angry at your partner for initiating changes.

- **Be civil.** If family members can be civil with one another on a regular basis this provides a solid foundation for healthy interaction.

- **Development considerations.** If you and your partner both have children they may be at various life stages and have different needs (for example, the needs of a teenager will differ greatly to a toddler or young child). They may also be at different stages in accepting a new relationship or family unit so it's important to understand any needs the child may have.

- **Appreciated and encouraged.** Children of all ages generally respond positively to praise and encouragement. They like to feel appreciated for their contributions, so be generous with your praise and encouragement whenever possible.

Children can often feel unimportant or invisible when it comes to decision-making in a new family unit. It is your responsibility to communicate openly, meet their needs for security, and give a child or children enough time to make a successful transition. Creating an honest and open environment free of judgment can help children feel heard and emotionally connected to a new step-parent. Children of a certain age have a right to be consulted, respected and heard but this doesn't mean you have to agree with everything they may say. It does mean you have to make a genuine effort with any stepchildren, which should be equal to the effort you put into the relationship with your partner. Children respect honesty and will often accept straight-talking even if it's not what they want to hear so always be direct, honest and approachable allowing the child to express themselves as well. **Understand this: if there are problems, ignoring the issues will not make them go away.**

A General Guide To How Children Adjust

Children of different ages and genders often adjust differently to a new step-parent or living arrangements. A teenager may take a long time accepting your love and affection but that doesn't mean he or she doesn't want it. You will probably need to adjust your approach depending the age and gender of the child, but your goal should be establishing a trusting relationship.

Children under 10	• Requires more daily needs to be catered for.
	• Can adjust more easily as this age group usually thrives in cohesive partnerships or family relationships.
	• Tend to be more accepting of a new adult.
	• Can feel competitive for their parent's attention.
Teenagers aged 10-14	• May be reluctant to demonstrate his or her feelings openly, but may be as sensitive regarding needing love, support, discipline and attention.
	• May have a very difficult time adjusting to a step-parent or new family.
	• Will probably require more time to bond before accepting a new partner as the disciplinarian.
Teenagers aged 15 plus	• May prefer to be on his/her own or to pull away from their biological parent as he/she begins to form their own identity.
	• There may be a tendency for less involvement with both parents or to reduce interaction.
	• Might not express his or her affection or sensitivity, but will still want to feel loved, important and secure.

General Tendencies:

- Boys appear to accept a stepfather more quickly.
- Girls and boys tend to prefer verbal affection, such as compliments and praise rather than physical closeness such as kisses or hugs.
- Girls tend to be uncomfortable with any physical displays of affection from a stepfather.

A major challenge for most step-parents is establishing trust. An important part of building trust is discipline and couples should discuss the role each step-parent will play in raising their respective children, as well as changes in household rules.

Observe: Let The Child Set The Pace

Every child is different and will show a step-parent how and when they're prepared to engage as the relationship develops. Some children may be more open or willing to engage than others and may require a step-parent to give them some space. Given enough time, patience, and interest, most children will eventually give the new adult in their lives a chance.

The following guidance can help make a potentially difficult transition easier:

- It is prudent to allow the biological parent to remain primarily responsible for discipline until the step-parent has developed a firm connection with the child or children.
- The step-parent should establish themselves as a friend or counselor rather than a disciplinarian.
- Creating a list of rules can be useful. These rules should be discussed with your partner and then jointly with the child or children. After this discussion place the list of rules somewhere prominent within the home.

These three fundamental strategies are important when stepchildren are involved but presenting a united front is also vital. Children can be very skilled at playing one parent against the other and will often exploit any weakness they discover to gain an advantage; a consistent failure to present a united front will leave the relationship open to ruthless manipulation that may be very difficult to survive. Regular family meetings and discussions where everyone concerned can express their views is an effective strategy for maintaining communication and resolving any issues. Family meetings also present excellent opportunities to reiterate any boundaries that may have been breached.

The creation of a strong family unit depends on those who lead it. Children often believe they don't need limits, but a lack of boundaries often sends a message that says the child is unworthy of time, care or attention. As a new step-parent, you shouldn't step in as the enforcer at first, but work with your partner to set required limits. When leadership and effective parenting are lacking in crucial areas, this can damage the relationship between the stepchildren and parents. These children can become adults with varying degrees of emotional damage or even some type of personality disorder; never underestimate how children can be influenced by their upbringing, environment and a lack of clear boundaries. According to psychologists it can take between five to seven years for a step family to become cohesive and function consistently. Establishing and maintaining boundaries is essential when dealing with children. They need to be established very early on in the relationship regarding how you as a step-parent will interact with your partner's children and how your partner's children will interact with you.

It might be time to seek outside help from a therapist if:

- Both partners have children and one step-parent or parent openly favors one child over another.
- A child directs their anger openly and resents a step-parent, parent or step-sibling.
- There is constant tension or feelings of resentment.

If you're already in an established relationship with stepchildren and find yourself struggling this is nothing to be ashamed of. Arrange professional therapy/counseling as a family if the situation becomes difficult but be prepared to walk away if your partner refuses to support you when his child or children are out of control.

Toxic In-Laws

"The first thing you've got to do is, you truly have to believe yourself. Call it gut feeling, intuition, instinct, whatever-when you get that feeling, that should send off bells. Listen, listen, listen, listen." – Dr. Phil, American TV Personality, Author & Psychologist

Over the years there have been numerous jokes told about dealing with difficult in-laws, but if you have the father or mother in-law from hell it's definitely not a laughing matter! Toxic in-laws can include anyone from your partner's extended family and you will probably have no idea what to expect. They often see a partner as some type of threat or sometimes just decide they don't approve of their adult child's choice. In certain cases they try to sabotage the relationship at the very beginning or may wait until you start living together or get married. In other scenarios, toxic in-laws become actively hostile or interfering when the woman falls pregnant or a child is born so be warned; these people can create a great deal of tension and conflict in any relationship. It doesn't matter how much your partner may say he loves you because serious conflicts with in-laws will cause you stress, distress, frustration and anger.

Interfering In The Relationship

Toxic in-laws do not respect boundaries, and usually because they haven't been given any in the first place. That's one of the main problems. These types often feel empowered to disrespect a relationship and the partner of their adult child without suffering any real consequences. They will often interfere in their adult child's life and your relationship by frequently providing advice you didn't ask for and don't want.

If you have in-laws who provide unwanted advice on a regular basis this is a very clear warning sign of toxic behavior. This "advice" will usually be about how to:

- Raise your children
- Spend or invest your money
- Decorate your home
- Dress and what to wear
- Cook and eat the right food (or even how to eat it!)

...and that's just for starters! The "advice" can cover a wide range of topics and have the potential to cause huge disagreements. Instead of treating you like an adult, toxic in-laws will treat you like a child who is incapable of making your own decisions. Friendly advice is generally acceptable, but you should never allow someone else to deliberately interfere with your personal choices. Excessive in-law interference will place serious stress on a relationship.

Parental Invasion

In-laws can disrespect a relationship by invading your time and space. They can believe the purpose of their adult child's life is to look after their desires and can become very aggrieved or even angry if their "needs" are not catered for. The fallout from their unreasonable demands will negatively impact on you if the toxic behavior is allowed to continue. When toxic in-laws constantly make unreasonable demands on a couple's time and energy the relationship can come under intolerable strain. Toxic in-laws often refuse to let their children go failing to respect the independent life their adult child has created with their partner. Subconsciously or with deliberate intent, they will demand constant time and attention, which sucks essential time and energy out of the relationship with your partner. The only situation where in-laws deserve as much time, love and support as possible is where he or she is suffering moderate to severe ill health. However, understand catering for the needs of an infirm and elderly person can consume vast amounts of time and energy.

The "Cold War" – Ignoring The Relationship

Toxic in-laws may refuse to acknowledge your relationship with their adult child even exists! There can be deep resentment their child is no longer dependent and is getting on with building their own life. When parents refuse to let their adult children go, they may seek to punish the partner for "taking away" their child. Any partner of their adult child is seen as reducing the attention the parent used to receive and you will be considered to be a dangerous threat. This disrespectful and possessive behavior is usually motivated by a parent using their child as a love-substitute. The adult child is still being used to provide a warped kind of love the parent didn't receive from their own partner. The result of this dysfunctional mindset is to seek revenge against their child's partner by ignoring, insulting or treating you with complete disdain.

The "divide and rule" strategy is another favorite of tactics used by toxic in-laws to try and create extreme discord. Arguing with your partner over his parents means your toxic in-laws have won an important victory as far as they're concerned. How do they do this? His parents deliberately upset you in some way and you complain to your partner, but instead of supporting you or considering the situation objectively he automatically takes his parents' side or make excuses for them.

Toxic In-Law Tactics include:

- Concealing their intentions to keep you off guard – if you don't know what they're plotting it is impossible to prepare a defense.
- Restricting conversations so you lack information that may be important.
- Constantly seeking attention.
- Trying to make you and your partner dependent on them.
- Acting friendly in order to spy on you.
- Seeking to crush you mentally, emotionally or spiritually.
- Frequently cultivating an air of unpredictability to keep you off balance and always trying to intimidate or even terrorize.
- Pretending they're innocent of any wrong-doing and not guilty of any nasty deeds.
- Accusing you of over-reacting.
- Insists on presenting controlled choices so whatever you choose is to their advantage or leaving you with a lose-lose decision.
- Disdaining things they cannot have: this provides a feeling of superiority.
- Stirring up arguments to gain an advantage and keep you off balance.

Toxic people often use an attitude of indifference to infuriate and to frustrate while they try to control the terms of any interaction. The behaviors of ignoring, demeaning and criticizing while showing disdain and contempt are designed to make you feel unworthy of respect, attack your self-esteem and to generally undermine you. In their minds, limiting or cutting communication or failing to acknowledge you gives them a feeling of superiority.

Strategies For Dealing With Toxic In-Laws

The following tactics are "power plays" or put-downs, which can be used against you overtly or covertly. Do any of these scenarios sound familiar?

During Visits:

- You are treated like a maid or some sort of hired help
- His parents usually ignore you
- They talk about you in the third person context when you are present
- They focus their complete attention on your partner

Watch out for:

- **Phone calls:** When they call your home they immediately ask to speak to your partner without engaging you in any conversation.
- **Post:** Clearly address letters or cards only for your partner's attention.
- **"Mistakes":** Constantly makes the "mistake" of forgetting your name.
- **"Forgetfulness":** Often makes the "mistake" of referring to you by his *ex-partner's* name.
- **Critic:** Frequently criticizes you openly in front of your partner and/or children.
- **Ownership:** If you have children with your partner the in-laws act as if they only belong to your partner's side of the family.
- **Exclusion:** You're usually left out of his family events as they only invite your partner.
- **Hypocrisy:** Talking negatively to your partner about you behind your back while being polite to your face.
- **Disinformation:** Telling you things but leaving out essential or important information that leaves you with the wrong impression, causing you to reach totally wrong conclusions.

Toxic in-laws often try to cover up an indirect insult or disrespect by pretending a comment was just an innocent "mistake" or "oversight." The attitude of contempt is frequently motivated by a desire for revenge by someone who feels they have been hurt or cheated and is looking for "payback." Passive-aggressive behavior can be a devious and underhanded verbal attack or sulking or sullenness used by someone to cope with their feelings of anger or hostility. The attack could be conscious or triggered subconsciously and a compulsive reaction to real or perceived hurt. These attacks can be very difficult to identify and you may not even be sure if you have been targeted. The perpetrator will usually have excuses and justifications that on the surface can seem very plausible.

The toxic in-law might have a habit of making sarcastic remarks that are hostile comments disguised as "humor" or pretending not to understand something to gain an advantage or to frustrate you. When someone intends disrespect this is often portrayed by the tone of their voice and not by what they may actually say. The person launching the attack may not be aware how deeply damaging their behavior can be to others and these types of attacks are usually very difficult to prove. The aim is to infiltrate and sabotage the victim's thinking to make them to feel demeaned or insulted. Always assume the attack is deliberate until you have clear evidence to the contrary.

It can be extremely challenging to identify and deal with someone who is skilled at being passive-aggressive because they are highly evasive and slippery. A passive-aggressive attack often leaves the victim feeling uncomfortable or bad without actually understanding why they feel this way. A good way to tell is to see how you feel after an encounter because you will probably be upset or angry but not sure why you feel that way. Always trust your feelings even if you are not sure why you feel how you feel. Pay attention to any patterns of behavior and trust your own commonsense and instincts.

The toxic in-law is often a master of making the perpetrator look like the victim and the victim look like the perpetrator.

Constantly having to deal with toxic in-laws will result in you often feeling:

- Rejected
- Inferior
- Insulted
- Angry

Insults, intimidation and manipulation are designed to upset you so you lose control and get involved in arguments; in their mind when you lose self-control and argue with your partner or them they have "won."

Remember

- It's their problem not yours
- Do not allow anyone to dictate to you
- Never allow anyone to manipulate you
- You don't have to engage in any mind games if you don't want to
- You always have a choice regarding how you will respond

Highly toxic in-laws are usually insecure (this is an explanation of their behavior and not an excuse for it!) and often have a strong desire to be in control and to win – and that victory will be at any cost. Dealing with people with this type of mindset can be very difficult and you will have to develop certain coping skills for a period of time if your partner is reluctant to confront their behavior. Constantly arguing with toxic in-laws will eventually wear you down and is a no-win game. The only way to maintain your sanity and come out ahead until a strategy is agreed with your partner is to refuse to play their mind games.

When dealing with anyone you suspect is toxic maintain eye contact, speak clearly in a firm voice and remain impersonal at all times. This approach will greatly help to avoid introspecting leaving you feeling miserable, hostile and resentful; it is vital to maintain your composure and self-esteem, which could be constantly under attack. Many relationships struggle or collapse under the pressure of dealing with toxic in-laws and the ONLY constructive way forward is to confront the issue head on – and the sooner the better! Taking action to stop or reduce the interference will benefit the relationship enormously providing there aren't any other major issues.

Your Partner's Responsibilities

A partner who allows his parents to interfere in his relationships may have been very spoilt as a child and very used to having his own way. He may be allowing his parents to interfere because they usually support his position. Children who are excessively protected and pampered by their parents grow into adults who don't usually cope well with life. This parental approach does not empower their children to be effective adults generally and to learn from the painful experiences of life that frequently provide valuable lessons. A relationship with a partner with poor coping abilities will probably have parents who are always on red alert to intervene if there is a "problem" robbing their children of the opportunity to build character. Negotiations, compromises and challenges have to be dealt with in every relationship and when issues come up his protective parent is going to think *you* are the problem as they step in to "rescue" their adult child. If your partner has a pattern of avoiding confrontations with his parents or is emotionally dominated by them, don't be surprised if you receive little or zero support.

If you're in a relationship and realize your in-laws are toxic, the most effective solution is to ask your partner to confront his parents and set very clear boundaries around you to stop the psychological attacks. Clear boundaries must be established and respected to allow the time and privacy the relationship deserves. Numerous daily phone calls or frequent unannounced visits are not acceptable; his parents should call and arrange appropriate visits unless there is a genuine emergency. He should make it clear his parents are welcome when they respect the boundaries, rules, standards and requirements, but if they cannot respect you or the relationship they will not be welcome. Understand this clearly: if this approach is merely a bluff that lacks consequences things will only get worse.

He has to establish certain boundaries and make it very clear that:

- As his partner you should be treated with respect and courtesy at all times
- You are an important priority his life
- When they criticize you they are also disrespecting him
- He will see them with you or not at all

Toxic in-laws must agree that when they visit they will not interfere or make any negative comments about you, the relationship or lifestyle choices including how any children are raised. If they refuse to accept these conditions then there should be consequences such as reduced or ceased contact.

This is not about your partner choosing you over his parents but a decision to be an adult and claim his independence. Toxic parents may try a variety of tactics to maintain control including guilt trips and claiming they aren't being shown enough love or respect; they might say he's ungrateful after all they have done or accuse him of betraying their love and trust. They might even demand he makes a choice between being with you and losing their love. These threats are usually made to test the new boundaries to see if they are firm and your partner is serious. They may protest, complain or claim they don't understand but he must stick to the conditions. At first, the toxic in-laws will probably be upset or even furious for being criticized and having their power to interfere curtailed, or may even sulk and refuse to communicate for a while. Eventually they often comply with the new boundaries without discussing the matter further or acknowledging they are sticking to the new rules.

You must be determined about your partner taking action and confronting his parents and he must establish firm boundaries to protect you and the relationship. If your partner truly loves you and is serious about the relationship succeeding, he has to give his parents an ultimatum. This is the only realistic strategy that can support your partnership. Allowing the toxic behavior and interference to continue unchecked is not a realistic option because it will destroy the relationship. Counseling can be an option if your partner will not challenge his parents but he might resist the idea of "outsiders" passing "judgment" on him or his parents.

▌Reality Check!

"I've always assumed that my parents and my in-laws would live with me when I get older and have children. I just assume it will happen and that it's the right way to do things. It's a deeply Indian custom that you kind of inherit your parents and your spouse's parents and you take care of them eventually." – Mindy Kaling, American Indian Actress, Comedian & Writer

It can be quite daunting when you're going to meet members of a new partner's family for the first time. Will they like you? Will they accept you? Will your relationship with his family be harmonious or a total nightmare? It can be difficult to spot any clues that indicate his parents might be toxic. You could be totally blindsided by your partner's stories of how wonderful his family members are only to discover the complete opposite when you have committed to the relationship. This problem can remain hidden until you are already involved or even deeply in love, by which time it will be very difficult to walk away if his parent's behavior becomes a problem. When you have been caught off guard it can be difficult to cope with and manage the problem and it will be very difficult to maintain a relationship when his parents are always rushing in to "protect" their adult child.

When a relationship suffers from persistent toxic in-law interference and a complacent partner these types of relationships can often end quite abruptly.

Already Involved

"Of all the peoples whom I have studied, from city dwellers to cliff dwellers, I always find at least 50 percent would prefer to have at least one jungle between themselves and their mother-in-law." – Margaret Mead (1901-1978), American Anthropologist

If he refuses to challenge his parents' behavior or to seek counseling/therapy to understand why this type of interaction is dysfunctional, you have to seriously consider walking away.

This may seem harsh but it will become an intolerable situation caused by your partners "arrested development" mindset; he might look like a fully-grown adult but is still a child reliant on his parents' acceptance and approval. Allowing a parent to dominate your adult life is a very unhealthy parent/child dynamic so unless he is prepared to "man up" very quickly, the prospects for enjoying a viable relationship are severely limited.

Partner Excuses

When your partner makes constant excuses for a toxic parent you will feel unsupported, misunderstood, frustrated or angry as he refuses to recognize the disrespect and manipulation being used against you.

Standard excuses include:

- My parent is getting old so let him/her have their own way
- My parent is growing old so you should be nice to him/her
- You should make more of an effort to get on with him/her
- It's up to you to sort out any differences

Your partner may try to excuse parental toxic behavior, but it's his responsibility to acknowledge and confront any attitudes or behaviors that are impacting negatively on you or the relationship. He has to take firm action to stop the interference by explaining clearly to his family members what type of behavior is unacceptable. Allowing your partner to avoid the issue, blame you for the problem or resist becoming involved is not a realistic option.

The truth is, if he can't understand why his parents are a serious problem without someone else explaining why this type of behavior is dysfunctional, you're probably wasting your time. At the end you will probably be emotionally bruised and battered but learn valuable lessons from the experience. Your ex-partner, however, will repeat the cycle because he has never taken the opportunity to learn and grow; nothing will change for him until he decides to be his own person and grow up. A relationship with a partner who will not support you while his parents or family members interfere in the relationship is a battle you cannot win and the only sensible solution is to walk away. Adult children of toxic parents have to understand their partners deserve to be respected.

Your Parents Or Family Are Toxic In-laws

If your own parents or family members are causing problems in your relationship it's your responsibility to establish healthy boundaries and demand respect for your partner. Adults who allow their parents to control their lives have an "arrested development" mindset; they have an unhealthy need to seek the approval and acceptance of their parents. They have to learn how to empower themselves, be independent and "cut the apron strings" otherwise the dysfunctional adult child/parent dynamic will continue to cause negative effects in your intimate relationships.

Allowing this type of parental control over your adult life is usually deeply embedded inside your Emotional Programming. It won't be easy for you to break the pattern, begin the process of healing and challenge your parents' or family members' toxic behavior, but it is

258

possible. It is a type of dysfunctional relating that has to be changed if you want your relationship to be healthy and more importantly to survive.

Assessing Overall Compatibility

"It is not until you rhyme with a person that makes you their perfect match, it is when you are satisfied with each other's peculiarities, and find jewels in their loopholes." – Michael Bassey Johnson, Poet, Playwright & Novelist

Pay attention to any warning signs that may indicate there may be issues that could seriously sabotage your relationship. When there is a serious lack of overall compatibility a relationship is unlikely to work. The best way to avoid any major potential compatibility hazards is to carry out due diligence before you become too deeply involved. In the dating game there are several key areas that should be considered when assessing a potential partner for overall compatibility.

Core Values

While sharing positive chemistry and mutual compatibility are two key components to getting beyond the dating stage, having similar core values is the basic foundation upon which many successful relationships are built. Core values are a mix of fundamental beliefs that make each person unique with many of these personal views being formed during childhood. Parents or caretakers usually have a strong influence on their children's values which can change as we mature and learn more about the various topics that are important to us. Core values affect all of the major decisions and choices you make as an adult, including your spiritual or religious beliefs, career choices and political beliefs. Each of us constantly make decisions based on our core values and this is demonstrated by our consistent attitudes and behavior as we do what feels "right" for us as individuals.

Defining Your Core Values

Many psychologists advocate that taking some time to know yourself is the best way to prepare for a healthy relationship. Clearly understanding your own core values is vital for being very aware of what you stand for and believe in. If you find yourself having to agree to something that doesn't fit with one of your core values you will usually feel very uncomfortable with the situation. What are your core values? Do the core values you're looking for in a partner actually match your own values or the values you aspire to emulate in the future? Having a list of personal qualities you may prefer in a potential partner who has similar interests is a good start, but finding someone who shares your core values is the best way to give a relationship a real chance of succeeding. One of the biggest mistakes people make is looking for a partner who enjoys the same type of hobbies, activities, or holidays but who doesn't believe in similar core values.

Many of us tend to judge people on how they spend their time because it is widely assumed a person's interests will reflect their core values, but this can be very misleading; for example, someone could be involved with charity work in their spare time because they passionately believe in the cause but may also be there just to socialize and meet new people not having any real interest in the goals of the organization. While it is important personal interests shouldn't cause any deep concerns or conflicts the fact is there are many healthy relationships where couples have very diverse interests. What creates a solid bond between partners isn't shared interests, but a couple sharing key core values as this greatly reduces the potential for serious disagreements. Sharing a variety of common interests will probably create good times together at first but the real test of each person's core values in a relationship usually occurs when fundamental shared decisions have to be made. This includes decisions regarding issues such as spiritual beliefs, finances, politics or how children should be raised. Major differences in values can cause serious conflicts that can completely sabotage the relationship.

Despite parental influences, there are men and women who have failed to define their core values for a variety of reasons so may not have strong views about a particular value until it is actually challenged or feels threatened. You may be tempted into compromising yourself after meeting someone who shares similar interests but not necessarily the same core values. For example, if you decide to radically change your religious beliefs to fit with your partner's views you will eventually feel compromised as you will just be pretending in order to keep the relationship going. It's important to discover what his or her values are before the dating stage becomes too serious. Couples who share core values work on setting short, medium and long-term goals together and this strengthens the bond within a relationship. They may have different religious beliefs (or one partner may not follow any particular faith) or come from different cultural backgrounds but what will support the relationship is the couple sharing core beliefs.

It is essential to spend some time understanding yourself and deciding what kind of values you're looking for in a partner as this will greatly increase your prospects of finding a partner who is a truly compatible match. Shared values create one of the major foundation stones of an enduring relationship. A significant difference in fundamental values inevitably results in conflicts and feelings of being undermined; the bottom line is it is very unlikely that you will be happy in a relationship with someone whose core values deeply conflict with your own.

Effective Communication

"The single biggest problem in communication is the illusion that it has taken place." – George Bernard Shaw (1856-1950), *Playwright*

It is virtually impossible to have a healthy relationship without effective communication. Making time for meaningful communication is one of the major keys to a successful relationship. It is the bridge between partners that helps them create mutual understanding in order to foster love and intimacy. Without effective communication, a couple will just go through the motions, lacking any genuine intimacy. Learn how to negotiate effectively. When communication in a relationship is difficult, effective negotiation skills can make all the difference and even retrieve what appears to be an impossible situation. Both partners must be able and willing to negotiate with respect and awareness and be prepared to consider their partner's position. Effective negotiations can even retrieve a failing relationship if it's worth saving providing each person is willing to compromise. First seek to understand and then to be understood; always take the time to listen and communicate with your partner. If your partner doesn't treat you with the same respect this is a relationship that you shouldn't be involved with.

Friendship

Don't allow yourself to be blinded by sexual attraction. Ask yourself whether if it were not for the sexual chemistry or connection if you would still like him as a friend. Step back, slow down and look at the dating process or early stages of the relationship objectively.

Personality

While your partner may enjoy a good argument you may prefer negotiating mutual agreements and consensus. If you're badly matched and the relationship fails, you may believe there is something "wrong" with you and brand yourself accordingly. This can damage your self-image or self-esteem especially if it was shaky before you became involved.

Intellect And Compatibility

There are different types of intelligence and it's a definite advantage when partners bring different skills into a relationship but it's the core areas that are important. Identify your core areas from your past relationships so you know what to look for in a partner. Strong compatibility is essential to building a successful relationship along with highly effective communication.

Correct Focus

Learn to enjoy and relish the great times in your relationship so the occasions that may feel dull and routine don't become your primary focus. Mutual support through the ups and downs of life can make a great deal of difference regarding the quality of a relationship.

Life Goals

If you're young and want to get married or enjoy a long-term relationship the key areas will be children, career and money. Goals and agendas change as we grow older but you should be with a partner who inspires and supports you.

Conflicts

Every relationship experiences conflicts and disagreements. Always aim to resolve any issues without hostility or using personal attacks and deal with any disputes calmly and look for win-win solutions.

Thoughtless Cheating

Sometimes people get bored even when they're in a good relationship or begin to wonder if there is someone more exciting or compatible out there. The grass can often look greener and more appealing on the other side of the fence but remember all that glitters isn't necessarily gold. You could jeopardize a perfectly good relationship for someone who appears attractive and exciting but is ultimately far less compatible than your current partner.

The prospect of achieving happiness in a relationship may frighten you at some level and this fear makes you back off. These negative patterns of relating probably happen when your relationships are actually going well but you sabotage yourself subconsciously fearing genuine emotional intimacy. You may have been involved with highly compatible partners in the past but push love away returning to your lonely but familiar comfort zone. If this sounds familiar, explore your relationship history objectively with support if necessary to uncover and heal issues any that may be damaging or destroying your relationship prospects.

CHAPTER 23:

Sexual Compatibility Issues

"No woman gets an orgasm from shining the kitchen floor." – Betty Friedan, Writer, Activist & Feminist

You could share strong feelings of chemistry with a man and experience intense sexual attraction but discover you're both sexually incompatible. Complementary sexual styles greatly increase the potential for a mutually satisfying relationship but a lack of sexual compatibility can set the scene for potential conflicts which can be very difficult to resolve.

- If you are planning to get married and decide to remain celibate until after you are legally joined in matrimony then a candid conversation with your partner regarding sexual chemistry and physical compatibility is vital. This can help to prevent the possibility of any unforeseen sexual complications or consequences.
- If you are currently in a relationship and considering getting married make sure you are confident good sexual compatibility exists between you and your partner.
- If there are any doubts it's important to discuss whether you're both confident a certain level of sexual chemistry and compatibility, which is mutually satisfying, can be maintained.

Where there are significant sexual compatibility issues it will be very difficult for both partners to enjoy a fulfilling relationship. A couple can improve their sexual chemistry and find solutions to any problems when they communicate effectively to adjust their sexual preferences so both partners feel sexually fulfilled.

There will be issues regarding sexual incompatibility when there is a significant difference in:

- Sexual styles
- Sexual frequency requirements
- Sexual dysfunctional or addiction issues
- Physical incompatibility issues

For sex to be enjoyed by both partners the relationship requires a positive blend of each person's sexual style; compromises are sometimes necessary but not total capitulation where one partner is satisfied while the other is deeply unhappy!

Significant Difference In Sexual Styles

Each individual has their own sexual style which is influenced by:

- The degree of positive self-esteem (do they feel they deserve pleasure and love)
- The degree of knowledge they possess about sex
- The degree of self-confidence
- The degree of self-acceptance regarding their body
- The degree of fear or openness regarding sexual interaction
- Their of attitude regarding intimacy
- Previous sexual experiences
- Previous childhood Emotional Programming that may have influenced attitudes towards sex

Everyone possesses different sexual rhythms and cycles of desire. It's quite normal during a long-term relationship for there to be occasions when one partner's desire for sex will not correspond with their partner's mood or pattern but a significant difference in sexual frequency preferences and this will eventually cause major problems.

- If you're currently involved in a relationship and there is a problem regarding sexual frequency preferences there is no point avoiding the subject or trying to live in denial.
- If your partner refuses to discuss the dilemma and is not prepared to seek and agree to some kind of compromise that is mutually acceptable, you have to consider very seriously if the relationship is actually viable.

A couple with a significant difference in sexual frequency preferences needs to communicate with each other truthfully and sensitively; they should also seek professional support and guidance if required. While it's possible to resolve this type of issue, differences in sexual appetites and frequency may prove to be an intractable problem which results in the failure of the relationship.

The sexual aspects of a relationship are unhealthy when:

- A partner totally surrenders their sexual style and preferences
- A partner is dominated by their partner's preferences and wishes
- A partner drastically changes their sexual style to accommodate their partner
- A partner drastically changes their sexual style to avoid conflict

Any of these scenarios indicates a very dysfunctional sexual relationship. Whenever a person experiences problems regarding very different sexual styles with their partner they have to be totally honest. While it's true sexual incompatibility can destroy a relationship it can also provide an opportunity for the positive evolution of the relationship. It is possible for a couple to grow and evolve together despite there being a significant difference in sexual styles. This variance can provide the opportunity for mutual growth based on mutual love and respect but the reality is a significant difference often presents serious challenges.

Sexual Dysfunction Issues

"Remember, sex is like a Chinese dinner. It ain't over 'til you both get your cookie." – Alec Baldwin, American Actor

The term "sexual dysfunction" doesn't just cover male erection problems or mental inhibitions regarding sex and intimacy, but also includes sexual addiction, sexual obsession or a lack of sexual integrity. Fulfilling sexual relations and shared intimacy are very important foundations for the vast majority of relationships; the act of having sex with your partner differentiates your primary relationship from all of your other relationships. Within a loving relationship, the sexual act represents a physical, mental, emotional (and I believe spiritual) bonding where a couple mutually enjoy and explore the chemistry and attraction they share. The majority of healthy humans have a strong desire for intimacy and sex and a lack of interest in sex or a low sex drive may indicate medical problems or underlying psychological issues.

The three main areas of sexual dysfunction:

- Problems performing sexually
- Sexual obsessions and addictions
- Little or zero sexual integrity

Male Sex Problems

Enjoying a satisfying sex life is an important part of a relationship, but there can be problems that can cause enormous tension and frustration. The male sex drive and sexual potency can diminish over time due to a number of factors. If your partner experiences "performance problems" you should talk about it while approaching the subject with sensitivity. Don't avoid discussing the issue just because you feel embarrassed or think talking about it will crush his Ego.

The two most common problems experienced by men:

Failure To Achieve Or Maintain An Erection (Erectile Dysfunction)

Many people struggle with the fear of intimacy and in some cases a man will be unable to achieve or sustain a meaningful or strong erection.

- If your partner feels overly mothered or controlled or felt this way in the past, he may have difficulties getting an erection as his body is reflecting the emotional state of feeling incapable and powerless. You could be treating him like a child or he may be recreating the role of his "mother"; subconsciously he will struggle to achieve an erection because a man is not supposed to have sexual relations with his mother.
- If your partner struggles to perform sexually he could be suppressing a huge amount of resentment, anger or rage towards you e.g. you cheated on him or hurt him deeply in some other way. The anger might be about his mother, an ex-partner or women in general.

Premature Ejaculation

The problem of premature ejaculation can be very frustrating for both partners. This often happens when a man feels very tense mentally, emotionally or physically and it may contribute to poor or inappropriate sexual techniques.

Problems with premature ejaculation may be caused by:

- Hiding negative emotions such as fear, guilt or anger or perhaps concealing a secret will tend to make a man ejaculate prematurely. If a man struggles to share his feelings with his partner this may result in "coming too quickly" as suppressing emotions or information creates physical tension.

- If a man was ever taught sex was "dirty" or was sexually molested as a child he may want to get the sex over with very quickly due to a strong aversion or actual fear about having sex.

- A sexual history including previously having sex with women he didn't like or paying prostitutes for sex to avoid getting close during sex due to a fear of intimacy.

- The fear of letting go and being out of control can interfere with a man's ability to experience orgasms.

- A poor diet that is high in fat or the side effects from certain medications can cause physical erectile dysfunction.

A great deal will depend on how severe the problem is and the willingness of your partner to get help and support to change. Of course if you're the one with the problem the same applies. Sexual dysfunction within a relationship is usually a very difficult and sensitive subject to discuss and manage. Singer Tina Turner may have had a hit with the song *What's Love Got to Do With It?* but it can be very distressing for both partners no matter how much love they may feel for each other.

Childhood Sexual Abuse

Sexual abuse victims can lose their desire for sex, have an aversion to sex or have an obsession with their sexuality that can result in sexual dysfunction or addiction. Sadly, people who have been sexually abused are often emotionally unavailable and experience problems being intimate. Frequent abuse leaves the victim feeling helpless, leading to deep feelings of possible guilt, anger and rage. Professional counseling to assist the recovery from sexual abuse is vital as it can be very difficult to heal these types of issues. Emotional damage is likely if a child witnesses inappropriate sexual activities or behaviors even if there was no actual physical sexual abuse. Being emotionally available, sexually open and sharing intimacy can also be a problem for an adult if they were punished for exploring their sexuality as a child. Other issues can be a result of suffering excessive parental discipline, being restricted or being made to feel guilty about sex through religious teachings or indoctrination. Children who are taught or conditioned to feel bad or guilty about sex will often carry the emotional damage into adulthood. Men and women who are overweight may have been abused when they were children. These individuals try to unconsciously protect themselves by building heavy physical defenses to protect their inner child who has been damaged in the past. The excess weight insulates them further from emotional and physical pain.

Adult Survivors Of Abuse And Pornography

"It's all free, easy to access, available within seconds, 24 hours a day, seven days a week. In some porn users, the response to dopamine is dropping so low that they can't achieve an erection without constant hits of dopamine via the internet. When they try to have actual intercourse and cannot, they understandably panic. Most men are astonished to learn that pornography use can be a source of sexual performance problems." – Marnia Robinson, *Report Author: Porn-Induced Sexual Dysfunction is a Growing Problem*

Adult survivors of sexual abuse may be attracted to pornography or have a strong tendency to become promiscuous. They may experience confusion trying to understand appropriate sexual behavior. A sexual fetish is generally considered to be a form of sexual desire in which gratification is linked to a particular object e.g. a certain part of the body or an activity. Sexual perversions are generally considered to be abnormal or unacceptable sexual behavior. However, one person's sexual fetish can be considered by another to be a sexual perversion; what may be considered acceptable sexual behavior can be very subjective so it's important to make it clear to a partner what you may find enjoyable or unacceptable. Men who constantly use pornography and surf the net for porn are less likely to be stimulated by ordinary sexual encounters while internet pornography is creating a generation of young men who struggle to perform sexually. Exposure to pornographic images and films on the internet is de-sensitizing many young people. Impotence is no longer a problem associated with middle-aged men with health issues but affecting young men in the prime of their lives.

A report in the respected US journal *Psychology Today* during October 2011, titled "Porn-Induced Sexual Dysfunction is a Growing Problem," claimed the inability of young men in their 20's to perform sexually was becoming "normal" precisely due to this reason. The author of the report, Marnia Robinson, said the repeated viewing of pornography online causes the over-stimulation of dopamine, the neurotransmitter that activates the body's reaction to sexual pleasure. The brain begins to lose its ability to respond to dopamine signals, resulting in an increased demand for extreme experiences to stimulate sexual arousal. Recovering pornography addicts were found to be more likely to experience a temporary loss of libido along with insomnia, irritability, panic, despair, concentration problems, and even flu-like symptoms. Robinson said recovery was possible by shunning pornography completely over a period of months which gives the brain a chance to "reboot" itself.

When pornography or third person fantasies are consistently introduced into a relationship this often severely damages the other person's trust, faith and love. Making love to their partner but having fantasies about having sex with someone else is a form of infidelity and this includes frequently reading or watching pornographic material. A commitment to a relationship includes being faithful to your partner emotionally, mentally and sexually. When your partner is concentrating his sexual attention on someone else, even if he isn't having sex with another woman, he is still cheating on a mental and emotional level.

Physical Incompatibility Issues

Some couples are a naturally good physical fit sexually while others are not. Sexual incompatibility problems of this nature usually cause a great deal of tension within the relationship. Where the physical differences aren't extreme a couple can work together to adapt their sexual behavior and styles to alleviate the problem, but when the differences are great and sex is uncomfortable or unsatisfying it will be very difficult for the relationship to succeed.

Reality Check!

"Sex is always about emotions. Good sex is about free emotions; bad sex is about blocked emotions. "– Deepak Chopra, Author & Public Speaker

It can be awkward discussing sex but if you are in a relationship and your partner is experiencing sexual performance issues pertinent questions can help to understand the roots of the problem.

Important Questions:

- What were his parents/caretakers' values and attitudes regarding sexuality?
- What was he told or taught regarding sex?
- Did his parents/caretakers indulge openly in inappropriate sexual interaction or activities e.g. prostitution, multiple partners or extra marital affairs?

Also, was he:

- Punished for having sex or masturbating?
- Abused or sexually molested?

If yes:

- Was the abuser a family member, an authority figure e.g. teacher, a priest or a stranger?
- Has he told family members what happened?
- Has he received therapy or is he in recovery?
- Has he confronted the abuser?
- Were there other siblings/family members who suffered sexual abuse? If so, have they received therapy to help their recovery?
- If your partner has suffered rape in the past, has he/she received individual counseling, or attended a support group or rape crisis center?

Sadly for victims of sexual abuse it can be very difficult to enjoy intimacy and a normal sex life. They can also have problems with blurred boundaries, which can be very rigid preventing intimacy or leaving them weak and vulnerable to further emotional or sexual abuse. If your partner has been sexually abused as a child or teenager it is essential to arrange professional counseling/therapy and support as a matter of urgency to heal any psychological issues.

Avoiding Sex And Genuine Intimacy

"It wasn't a thing I had consciously missed, but having it now reminded me of the joy of it; that drowsy intimacy in which a man's body is accessible to you as your own, the strange shapes and textures of it like a sudden extension of your own limbs." – Diana Gabaldon, Author

Sexual interaction exposes each partner fully to the other and creates an incredible amount of mutual intimacy due to the emotional and of course the physical sharing of two bodies. A partner who appears to be avoiding sex within a relationship could be subconsciously avoiding intimacy. People who have experienced some kind of sexual trauma or had their attitude towards sex corrupted by their parents or caretakers may consciously or subconsciously choose partners who they find sexually unattractive. They often prefer relationships where there is very low or nonexistent sexual chemistry that allows them to avoid sharing genuine intimacy.

This mindset is typical when your partner:

- Experienced negative Emotional Programming regarding sex as a child
- Experienced some kind of sexual abuse or molestation
- Felt sexually controlled or repressed by a previous partner(s)
- Suffered rape

The outcome of these types of experiences can be an adult who subconsciously seeks to protect his or herself from feeling vulnerable. A person with a tendency to become involved with partners when there is a lack of sexually chemistry and attraction needs to seriously consider seeking professional counseling or therapy to heal their aversion to sex and intimacy.

Control Issues

When someone seeks to be constantly in control or feels afraid of losing control they may consciously or subconsciously select partners with limited or zero sexual attraction as a defense mechanism to maintain emotional distance. The emotional distance gives the person a feeling of security and power within their relationships by withholding or hiding themselves and their sexuality. Men and women can be motivated to choose partners who they don't feel a great deal of sexual attraction or chemistry toward which protects them from becoming vulnerable emotionally. The fear of letting go and being out of control can interfere with a woman's ability to experience orgasms. We usually lose control briefly during an orgasm so the desire to remain "in control" during sex is clearly a barrier to intimacy and spontaneity. A woman who insists on remaining in control during sex could be making a passive-aggressive statement that sends a message to her partner that says: "You can't arouse me sexually unless I 'allow' it to happen." She may believe (perhaps with good reasons) her partner is too controlling in other areas of the relationship or may have felt victimized in the past.

- Suppressed anger or rage can interfere with a woman's ability to experience orgasms.
- A poor diet that is high in fat can make it difficult for a woman to achieve an orgasm. Effective sexual arousal for both men and women primarily relies on efficient blood flow.

Intimacy involves letting go of emotional and physical control, which means you trust your partner enough to allow yourself to be exposed and vulnerable. Maintaining control while suppressing emotions and expressions of intimacy restricts the development of a healthy relationship.

Faking Orgasms

"This is something that we talk about happening in popular culture, in the movies and magazines...we know that this is pretty prevalent in our culture, but we don't know much about it from a scientific standpoint. That to me is a real catastrophe." – Erin Cooper, Temple University, US

In the classic movie *When Harry Met Sally,* Meg Ryan's character performs a very convincing orgasm during a hilarious scene while sitting in a restaurant. Faking orgasms is not so funny in real life and fake screams of ecstasy during sex may be motivated by a fear of intimacy or personal insecurities rather than trying to protect a fragile male Ego. Erin Cooper of Temple University estimates that around 60 percent of women have faked an orgasm during intercourse or oral sex. Cooper surveyed 366 females ages 18 to 32 regarding their feelings about intimacy, sexual habits, faking orgasms and reasons for faking during previous relationships.

Around 25 percent of the men surveyed also admitted faking orgasms. Many of the women said they faked orgasms due to a fear of intimacy, because they felt insecure about their sexual performance or just wanted the sex to be finished as quickly as possible. A small group of those surveyed said they faked it to enhance the experience and to increase their own arousal resulting in higher levels of sexual satisfaction. Cooper suggested faking could be used to create distance when a woman has issues around intimacy or when she lacks confidence sexually to protect her Ego. Women who try to have sexual intercourse quickly may have difficulty allowing a man to get too close and feel disconnected from their partner or the sexual experience so unable to enjoy sex. Increased communication and work to bolster trust and intimacy could help these women overcome their need to fake it in the bedroom. Faking intimacy and orgasms can have a negative impact that may cause wider problems in the relationship.

Ignoring sexual issues just means storing up serious trouble for later on. Sexual problems can be discussed and resolved with support if necessary. Failing to address any issues allows the problem to fester often placing an intolerable strain on the relationship.

Lack of Sexual Activity

"Good sex is like good bridge. If you don't have a good partner, you'd better have a good hand." – Mae West (1893-1980), American Actress, Singer & Playwright

In his book *Relationship Rescue* Dr. Phillip C. McGraw says if we enjoy a satisfying sex life with our partner, this only registers as important at around 10 percent when considering the overall relationship. However, when there is little or no positive sexual interaction the lack of sex becomes a major problem regardless of what else may be happening within the relationship. Enjoying healthy sexual relations with a partner is generally considered to be essential for most people but when there is a lack of sex within a relationship couples sometimes may ignore the issue, rationalize or make excuses. The choices men and women make when deciding to embark on a relationship can be based on a variety of factors. There may be an obvious lack of sexual attraction or chemistry but some women may decide to choose a man who is a good provider, assuming he is a relatively safe bet for a stable and enduring relationship of security and contentment. Couples can find themselves in a relationship lacking sexual attraction, chemistry and activity by becoming involved on the rebound. They go looking for someone who is the exact opposite of their previous partner believing pursuing strong feelings of sexual attraction led them into making a poor relationship decision. While the mistake of embarking on a relationship based purely on sex or lust has been acknowledged becoming involved with someone where there is a serious lack of sexual chemistry and attraction compounds the previous mistake.

Partners who are avoiding discussing a lack of sexual intimacy within their relationship may claim they're both under too much "time pressure" and cannot find opportunities in their busy schedules. One or both partners may claim their lack of sexual activity is "normal" for most couples and not particularly unusual even though they feel unfulfilled or the lack intimacy is causing underlying tensions within the relationship. Others avoid acknowledging a lack of chemistry and sexual activity within their relationships by presenting a "united front" motivated by the desire to maintain the financial and material status of the partnership. This is a living arrangement or a lifestyle choice and all about presentation and appearances but possesses very little love or authenticity. Emotionally, either partner may feel constantly rejected providing the incentive for cheating or living separate lives. Ignoring a lack of sexual activity within a relationship usually causes enormous problems and makes it much more likely that one or both partners will seek sexual intimacy, satisfaction and fulfillment with someone else.

▌ Reality Check!

"Sex is a part of nature. I go along with nature." – Marilyn Monroe (1926-1962), Actress, Model & Singer

A lack of sexual chemistry and activity within a relationship makes it very difficult to renew the bonds and maintain a strong emotional connection with your partner. If you decided to embark on a relationship knowing there was very little or zero sexual chemistry attraction at the beginning it will be very difficult to create or develop those feelings. When a reasonable period of time has passed and there is still a serious lack of sexual attraction it's very unlikely matters will improve without the matter being addressed. Alternatively, strong chemistry may have existed at the beginning and you both enjoyed having sex but during the relationship feelings and activity began to fade, which is quite normal in this type of relationship.

Sexual relationship problems can be caused by suppressing underlying issues or grievances, which should be explored and addressed instead of being left to fester. The reality is pretending a lack of sexual activity or intimacy is "not a big deal" is a form of denial. Effective, honest communication can help to rediscover and revive sexual chemistry, attraction and activity. If both parties are prepared to make a genuine effort with the support of professional therapy or counseling if necessary it is quite feasible to rekindle and enjoy the passion and benefits of intimacy. If he refuses to discuss the matter or to seek support it's possible he has already decided the relationship is over but lacks the courage to tell you. A partner who claims not to be interested in sex or sharing intimacy strongly indicates there is an underlying issue and if there is a refusal to address the problem the relationship is probably doomed.

CHAPTER 24:

Friends With Benefits: Can It Work For You?

"Lust is easy. Love is hard. Like is most important." – Carl Reiner, Comedian, Actor & Director

We live in an era where a committed relationship can often be very difficult to find and even harder to keep. As a result many opt for a casual relationship or "Friends With Benefits" (FWB) arrangement where they have recreational sex but little else. The FWB concept has been around for a very long time but the term has become very popular over the last few decades. The idea is two adults can agree to "no strings attached" consenting sex without any problems, providing both parties are clear about what they are doing and no one is being misled. The general rules are both parties agree to have sex without either person becoming emotionally involved or having any expectations for the future. There is a mutual understanding it's a sexual agreement for a limited period of time without any consequences and some people believe this arrangement can even help to prepare you for your next serious relationship. A FWB arrangement can be mutually enjoyable, suit your needs for a period of time and not necessarily be motivated by trying to avoid commitment.

Having sex without any emotional attachments can be a very tempting idea especially when it's widely accepted that a good sex session is a great way to relieve stress! In a nutshell, you can have sex with someone at your mutual convenience with no strings attached, have a lot of sexual fun, experiment sexually, and no one gets hurt so it appears to be a win-win deal! Enjoying sex is nothing to be ashamed of and sex certainly does not have to be confined within a marriage or committed relationship with women generally enjoying greater social and financial independence while practicing more sexual freedoms than ever before.

Many women today have a totally different attitude regarding sex compared to previous generations. Less than fifty years ago a woman would generally make a man prove he was serious about having a relationship before allowing any physical or sexual interaction. It is now widely accepted things have changed. There has been a significant increase of females having recreational sex just like many men and choosing Friends With Benefits rather than looking for a committed relationship. In a poll of 2,168 single women by MycelebrityFashion.co.uk during November 2011 one in three women surveyed admitted having casual sex with a male friend. They were asked: What kind of relationship do you have with your male friends?

Top five answers were:

- Only Friends 62 %

- Friends With Benefits 34%
- Ex-Boyfriend 29%
- Male Colleague 23%
- Male Best Friend 19%

Of the women who admitted having a FWB they were also asked why they agreed to a "no-strings" sexual arrangement. They said:

- Not looking for a serious relationship 51%
- It wasn't planned 22%
- Just wanted to have fun 19 %
- Had feelings for him and was hoping for more 8%

While there is no doubt women are enjoying greater sexual liberation which should be celebrated there is another side to the story. Sadly, some women who are motivated to have casual sex come from a broken or dysfunctional family background while others may be trying to protect their emotions after a relationship failure. It can be difficult and even frightening to consider taking a chance on love again after being betrayed while low self-esteem or desperation can also influence a woman to decide to embark on a FWB arrangement. In extreme cases sexual addiction can motivate men and women to seek out casual sexual adventures. Even if the factors described don't apply to you personally a woman can still find herself at an emotional disadvantage when she has regular casual sex with the same man.

The Oxytocin Effect

During 2011 American researchers from Rutgers University, New Jersey, conducted experiments using scans to monitor women's brains when they were sexually aroused and discovered different parts of their brains were activated. The scientists also found sexual arousal tends to numb the female nervous system so a woman doesn't feel as much pain but only pleasure. When a man has an orgasm the main hormone released is dopamine which provides a surge of very pleasant feelings. Men and women have a hormone called oxytocin, sometimes referred to as the cuddle or "love" hormone which is released every time we hold hands or snuggle up close to someone. It bonds us to the significant people in our lives including children, family members, friends or lovers. Whenever we hug or kiss a loved one the oxytocin levels go up which increases our sensitivity to touch, encourages cuddling in both sexes and is a huge factor in couples bonding. Touching someone is a key element of producing this hormone and touch deprivation will significantly deplete the supply. The hormone tends to make women desire regular non-sexual physical contact, to talk about the relationship and to connect on an emotional level. Studies have shown levels of oxytocin increase dramatically for both genders during orgasm while research has also shown men who stimulate their partners with more physical non-sexual touching regularly are treated with greater love and affection. For women it plays an important role in forming a monogamous bond with their partner evoking feelings of contentment, calmness, trust and security while reducing feelings of doubt or anxiety. This hormone is increasingly stimulated by other physical activities such as giving birth or breast feeding.

The oxytocin effect is more powerful in women, probably because it works in concert with estrogen which is more plentiful in the female body but is subdued by testosterone which is much higher in men. It can also lower a woman's defenses and makes her trust people more. It is the key to the bonding process and increases levels of empathy. As a result women will often want more after agreeing to casual sex or being involved with a FWB arrangement and are more likely to start falling in love with a man after having sex. The male species is simply not driven by oxytocin in the same way, just as they are not designed or equipped by nature for the process of child birth. With lower levels of oxytocin men are unlikely to experience a similar surge of the hormone compared to women during sex. The result is men generally don't bond with a woman they're having sex with as quickly or simply fail to have the same urges to seek being close on a physical or emotional level.

When this hormone is released within the female body the bonding process for a female usually begins regardless of the circumstances surrounding the physical contact or sexual activity. When the oxytocin is released it doesn't distinguish between having casual sex in a FWB arrangement or sexual intercourse within a committed relationship.

The key advantage of this hormone in a stable relationship is it helps a woman to bond with her partner relatively quickly but the disadvantages can be difficult to manage when you're having regular but casual sex, which may leave you feeling as if something is "missing." Some women will choose a sex partner they're not really attracted to for regular "no strings attached" sex thinking it will be easier to manage or end the arrangement. However, because the Oxytocin effect doesn't discriminate when it's released during sexual activity a woman can still end up having genuine feelings for a sex partner who she didn't like that much in the first place! Great sex can make you feel fantastic and you could end up wanting to spend time with your FWB partner.

When a woman continues to have sex with the same man over a relatively short period of time she is probably going to become emotionally involved. The desire for emotional intimacy, motivated by the oxytocin hormone, will probably increase while her sexual partner is just having a good time. What usually happens is the man eventually terminates the arrangement because the woman begins to imply or demand she wants more than just a sexual arrangement. Instead of walking away some women can find it difficult to terminate a FWB as they become emotionally engaged wanting more from the man than just sex.

Casual Sex: Benefits

- Having someone available for sex at your mutual convenience.
- A chance to experiment sexually and to some extent emotionally.
- Having sex with someone you know, like, and trust as opposed to a series of one-night stands.
- Enjoying sex without commitment.
- Indulging in some of the perks of a relationship while remaining officially single.
- When the arrangement no longer suits you it can be quite easy to move on providing your emotions have not become too involved.

Casual Sex: Risks

Before you decide to enter a "sex with no strings" agreement there are a few important points to consider:

- If you have a tendency to be jealous, to strongly associate sex with love or to become emotionally attached to partners after sharing great sex, FWB is probably not for you.
- Friends With Benefits are not necessarily exclusive and he may be having sex with someone else. Even if exclusivity has been agreed there are no guarantees he will honor the agreement.
- If you want sex without commitment recognize the older you are the greater the risk of eventually ending up alone.
- FWB sex often confuses the boundaries of male/female friendships; many do not survive after the sexual arrangement comes to an end.
- FWB becomes a serious risk if you are developing romantic feelings.
- You can become unhappy and develop feelings of being used from the lack of commitment.
- Feeling guilty about having sex outside of an official relationship.

If you are contemplating having casual sex or a FWB arrangement you have to ask yourself honestly if this is really what you want to do or if you are just considering it because there is nothing else better on offer. If you have a fear of commitment or suffer from low self-esteem seriously consider having counseling or therapy to work out what the real issues are.

Casual sex can be great fun providing you protect your emotional and physical health and are confident you are not being motivated by any underlying issues. Regular casual sex or a Friends With Benefits agreement usually means your "partner" considers you great fun for their sexual convenience but not good enough for a genuine committed relationship. The only way to emerge from a casual sex agreement emotionally unscathed is to set very firm boundaries at the very beginning and stick to them. Decide to indulge yourself for a limited period of time and make sure you end the arrangement within a couple of months. Whether it's casual sex or a FWB deal practicing safe sex is absolutely essential. The motivation for agreeing to some sexual fun makes the concept and activity very popular, but the reality can be very harsh if it results in an unplanned pregnancy or a serious sexual infection.

Friends With Benefits Strategies

- You can consider having more than one FWB at a time. This can help prevent becoming too emotionally attached to one man but may not be an acceptable option for you.
- Don't spend any quality time together.
- Don't think or plan for the future.
- Don't meet their friends or family.
- Don't discuss anything on an emotional level.

Reality Check!

"There can be no happiness if the things we believe in are different from the things we do." – Freya Stark, British Explorer & Travel Writer

I have been involved with several Friends With Benefits and always made it very clear it was just about sex. Most of the women tried to persuade me to commit to a relationship which was not what I had "signed up" for. This had nothing to do with my sexual prowess (although at the time I did convince myself to believe otherwise!) but the fact that for the majority of women having sex is usually a physical **and** emotional act. I have spoken to many women about their Friend With Benefits experiences and the vast majority have told me agreeing to this type of arrangement has often been the most disappointing and unfulfilling "relationship" choices they have ever made. While a man can often have sex without any emotional content a woman sleeping with a guy who isn't her "official" partner usually develops feelings for him and begins hoping for something more.

Already Involved

If you're currently involved with a sexual arrangement and feeling dissatisfied it's time to have a long hard look at your values and relationship expectations. Research conducted during 2009 at Wayne State University in Detroit, US, found it was highly unlikely for FWB couples to progress into having a committed relationship, so if you are hoping the arrangement is going to provide a long-term partner you're probably wasting your time. Having sex with a man hoping this is going to persuade him to commit to a relationship is usually futile and often causes a woman to feel used, bitter, resentful or even angry.

Reviewing Your Expectations

If you're serious about finding a committed relationship you should expect:

- To be treated with respect
- A potential partner who is available (not dating or physically/emotionally involved with another woman)
- A potential partner who is interested in a committed relationship and ready to explore the potential of embarking on one
- The dating stage is not going to continue indefinitely and will lead to a serious/committed relationship
- To have confidence a partner will be faithful and honest

Denying what you really want while accepting far less is guaranteed to end in tears. Often a woman's intentions and expectations for herself are totally out of sync with the sexual arrangement as she holds onto the hope that somehow it will develop into a committed relationship. The majority of women know they want to be loved, treated with respect and most importantly for their partner to be faithful. These types of circumstances often cause internal conflicts because on the one hand you know what you want but on the other you know deep down the casual sex arrangement is not really working for you. Investing emotionally in a relationship when your true expectations and needs are not being fulfilled inevitably leads to feelings of frustration and resentment. Be honest with yourself about what type of relationship you're looking for and stick to the plan. It can be very easy to drift into a FWB arrangement by just accepting whoever might be available or convenient.

If you feel unsure about:

- Your status when you're having regular sex with a man
- The status of the relationship
- His activities with other women including dating and sex

Then you're not really in a relationship no matter how much you try to convince yourself that you are. Sleeping with a man when you're unsure of the status of the relationship can be an extremely frustrating and demoralizing experience. A lack of trust and confidence inevitably causes instability because when someone feels insecure or uncomfortable in a relationship they're not going to be able to relax and be themselves.

It's not unusual for a woman to want more once she is involved with a FWB so don't be afraid to talk about the possibility of a committed relationship, while clearly understanding trying to elevate this type of sexual arrangement to full relationship status is very unlikely to succeed. If he's prepared to take you seriously any negotiations should be on your terms so be strong and make sure you're clear about your future expectations. Of course you run the risk of being rejected if your sex buddy doesn't want to be in a relationship but this isn't a bad thing – in fact it's a very good thing! Feelings of desperation fueled by the fear of being left on the shelf can cause a woman to accept or tolerate a sexual arrangement that can be very detrimental to her emotional health.

Females are generally much more emotional than men but some women like to deceive themselves into thinking they can handle this type of situation. Others hope this approach will eventually persuade a man to make a commitment. Many men will take whatever is on offer and then leave the arrangement at their convenience. This leaves many women feeling sad and empty, especially if the guy moves onto a successful relationship or marries another woman. There comes a time when you have to face reality and stop believing your frog is going to turn into a loving prince.

If you agreed to a FWB and now find yourself struggling emotionally with having casual sex with a man who doesn't love you, accept responsibility for your decision. It's very unfair to blame your FWB sex buddy; he was just acting like a typical man who found a woman prepared to provide no strings attached sex. Perhaps you were naïve, misguided or even desperate to be loved when you agreed to the FWB arrangement but at this stage there's no point in beating yourself up about making a mistake. You thought you could handle it but now the arrangement is making you feel unfulfilled, uncomfortable or even very emotionally conflicted. When a person begins to compromise their true relationship desires and expectations they eventually end up compromising themselves. Denying what you really want in a FWB arrangement is almost guaranteed to end in tears eventually and it's usually the woman who ends up crying.

"Commitment is inherent in any genuinely loving relationship." – M. Scott Peck (1936-2005), Psychiatrist & Author

Leaving a Friends With Benefits arrangement when a man isn't prepared to commit means you are taking control. Regaining your emotional independence will give you real options, instead of wasting your time hoping the man you're sleeping with eventually decides he wants more than just sex. The majority of women usually prefer sexual activity within a committed, stable relationship. You deserve so much more than just being available for mutually convenient sex so set your intentions, work on your strategy and believe you will find the kind of relationship that you *really* want.

FWB By Default

"Some of the biggest challenges in relationships come from the fact that most people enter a relationship in order to get something. They're trying to find someone who's going to make them feel good. In reality, the only way a relationship will last is if you see your relationship as a place that you go to give, and not a place that you go to take." – Anthony Robbins, Author & Life Coach

Whether a woman decides to have a Friends With Benefits arrangement or drifts into having casual sex she can experience unforeseen emotional pitfalls. One of the most common clichés around today is hearing a woman claiming "it's complicated" when describing her relationship. What this usually means is she's having regular sex with a man but is unclear about her status. In other words she is involved with a FWB by default and doesn't even know it!

Women end up in FWB by default situations for a variety of reasons:

- Engages in sexual activity too early during the dating phase hoping this will entice a man into committing to a relationship
- Assumes by having sex with a man means she is in a serious relationship
- Low self-esteem or lack of self-respect
- Unaware or in denial about her FWB status
- Previous relationship downgraded to FWB status
- Failure to clarify a man's intentions
- Has been lied to regarding the FWB's status

Engages in sexual activity too quickly hoping this will entice a man into a relationship

A woman who sleeps with a man too quickly and easily will not usually be considered seriously for a long-term relationship and it doesn't really matter how mind blowing the sex is. The majority of physically healthy people want to enjoy a great time between the sheets but a man isn't going to commit just because a woman satisfies him sexually. Some women believe that by providing "good sex" this will eventually persuade a man to give them the commitment they crave. Eventually they have to confront their true feelings, desires and relationship expectations. This is what usually happens: the man just takes whatever sex is on offer, does not consider the woman seriously and eventually just walks away. Trying to use sex in the hope of enticing a man into a relationship is an extremely misguided short-term strategy that often ends with a woman feeling used and disappointed with herself.

Assumes having sex with a man means she is in a serious relationship

Women are usually emotionally engaged at some level when they decide to sleep with a man and a woman having regular sex with the same guy is probably going to want more after a period of time. The majority of men who are enjoying no hassle, commitment-free sex for three months or more will probably be very reluctant to make a relationship commitment. A woman who fails to clarify a man's intentions is setting herself up to be used because for the average male, a woman who has casual sex is just a "good time girl" not a potential long-term partner. Sharing hot sex sessions doesn't mean you're involved in the greatest love affair of the 21st century and doesn't mean he's in love with you. Many men can indulge in sexual activity without feeling any real emotional content and for many men sex can have absolutely nothing to do with love or romance. While the woman gets busy behaving like she's in a serious relationship, he just sits backs and enjoys whatever sexual and other perks are on offer until he decides it's time to move on. The qualities that attract most men include a good personality, high self-esteem, charisma, loyalty, integrity and self-respect. Using sex in the hope the FWB arrangement will eventually start "going somewhere" is just setting yourself up for a big disappointment.

Low self-esteem or lack of self-respect

"Low self-esteem is like driving through life with your handbrake on. " – Maxwell Malz

Low self-esteem issues can trap a woman inside an unhealthy FWB arrangement if she believes she doesn't deserve to be loved and respected. Rushing into sexual activity on a desperate mission to be with "Mr. Right" often ends in tears; these women often sleep with men prematurely hoping to secure an agreement of commitment from the new man in their life. Of course there is no obligation for a man to commit which is very unlikely when he is receiving easy sex. Men respect women who respect themselves; women who "give it all away" while desperately hoping to create a viable relationship often end up feeling cheated. A woman with low self-esteem is often highly likely to drift into a FWB by default situation.

Unaware or in denial about their FWB status

Some women become sexually involved with men but remain uncertain about their relationship status while others are not sure if the arrangement is sexually exclusive. This type of FWB by default usually happens due to:

- Failing to maintain effective personal boundaries
- Failing to clearly explain her expectations and requirements
- Having sex too quickly
- Failing to ask questions to discover his true intentions and making assumptions

Maintaining healthy boundaries while clearly expressing your expectations effectively filters out Players and timewasters. The failure to clarify intentions often occurs when sex happens too quickly without discovering what the man's intentions are besides just having a good time. As the arrangement progresses the woman becomes increasingly emotionally involved and finds it difficult to walk away. A failure to ask pertinent questions and clarify a man's intentions at the beginning often results in FWB by default. There are women who are in a FWB arrangement who believe they're involved with a genuine, exclusive relationship despite very obvious clues or warning signs. This is a form of denial motivated by a desperate attempt to sustain the illusion of a relationship.

Lied to regarding FWB status

This scenario is very common: the man claims to be single and available but is actually a Player with one or several women, or possibly even married. Alternatively, he pretends to be fully committed to the relationship but is really just biding his time until he meets someone new.

With a man who is already involved but claims to be unhappy with his current partner, he will often say the relationship is not working out, he no longer has sex with his partner or if married is filing for a divorce. None of these stories are actually true but are used to give the appearance of a man who is emotionally available, which is what entices the woman to entertain the idea of having an affair. He then convinces her she is the "love of his life" and everything will be different when they're together "officially." They begin having sex which is great for a while but eventually he begins to create distance as it becomes clear he has no intention of leaving his partner or wife. After a period of time and several broken promises later it becomes apparent the woman is in fact a mistress and in a FWB by default situation. By this time she has become so emotionally invested it feels increasingly difficult to break away. This can go on for months or even years with the woman hoping the man she has fallen in love with will eventually be hers.

Downgraded to FWB status after a failed relationship

This is one of the most common FWB by default scenarios. After a break up a woman continues to have sex with her ex-partner hoping he will recommit to the relationship. This strategy is very unlikely to succeed because it's quite easy for most men to transition from having sex within a committed relationship to having casual sex with the same woman.

If you're in this kind of situation you will probably experience a range of emotions. There will be occasions when you feel happy because there is hope for rekindling the relationship so will accept the FWB status but at other times feel frustrated and used. Deep down inside you're unlikely to be happy with just having sex so there will probably be feelings of frustration or resentment mixed with an underlying fear. This fear is caused by knowing that if you actually express your dissatisfaction and start making demands the man might walk away for good. Becoming caught up in this cycle can be very confusing, emotionally draining and often results in erratic behavior.

Being downgraded to a FWB and then trying to get an upgrade back to committed relationship status is possible but not very likely. If you're in this type of situation with strong feelings for your ex-partner understand that continuing to have sex with him in the hope of persuading him to recommit to the relationship is probably a waste of time. The eventual realization you have only been used for sex may be a very painful emotional experience.

▌ FWB By Default Reality Check!

"There can be no trust without confidence. And there can be no confidence without integrity." – Samuel Johnson (1709-1784), Poet & Essayist

Women often stay in sexual arrangements that are negative and unhealthy because they believe the man will eventually "see the light" and realize he wants a committed relationship. If you are unsure about whether you're in a FWB by default situation there are several warning signs that will help you to identify his intentions.

Warning Signs

You are probably in a FWB if:

- You do not know his address and have never been invited to his place.
- He has never slept over at your place using the excuse he can't sleep properly except in his own bed.
- He sleeps at your place sometimes but often has to get up and leave really early while providing a variety of excuses.
- He is often difficult to contact on his mobile after a certain time during the evening, it goes straight to voicemail or he never returns your calls until the following day.
- You do not go out as a couple and the only place you meet up is at your place ending up in the bedroom.
- You're out with him and he introduces you by your first name but not as his girlfriend or any other term that indicates you are in a relationship.
- Having children has been discussed and you're both at a reasonable age to start a family but it has been made very clear he does not want any with you.
- Marriage has been discussed and it has been made very clear he does not want to marry you, that he is keeping his options open.
- He does not seek your advice about anything important, conversation is mostly shallow and he does not expect or ask for your support during difficult times.
- You have been seeing him for a period of time (two to three months) and he has never invited you to meet any of his friends or family members.
- If he does introduce you to his parents and his mother seems unexcited or distant this is probably due to him introducing various women to her previously. The lack of enthusiasm is due to his mother expecting you to be replaced in the not too distant future. Fathers tend to be more welcoming regardless of the number of women his son has brought home previously so it is unwise to assume a feeling of acceptance or to start making plans for the future based on an enthusiastic response from his Dad!

Generally from a man's perspective having a FWB will always be a win-win arrangement as he enjoys having sex without any responsibilities or commitment; he gets all the perks with very little "downside." For the woman it is a lose-lose arrangement; not only does this type of sexual arrangement raise false hopes of a lasting relationship, it will probably erode her self-esteem (which may have been shaky anyway) and can cause a loss of self-respect. Being in denial about your status will just prolong the arrangement at his convenience. If you're unhappy with having sex without any relationship commitment terminate seeing him immediately and find a man who will treat you with the respect you deserve instead of being a FWB.

Toxic FWB

"No one can make you feel inferior without your consent." – Eleanor Roosevelt (1884-1962), Politician & Activist

A FWB sexual arrangement always has the potential to turn into a toxic "relationship" where the experience is usually filled with extreme feelings of uncertainty, disappointment and possibly abuse. A toxic FWB can happen when an ex-partner tries to assert overt or covert control to maintain sexual activity. Alternatively, the same tactics can be used in a previously agreed sexual agreement to "encourage" you to continue the arrangement. For example, after the relationship is over you continue sleeping with your ex-partner because you still have feelings for him. It may be implied or even mutually agreed you're in a FWB arrangement but there usually isn't any discussions about having sex with each other just as "friends."

There may also be promises to recommit to the relationship at some unspecified future date but he says he needs time to "sort himself out." You might assume or hope you're officially back together as a couple and decide to see if the relationship deserves another chance. Alternatively, the ex-partner starts to use mind games to manipulate you into accepting the arrangement. He may gradually begin to imply or insist on being treated like your "official" partner even though he isn't or might try to undermine your confidence and self-esteem by suggesting no other man will want you.

When it has been mutually agreed the relationship is over and is now a FWB **but** you're both free to date other people, he may become jealous if he finds out you're seeing another man or considering other options.

Other tactics to assert and maintain control include:

- He often gives you mixed and confusing messages.
- He wants to dictate the terms of the FWB with very few if any compromises.
- He appears to have mood swings, which keep you off-balance either mentally or emotionally.
- He makes subtle criticisms designed to undermine your confidence.
- He generally treats you like a sexual object.
- He usually disregards your personal feelings.
- He frequently makes you feel as if your opinion is worthless.
- He asks a lot of questions about your whereabouts (or there are periods of relentless questioning).
- He acts like he is doing you a favor by continuing the arrangement.
- There are frequently huge inconsistencies between what he says and what he actually does.
- He is highly unreliable or makes promises that are broken.
- He is rigid and inflexible about when he can see you.
- He implies you're using him or taking advantage.
- He blames you for the previous relationship failing.
- He often insists on having sex even when you make it clear you're not interested.

- He may ignore any meaningful foreplay and rush sex before you're ready resulting in painful intercourse.
- He uses guilt trips, for example, often pretending to be "hurt" when you say you're unhappy with the FWB arrangement. When you express yourself you're made to feel guilty so avoid confronting him about the "relationship" to avoid creating tension. Any type of guilt trip is designed to put you on the defensive while keeping you engaged in the FWB arrangement.
- He seeks sympathy by making statements such as, "You're too good for me" or "You can do better than me." This is designed to make you feel sorry for him.
- He uses projection where he accuses you of being selfish, unkind etc. Projection is a psychological strategy used to avoid ownership of feelings or behaviors. For example, he accuses you of being upset when the truth is HE is the one who is feeling upset. If he constantly and unfairly accuses you of having sex with someone else this probably indicates that's exactly what HE is doing.
- He is prone to sulking if he doesn't get his own way. Sulking is a form of passive-aggressive behavior used to try and make the target feel uncomfortable or bad about themselves.
- He is oblivious to or disrespects your feelings and opinions.
- He says things he claims are "very honest" but are really blunt and hurtful.
- He uses disapproval, name-calling, putdowns, blame and guilt to manipulate you to the point where you begin to doubt yourself.
- He is possessive – but this can be overt or covert. He may constantly make surprise visits to your home or work place. He is also likely to call, email or text frequently because he wants to know you're "OK."
- He generally has a low opinion or degrading views about women. He frequently makes negative comments about women, his mother, female relatives or previous girlfriends. He always blames ex-partners for relationship failures and has a history of being rejected by previous partners.

These tactics and strategies are designed to maintain control and many women don't realize they're being manipulated to have sex. Pay attention to your sex buddy's behavior and if you suspect you're a victim of toxic behavior and manipulation terminate the arrangement immediately. There are women who will endure a toxic FWB believing the arrangement has "potential" to become a serious relationship. Remaining in a situation where a man manipulates you into having sex at his convenience means you're leaving yourself open to being abused.

FWB Exit Strategies

The first step towards escaping an unhappy FWB is to confront your true feelings, desires and relationship expectations. Then you should clarify your sex buddy's intentions as soon as possible. A woman in a FWB arrangement who decides she wants more will probably be tempted to start dropping hints or even making demands for some type of real commitment. She might be scared of asking too many questions fearing this could upset her sex buddy or scare him away or begin issuing ultimatums hoping to get the FWB upgraded to committed relationship status.

His Typical Response:

- Complains about too much "pressure" and threatens to leave.
- Accuses the woman of being unreasonable, needy, pushy or desperate.
- Withdraws sexually either gradually or suddenly.
- Sabotages the "relationship" by causing arguments or by using other tactics designed to manipulate the woman into ending the arrangement.

When a man feels "pressured" into making a commitment he might pull back or even decide to end it so you have to be emotionally prepared for that type of response. Whether you're in a FWB by design or default and want more than just sex it's time to make a decision: continue to allow yourself to be used or decide you want and deserve more. Instead of issuing ultimatums or threats the most effective strategy is to give a man an ultimatum disguised as a choice.

His "choices" are:

- He agrees to a serious, exclusive relationship.
- The FWB arrangement will be terminated immediately with absolutely no contact for a minimum of three months.

Remember this is not a negotiation! For this strategy to succeed you cannot allow him to make any further suggestions or present any additional options. If you allow alternative options to be considered or accepted for discussion he will probably try and persuade you to continue with the FWB. You must persist with presenting only *your two preferred choices* and limit any discussion to your agenda regardless of his responses. When a straight two-way choice is presented, you retain control of the situation because whatever he chooses, the outcome will be to your advantage. If he agrees to a serious relationship you have the chance of working towards a real relationship with a man you have feelings for. If he decides he doesn't want to be more than a FWB that sets you free to find the kind of love you want and deserve.

Present your terms firmly, clearly and briefly. Many people believe they have to talk a great deal to get their point across, but you don't. A person who keeps their speech and responses brief will command greater authority. If he doesn't have much to say don't be tempted to fill in the gaps; when faced with periods of silence people often speak more as the silence makes them feel uncomfortable. Allow periods of silence if they occur as by encouraging him to fill the silence he may reveal useful information about his mindset and intentions. To maintain control of the situation always say less than necessary and be careful about what *you* do say; once words are spoken they cannot be taken back. The truth is the *more* you say the *less* control you will appear to have while also running the risk of becoming too emotional.

So when your terms are offered in the correct manner they will be brief, to the point and *final*. There are no demands or ultimatums made or implied and not a hint of neediness or desperation. By presenting a restricted choice he either agrees to engage in a serious relationship or you terminate the arrangement. He has to choose from the options presented and make a decision; if he agrees to commit to a serious relationship any further discussions or negotiations will be on your terms, but if he doesn't agree to a committed relationship you *have* to be prepared walk away for good! This strategy won't work if you're weak and fail to follow through; if he doesn't want to be in a relationship with you, it's better to find out sooner rather than later. This saves wasting even more time on a dead-end FWB that isn't going anywhere. This is a win-win strategy – if he agrees to a relationship (and is serious) you get what you want and if he doesn't you get what you need e.g. to leave a FWB that isn't going anywhere.

▌ Reality Check!

"What exactly does that expression mean, "Friends With Benefits'? Does he provide her with health insurance?" – Chuck Lorre, American TV Writer, Director & Producer

Many men, whether they're single or attached, will happily spend time with a woman who appears to be "flexible" and accommodating as far as sex is concerned. A man who is getting convenient no-questions-asked sex is going to continue the arrangement for as long as possible! Women who try to change a casual sexual arrangement into a committed relationship are very unlikely to succeed and that's why it can be a big relationship mistake. Having sex with a man who is just a "friend" is a woman's personal choice but expecting a man to commit to a relationship after a FWB arrangement is not realistic. The most likely outcome is he will decide (at his convenience) that he doesn't want to be in a committed relationship, at least not with the woman he's having sex with. The anecdotal evidence strongly suggests that while many women make sexual agreements in good faith they can often struggle to play by the agreed "rules." Casual sex agreements usually work out much better for men who tend to adhere to the arrangement and are far less likely to become emotionally involved. Men often compartmentalize their lives in their minds so sex can be an expression of genuine love and affection, enjoyed strictly for pleasure or used as a stress reliever.

From a man's perspective it is a win-win arrangement because he is enjoying sex without any responsibilities toward the woman, which means he gets all the perks with absolutely no "downsides." For the woman it's a lose-lose strategy because not only does this type of situation erode her self-respect but she usually loses the man anyway. A woman who "gives it all away" desperately hoping for more will eventually feel cheated even though in reality she actually cheated herself! Others make the mistake of believing they can convince their sex buddy to take the arrangement to the next level, but when there is no real emotional connection a serious relationship is very unlikely. Many women simply don't want to believe having casual sex might be a bad idea but down the line when you realize you have just been used sexually and emotionally it can be very damaging to your self-esteem and self-respect. Falling in love with a man after having a bit of sexual fun can be a very painful experience when it becomes clear he is not prepared to provide the kind of love and emotional fulfilment you really want.

CHAPTER 25:

13 Big Relationship Mistakes

"Most people would learn from their mistakes if they weren't so busy denying them." – Harold J. Smith (1910-2001), Southern Baptist Evangelist & Founder of Radio Bible Hour

Falling in love can be a breathtaking experience, yet the word "fall" is usually associated with accidents such as "falling over" or "falling off" something, like a building or chair; and negativity like defeat or some other kind of mishap. However, when a person falls in love too quickly while ignoring clear warning signs there is often an accident ahead just waiting to happen! Relationship mistakes are a part of life and learning how to avoid them is wise and a much smarter strategy than having to deal with the emotional wreckage in the aftermath. The longer a romantic relationship lasts the more likely you will become emotionally involved, risking a great deal if it goes wrong.

Many men and women make one or more common mistakes or sadly repeat the same patterns of relating because they have not learnt the lessons provided by previous relationship experiences or failed to cultivate a certain degree of self-awareness. The following major mistakes can happen during the dating phase or emerge after you're already involved so watch out for the warning signs!

Not Trusting Your Intuition And Instincts

"Trust your own instinct. Your mistakes might as well be your own, instead of someone else's." – Billy Wilder, Actor

Your sixth sense is your intuition. We all have this gift but not everyone uses it. Listening to and following your intuition can lead you to discover a greater purpose in your life. There are other words that describe intuition such as your:

- Instincts
- Gut Feelings
- Hunches
- Sixth Sense
- Inner Voice

Intuition has absolutely nothing in common with logic but can certainly work in harmony with it. The dictionary definition of intuition is the ability to understand or know something without conscious reasoning. Many people pursue the logical, rational approach to a situation and pay very little attention to their "gut feelings" and yet intuition can be applied in many important areas in life including your relationships.

We can allow intuition to guide us through our lives but first we must learn how to connect and listen to it. It's quite common for most people to "hear" their intuitive voice or experience that "gut feeling" but then allow doubt or logical reasoning to block the promptings of their inner guidance.

Examples:

- You meet someone new who seems very nice, charming and attractive but "something" does not quite feel right.
- You're in a relationship and your instincts keep telling you something is wrong but there is no tangible evidence to substantiate how you're feeling.

For many of us that "feeling" frequently turns out to be very accurate. There will always be a certain feeling or emotion behind any intuitive thought you have as this is how your sixth sense communicates to you. If you have not fully acknowledged your gift of intuition it is important to learn what your inner voice feels like.

Reality Check!

"The only real valuable thing is intuition." – Albert Einstein (1879-1955), German Theoretical Physicist

Pay close attention to all of your feelings of positive expectancy as well as any negative feelings or "vibes" you may have about a place or person. Ignoring or dismissing your intuition can often result in making the wrong decisions resulting in unhappy, disappointing or even toxic relationship choices. In my experience, women seem to be more naturally in touch with their intuition than men but anyone can learn to listen and follow their own inner guidance.

Five Ways To Tune Into Your Intuition

- Set aside a few minutes to listen to your intuition and try and turn down the constant chatter of the conscious mind.
- Follow your gut instinct a few times to see what happens. Each time you try you will learn to feel what you should do.
- Be open to other people's opinions but don't believe everything you hear straight away.
- Pay attention to your first thought even if you do not like it. Self-persuasion is a powerful thing especially when you meet someone you feel strongly attracted to. Do not ignore your intuition even if the "feeling" doesn't make sense straight away.
- Trust yourself. Try not to waste too much time weighing up whether or not you're right. Trust your inner voice and your relationship choices will improve. In addition, your life challenges generally will become easier to navigate.

When you experience feelings of emotional discomfort while considering a decision or choice, pay attention! That feeling will probably continue to linger (in some cases the emotional discomfort or unease will be very strong) if you have made a decision that is probably not in your best interests.

Four simple steps to learning to follow your intuition:

1. Listen
2. Trust everything you perceive
3. Respond to your intuitive voice
4. Investigate the results

Discovering how to follow your intuition means educating yourself through conscious observation of the results and the price you may pay for ignoring it. With consistent practice and application you will learn how to work with and respect your inner emotional currents of energy and what it is trying to tell you. With consistent practice you can learn to listen to and trust the voice of your intuition. Regular experimentation usually provides consistent results. Get into the habit of listening to your instincts and only make decisions that make you feel positive.

"I feel there are two people inside me: me and my intuition. If I go against her, she'll screw me every time, and if I follow her, we get along quite nicely." – Kim Basinger, Actress

The gift of intuition can guide and protect you but you have to listen to the messages and follow any guidance you receive. Following the promptings of your inner voice can provide warnings of possible dangers you may not even be aware of and could even save your life. Listening and acting on your intuition can help you to make the right decisions and avoid making a major relationship mistake.

Failure To Ask Enough Questions

"No investigation, no right to speak" – Confucius (551-479 BC), Philosopher

One of the biggest mistakes is the failure to ask pertinent questions during the dating stages to save wasting time with a man who isn't compatible. Asking the right questions at the right time can help you to discover important information that could warn of potential problems in the future.

Obtaining reliable information is absolutely vital to find out:

- What type of person is he?
- Is he a viable candidate?

Employers routinely carry out background checks on potential employees to filter out weak candidates and conduct interviews to get an impression of prospective employees. This is done to assess whether he or she is likely to be productive, reliable and capable of contributing to the organization's goals. There are companies and organizations that invest considerable time and expense recruiting new employees to make sure they select the right candidates.

Conducting some sort of prolonged interview with a potential partner does not sound very appealing, spontaneous or romantic but dating someone new and getting to know them *is* an extended interviewing process. Your initial reaction after reading this may be, *"I'm looking for a partner not an employee!"* and it might appear to be very unromantic to act like an employer hiring new staff but asking important questions doesn't have to be conducted like a job interview; but just like any good interviewer you're after information that will assist you in making an educated and informed decision.

If you want to discover if the man you are dating is a viable candidate for a long term relationship questions have to be asked. Asking a potential partner about his past can be tricky sometimes and you should definitely avoid a situation that looks like an FBI interrogation! A good strategy is to encourage a person to discuss themselves; this gives you opportunity to learn about his history and life.

General Questions

- What did you enjoy (or hate) about school?
- What's the earliest memory you have?
- Who is your best friend?
- Where's the best place you ever went with your parents, and what did you do there?
- What kind of books (TV shows/movies/video games) do you like?
- What's the worst job you've ever had?
- What's the most embarrassing moment of your life?
- If I asked you to cook dinner for me, what would you make?
- What do you think is the biggest problem in the world today? How do you think people should respond?
- If you could have lunch with anyone in the world, alive or dead, who would it be with?
- If you won the lottery tomorrow, what would be the first thing you would do with the money?
- Who's your favorite movie character? What do you like about him/her?
- What's the biggest goal you're working on now?
- Have you ever had your heart broken? What happened?
- Have you ever cheated on a partner? Why did you cheat? Did you get caught? What happened?
- Do you think there is a difference between having sex and making love? What is it?

These type of questions can give you some important insights without appearing to be overly intrusive. Avoid rattling off the questions quickly and don't interrupt a good conversation just to ask the questions! If he is engaged in talking to you just listen and learn about him that way. The truth is you have to be pretty ruthless when you're screening potential candidates in the dating game. Understand those applying to become a part of your life could easily be Players, time wasters or simply not compatible with you for a variety of other reasons. The only intelligent strategy for finding out information is to ask questions - this may seem very unromantic but it is very practical and sensible!

Why do so many women fail to ask sensible questions before they become deeply involved?

The quest to find the elusive "soul mate" can over-rule commonsense so instead of asking the right type of questions and paying attention women can often indulge themselves in the dating rituals of socializing, flirting and fantasizing.

There are women who truly believe meeting the true "love of their life" will be magical and effortless allowing them to experience their own private fairy tale. While the romantic dreams are pursued practical issues can be pushed aside and ignored.

Reasons Why You Might Avoid Asking Too Many Questions

- You're desperate to find love and think too many questions might scare off a potential partner. When you're desperate to be involved it's very easy to fall into the trap of not asking too many questions fearing this will create problems and prevent the relationship from moving forward.

- When dating a new man, you avoid asking questions because you're too busy enjoying the possibility of your romantic fantasies being fulfilled. Trying to pursue or maintain a romantic fantasy, you concentrate on the reasons to stay with him convincing yourself he is the right guy for you, while ignoring the possibility he could be wrong for a relationship.

Whether you're dating or in a relationship a reluctance to ask questions is a form of denial which can eventually lead to a variety of dramas that have the potential to be very damaging and even dangerous. A failure to ask questions may be motivated by the desire to avoid being asked too many questions about yourself. This can indicate low self-esteem issues. A potential partner may decide you're not very attractive if you reveal too much about yourself so this strategy can also be used as a form of self-protection caused by a fear of rejection. If you're uncomfortable asking questions review your personal and relationship history to see why this is a difficult issue for you. Seek professional support if resolving this problem becomes too difficult to tackle on your own.

Both Partners Avoid Asking Questions

When two people are dating or get together they may both avoid asking relevant questions, which often results in misunderstandings and confusion. A couple with very little information about each other can delude themselves about a variety of important issues. A relationship where partners avoid asking each other questions is disingenuous, unhealthy and can even be dangerous.

In the dating game the most sensible and prudent policy is to ask lots of questions; the more information you have, the better your relationship choices will be. Failing to make enquiries about a man's background or attitude towards certain subjects is a major mistake. Assumptions can waste a great deal of time and can lead to some very unpleasant surprises! If you're making decisions on poor or very little information you can end up with a man who is very unsuitable or even worse, toxic. Intelligent women take nothing for granted.

"Those questions you have? Whether he's the one, whether you feel about him the way you should, or whether the relationship is going okay? When you're not sure whether you're in love with someone or not, the answer is not." – Deb Caletti, *The Secret Life of Prince Charming*

The dating process would be a lot easier if men had a clear warning sign on their foreheads listing their positive and negative personality traits, habits and agendas – but they don't. To avoid making a major mistake you can't allow yourself to be influenced by slick presentation, romantic fantasies or enticed into becoming involved prematurely just by being told what you may want to hear.

The Biggest Relationship Mistakes Often Happen When Women:

- Fail to ask the right questions
- Become emotionally or sexually involved too quickly
- Fail to investigate
- Make assumptions

Many women simply fail to ask the man she is dating his views on relationships or marriage. Disappointing and distressing dramas inevitably happen when a woman wants marriage but discovers her partner is not looking for the same thing or is completely against the idea. It's always prudent to find out a potential partner's life goals and intentions during the dating stage or you could end up drifting along in a relationship that isn't going anywhere.

Dating someone new isn't about trying to win him over; your mission is to gather as much relevant information as possible so you can decide if he is a suitable candidate. Always pay attention and act on whatever you discover so your decisions and relationship choices are sensible and informed.

Already Involved

If you're currently involved and have avoided asking your partner the right questions this isn't healthy. You probably fear asking too many questions could expose information that might endanger the relationship so ignore any suspicious or obvious signs of cheating. Trying to avoid the truth while attempting to manufacture greater harmony or compatibility when it doesn't really exists or constantly giving a man the benefit of the doubt results in living a lie. A woman should never be scared of asking questions because she thinks this will scare her partner away; when a relationship isn't honest and communication is poor it's probably going to fail anyway so you have nothing to lose by pursuing the truth. When you're with a partner and scared to ask questions due to a fear of being abused this isn't a healthy relationship, it's a dictatorship. Make plans to leave *now* and when you do, don't look back.

Giving Into Feelings Of Sexual Lust

"If they substituted the word 'Lust' for 'Love' in the popular songs it would come nearer the truth." – Sylvia Plath, *The Unabridged Journals of Sylvia Plath*

The classic movie *Fatal Attraction* starring Michael Douglas and Glen Close tells the dramatic story of two people giving into lust and strong sexual chemistry which results in very tragic consequences. We live in very liberal times with many men and women enjoying recreational sex without any emotional investment and it's hardly a secret women enjoy sex just as much as men! Sex is one of the most glorious experiences a human being can have and feeling an urge for sexual activity or feeling "horny" is perfectly natural. If you have been sexually inactive and single for a while, feeling lonely and experiencing strong sexual yearnings, you might feel as if there is something "missing" from your life. It can be tempting to consider taking the easy option of a one night stand with "no strings attached", believing this will satisfy the feelings of desire. Finding a man who is willing to satisfy a woman's sexual urges isn't usually a problem but there can be unforeseen consequences.

Typical Scenarios

- You indulge in a one night stand after a moment of "weakness" and begin to feel guilty. You therefore start telling yourself, "I'm not that type of woman" and try to justify sleeping with him by making it into a "relationship."

- The emotions triggered by having sex convince you the feelings are actually deeper than they really are.

- Your desire for sex motivates you to continue sleeping with a guy you don't particularly like. The sex might be fantastic but you cannot spend all of your free time copulating!

- The man is physically attractive but isn't really compatible with you. Gradually it becomes clear there isn't a great deal in common and you start to regret getting into a relationship or a Friends With Benefits arrangement based purely on sex. You begin to realize having sex without any feelings or commitment can't provide what you really want.

Many women convince themselves they can have sex without becoming emotionally involved but learn through bitter experience that indulging their sexual yearnings on a whim isn't a very good idea. While casual sex can be a great deal of fun it can also lead to a great deal confusion and drama.

▌ Reality Check!

"For men, I think, love is a thing formed of equal parts lust and astonishment. The astonishment part women understand. The lust part they only think they understand." – Stephen King, Author

Everyone has their personal "code", moral beliefs and attitudes regarding sexual activity and our individual conscience dictates how we each respond. Feelings of lust are a natural part of the human experience – it's whether we choose to act on those impulses or not that matters.

There is nothing wrong with consenting adults indulging in casual sexual activity providing they are both clear about what they're doing but if you are constantly giving in to those "feeling horny" urges this indicates you have a problem. Many people use sex as a substitute for real intimacy or even as a way to avoid intimacy, but the act alone cannot replace a genuine emotional connection or true intimacy. Sleeping with a man just for sex or to feel physically close to him isn't a smart decision, especially if you're looking for a serious relationship.

Each of us has a "sexual cycle." Some people like to have sex three times a week while others prefer to have sex once or twice a month. It's important to understand your unique sexual cycle, urges and desires which are motivated by certain psychological aspects of your personality. If the urges become very strong learn to be disciplined and to resist any temptations to indulge yourself. Giving into sexual yearnings can get you into a relationship for all the wrong reasons, resulting in drama, emotional distress and massive disappointments.

The Falling In Lust Trap

Falling in lust is one of the major pitfalls associated with deciding to give in to powerful sexual yearnings. Indulging in some convenient sex can seem like a good idea but women and men are biologically and emotionally very different. For some women it can seem quite easy to act like a man and think like one too when it comes to sex but the reality is very different with unseen issues arising that can be very difficult to resolve.

Men and women who have a pattern of falling in lust are not concerned about overall compatibility or the other important qualities each of us should be looking for in a potential partner. The danger of becoming involved with men purely based on physical attraction and lust is women end up trying to convince themselves everything else will just "work out" for the best. It can be very tempting to believe appearances or feelings of strong sexual chemistry can guarantee compatibility in the other key areas of a relationship but this simply isn't true.

▌ Reality Check!

"The more we are filled with thoughts of lust the less we find true romantic love." – Douglas Horton (1891-1968), American Clergy Man

Giving in to strong feelings of physical attraction and sexual chemistry usually results in falling in lust. When someone is "in lust" they're actually "in love" with the sexual chemistry and passion they feel for the other person. They make the mistake of believing what they are feeling is "love" and the experience can be so intense for some people they can be in denial about what is really happening.

After falling in lust women can feel obliged to continue having sex trying to create a relationship for a variety of reasons. They may:

- Refuse to face the reality of the situation
- Develop feelings so find it difficult to end it and let go
- Fear being alone or starting again
- Be desperate to make the relationship succeed
- Refuse to admit they've made a mistake
- Ignore any potential warning signs regarding his personality or lifestyle

Some women commit to a man quite quickly based on their feelings of lust or strong physical attraction, only to gradually discover overall compatibility is severely lacking. Of course sexual compatibility is very important but couples spend the majority of their time doing other things.

Finding a man very attractive is perfectly natural but constantly allowing lust to govern your relationship decisions is just being irresponsible. Sharing powerful sexual chemistry and enjoying mind blowing sex is great but sex alone cannot maintain a relationship or contribute to its growth.

To find a relationship that has real and enduring potential you have to look beyond physical appearance or feelings of sexual attraction and take the time to investigate what type of personality and character a man possesses.

If your relationship history indicates a tendency to be heavily influenced by appearances, feelings of physical attraction and a habit of becoming sexually involved quite quickly, slow yourself down and take any dating one step at a time. Becoming involved with men based purely on appearances or strong feelings of physical attraction has almost zero percent chance of relationship success. Rushing into sexual intimacy often causes problems, disappointment or heartbreak – problems that can be very easily avoided. Getting to know someone takes time so make this your first priority; falling in lust is a very shallow reason to have sex with a man and usually leaves women who succumb to those urges being used, abused and ultimately abandoned.

Giving Into Family Members' Opinions Or Peer Pressure

"The individual has always had to struggle to keep from being overwhelmed by the tribe. If you try it, you will be lonely often, and sometimes frightened. But no price is too high to pay for the privilege of owning yourself." – Friedrich Nietzsche (1844-1900), Philosopher, Poet & Composer

The majority of people follow the crowd because it's generally much easier and requires very little independent thinking. When your family or friends share similar beliefs there can be pressure to agree with their opinions and to conform fearing they might disapprove. The opinions of family members can be influenced or formed by a variety of factors including childhood conditioning, cultural expectations and the wider society in which they live. Family members may think it's a bit "strange" if you're a certain age and have been single for a while or not married. They may begin to drop hints, make comments that make you feel uncomfortable or question you directly regarding your single status. Age pressure can come from family, friends and wider society and can make some women begin to panic about the lack of having a partner in their lives. Women generally have a target age when they expect to be married or in a long-term, serious relationship. This goal may be conscious or subconscious but most women have strong maternal instincts and are conscious of the legendary "body clock" that counts down towards having children. If you're single while several of your female friends are in serious or long-term relationships, you might begin to compare yourself with them and start to worry about being "left on the shelf." You may even feel slightly jealous of your friends who are in relationships at times, especially when you're invited to social events and don't have a partner to go with.

You can be influenced by a combination of family, friend and age pressure when:

- You're the last person in your family to get married or to be involved in a serious long-term relationship.
- The majority of your friends are in stable relationships but you're still single.
- You're over thirty years old, still unmarried or not in a serious relationship.
- You have been recently divorced.

It can be easy to fall into the trap of believing you must have some kind of "problem" because you're not in a serious relationship. For some women a combination of family, friend and age pressure can cause feelings of mild depression or even panic. Buckling under the pressure often creates a sense of urgency which can badly affect your judgment where you miss obvious warning signs and become involved in a relationship motivated by fear, insecurity or self-doubt. Feelings of desperation or the fear of being alone can send you on a mission to find a man before it's "too late."

Men and women can end up in unhappy relationships because they let other people influence their thinking and choices!

| Reality Check!

"A year or so ago I went through all the people in my life and asked myself: does this person inspire me, genuinely love me and support me unconditionally? I wanted nothing but positive influences in my life." – Mena Suvari, American Actress

We can all be influenced negatively or positively by the expectations or cultural preferences of family and friends. There can be a variety of pressures to conform to their opinions because we fear disapproval. Many men and women make the mistake of succumbing to these pressures and find themselves enduring deeply unhappy relationships. Sadly these individuals were not assertive enough to resist family expectations or the opinions of others and allowed this to influence their thinking and choices. Allowing these pressures to dictate your choices can result in choosing a partner you're not really compatible with or even worse staying in a relationship with a man you don't love. The expectations of friends, family and wider society can also impose so many requirements and expectations regarding what type of man is a "good catch" and this can make it very difficult to know if you're making a sensible choice. The influence of others on your relationship choices can be very strong if you lack self-awareness. This leads to making relationship decisions that may look great on the surface and suit the opinions of others but which are ultimately misguided.

Your priority should always be to choose when you're ready for a relationship free from the opinions, influences and expectations of other people. It's your life so make sure you choose a partner you truly want to be with instead of making choices influenced by the opinions of others. It's also important to discover if you are putting yourself under unnecessary pressure by your own idealistic expectations, hopes and dreams. If you're feeling pressured to find a partner, spend some time exploring why you're unhappy being single and any other factors that may be influencing your mindset.

Deeply Desperate

"As long as we believe that we have to have the other in our life to be happy, we are really just an addict trying to protect our supply-using another person as our drug of choice. That is not True Love-nor is it Loving." – Robert Burney, *The Dance of Wounded Souls*

Are you desperately searching for your "soul mate?" Do you hope to find someone who will validate you as a person and help you to feel better about yourself while struggling with feelings of loneliness? Are you looking for a romantic fantasy believing a relationship will satisfy and fill the "hole" in your heart? There are women who allow their feelings of insecurity or desperation to control their perspective and choices instead of embracing the many opportunities being single provides. The deeply desperate often confuse **wanting** a partner with **needing** a man in their life and when a woman believes a relationship is vital for her happiness she will sacrifice many things, including her self-respect.

7 Major Signs Of The Deeply Desperate

1. Constantly seeking the "perfect partner"
2. Believes a relationship is a necessity
3. Unrealistic expectations
4. Poor boundaries
5. Falls "in love" quickly
6. Extreme emotional needs
7. Will *tell* their new partner they are in love quickly

The deeply desperate frequently frighten away potential partners with totally unrealistic dreams about how "true love" should be. Alternatively, they enter relationships with unrealistic expectations and begin to make unreasonable demands. These types often see themselves as overflowing with love and men can be suckered into a draining or dysfunctional relationship mistaking desperation for genuine connection. It can be easy to believe someone who is desperate to love will have plenty of love and affection to share. However, once involved they're likely to think of their partner as being unappreciative of their efforts and attention and have rigid views about how true love should be while believing fantasies about how the relationship will transform their lives for the better. This combination often places a great deal of pressure on the relationship and their partner will constantly feel drained, suffocated, or even trapped. The version of "love" the deeply desperate offers can come at a very high price and the majority of emotionally healthy people are unwilling or unable to stay in such a relationship.

Desperate For Commitment

In the dating game females are much more likely to want a committed relationship than the average man and have a greater tendency to fall into the trap of assuming a commitment has been made without actually discussing the matter. This is particularly true for women who constantly fantasize about being married and spend a lot of time fueling those dreams by:

- Constantly reading bridal magazines or researching wedding tips online.

- Fantasizing about marriage and children very soon after meeting a new man.
- Feeling resentful when their friends talk about the eligible men they've met recently.
- Feeling sad or anxious when completing applications and forms that require information about their relationship status.

Women desperate for love usually maintain very poor personal boundaries, especially when they begin to panic about being single. Desperation is rarely considered very attractive but predators in the dating game know how to identify the desperate types who leave themselves open to being used and abused by those who will ruthlessly exploit any obvious neediness. If you're in serious denial about your state of desperation it's easy to end up having sex with a man just to avoid your own company. To make matters worse, those with a desperate mindset often find it difficult to handle relationship failures leaving them feeling both deeply rejected and unworthy of love.

Reality Check!

"Chasing a man is not winning. The only thing you win is the loss of your dignity. Confidence is knowing your value, instead of expecting a man's love to provide you with value." – Shannon L. Alder, Author

Seeking to begin a relationship due to feelings of loneliness and desperation is a bad idea. Finding a partner can be quite easy when you're feeling desperate but it's unlikely to provide the kind of relationship you're really looking for. For those compelled by desperation to seek love, the prospects for a healthy, normal relationship are usually doomed from the very beginning.

When you enter a relationship insisting on having your needs met by a man instead of being whole and complete in your own right you will end up deceiving yourself and your partner. Eventually feelings of resentment will grow as you find and demand your other "needs" are also satisfied. It is impossible for one person to fulfill all of their partner's needs consistently and these unrealistic expectations will eventually leave you feeling disappointed and frustrated. Entering a relationship with a desperate mindset will often result in pain and confusion for both parties when it inevitably ends in tears and recriminations.

Becoming romantically involved when you're feeling intensely desperate will usually result in very poor relationship choices. A relationship should enhance your life instead of being some kind of emotional crutch to compensate for whatever feels missing inside. When you learn to truly accept, love and respect yourself any feelings of desperation will become a very distant memory.

A healthy relationship with yourself is the key to enjoying productive relationships with others. If you're feeling desperate for a relationship spend some time working on yourself, with support if necessary, to build up your self-esteem. Raising your self-awareness and self-esteem can help you to prepare for a healthy relationship that will have a genuine chance of succeeding. It's a big mistake to give into feelings of desperation. Maintain your standards and look for the kind of relationship that you want and deserve instead of settling for second best or just a man who happens to be available!

Relationship Distraction

"When we're incomplete, we're always searching for somebody to complete us. When, after a few years or a few months of a relationship, we find that we're still unfulfilled, we blame our partners and take up with somebody more promising. This can go on and on – series polygamy – until we admit that while a partner can add sweet dimensions to our lives, we, each of us, are responsible for our own fulfillment. Nobody else can provide it for us, and to believe otherwise is to delude ourselves dangerously and to program for eventual failure every relationship we enter." – Tom Robbins, American Novelist

Relationship distraction is when you distract yourself deliberately or unconsciously to avoid dealing with feelings of emptiness or loneliness. These are people who like to keep busy or pretend to be extremely preoccupied so they can avoid discovering who they really are. The quest for distraction can also be motivated by the feeling that "something" is missing so men and women go out looking for a relationship believing finding a partner will make them feel complete. Those who suffer from low self-esteem often feel unlovable so use situations or people to divert their attention away from having to consider their feelings of inadequacy. Frequently feeling uncomfortable with themselves, they are experts at finding something or someone to provide a distraction.

People who fall into the distraction trap are generally trying to:

- Receive attention and to feel important (motivated by the Ego)
- Escape feelings of loneliness
- Avoid feelings of emptiness
- Distract from feelings of depression
- Recover from a previous relationship (on the rebound)
- Provide excitement
- Re-establish a sex life
- Feel worthy of love

The Distraction Trap And The "Instant Relationship"

Men and women caught up in the distraction cycle frequently become involved with new partners quite quickly, spending only brief periods of time being single in between each relationship. You can begin to fall into this trap by giving into any feelings of loneliness and becoming gradually obsessed with finding that special soul mate, convincing yourself finding love will finally deliver lasting happiness.

When you begin dating a new man this provides a temporary distraction as a new relationship is usually a lot of fun and can be very exciting! There are great feelings of relief and joy now you have finally found that special man to share your life with, but eventually those negative feelings about yourself begin to haunt you once again. You also begin to blame your partner, believing he is not really fulfilling your "needs." Petty arguments fester and then develop into major conflicts as the feelings of loneliness or low self-worth come to the surface. The initial feelings of euphoria and state of bliss are swiftly replaced with unhappiness, drama and usually the end of a relationship that appeared to have promised so much at the beginning.

Are you caught up in a distraction cycle? Check yourself out:

- I prefer be with other people to avoid spending time alone.
- I tend to become romantically involved with a new partner very quickly.
- I have a history of unfulfilling relationships.
- I devote less time to my own interests and friends when involved in a relationship.
- I encourage and motivate others to solve their problems while neglecting my own.
- My romantic relationships or friendships tend to be very time consuming.
- I am easily distracted by other people's needs even if working on an important task or project.
- I usually abandon my personal projects or dreams when I am in a relationship or called upon by a friend.
- The emotional, mental or spiritual areas of my life tend to be neglected, especially when I am in a relationship.

Identifying strongly with several of the above statements indicates you're using your relationships or other activities as a distraction to avoid addressing certain personal issues.

Any kind of distraction that prevents you from exploring and healing yourself is ultimately futile. A new or current relationship can be used as a distraction from dealing with any personal issues honestly and thoroughly. People who try to keep themselves "busy" in relationships never truly discover what their genuine wants and needs are. They invest a great deal of time and energy into making their relationships "work" while distracting themselves from getting in touch with and understanding their true selves. Using your relationships as a distraction is totally counter-productive because you are just hiding from yourself.

▌ Reality Check!

"I needed something - the distraction of another life - to alleviate fear." – Bret Easton Ellis, *Lunar Park*

Negative patterns of thinking or Emotional Baggage that may be sabotaging your relationships are not just going to disappear because you decide to ignore the issue. When you're using a relationship to avoid looking at yourself, you run the risk of becoming involved with a man for reasons that have nothing to do with love. Men and women who lack any real purpose or passion in their lives also find it very convenient to become romantically involved. They use relationships as an excuse for failing to take some time to raise their levels of self-awareness and to discover who they really are. It is important to acknowledge it is emotionally dishonest to use partners as an excuse to avoid dealing with your own issues or a lack of life purpose. Sadly, for some people it can take many failed relationships before they decide to take some time out for a period of genuine reflection.

Consider these questions carefully:

- If you feel uncomfortable or really don't like being single why should a man be genuinely interested in getting to know you?
- Why should a man want to be in a relationship with you when you don't really enjoy being with yourself?
- Why do your relationships keep failing even though you keep making your partner a priority in your life?
- How many more "romances" will it take before you recognize the importance of taking some time out for yourself to discover if there is any Emotional Baggage motivating your decisions and behavior?

When you fail to deal with any underlying issues before becoming involved they will inevitably resurface in your relationships. Work on yourself and release any fears of being alone, being considered "different" or not being liked and learn to enjoy time being by yourself. Become your biggest fan and grow to realize that no one but you can make you feel whole and complete.

If you believe your happiness in life is dependent upon another, then you will leave yourself open to being manipulated, used and abused. You will never be ***truly*** happy because whoever you are with will always have the ability to hold you to an emotional ransom. Our relationships are supposed to enrich our lives, not *be* our lives. All the love you have to give begins with self-love; I am not talking about the negative personality traits of arrogance or conceit but a healthy nurturing love of self. Cultivating qualities such as high self-esteem, self-awareness and feeling good about yourself will provide a solid foundation for entering a satisfying and loving relationship.

Guilt

"There is a luxury in self-reproach. When we blame ourselves, we feel that no one else has a right to blame us." – Oscar Wilde (1854-1900), Irish Author, Playwright & Poet

As children, many of us are taught that feeling guilt is natural or even a virtue. Cultures and societies over the centuries have used guilt, shame and blame to control their children. Certain religions still teach their believers to feel guilty about certain behaviors such as having sex or teach it is a "sin" to do anything that feels good. Many people have even been conditioned as children to believe it's bad *not* to feel guilty! This can be true in certain circumstances, for example feeling guilty can compel us to act properly or do the right thing. A guilty conscience can also cause feelings of deep regret and can demonstrate to another person we feel sorry if we have hurt them in some way. But there are also times when guilt can be used in ways that cause unnecessarily pain and blockages.

Are you motivated or controlled by guilt? Check yourself out:

Did you:

- Grow up in a home or environment feeling responsible for the happiness of others; perhaps you had a single parent who relied heavily on you for support or affection or you had a parent who required constant rescuing and attention?

- Grow up in a dysfunctional family where your feelings were dismissed e.g. your parents were controlling, critical or alcoholic?

Do you:

- Take great pride in being considered a sensitive person?
- Feel deeply hurt if accused of being selfish?
- Have difficulties expressing your opinions if you think this will upset your partner?
- Struggle to identify your needs or find it difficult to ask for what you want especially from your loved ones?
- Find it difficult to assert yourself by refusing requests from others especially those who are close to you?
- Feel compelled to offer assistance and seek solutions for others?
- Feel comfortable spending your time and money on other people but not on yourself?
- Feel uncomfortable being more successful or happier than your partner or people who you know well?

If you agree with even a few of the above statements it's likely you experience feelings of guilt occasionally and this is normal for the majority of people.

Agreeing with four or more of these statements indicates you're permitting guilt to either

a) Influence your relationship choices, or

b) Keep you in relationships because you feel guilty

If the majority of these statements apply to you, you're probably allowing guilt to motivate your relationship choices for all the wrong reasons and have some serious work to do in this area.

By their very nature women can stay with partners due to deep feelings of sympathy, guilt or even pity but, unfortunately, this can mean staying in relationships way past their "sell by date." Denial often plays a large part in these scenarios as they deceive themselves into believing they're staying for reasons of "love." Others become a hostage of their guilty feelings, wanting to leave but scared of how their partner may react if they're rejected.

▌ Reality Check!

"Guilt isn't always a rational thing, Clio realized. Guilt is a weight that will crush you whether you deserve it or not." – Maureen Johnson, *Girl at Sea*

Relationships end all the time for a variety of reasons. Deciding to leave doesn't make you evil or a bad person but you may fear being judged by your soon to be ex-partner who will be deeply hurt or even angry. Break-ups are seldom mutual agreements and often leave one partner with feelings of rejection and loss. Many people find deciding to end a relationship difficult and the announcement can be delayed for weeks, months or in some cases even years.

The cycle of thoughts that can keep you trapped include:

- I don't want to upset him
- He is a good person and doesn't deserve to have his heart broken
- I don't want to hurt him
- I feel responsible for him
- He doesn't have a good support system to get through this when I leave
- He won't be able to cope without me
- He is going to hate me

These thoughts and feelings are perfectly natural and show you're a compassionate person but the desire to protect a partner can keep you trapped inside living a lie.

Examine your relationship history to see if you have a tendency of dating men you feel sorry for or a habit of staying with partners when you knew it wasn't working because you didn't want hurt their feelings by leaving. Perhaps you felt your rejection would cause a previous partner great pain or you believed they had deeper feelings for you than you had for them. Staying in a relationship due to feelings of guilt or sympathy doesn't help anyone; in fact, it disempowers the person on the receiving end of this type of "kindness." When guilt is the motivating factor for staying you're not doing yourself any favors and if you're convinced your partner cannot survive without you, the feelings of guilt will eventually turn into feelings of resentment or even disdain.

Ask yourself this question: "Would I want to be in a relationship with a man who didn't really want me?" Each person deserves to be with a partner who wants to be in a relationship with them. When we enter a relationship there is always the possibility it isn't going to work out and someone is going to get hurt. It's futile trying to protect a partner from this reality and any attempt to delay expressing your true feelings will usually result in the break up being even more painful. Your partner deserves honesty and respect; delaying ending the relationship through misguided devotion when you're no longer in love is being emotionally dishonest. Trying to fake how you feel and pretending everything is just fine inevitably becomes very stressful and while men are often accused of failing to pick up signals or being emotionally insensitive this generally isn't true. Your partner probably senses something is wrong and once you reveal the truth he may even say he noticed a change in the relationship. He may even be upset that you have been faking your feelings for him. Once you know in your heart it's over make a decision to tell your partner as soon as possible to avoid the mistake of remaining in an unhappy relationship.

While remaining in a relationship due to feelings of guilt is a very bad idea, using guilt trips to manipulate others is devious and unethical. Those who employ guilt trip tactics seeking to control others actually teach themselves to feel guilty. At the creative level of consciousness intentions and thoughts are never just given away, they are always shared. Every thought and intention generated by each individual is kept as a "copy" of the intent and eventually returns to the sender in one way or another. In other words, what goes around comes around. On a practical level guilt trips may work on others in the short-term but eventually people see through this strategy and distance themselves, often feeling disgust at such behavior. Feeling guilty or trying to make others feel bad about themselves cannot take you to a place of love, peace or happiness.

During your personal self-development you may find a variety of issues you have been conditioned to feel badly about. "Feeling guilty" is often a conditioned response and many of us are taught to feel bad or guilty when someone judges us. These judgments can be about a wide range of issues, including what we might say or how we dress, think or behave. When you believe you have done something wrong feelings of guilt may compel you to judge yourself very harshly. The feelings of guilt can pull you in several different directions at the same time, draining your energy. Excessive guilt can leave you feeling very stuck and engaged in an intense inner conflict where you lose yourself in an ocean of recriminations. This type of thinking doesn't actually make a great deal of sense! If another human being isn't being intentionally hurt, exploited or damaged in some way, we should all feel comfortable and totally guilt-free pursuing the activities that make us happy.

The best way to avoid falling into the trap of guilt is to become conscious of your own judgments about yourself and to stop accepting the judgments of others. Get in touch with your authentic feelings and do what is right for you instead of responding to any childhood conditioning influencing what you think you should do. The bottom line is becoming involved or staying with a man motivated by guilt means you're cheating yourself out of the kind of love you want and deserve.

Compromising Standards, Values And Requirements

"Commitment in a relationship needs to be based on a commitment to myself – to love, honor, obey and cherish my own being." – Shakti Gawain, *Living in the Light*

When you first meet someone new it's natural to share your beliefs and values to discover how much compatibility there may be. However, if substantial differences are discovered but you really want to pursue the relationship, you may decide to make unhealthy compromises to avoid potential conflicts. He might tick many of the right boxes and you may even find him attractive, so it can be very tempting to reduce or dismiss certain points that are really important by trying to create more compatibility than actually exists.

Premature compromises generally begin to happen during the dating phase of the relationship.

- *You make major adjustments to your standards, requirements and expectations.*
- *You make major adjustments to your behaviors and habits.*

Certain compromises are not made consciously but can be motivated by the hope of really wanting the relationship to work. So agreements are made regarding things you're not really happy with or you ignore particular issues hoping this will help the relationship to succeed. Healthy relationships require a certain degree of compromise and being a partner means you're likely to seek agreements on certain issues but making ***premature compromises*** often results in storing up problems for the future and can even be dangerous.

How Premature Compromises Happen

- Feeling desperate you make compromises at the beginning to keep the relationship going.

- Over time it becomes obvious there are major differences but you compromise your standards, values and requirements to keep the relationship intact.
- You have sex too early because you feel pressured or because you want to take the relationship to the next level.
- He didn't put you under any pressure to compromise but you were scared this might be your last chance to find "true love" so adjusted your standards and behavior to make yourself a better "fit" with him.
- You modify, deny or fail to express your opinions and beliefs regarding personal and general topics such as religion, politics, the environment, abortion or homosexuality to avoid any potential conflicts.
- You decline to express your opinion even when you strongly disagree with your partner.
- You fail to challenge your partner when you feel he is doing something wrong.
- You get involved in activities and pastimes that didn't interest you before, such as using illicit drugs, drinking excessively or watching pornography to appear highly compatible with your partner.
- You become drawn into the personal dramas of his friends.

Making major premature compromises to please your partner in the short-term is to create a fantasy where you imagine more compatibility than actually exists. Compatibility based on a fantasy means pretending the connection you share with your partner is deeper than it really is and this is a very unstable foundation for any relationship.

You Are Compromising Too Much When

- Your partner says he isn't comfortable spending time with your family and friends so you greatly reduce the actual time you spend in their company or stop seeing them.
- You try to please him by spending more time with his family and friends even though it makes you feel uncomfortable.
- He puts pressure on you and threatens to end the relationship if you don't comply with his wishes.
- Any decision you make is based on desperation to be loved and accepted by your new partner and make the relationship work.

When your beliefs and interests are suppressed because your views are not acceptable to your partner or he doesn't like your family or friends, you may tend to make these less of a priority in your life to create the illusion the relationship is working and everything is just fine. Excessive compromises inevitably result in not being true to yourself and eventually *losing* yourself in a relationship. Compromising excessively out of a desire to avoid conflict will inevitably leave you feeling very frustrated and resentful.

Honest Relationships

"You cannot belong to anyone else until you belong to yourself." – Pearl Bailey (1918-1990), Actress & Singer

When there are serious differences regarding values and expectations, conflicts are inevitable. Premature compromises will eventually leave you with three choices:

- Continue to sacrifice your values and beliefs for the preservation of the relationship.
- Try and change your partner (not a good idea!).
- Stand by your values and beliefs risking tension, conflict or even the failure of the relationship.

One of the main benefits of cultivating strong personal boundaries and self-awareness is that you will really know yourself. You will have firm standards, values and requirements and your core principles and beliefs will not be negotiable. The best way to give a new relationship a real chance of succeeding is not to compromise your most important personal values and peace of mind for the sole purpose of being with someone. When you start dating or begin a new relationship, be honest about who you are and what your expectations are. If it's moving too fast for you, be truthful and say so. Respect your own feelings and don't let desperation for a relationship prevent you from expressing how you feel. Remember your agenda, and accept total responsibility for implementing that agenda. Once you begin to suppress what is important to you in the hope of creating a false sense of compatibility and unity, you're not being true to yourself. Compromises and adjustments should happen as you get to know someone new but not to the extent you lose yourself in the process.

Reality Check!

"I cannot compromise my respect for your love. You can keep your love, I will keep my respect." – Amit Kalantri, *I Love You Too*

Compromising your beliefs and values for the sake of finding or keeping a relationship is self-defeating. If you're currently involved and now realize you have made major compromises just to please your partner or to "keep the peace," it's time to seriously reevaluate the relationship. Being committed to yourself first and your partner second isn't advocating selfishness, just plain commonsense. The most important relationship you will ever have is the relationship you have with yourself. Loving yourself means you set the standard as to how you will be treated and what you expect. Loving yourself always means you accept your strengths (which you celebrate) as well as your weaknesses (which you work on) while making sure you're very clear about your own values, standards and interests.

Material Seduction

"When we are motivated by fear, we can easily be seduced by the false gods of sex, power and money and all they represent. Once seduced we abdicate our control to the seductive authority: the dysfunctional relationship, the external source of money and security." – Caroline Myss, *The Anatomy of the Spirit*

One of the primary drives of the Ego is the desire to feel important. You have probably heard someone being accused of having a "big Ego," which usually means he or she is conceited or has a high opinion of themselves. The Ego is the part of your personality that seeks to separate you from others, which is necessary for your physical survival and helps to provide a sense of independence from others. It provides the motivation to feed and clothe yourself and also attempts to keep you safe from harm. These positive functions are primal, natural and greatly assist each of us to define ourselves in the world.

When the Ego becomes too big and out of control it isn't satisfied with food but demands to consume the *best* food or a home that must be the *largest or most expensive*. A car is no longer seen as a convenient way of getting around but is transformed into a status symbol. The Ego's appetite must be catered for at all times as it constantly seeks external validation of self-worth. The measurements of personal success are always money, power, fame and glamour while the ideals of love, peace, cooperation, harmonious relationships or ethics are often considered worthless. The Ego always seeks to compromise or sacrifice the ideals that are truly important in life while seeking to satisfy superficial needs. Ego's that are out of control constantly need to defend themselves as they seek to compete, trying to "prove" they are "better" than other people instead of wishing to cooperate. If your Ego remains unchecked and running wild it will drive you to relentlessly compare yourself with others and the desire to feel superior will lead to judgments about other people being inferior.

Allowing your Ego to rule your life can be very tiring. There may be brief moments when its demands are satisfied but you can never really relax because it always wants more! Everyone has an Ego just as each of us have narcissistic traits to varying degrees, but this part of your personality is not some kind of uncontrollable monster! The Ego can be tamed by applying personal discipline, cultivating greater self-awareness and developing a deep sense of humility. This combination helps to create a mindset that seeks to cooperate with others instead of wanting to constantly compete and win.

Now you're probably thinking, "What has my Ego and the desire to feel important got to do with my relationship choices?" Your relationship with yourself sets the tone for every other relationship you have. *When your Ego is dominating your relationship choices it will drive an unreasonable desire for greater social status, which can lead to making some of the biggest relationship mistakes.*

The Status Trap

"It is a brave and honest person who can stand apart from the masses and openly challenge its most treasured beliefs." – Donna Evans, Author

For many people, status is relative to their social or professional standing. Their *status symbols* are the possessions that demonstrate their wealth, high status or a particular level of social standing. During December 2008 the *Evening Standard Magazine* published an article called "Status of Mind" by Helen Kirwan-Taylor that discussed how the loss of status impacted individuals. She predicted an epidemic of "status reversal" for many people caused by mass redundancies and unemployment due to the then "credit crunch." The term "status reversal" sounds very chic but it's just another way of describing the emotional investments many people make regarding their possessions and status. Michael Marmot, professor of Epidemiology and Public Health at University College of London, has spent 30 years looking at the effect of status on people's health and what he calls "status syndrome." He defines status as a person's position within a hierarchy, and the higher a person considers themselves to be, the greater the pain when he or she fails. According to professor Marmot any loss of status can result in feelings of humiliation and an increased risk to good health. Deep anxiety is usually the first symptom, which if left untreated can lead to serious long-term illnesses such as gastro-intestinal disorders or even cancer. His research also shows the loss of status can directly impact negatively on someone's health whatever their employment may be.

"It's all very well people saying we shouldn't be concerned with status, but we are all very sensitive to it." – Michael Marmot, Professor of Epidemiology and Public Health at University College of London

Richard Smith is a professor of psychology in the US who believes people are constantly comparing themselves to others. If the majority of human beings are endlessly comparing themselves to others while rarely feeling satisfied with their own performance, how can they ever expect to be content, happy and at peace? Clearly "status reversal" can cause emotional distress and ill health while reports of people committing suicide as a result of losing "everything" are quite common. Piers Bishop is a psychotherapist at Mindfields College who facilitates workshops on improving self-esteem. Bishop says there are two kinds of status, the first being natural where you love and respect yourself no matter what your external circumstances may be, and second being status by proxy. He concludes status by proxy usually causes issues for those who strongly connect their status with their possessions.

"People are rarely satisfied by simply knowing their own performance – they want to know how they stack up against others." – Richard Smith, Associate Professor of Psychology, University of Kentucky

There is nothing wrong in liking the finer things in life but many men and women often define themselves and their sense of self-worth according to:

- Possessions
- Occupation
- Social Status and Recognition

For example, a man who depends on his car as a status symbol will suffer if he suddenly loses it. People often buy things to help them feel good about themselves, gain attention or to feel important. Those who crave status symbols frequently believe material things or reputations represent their worth as a person. Achievements or possessions can never be a solution for low self-esteem; if your sense of self-worth is entirely dependent on the externals of life a feeling of genuine inner peace will always be elusive. Individuals who have cultivated a certain level of self-awareness are humble but assertive when necessary, kind but not weak and understand what is really important in life.

Games People Play

"If you compare yourself with others, you may become vain or bitter, for always there will be greater and lesser persons than yourself." – Max Ehrmann (1872-1945), American Writer & Poet

Many people are obsessed by status and being important. The next time you meet someone new at a social event try a little experiment. When you're asked what you do for a living, do not answer the question directly but be vague for as long as possible. It's likely the other person will gradually become uncomfortable, nervous, insistent or even annoyed! Those who are "status conscious" will evaluate your status by judging your occupation or career as this allows them to "slot" you into their personal "social paradigm" or world view. For these types it's a priority to find out quickly how well they compare to you and whether they should feel superior or inferior.

Once they know what you do for a living they will:

- Allocate you a level or position compared to what they consider their own position to be
- Judge your "worth" and treat you accordingly based on your "allocated" level or position

If you're a doctor, lawyer or a "professional" you will be probably considered higher in the social structure, but if you're bricklayer, cashier or hairdresser you're likely to be placed at a lower level of "worth." In many societies possessing the "correct" status is widely admired and envied in equal measure. Failing to possess any of the recognized symbols can lead to others labeling you as being a "loser" or not very high up the social ladder. Many people place high importance on external factors yet all can be very temporary. Money can be lost, physical appearances and attractiveness fade with time, careers can fail, reputations can be destroyed, power reduced or lost and lifestyles drastically reduced, altered or curtailed.

The truth is those who are "status conscious" are chasing an illusion because:

- Status is largely about perception
- Status can be complicated as it is relative
- Obtaining high status symbols do not necessarily make people happy

There are women who feel embarrassed or even ashamed because they think their partner's employment or career isn't impressive enough and doesn't reflect the required level of status. Those who are constantly comparing themselves with others usually suffer chronic negative feelings such as blame, depression, anxiety, perfectionism, resentment, self-pity, confusion and guilt.

What Type of Man Are You Looking For?

Single men who are rich or earn a very high income are rare. If you do meet a man who is single and financially comfortable he may:

- Know he is considered a "good catch" so may play hard to get
- Have extremely high expectations
- Only date highly attractive women so he can show them off as trophies
- Use his money to seduce women and could be a hard-core Player

Affluent men and those with power or influence usually know how to operate in the dating game and they don't always play fair. It can be very easy to be manipulated when you allow yourself to be seduced by money, fame or status.

Are You Looking For Love Or A Lifestyle Choice?

"Better the cottage where one is merry than the palace where one weeps." – Chinese Proverb

There have always been women seeking men with power, money or with good career prospects. You may be tempted to choose a partner influenced by factors such as:

- Money
- Appearance
- Lifestyle
- Career
- Reputation
- Power

When you become involved with a partner influenced primarily by status symbols this provides a very weak foundation on which to build a committed relationship. There is very little left to support the partnership if there is a lack of compatibility in key areas or if circumstances suddenly change for the worse. Many women stay in unhealthy relationships with men who are wealthy but not very nice people. Despite being desperately unhappy they stay in unhealthy or dysfunctional relationships fearing a loss of lifestyle or material status. The craving to keep the "right" status overrides all other considerations so they remain in deeply unhappy relationships living lives of quiet desperation in fear of losing the superficial stuff they hold dear.

The majority of single women interested in having a relationship would like a man with the following qualities:

- Interested in a serious committed relationship
- Positive personality
- High self-esteem
- Integrity
- Good sense of humor
- Emotionally available
- Caring
- Kind
- Emotionally healthy
- Sexually compatible

Are you the type of woman who rejects a man with most or all of these qualities because he doesn't have the "right" occupation or career that provides the "correct" status? These types of women are usually the ones who complain about a lack of any eligible men! This kind of mindset can cause you to dismiss great opportunities to meet a good man because he is not considered a "good catch" by you, your family, friends or wider society. The problem is not the lack of decent men but the use of materialistic or unrealistic criteria when looking for love. This doesn't mean you should severely compromise your personal values, principles and standards, but when your personal preferences are motivated purely by the desires of the Ego you could dismiss a man who is highly compatible or even end up in a toxic relationship. Concentrating on the externals and what a potential partner can offer materially is one of the biggest relationship mistakes men and women make. I know of many cases where women have been materially seduced by men promising a glamorous lifestyle and higher social status only to bitterly regret the decision later on, sometimes with very tragic results.

A man who doesn't have a desire or plan to earn extraordinary amounts of money isn't necessarily a bad thing and this certainly shouldn't result in his automatic rejection as a potential partner. He could be the "Steady Eddie" type who is happy with a regular job and regular income. Men committed to being in a loving relationship, enthusiastic about having a family and who take their potential or current parental responsibilities seriously should not be dismissed just because they do not earn substantial amounts of money. If a man has positive personal goals for his primary intimate relationship, strong positive character traits and appears to be very compatible in the right areas he should be considered as a serious candidate for a long-term relationship. When you're looking for someone to share your life with, important qualities such as compatibility, integrity and emotional availability should be on the top of your list of priorities. Living a truly successful and happy life cannot be achieved by pursuing status, money and all the other material things money can buy.

Reality Check!

"Money isn't the solution to your problems. It only lets you carry your unhappiness around in style." – Shannon L. Alder, Author

There are many good men out there but if you insist on looking for a high status "good catch" type this will automatically restrict your choices. If you have been feeling frustrated in your search for the right partner consider getting to know a man for his character before dismissing him due to his lack of financial status. Focusing on a date's personality traits instead of his wealth or career prospects will naturally increase your options for finding a viable relationship. You may even be very pleasantly surprised!

Putting Commitment Before Compatibility

"Always carry with you a little reasonable doubt, should you meet someone who needs to be found innocent." – Robert Brault, Author

Many women have been conditioned to seek a firm commitment from their partner as soon as possible. Mothers often bring up their daughters to believe securing a promise of commitment equals security but this can also result in women giving a premature commitment. Of course the man isn't under any obligation to return the commitment, so while the woman gets busy behaving like she is in a serious relationship, her partner may just sit back and enjoy whatever is being provided or be scared off by premature demands for commitment.

You may tend to rush into relationships and commit to a man prematurely when you:

- Are fed up of dating
- Want to settle down
- Feel you're running out of time to find a partner
- Allow other people to pressure you to be in a relationship
- Are not married or in a relationship but all your friends are

- Don't like being single and prefer to be in a relationship
- Feel "incomplete" unless involved in a relationship
- Want to feel loved and to belong to someone desperately due to unresolved childhood issues
- See "the good" in everyone you meet and quickly idealize them
- Want to have children before your biological clock runs out
- Are desperate to be in a relationship

If you're single and can identify with any of the above statements spend some time working on raising your self-esteem, expanding your self-awareness and exploring personal self-development. Allowing unresolved issues to motivate premature commitments usually leads to various types of relationship drama. When you're dating someone new you may feel there is the potential for a successful relationship but making premature commitments to a man you hardly know isn't sensible.

Warning signs you're moving too fast!

- Within a few weeks of dating you convince yourself your new partner is "The One."
- You spend more time thinking and fantasizing about your partner than actually spending time together.
- Within the first few weeks or months you are acting as if your new partner is "The One" and you have a tendency to act this way during the early phases of your previous relationships.
- Within the first few weeks or months you begin to fantasize and plan how you are going to spend the rest of your life with your new partner.
- Within a month you start having sex with your new partner.
- Within three or four months you begin living with your new partner.

Living with someone usually requires a great deal of adjustment and compromises have to be agreed. Learning how to resolve conflicts is an essential part of building a successful relationship and when a couple starts living together too quickly there hasn't been enough time to learn about and adapt to each other's personal style of conflict resolution. This can lead to reluctant or grudging compromises where underlying resentments begin to fester or minor disagreements quickly escalate into major arguments. One of the biggest mistakes men and women make with "commitment before compatibility" is deciding to live with a partner far too quickly.

Reasons why couples begin to live together prematurely:

- To spend more time together.
- One partner persuades the other to move in together because he or she fears the relationship is in trouble or is going to fail.
- Two people living together can save money – it's usually cheaper than maintaining two separate homes.
- If a person has a superior home or lives in an affluent area this can motivate their partner to suggest living together.

A couple deciding to live together prematurely is taking a huge risk. It takes time to really know a person and relationships which are rushed are rarely successful in the medium to long-term. During the early stages of living together a variety of circumstances or pressures can inflict serious damage as the partnership has not been properly established. There is a risk of complacency, where one person gives their partner less respect, appreciation and attention, where the relationship is taken for granted and emotional needs are neglected. Unrealistic expectations can also severely damage a relatively new relationship before it even has a chance to develop properly. Choosing to move in with a partner you hardly know is choosing to live with a virtual stranger before truly exploring compatibility. It means you're probably setting the relationship up to fail. Taking a relationship to the commitment level of living together should not be rushed under any circumstances. For couples who are both relatively young (e.g. 25-35 years old) and hoping to raise children or thinking about marriage, living together should be considered as a step towards greater commitment *at the appropriate time.*

Reality Check!

"Too many girls rush into relationships because of the fear of being single, then start making compromises, and losing their identity. Don't do that." – Katy Perry, Singer & Songwriter

When premature commitments are made there can be pressure to compromise inappropriately or accept things you're not totally happy with, leading to feelings of resentment. If you're dating someone new or have recently embarked on a relationship but things are moving too quickly step back and slow things down – now! Rushing into a commitment without taking the time to really know your partner is reckless and totally irresponsible if it leads to marriage and children within a relatively short period of time. It doesn't matter how much you may *want* marriage and commitment, marrying the *wrong* person isn't going to make it work.

Are you in an unhappy relationship and suspect premature commitments have been made? The first step is to explain to your partner you need a break from the relationship. If this isn't possible because you're living together make it clear you need to withdraw for a while. If your partner has your best interests at heart he will agree and respect your wishes. This will give you the space required to think about these issues and also give you the opportunity to get in touch with yourself. It is vital to spend some time considering the relationship with detachment. Being detached doesn't necessarily mean *you don't* care about the outcome or do not love or care about the people in your life. It means accepting you have a choice and a right to seek your own happiness and other people have the right to seek theirs.

You should try to:

- Understand if you have a pattern of becoming committed prematurely and what motivates this behavior.
- Ask your partner questions about how he feels and pay close attention to what is actually happening in the relationship.
- Consider realistically if you and your partner are truly compatible in key areas.

When there has been considerable emotional investment over a period of time it may seem silly to just "throw it all away." It can be very tempting to choose familiarity, convenience and perhaps fleeting moments of happiness instead of being honest. In relationships partners change their minds about what they want or decide to move on when they feel their needs are not being met or are unlikely to be fulfilled. Consider the relationship carefully and be honest with yourself about the prospects for happiness and success. If you're unhappy ignoring the facts will not change the situation or make it better.

The aftermath of a previous relationship where premature commitment has been a factor can be confusing and the emotional recovery may take some time. Some people begin to seriously doubt their own judgment or quickly become involved with someone else on the rebound trying to distract themselves from the pain of failure. Making premature commitments has taken many women down the road to relationship hell. Committing prematurely to a man before you really know him is a huge gamble which is likely to result in disappointment, distress and heartache.

Staying With A Serial Cheater

"People generally didn't cheat in good relationships." – Emily Giffin, *Something Blue*

The traditional relationship roles are for women to be faithful and sexually exclusive while the male role is to provide financial security, stability and protection. In the 21st century these gender roles are still generally expected to be fulfilled; if either partner fails to fulfil these basic requirements they're often rejected as being no longer suitable relationship "material."

In his book *His Needs, Her Needs* bestselling author Dr. Willard F. Harley Jr. Ph.D. explains that while conducting his therapy practice men caught cheating often found it difficult to give up the other woman frequently continuing the affair despite promising not to do so. Harley also observed women who are caught cheating usually remained faithful to their partner if the relationship survived the infidelity.

Discovering your partner has been unfaithful can be devastating and cheating has destroyed untold relationships which often appeared to be happy. Many people believe men are more likely to cheat on their partners but this isn't true according to recent research. Men and women generally approach the topic of infidelity very differently and society also plays a part in influencing our attitudes regarding cheating.

Why Men Lie About Cheating

Some men like the chase while others want the "best of all worlds." They can enjoy the comfort and privileges of a stable relationship while having sex with a woman who is considered more thrilling or exciting. Once he is enjoying the best of both worlds he is unlikely to give up cheating unless he is caught. There are no guarantees he won't cheat again regardless of what promises he may make.

For some, it's the sexual conquest that feeds the Ego. For others it is purely about seizing an opportunity that presents itself. Some men lie about their affairs because they don't want to hurt their partner and if there are children involved it's more likely a man will lie to prevent ripping his family apart. In this kind of scenario a man will rationalize his decision by convincing himself he is protecting the people he loves.

When a man cheats seeking attention or sex outside of his relationship this doesn't necessarily mean he wants to leave his partner. There are men who like the idea of having total sexual freedom and enjoying multiple partners while being married or in a long-term relationship. Some men make excuses about infidelity saying they have just made a "mistake" or it's just a "phase" they're going through that will end soon. The majority of men know if they get caught cheating their partner will not accept it so they will lie even when the evidence is solid. Provided they don't get caught it doesn't really matter as their primary relationship will not suffer any serious damage.

Understanding why your partner cheated may not save the relationship but the information can help you to identify any warning signs when you become involved again. If you decide to end it, embrace the bereavement process many people go through after a relationship fails and always remember forgiveness is a gift you give to yourself.

Why Men Find It Difficult To Forgive A Cheating Partner

So men who cheat do so for a variety of reasons and will try to hide their infidelity to protect their primary relationship, however, these men would probably not be very happy if their wives or partners were sharing sexual experiences with another man! We have all heard stories of men caught out cheating on their girlfriend or wife but given another chance. Yet when a wife cheats the husband usually ends the relationship immediately or demands a divorce. A man who is cheated on by his partner or wife is far more likely to be ridiculed for being unable to keep her satisfied sexually or otherwise. There is little stigma attached to a man caught cheating and the greater his status, wealth or power the more understanding society tends to be. The majority of men are very territorial regarding their partner's body while women generally tend to be territorial regarding a man's attention and resources. The average man will find it very difficult to accept another man has been having sex with his partner. There are experts who advise women who insist on having affairs to avoid any kind of penetration with a lover because if the affair is discovered there will be a higher chance of salvaging the relationship or marriage.

If a child is born as a result of an affair, a typical man isn't going to accept his resources or income being used to raise another man's child. Being in a relationship with a woman who is considered untrustworthy is usually seen as a threat to his status or even economic survival. Many men find it difficult when their ex-partner moves on if her cheating was the reason for the break-up: the male Ego can be very fragile in this type of scenario.

A man can just have a mere suspicion of infidelity and the image will probably be burnt into his brain and this alone can prompt a decision to end the relationship. He will find it very difficult to accept the idea of his partner with another man and most men are so territorial they're inclined to jump to the worst conclusions. This can be prompted by the slightest suggestion their partner has been unfaithful; once that seed of doubt has been planted in a man's mind it can grow very quickly indeed, even if absolutely nothing happened. Most men cannot cope with the public and private humiliation of a wife or partner who cheats. If there are children involved and the man feels a strong parental duty he may stay but it is more likely he will leave.

Men usually pursue affairs motivated by chemistry, sexual attraction or basic lust. Women frequently have affairs with men who listen and talk to them; in many ways a woman may subconsciously trade sex with a man because he makes her feel validated by providing conversation and attention. When a woman has an affair she will often claim it wasn't about the sex but it happened because she felt her lover was someone who really listened to her. Men often find this very difficult to understand as the motivation for having sex with another man.

When a man listens and pays attention many women assume he has connected intimately on an emotional level. Men can often be surprised when their lover says the sexual component of the affair wasn't as important to her as the feeling of an emotional connection. While men who cheat can come up with a variety of excuses, it isn't really socially acceptable for women to cheat because they're supposed to be virtuous – it doesn't matter what the excuse may be, it isn't really ever going to be good enough. A woman caught cheating trying to excuse or justify the betrayal to her partner is usually wasting her time. A typical man isn't going to be interested in hearing, "You were always at work" or "You didn't talk with me enough." When a man has been cheated on he will usually be stuck with images of his partner having sex with someone else running through his mind.

How The Suspicion Of Cheating Affects Women

A cheater will often lie and say, "It's all in your head" or even call his partner crazy when she confronts him. Most women are quite intuitive and can *feel* if something isn't quite right. Sensing lies and dishonesty can make a woman feel uncomfortable or even physically unwell. Most women desire or require total transparency, openness and honesty from their intimate partner to feel totally relaxed. Generally, men are not as sensitive when it comes to intuitions or gut feelings so both genders tend to have a very different experience when picking up on deceptions.

It's not that men do not value honesty and integrity in the same way as women but the fact that being lied to affects the genders in different ways. Many men assume a woman is being highly dramatic when she discovers she is being lied to, what they don't appreciate is how being lied to impacts on a woman mentally, emotionally and physically. Discovering lies or betrayals can cause women to behave in highly erratic and dramatic ways because of the feelings they are experiencing both physically and emotionally. Intuition can often be used to keep a woman and her child or children safe so when she is placed in a situation where she begins to question her instincts this can be very unnerving or even terrifying. Being told you're "imagining things" or "crazy" when your intuition is firing on all cylinders and your gut is telling you something is suspicious will affect you mentally, emotionally and physically. When a woman doubts her intuition and the signals her body is sending her this can result in illness and in some cases the symptoms can be very debilitating. By the time a woman discovers an affair and has irrefutable evidence or a confession she may have experienced all kinds of mental and emotional tortures struggling with her intuition.

A woman who discovers her suspicions have been correct and her partner has been cheating usually feels deeply hurt, betrayed and angry but conversely she will also feel better within herself. She knows she isn't going mad or crazy and feels confident her intuition hasn't failed her. Once the suspicions prompted by her intuition have been verified the self-doubt and tension she has been experiencing is replaced with feelings of balance and clarity. There is an old joke that says women are like the FBI: it doesn't matter how much evidence they have they always want a confession too! Many women will stay with a cheater after discovering the truth because the discovery brings a type of conclusion to the matter – she feels better about not being lied to anymore and knows she isn't going crazy. Women are also more likely to forgive infidelity so will often try again.

Major Cheating Signs

According to a variety of studies half of all men cheat and some experts say the percentage is actually closer to 75 percent. It can be a mistake to jump to conclusions but it is always prudent to pay attention if your observations or intuition begin to give you cause for concern.

Different Or Less Sex

Have you noticed that the way he makes love to you has changed? A man who is sleeping with another woman will probably continue to have sex with his partner to try and cover his tracks but something may be different about it. It's not just about the quantity of the sex but also the quality; sometimes a man may not change the frequency but the quality of the sex is noticeably different. For example, a man may have been a very romantic and attentive lover but his style changes and suddenly he just wants to have straight sex lacking any emotional content. If you notice a reduction in his sex drive this could indicate he has something that is troubling him but could also be a sign he is having an affair.

Demanding Increased Privacy

Does he want more privacy? Your partner suddenly becomes very territorial about his phone, begins having whispered phone calls, goes into another room to speak to someone, constantly has his cell phone on silent/vibrate, sleeps with his mobile very close by at all times (I have heard of cases where the man sleeps with his mobile phone under his pillow!) or begins using the bathroom like a public phone box. Perhaps he appears reluctant to check his emails in your presence or his mobile phone bill has been diverted to a different address. Any of these signs should alert you to some kind of deception and the possibility your partner is having an affair.

Attitude Change Or Acting Differently

Has his attitude or behavior changed subtly or significantly? One of the most obvious warning signs is when a man begins acting a great deal differently than he used to. When your partner has generally been romantic, kind and loving but suddenly becomes easily irritated, critical, annoyed or begins starting unnecessary arguments he could be having an affair. There could be work pressures or he could be distracted by personal problems but it's also possible your partner is actually feeling guilty about cheating. Something (or someone) will usually be motivating his change of attitude and you should investigate what has caused his change of attitude or behavior.

Avoidance

Does he seem to struggle to spend quality time with you? If you live together and he has changed his routine by suddenly coming home late, appears to be avoiding you, generally seems elusive or starts going away on weekends these could be signs of cheating. In his book, *The Truth About Cheating*, M. Gary Neuman, a licensed family counselor, discovered during his work that 50 percent of men who were thinking about cheating and 61 percent who were actually being unfaithful tended to spend less time at home. We can all be busy at times but when a man stops making an effort to spend quality time with you without a valid reason it's logical to assume he's probably in the company of another woman.

Unreliability

Does he change plans at short notice? If there is a consistent pattern of your partner not being where he says he should be he is obviously lying for a reason. He might claim to be spending time with a friend but the friend calls your home wanting to speak to him or you're told he has to go to work at an unusual time but when you call him at the office he isn't there. Plans change all the time and being flexible can be important, especially if your employer is suffering a down turn or the general economy is struggling, but when a partner is constantly not where he says he will be it's likely he is having an affair. If you suspect your partner is cheating there is no point ignoring it. If you lack solid evidence but feel "something" is not quite right pursue the matter; always confront the situation using tact and respect but it is important to be persistent.

Is He Telling The Truth? Dishonesty Indicators

Attitude and/or Voice Changes

If how he generally speaks or acts changes abruptly when you begin to ask him questions or he shifts from being calm to becoming agitated, or even vice versa, he is probably lying.

Physical Cues

Watch his body language for typical clues such as fidgeting, appearing distracted, nervous, anxiety or sweating.

Hostile

Liars tend to be unpleasant when they are put under pressure so can start complaining or making negative comments directed at you to try and deflect your questioning.

Avoids Eye Contact

If he will not make or maintain eye contact with you this is often a sign of deceit.

Constant Story Changes

When people lie their stories tend to lack details so ask him for specifics. The more information a liar is forced to provide, the more likely he is to make a mistake during his responses and expose his dishonesty.

Keeps Repeating He Is Telling the Truth

To convince another of the integrity of their answers, liars often use phrases such as "to tell the truth" and "to be perfectly honest." The majority of people who are telling the truth tend not to use these types of phrases.

Quick Answers

When you ask most people a question they will pause before providing a response; this pause is the space where they're formulating an answer. If he seems to respond too quickly without any hesitation this indicates the possibility of a dishonest and rehearsed response.

Intuition

Experts agree effective human lie detectors learn to develop, listen and trust their intuition. Women tend to be more in touch with their "sixth sense" than men so always pay attention to your feelings. Often your intuition will know he is lying but your mind is waiting for the evidence to show up! If you have clear evidence of his infidelity this should be discussed as failing to do so will make the average man believe his cheating is acceptable. Confrontations about suspected or actual infidelity can be very emotional so try to remain calm and talk to him to find out what is motivating his change of attitude or behavior. Explain that the relationship feels different and ask him why he has changed; if he claims there is nothing wrong, denies any change or claims "It's all in your head" don't accept these or any other deflections or excuses. Your partner may refuse to answer questions if there is a lack of any firm proof although there may be strong circumstantial evidence. Alternatively, he may not be having an affair yet but could be seriously considering cheating for a variety of reasons. Talking through any problems might prevent him from straying and together you may be able to repair the relationship.

If he has been cheating, it can help to find out why your partner has cheated – it may be the infidelity is a symptom of underlying issues in the relationship. For example, if you're in a marriage or long-term relationship with children you may have grown apart due to everyday commitments while failing to maintain a realistic work/life balance. Spending more time together and talking through the issues might rekindle the romance and save the relationship. You can also suggest therapy/counseling as a couple but if he is adamant nothing has changed and refuses to discuss your concerns it's time to seriously consider if the relationship is really viable. Effective communication is one of the major foundation stones of any healthy relationship; a lack of communication usually fuels even more suspicion and feelings of frustration as well as betrayal so honesty is always the best policy. Remember, women often have affairs due to feeling they're not being listened to so be careful you don't fall into the trap of cheating yourself.

Whenever cheating is discovered it's very important for you and your partner to be tested for any and all Sexually Transmitted Diseases (STDs). The fact is when a man or woman is unfaithful they're potentially exposing their partner to a variety of diseases such as gonorrhea, syphilis, Hepatitis, neo-natal Herpes or even HIV by having unprotected sex. There are many attractive people who carry the HIV virus or other very unpleasant STDs so don't be naive and believe it can't happen to you; diseases and infections do not discriminate regarding their hosts.

Top Reasons Women Stay With Cheaters

"Delusion detests focus and romance provides the veil." – Suzanne Finnamore, *Split: A Memoir of Divorce*

Lifestyle Choice

Whether she is in a steady relationship or married sometimes a woman can decide to stay with a cheater because of the lifestyle she enjoys. Exotic vacations or high-end status symbols can be very difficult for some women to give up. There are many married women who are extremely reluctant give up the security, resources and social status provided by the marriage so will stay with a cheating husband. A man who diverts time and resources away from his partner or wife and children is endangering their lifestyle so a woman may decide to stay with a cheater providing her partner's attention and financial resources are primarily focused on her and their child or children.

Children

A variety of studies indicate women who are married or in long-term relationships with children are more likely to have a cheating partner. However, many women can find it difficult to leave a straying husband or long-term partner when there are children involved and may decide to stay to provide stability and security for their children. Some women stay with a serial cheater until the "other woman" becomes pregnant. They decide to end the relationship once it becomes clear a significant amount of the man's financial resources and attention will probably be diverted towards his lover and new child. Ex-wives and girlfriends often monitor and consider how much money and attention their ex-partner is spending on his new woman and compare this to how they were treated.

Men Can Make Certain Women Feel Safe

The feminist movement has made great progress since the last century but traditionally men have been given the roles of protector and provider. There are clearly primal reasons for this perception by the vast majority of societies and cultures where men are still expected to be strong and provide stability. There are women who still believe having a man in their life makes them more physically safe and secure despite acceptance or approval of a woman being single and independent in the 21st century. Sadly they sacrifice self-respect for feelings of physical security while enduring constant emotional damage to their self-esteem. Some women are just emotionally programmed to want a man around whether he is fulfilling the traditional role of provider and protector or not. Others feel safer having a man in their life even though he is causing a great deal of pain. They believe their life will be empty and lonely without a partner or are simply blinded by love.

Cheater Playbook

It can be difficult for a woman to leave a hardcore cheater for a variety of reasons but many women are seduced by listening to what they want to hear.

Typical lines cheaters use include:

- I love you
- I'm so sorry
- She meant nothing to me
- You're beautiful
- You're the best thing that ever happened to me
- I can't live without you
- Don't leave me

These platitudes are standard operating procedure for a cheater. When certain women are told what they want to hear they forgive or go into denial hoping their partner won't cheat again. If you want to see how a typical cheater reacts when they're caught, watch the popular TV series *Cheaters* where they investigate unfaithful partners. Even when the evidence is damning and irrefutable the man often blames his wife or partner for his cheating combined with promises to change if she gives him another chance. The sad part is the woman usually believes him because it's exactly what she wants to hear so decides to stay with her cheater.

Cheater Guilt Trips

"If you are an approval addict, your behaviour is as easy to control as that of any other junkie. All a manipulator need do is a simple two-step process: Give you what you crave, and then threaten to take it away. Every drug dealer in the world plays this game." – Harriet B. Braiker, *Who›s Pulling Your Strings? How to Break the Cycle of Manipulation and Regain Control of Your Life*

There are women who aspire to be the "perfect woman" and who are very susceptible to being sent on guilt trips by their partners, and this provides cover for a cheater to operate.

Typical guilt trips include being accused of:

- Always being busy
- Always being tired
- Always coming in late from work
- Not wearing sexy clothes anymore
- Always paying a new baby or child too much attention so he felt ignored

These excuses can trigger a guilt trip in a woman with a mindset that constantly tells her she has to be perfect. When a man attempts to deflect blame for his betrayal a woman with the "I must be the perfect woman" program running through her mind will often accept the responsibility for her partner's cheating. A cheater doesn't even have to try to give his partner the total blame, just plant a seed that suggests it's not all his fault and a woman might begin to doubt herself. Women who are "guilt tripped" blame themselves when their man cheats asking themselves why they were not good enough to keep him faithful. When a woman accepts the blame for her partner's cheating she often feels responsible in some way so will feel obliged to stay in the relationship.

Another factor that can come into play is when a woman has a "Daddy Complex" emotional program running, where she wants to be "Daddy's Little Girl" all over again. Others are hoping deep inside to win the approval of their father all over again by seeking to be truly loved and adored by their partner or subconsciously attempting to change unsatisfactory childhood scenarios. Many of these women believe if they're just loving enough or demonstrate enough patience they will be loved just how their father loved them or how they wished their father had loved them.

Consequently, for one reason or another, these women will simply accept excuses or avoid any major confrontations to keep the relationship intact, especially if there are children involved. They tend to make excuses to their family and friends who know about their partner's infidelity and will usually be defensive or claim that "things are much better" now when in reality she knows she's with a serial cheat. Staying with a partner who cheats is often a tiring and painful experience yet many women do.

Misplaced Emotional Commitment

Most women are emotionally committed to their partner and the relationship. It is generally accepted having sex doesn't necessarily have the same emotional content for a man as it does for a woman. If it has been a long-term relationship it can be very difficult to walk away.

Religion

There are wives who believe it is against the rules of their faith to divorce a husband. For example, there is a Jewish tradition where the wife cannot divorce her husband without his consent.

Fear

There are women who are scared of being alone or single so are motivated by fear to stay with a cheater. They may suffer from low self-esteem and believe having a man who cheats is better than not having a partner at all but underlying this belief is fear.

Can Cheating Improve A Relationship?

Cheating is usually a deal breaker for many women but some believe having an affair can actually improve a relationship. Bestselling author Cathrine Hakim's book, *The New Rules of Marriage: Internet Dating, Playfairs and Erotic Power,* claims the British in particular are unrealistic regarding affairs. She compares fidelity and long-term sexual exclusivity in relationships to "traps" which make many people feel like "caged animals." According to Hakim because of this millions of people are being condemned to lives lacking passion, excitement and the kind of sex everyone deserves to experience. She believes meeting a lover for sex should be as normal as going out for a pleasurable meal in a fancy restaurant and claims affairs can improve relationships rather than destroy them. So is having an affair ever a good idea? Is cheating acceptable? These are important questions that deserve to be explored.

Successful Affairs

Hakim believes it is possible to have "successful affairs" where both partners benefit and nobody gets hurt. She says affairs can make relationships more stable and home lives happier. In advocating affairs Hakim claims those who reject a fresh approach to marriage and adultery fail to recognize the benefits of a revitalized sex life outside the home. Affairs are good for relationships and couples have to learn a new set of rules to reflect this reality. She uses France and other southern European countries as examples of societies where accepting infidelity is widely practiced and couples are happier as a result.

Hakim claims monogamy and being faithful is defunct and expecting infidelity is simply a "21st century approach to marriage." She points out there has been a great increase of websites promoting infidelity where people in relationships can meet up for illicit sex and believes this will cause a major shift in sexual behavior. According to Hakim more people will openly have and accept their partners having affairs and appreciate the advantages this can provide to their primary relationships.

Is Expecting Monogamy Unrealistic?

Catherine Hakim isn't the only expert to defunct the monogamous relationship. Helen Croydon, author of *The Sugar Daddy Diaries*, is another expert to question the merits of a traditional monogamous relationship where expecting your partner to be faithful is a basic standard requirement.

Croydon says: "As much as we love to feast on the Hollywood-inspired fairytales (there is a soulmate out there who can make our dreams come true, and still make us quiver between the sheets every night), I'm afraid my research finds more evidence of boredom, bickering and monosyllabic TV dinners than passion, princes and someone who massages your feet every night." In their book *Sex at Dawn*, sex researchers Cacilda Jethá and Christopher Ryan claim expecting monogamy is not natural. They question if it is even possible for two people to stay together over an extended period of time and remain happy; they argue expecting sexual monogamy is unnatural and always has been.

Philosopher Alain de Botton has also claimed there is a variety of advantages to practicing adultery in his book *How to Think More About Sex*. These experts and others blame monogamy for the increasing divorce figures that reflect sad, cold, passionless marriages. Interestingly, none of the experts mentioned claim you shouldn't be monogamous if this has been mutually agreed with your partner, but we should all face reality and be more accepting and less judgmental of those who want additional sexual activities. Hakim even suggests partners who are upset or bitter at a partner's infidelity should simply go out and have an affair themselves instead of splitting families apart.

What About Trust?

Hakim and others suggest the thrill experienced by both men and women from infidelity can improve their primary relationships and make them happier. For example, they argue sexual curiosity can be satisfied by having affairs or if a couple have different sexual appetites both partners can feel fulfilled and content without threatening the primary relationship. In other words, if everyone became more accepting of affairs, this shift in attitude could support relationships in lasting for longer or even succeeding.

It sounds like a feasible concept in theory and might work if you're a Vulcan or an android who lacks emotions but believing having an affair will not hurt your partner is misguided. If he or she doesn't care the bottom line is they're not in love with you, which is one of the common reasons people have affairs. One of the fundamental foundations of any relationship is trust. When this is deliberately broken the impact on the partner who has been betrayed can be devastating.

Betrayal is a potent destroyer of any type of relationship, intimate or otherwise. What ultimately causes the damage is not the actual act of cheating but the lies and deceit required to be unfaithful. The secrecy that surrounds an affair and the associated betrayal often damages a relationship beyond repair.

Many experts claim it's not just the sexual and emotional betrayal that damages relationships. There are the possible financial costs of conducting an affair, like hotel rooms or expensive meals associated with maintaining a mistress, and an affair that may have impacted on the household finances in other ways. Also, time with a lover may have meant spending less quality time with any children of the marriage or primary relationship.

Can Affairs Be Constructive?

Despite the radical views of Hakim and others, the majority of relationship experts agree affairs are a serious breach of trust and a deep betrayal that is very unlikely to make couples feel closer. If it's a Friends With Benefits arrangement there might be some resentment if it was agreed the arrangement was exclusive. When it's an open relationship where there is a mutual agreement to having sex with other people there shouldn't be a problem. These types of relationships can work if both partners agree and may provide some benefits in the short to medium-term but such agreements and relationships are very rare. There are experts who concede there may be advantages to having an affair at least in the short-term; the person having the affair might feel happier which may ease tensions if he (or she) lives with a partner. However, the damage caused by the discovery of an affair usually far outweigh any nebulous benefits.

Should You Forgive A Cheater?

Affairs happen all the time for a variety of reasons. We are all human beings who make mistakes sometimes and many women will consider this when giving a cheating partner another chance. They also want to believe if the cheater is forgiven he will change his ways, but a woman can also stay with a cheater because love clouds her better judgment. Each case can be very different. People decide to cheat for different reasons so it really depends on each person's value system. If trust is very important to someone the deception is often too much for the betrayed party to accept.

It can be very easy to be judgmental and claim it could never happen to you but no one ever really knows the full truth about what happens in a relationship. We might be able to make an educated guess based on observation or information shared, but always remember if a friend is confiding in you they're probably going to be biased as they provide their *version* of events. If a woman decides to forgive her partner for cheating, we can't really know the emotions she may be struggling with such as fear, shame, pain and anger. We can never truly know how hard her husband or partner is working to try and rebuild the trust and make the relationship work. If you have a female friend who decides to stay with a man who has cheated on her once, try to be supportive instead of judging her.

The majority of couples experience problems in their relationship at some stage but discovering infidelity can be very painful and it is often considered to be the ultimate betrayal. For some women discovering their partner has been cheating can result in feelings of not being "good enough" or even depression. Typically a woman wants to know if her man is in love with the other woman while men are usually more concerned about the physical act of sexual betrayal as opposed to whether their partner is actually in love with someone else.

When a woman decides to forgive her partner for cheating she has to be confident he is truly sorry. This means he deeply regrets betraying her trust and is not sorry simply because he has been caught! If you can secure sincere promises he will not cheat again it may be worth giving him another chance but to continue with the relationship will depend on a variety of factors. For example, when there are children involved it might be worth trying to work things out and rebuild the shattered trust. However, staying together because there may be a child or children involved is not recommended; for many women and men the decision to leave if they discover their partner cheating is non-negotiable.

▎Reality Check

"Cheating and lying aren't struggles, they're reasons to break up." – Patti Callahan Henry, *Between the Tides*

A relationship can survive one act of betrayal but staying with a serial cheater is usually a big relationship mistake. A person who discovers they have been cheated on has to weigh up their options and decide whether to try and rebuild the trust or leave. If the relationship is strong it might survive one act of betrayal but staying with a serial cheater when fidelity is important to you can place the relationship under enormous strain.

Refusing to Leave A Dead Relationship (Knowing When To Quit!)

"The truth is, unless you let go, unless you forgive yourself, unless you forgive the situation, unless you realize that the situation is over, you cannot move forward." – Steve Maraboli, *Unapologetically You: Reflections on Life and the Human Experience*

Men and women all over the world endure unhappy relationships due to a lack of finances to break free or they may simply be too scared to walk away. Many people prefer what feels familiar even if it is dysfunctional so remain in unhealthy relationships feeling unhappy or scared to make a decision while prolonging their own pain, distress and heartache. There may be constant incidents of breaking-up and making-up or a partner decides to end it but is persuaded to try again. Does this sound like you? Have you been in a situation where numerous promises have been made by your partner to change and convinced yourself this time it will be different, this time it will be better but the relationship has failed to improve? Perhaps you kept excessively compromising in a futile attempt to please your partner and make the relationship work but eventually ended up feeling frustrated, trapped or extremely unhappy. After trying to make it work several times it can feel like you're on a roundabout spinning so quickly it seems very difficult to get off.

Signs You Should End It

A Lack Of Sex

This is one of the obvious warning signs a relationship is on the way out. There are a variety reasons for a lack of sexual activity within a relationship but if the sex feels boring, routine, dries up or you no longer find your partner attractive then ignoring this type of problem is not going to make it go away.

Lack Of Physical Intimacy

Showing affection, tenderness and being intimate isn't just about having sex. Passionately kissing your partner can often be more emotionally intimate than having sex; when two people begin to drift apart a lack of kissing or affectionate touching is usually one of the first warning signs the relationship could be heading for trouble. Touching, kissing, holding hands and hugging are all signs of a healthy relationship. If you tend to cringe when your partner comes near or tries to touch you the relationship is in serious trouble.

False Declarations Of Love

Saying you love someone when it's not true is another big warning sign because not only are you misleading your partner but also lying to yourself. The words "I love you" are an expression of a deep and profound emotion for another human being so if you don't mean it don't say it. When you know you are pretending to be in love and faking how you really feel it's time to be by yourself for a while.

The Jokes And Joy Have Disappeared

Making your partner laugh is one of the shared joys of a relationship. If you often feel irritated, annoyed or frustrated when your partner speaks to you, you need to seriously consider if you are with the right person.

You No Longer Communicate

Effective communication is the key to a successful relationship and that means talking about trivia or occasional gossip as well as all the other more serious and challenging issues. If there is little or a total lack of discussing the small things in life this indicates you don't really see your partner as a friend. When you stop talking to each other about the little things, it's a sign the friendship factor of the relationship is declining or has disappeared.

You're Always Finding Fault

If you are always finding fault with your partner this is a serious warning sign. This behavior is definitely not good for your emotional health or your partner's self-esteem. Subconsciously you may want to walk away from the relationship but lack the courage to make the decision. If your partner frequently finds fault with what you say or do, he may want to end it but may be too scared to make a decision or perhaps has decided to stay in the relationship for reasons that have nothing to do with being in love. Your partner could be also trying to provoke you into ending the relationship so he does not feel responsible for hurting or rejecting you. When either partner is constantly finding fault with the other this is a negative and destructive pattern of relating and a big warning sign the relationship is failing.

Trying To Change Your Partner

All relationships begin with great promise and imagined potential but once the early glow has passed compatibility issues often begin to surface. Trying to change someone is a very bad idea and will lead to unnecessary conflicts. Big differences regarding values or beliefs serve as clear warning signs the relationship is probably doomed to fail. The perfect match in relationships do not exist but trying to make a relationship work with someone who is clearly incompatible is going increase the chances that it will not work. It is impossible for one person to fulfill all the needs of their partner but if you are motivated by unrealistic expectations it's easy to make this mistake, which results in feelings of disappointment and frustration. Trying to change your partner invariably results in conflicts and feelings of resentment but you may feel it's easier to stay in the relationship while constantly complaining. The perfect match is a fairytale that doesn't exist. The sensible strategy is to cut your losses and look for someone who is a better overall match where you share more key areas of compatibility.

Comparing Your Partner To Other People

If you find yourself constantly comparing your partner unfavorably to other men, find other guys more attractive or keep daydreaming about being with someone else you're cheating on your partner. While you may continue to be faithful physically, you're being emotionally dishonest. Deep down inside you know you're unhappy with the relationship and a failure to acknowledge the truth means you're in denial. Continuing with this type of behavior means you're not doing yourself any favors.

Separate Social Lives

Going out together keeps the relationship alive even if you're living with your partner. Dating or enjoying social activities together should not stop just because the relationship has been established. When a relationship is solid both partners should enjoy socializing together and with their own friends. If you prefer to socialize with your friends this indicates you dislike your partner or are trying to avoid issues that need to be dealt with.

Your Friends Think You Are Unhappy

Genuine friends want the very best for you so if they have doubts or concerns about your partner listen carefully to what they have to say. Often we can be too loved up or emotionally involved to look at a partner or the relationship objectively. When a family member or close friend has genuine concerns that are clearly justified always remember the people who love you will always support you long after the relationship is just a distant memory.

You Want To Be Alone

Everyone needs personal time and space to explore their hobbies, interests and of course themselves. It is quite normal to enjoy some time alone but if you're constantly avoiding your partner preferring to spend more time alone instead of with your partner this is a very serious problem. The relationship is clearly not working and you're probably feeling frustrated, disappointed and resentful.

Relationship Imbalance

The majority of relationships go through a phase where one partner is giving more than the other. This is quite normal but should not be a permanent state of affairs. If one partner is doing all the work to keep the relationship going this is a dysfunctional dynamic; if you're the one making all the effort or being treated like a doormat most of the time, the time has come to insist on some very drastic changes. A failure to reach an agreement where the balance in the relationship is more equitable means it is time to leave.

Unequal Responsibilities And Chores

Domestic bliss is a great concept but can be very difficult to achieve for some couples. If you're living with someone there may be disagreements regarding housework and other general chores that help the household to run smoothly. Compromises have to be agreed but when your partner expects you to take on unreasonable responsibilities while refusing to do their fair share this will probably result in feelings of frustration and resentment.

Feeling Bad About Yourself

Being with someone who constantly criticizes you will eventually destroy your self-esteem and the emotional recovery could take quite a long time. A relationship is meant to be life-affirming and empowering. Control freaks often try to brainwash their partners to maintain a feeling of superiority. If he makes you feel unattractive, unloved or bad about yourself end the relationship now!

Letting Yourself Go

Being in a relationship doesn't mean you should stop taking pride in your appearance. If you no longer care whether your partner still finds you attractive this will probably cause problems for your sex life and inevitably for the relationship. When you're deliberately attempting to appear less attractive to avoid sexual intimacy the relationship is probably doomed.

Forgetting Important Dates

Special days such as anniversaries, birthdays and Valentine's Day may seem trivial, but a couple who intend to stay together will acknowledge and share important dates in some way. If someone forgets their partner's birthday or another significant date the relationship is probably past its sell-by date.

Flirting Online

Katherine Hertlein, a licensed marriage and family therapist, believes cyber cheating is especially appealing to women as they can have their emotional needs met using a computer or smart phone in the comfort of their home. Various polls have indicated seemingly harmless online friendships often develop into intense affairs.

Secretive

If you're deleting your text messages or emails from someone of the opposite sex this indicates you know your partner will be upset if he reads them. Ask yourself how you would feel if the situation were reversed; if the answer makes you feel uncomfortable it's obvious the correspondence is inappropriate.

The Time Factor

You need to consider not only the *content* of the messages but also the *amount* of the communication. For example, spending two hours per night on Facebook chatting with an online buddy of the opposite sex may not be acceptable to your partner if he knew about it.

Rationalizing

Justifying what's happening by saying, "He's just a friend," is a statement you shouldn't have to say to yourself or others when the communication is innocent. Having to constantly wrestle with guilt or feeling the need to rationalize your actions is a clear warning sign the flirting is inappropriate.

Indulging or Fulfilling Your Personal Needs

If your need for intimacy is being met by an online relationship or with a co-worker based on playful or sexual banter ask yourself why. Be careful if you're sharing intimate sentiments because you feel the other man understands you in ways your partner doesn't. Pay attention if the other man is feeding your needs in ways you believe your partner isn't. This can be dangerous territory.

Wrong Intentions

If you think your partner isn't paying you enough attention it can be easy to find someone else to feed your Ego by saying you're sexy, funny, clever, etc. Some people may unconsciously seek out an admirer to get their partner's attention and this strategy can be effective but is also manipulative. There are healthier ways to try and boost your self-esteem.

Sexual Agenda

This may seem obvious but if you notice that your correspondence fuels your sexual fantasies (affairs are often motivated by such thoughts) you're probably in danger of cheating. If there are any subtle or overt sexual overtones or the banter feels like virtual foreplay in anyway, you may be tempted to stray.

Friend(s) Are Concerned

If a good friend or close member of your family asks why you're talking about the other man so much, pay attention. Family members and friends can often identify the red flags before you may be willing to recognize them yourself.

Your Partner Disapproves

If your partner is aware of the communication and disapproves (especially if the communication is with an ex-partner) this should serve as a red flag. This usually means the content or the amount of time (online or offline) is excessive or the interaction isn't really appropriate and is impacting negatively on the relationship.

Sharing Relationship Information

Generally, it is disrespectful to share intimate details regarding your relationship. Consider how you would feel if your partner overheard these types of conversations and whether he would find them acceptable.

Meeting Up With Ex-Partners

Being friends with an ex-partner can be a sign of maturity and demonstrates you have moved on emotionally. It is quite acceptable to remain friends providing certain boundaries are respected. If you're in constant contact with an ex-partner, meeting up regularly, flirting with him or thinking about what could have been, you're disrespecting your partner. Subconsciously you may even want to get caught so your partner decides to end it. Meeting up and flirting with an ex-partner is a serious warning sign you're with the wrong person. If you have fallen out of love be honest with your current partner instead of running the risk of creating unnecessary drama or compromising your integrity and self-respect.

Tempted To Cheat

It is often said men only need a place to have an affair whereas a woman needs a reason. It can be tempting to stray due to feelings of loneliness in a relationship. If a woman's partner is a workaholic or works away from home a great deal she may decide to compensate for neglect or lack of attention from her man by cheating. If another man starts to show care and concern to her, this could lead to an affair outside.

A Lack Of Love And Romance

Many women seek emotional security so when a woman feels unloved, ignored or taken for granted by her partner it's possible she may be tempted to cheat. Women generally like to be courted and romanced; it can be tempting to try and replace romance with an attractive man who provides compliments. If a woman is not receiving the kind of attention she expects in her relationship she may decide to cheat instead.

Unsatisfactory Sex

There are women who get involved in extramarital relationships purely for sex. If her partner is unable to satisfy her sexually a woman may decide to seek that attention elsewhere and become involved in an affair.

Excitement

Boredom may also factor into why women cheat. Seeking to make their lives more exciting some women turn to other men trying to rekindle the feelings they experienced during the early stages of their relationship.

Money & Power

Women often pursue affairs with men who hold powerful positions or who are financially secure. These men can be willing to provide presents and the material items she feels are missing in her life.

Genuine Attraction Or Falling In Love

Many women manage both home and work efficiently, so are likely to meet other men. If a woman is in an unhappy relationship falling for another man she spends time with outside the home is quite possible.

Lack Of Self-Esteem

If a woman feels she is not receiving the amount of attention and admiration she needs from her current partner, she can end up cheating to reaffirm to herself that she is still attractive and desirable.

Revenge

Some women cheat to take revenge for their partner or husband cheating on them. These women decide cheating on a partner is justified if their partner has done the same thing.

Having an affair is a cowardly act which demonstrates a clear lack of integrity and respect. There are seldom any "winners" when affairs are pursued – someone usually gets hurt and the pain of discovering your partner has been unfaithful often compounds the pain of the failing relationship.

When a relationship is in trouble it is often not why it fails but how it comes to an end which can cause unnecessary pain, distress and drama. Once you have made a decision the relationship is over communicate this to your partner as soon as possible to show him respect and to maintain your own integrity.

▎ Reality Check!

"Sometimes you have to get to know someone really well to realize you're really strangers." – Mary Tyler Moore, American Actress

If you're experiencing one or a few of the above signs regularly, it may be time to move on. Life is too short to waste valuable time in a dead end relationship that isn't going anywhere. It's time for a relationship to come to an end when your main emotional needs have not been met for a while and your partner is not interested in discussing or compromising with you. It is important to be fair, responsible and reasonable and to be confident the problem has become a pattern and is not just an isolated event, unless he has done something serious such as having an affair. Once a pattern has been observed talk to your partner and be specific about what you are unhappy about and the behaviors that you want him to change. If he agrees to address your concerns be specific regarding a time frame that is acceptable to you. You may decide to give him a few weeks or a couple of months but at the end of that time period, it should be clear whether you should stay or go. If there are children involved, deciding to end the relationship can be difficult and complicated, but children can often sense or know when their parents are unhappy together. Staying in an unhappy relationship for the sake of the children is not healthy for parents or the children and can expose them to a dysfunctional relationship model they may reenact as adults.

It's definitely time to seriously consider ending a relationship when:

- The love seems to have died
- You feel deeply betrayed due to infidelity
- It becomes clear you and your partner are incompatible
- There is a lack of sexual chemistry
- You and your partner have grown apart

If you're in an unhappy relationship, evaluate the situation, make certain decisions and take action. A couple who stays together for all the wrong reasons eventually create a battleground filled with resentment, bitterness or even hatred. Ignoring any major problems will not make them magically disappear. Counseling, therapy or attending relationship coaching as a couple may help if you're both serious about improving or even saving the relationship. Attending therapy on your own can also be very beneficial and if you're struggling in an unhappy relationship or with emotional issues.

Honesty is always the best policy regarding your partner and yourself. If you embarked on your current relationship carrying unresolved Emotional Baggage it's likely you're contributing to any difficulties.

Review how you felt before you became involved.

Did you:

- Feel reluctant to express your feelings to other people?
- Find it very difficult to connect with your own emotions?
- Suffer from feelings of low self-esteem or dislike yourself?
- Have any type of addiction problem which hasn't been dealt with?
- Feel lonely, desperate or completely miserable without a partner?
- Still have love, feelings or romantic desires for an ex-partner?
- Have a great deal of rage and resentment regarding an ex-partner?
- Believe whatever you had to offer a relationship was not worth a great deal?

- Believe no one would seriously want to be in a relationship with you?
- Ever feel "empty" or as if there was "something" missing inside emotionally or spiritually?

If you can strongly identify with any of the above statements, you were probably emotionally unprepared for your current relationship.

Seriously consider taking a break for a period of reflection to explore your personal self-development to see why you became involved when you were not ready. Taking time out for yourself may not be practical if you're actually living with a partner but you should still discuss your feelings or concerns candidly and arrange counseling for yourself or as a couple. If a relationship or marriage is in serious trouble there are various resources available to try to help it including books, online advice and information or support groups. Counseling or therapy as a couple can also be seriously considered and pursued if you're very unhappy but still believe the relationship can be saved, however you have to be realistic. If you're desperately unhappy and your partner will not make an effort to save the relationship or marriage the best thing to do is walk away. Sometimes it can seem easier to hold on to an unhealthy relationship out of fear of the unknown, feeling frightened by what may seem to be a very uncertain future. Fear of the future or being alone can make the option of trying to keep a relationship on life support much easier when it's clearly dead and should be given the last rites. Instead of walking away, you might decide to struggle on in vain due to unhealed emotional issues, hoping things will change and wishing things were different while constantly feeling tense and frustrated, losing your temper at times or frequently crying yourself to sleep.

Being involved with an unhappy relationship often feels like a very lonely place and can eventually become a soul-destroying experience. Sometimes it can be difficult to know when to end it and walk away as doubts can creep into the mind as you question yourself about whether you are making the right decision. Are you being unreasonable? Will anyone else want you? Are you making the right decision? Do you really want to be single? Will your partner be crushed by the rejection? Is this a decision you are going to regret later on? What if you realize you have made a mistake by ending it and want your partner back? You can end up staying in an unhealthy relationship for all the wrong reasons. Ending a relationship can be very sad or even heart-breaking but if it's clearly not working doubts and fears are not good enough reasons for staying.

When a relationship or marriage begins to fail the love, respect and trust is often replaced by suspicion, resentment or anger. Deciding a relationship has "run its course" and is no longer viable can frequently be a very sad and painful decision but it is important to know when to quit. With a terminally ill patient on life support there comes a time when the only option is to pull the plug. When you're satisfied you have done your best to try and maintain or rescue a relationship the reality of the situation must be faced with courage and honesty. When a relationship reaches this stage difficult decisions have to be made; failing to respect yourself by staying in a dead relationship means you're giving away your power. Sometimes the smartest move you can make is to quit, especially if you feel miserable most of the time, lack peace of mind, feel it is a huge struggle to make the relationship succeed or, worse, you are suffering physical, mental or emotional abuse.

Always remember if you decide to end a relationship you're not a failure. There may come a time when you know you have tried your best and it just isn't working. The aftermath of a break-up can be painful but any relationship failure can be transformed into a positive learning experience. Your past mistakes are supposed to guide you, not define you. Cultivating self-awareness, knowing what you want and asserting yourself are all signs of emotional maturity. The only true "mistake" in relationship failures is holding on to the same beliefs which may not be serving you while repeating the same patterns and expecting a different result. We can all learn from our failed relationships and each "failure" can provide great opportunities for personal growth. Each relationship can be a learning experience that can help you to make better and more informed choices in the future. There are no "failures" when a relationship ends, only lessons. "As one door closes another door opens" is an old and very true saying; a different path has great potential to bring you new experiences, greater personal growth and shared happiness with someone else. One of the biggest mistakes many people make is hanging on to a relationship that isn't going anywhere. Being committed is one thing; staying when a relationship has gone way past its sell by date doesn't make any sense.

It's a fact of life that couples grow apart, relationships fail every day and becoming romantically involved always carries with it a certain element of risk. When two people are growing together there are fewer opportunities for conflicts but individuals change and evolve constantly and as they do so do the dynamics of their relationships. It can be difficult for some people to understand what they're feeling or to share their thoughts so it can feel easier to withdraw from their partner instead of expressing themselves honestly. This can cause disappointment, despair and even guilt which results in conflict and confusion. Issues should always be discussed honestly with the belief this will ultimately benefit both partners even if the eventual outcome is the actual end of the relationship.

"Don't confuse poor decision-making with destiny. Own your mistakes. It's OK; we all make them. Learn from them so they can empower you!" – Steve Maraboli, Speaker, Author & Behavioral Science Academic

A separation or divorce can bring up many feelings which are often painful or distressing. When it becomes clear a relationship is no longer working but a degree of love and respect still remain it can be extremely difficult to walk away. The relationship might be over but that doesn't necessarily mean the feelings will be totally dead even if you made the decision to leave; it is still possible to have a degree of love, affection and respect for an ex-partner. When the emotions of both partners have settled and don't feel so raw, both parties can eventually become friends and supportive of each other. With mutual respect both partners can acknowledge the relationship is over without bitterness or blaming while truly wishing each other the very best for the future. While there are certain relationship breakdowns where this type of attitude can take a while to embrace it is possible! Caring for your ex-partner and wanting them to be happy is real love because you recognize even if he couldn't be happy with you he could be happy with someone else. Real love is wishing him well and letting him go. If there are children involved this is clearly a win–win situation for all concerned. The emotional wellbeing of any children should always be the first priority and if issues such as visitation cannot be resolved amicably, it is always best to seek professional advice and support.

In the final analysis ending a relationship is a practical as well as emotional decision and it's always wise to acknowledge when a partnership has run its course. Taking the decision to leave a failing relationship is the first step in taking personal responsibility. Although the end of a relationship can be difficult and painful eventually you will appreciate leaving a dead or dying relationship is the right decision for yourself as well as your partner. Most of us have made at least one major relationship mistake in our lives but that doesn't mean we have to beat ourselves up. Understanding what may have motivated you to make poor relationship decisions in the past can help you to avoid making the same mistakes in the future.

CHAPTER 26:

Relationships Probably Doomed to Fail

"Common sense is not so common." – Voltaire Writer (1694-1778), Historian & Philosopher

There are certain types of relationships that are more likely to fail than succeed despite whatever sacrifices you're prepared to make or how much love you may feel.

The Commitment Phobic Relationship

Individuals who have phobias constantly worry about what may happen if they get too close to whatever they're afraid of. Many people suffer from a fear of something and some are more rational, reasonable or understandable than others.

Fears Come In All Shapes and Sizes!

- Acrophobia – Heights
- Claustrophobia – Confined or enclosed spaces
- Arachnophobia – Spiders
- Agoraphobia – Open spaces or public places
- Technophobia – New technology
- Hydrophobia – Water
- Nyctophobia – Night or darkness
- Xenophobia – Foreigners or strangers
- Homophobia – Gays/Homosexuals
- Islamophobia – Muslims/Religion of Islam

There are some people who are afraid of dogs, but this fear is understandable as a dog can give you a nasty bite or even inflict serious physical damage. I'm quite wary around dogs myself but that doesn't stop me from going jogging in my local park or talking to someone who has one. There are others who are so petrified of flying they have never been to another country, even though traveling on a plane is statistically proven to be much safer than driving a car. I used to date a woman who was absolutely terrified of spiders, and who would run screaming from her apartment if she saw one of our little eight-legged friends. Unfortunately, her 12-year-old son would also run behind his mother screaming, assuming they were both in imminent danger; her irrational fear had been transferred to her child. Many fears can be traced back to childhood experiences combined with a vivid imagination. The mind creates an image of a threat or some kind of negative outcome and this produces fear. Often fully grown adults cannot remember how or why they have a particular fear or phobia, which has its roots in their childhood, but the image is still very deeply imbedded within their minds.

The symptoms generally associated with any medium to intense phobic response:

- Nervousness
- Excessive sweating
- Headaches
- Palpitations
- Nausea

Whatever causes the phobia, there will be emotional and physical responses when the source of the fear is encountered that will result in tension, fear or even severe panic attacks. These reactions are often highly disproportionate to the trigger causing the fear or phobia.

Commitment Phobia is a *claustrophobic* response to intimate relationships. One or all of the symptoms listed above can be experienced by someone who is Commitment Phobic when the relationship feels like it's becoming too close or their partner expects a greater commitment. When a Commitment Phobic is gripped by fear it can be very difficult to believe it is the same person. A relationship with this type will be confusing because they're not consistent; at the beginning they can't get enough of you and then for no apparent reason they become "unavailable" both emotionally and physically. Most people have commitment fears and conflicts to varying degrees. How these fears and conflicts are managed makes the difference between embracing a real opportunity for building a solid, enduring relationship or destroying it. Commitment Phobics are sometimes referred to as Love Avoidants but this can be misleading; while both types have very similar patterns of behavior, each mindset can be motivated by different factors. Love Avoidants often have issues that stem from their childhood experiences, their temperament or a combination of both. Commitment Phobic behavior can be caused by a bad relationship experience so he or she is reluctant to let anyone get too close, fearing being hurt again.

Men & Women

While both men and women can be Commitment Phobic, women with commitment conflicts can face problems and consequences that often put them at a disadvantage to men with similar issues. If a man struggles with commitment he doesn't usually face the same pressures as a woman with similar issues. In the past, Western society promoted cultural myths regarding how women should think about love or interact with their partners. Women were taught to be loving, loyal, understanding and supportive to carry out the role of being the "power behind the throne." The male was the "head of the household" in the traditional view of the family unit, but this model is rarely the case in these modern times where a relationship is generally considered to be a partnership of equals. Times may have changed a great deal but men still don't have the same biological pressures to produce children. A man has more time to consider his options or can simply wait until he is ready to make a commitment. He can convince himself that any anxieties about making a relationship commitment will eventually fade away or may decide to sow his wild oats through his thirties or even mid-forties and beyond!

For women, they can be under various types of pressures to conform and "perform." There may be parental or cultural pressure to get married and have children within a traditional family unit. Some women resist marriage or a committed relationship because they dislike what they see as the "traditional" role they will be forced to adopt with the man being the "boss." Many women have chosen to have a child or children outside marriage as society no longer stigmatizes unmarried mothers. This allows a woman to act on their "biological clock" if they want a child outside of marriage or a stable relationship. There are men who still believe the main life goal of most women is to meet a man, settle down or get married and create a family. This can be a dangerous stereotype to believe and men have to be aware of becoming involved with a woman who is Commitment Phobic, or worse narcissistic. A woman with deep commitment issues can come on strong at first, being very enthusiastic about the possibility of having a relationship, being highly seductive and even sexually aggressive. Eventually, she will pull back, sometimes quite suddenly and reject her partner. This type of behavior often leaves a man shocked and confused because it doesn't fit their world view of a "normal" female. I have been through this kind of relationship experience myself, but generally men tend to be more Commitment Phobic than women.

The Commitment Phobic Relationship Pattern

I examined my relationship history and realized I had been deeply Commitment Phobic over a period of several years after discovering the child of my marriage was not my son. The emotional pain was very deep and while I conducted relationships after the shocking revelation, I refused to let a woman get too close to me intimately. I came to a point in my life where I wanted to really understand why I had avoided commitment for several years and read the best-selling book *Men Who Can't Love* by Steven Carter & Julia Sokol. The information provided enlightening insights regarding men who struggle with commitment issues and more importantly helped me to recognize how I had allowed my own unresolved Emotional Baggage to sabotage several of my previous relationships.

Four Typical Stages In A Commitment Phobic Relationship

1. The Beginning: Hot pursuit and obsessed with having you.
2. The Middle: Knows you have become emotionally involved and is expecting a commitment so feelings of panic and fear begin.
3. The End Game: Fear makes him start to back off from the relationship but at this stage you probably want more.
4. Toxic Termination: Withdraws from the relationship (sometimes very suddenly) leaving you very confused and hurt.

Stage 1: The Beginning - Hot Pursuit

This stage is all about the Commitment Phobic's presentation and pursuit. He is on a mission and will do whatever it takes to get your attention and interest, so it all depends on how long it takes you to respond.

The Commitment Phobic will entice you into a relationship by using one or a combination of the following strategies or behaviors:

- Very enthusiastic about pursuing you.
- Often much more interested in pursuing the relationship than you are.
- Implies or indicates he is not interested in a fling or superficial affair and is looking for an exclusive and meaningful relationship.
- Declares you are "special" within a very short time.
- Very attentive to all of your desires or needs.
- Prioritizes the relationship and makes a genuine effort to spend time with you.
- Tries to impress in whatever way he can and tells you about any talents he may have.
- Happily spends money on gifts or special occasions.
- Constantly stays in touch by phone, text or email. Will call you because he "misses your voice" or "just to say hello" or to see "how you are".
- Often displays the positive aspects of his character including depth, sensitivity and vulnerability.
- Appears to be thoughtful and sensitive regarding female issues and will complain about men who are unkind or thoughtless towards women.
- Talks often about making plans for the future as a couple.
- Wants you to trust him and eventually convinces you he is trustworthy.
- Probably has a patchy relationship history but convinces you this time it will be different and special.
- Persuades you to accept his intentions are genuine.

If you respond to all of this positive attention, it's likely to be the beginning of a whirlwind romance. You may decide to make an emotional commitment or become sexually involved too quickly.

Stage 2: The Middle - The Initial Feelings Of Panic

While in "hot pursuit" this man was very confident he wanted you but now a relationship has been established he feels unsure or even frightened. You're expecting a real and tangible commitment based on his promises, which is totally reasonable. He knows you expect the relationship to move forward based on his promises; he also knows the fear and anxiety he is beginning to feel is very real and it's going to be very difficult to keep those promises. Second thoughts and doubts are creeping into his mind. The feelings of panic may be mild, moderate or severe but signs of anxiety will probably be noticeable. These feelings of intense panic and fear might motivate him to immediately go to The End Game phase of the cycle if he definitely decides he can't keep the promises he made during Stage 1. If he is considering leaving the relationship he will be constantly questioning himself about whether it's the right decision, which creates a great deal of inner conflict and confusion. The contradictory nature of a man with deep commitment conflicts means he seeks the intimacy of a relationship but then begins to panic when he gets too close. These men have to find an "escape route" quickly or create some distance until the feelings of being "trapped" have faded.

Problems With Special Occasions

Relationships with a Commitment Phobic tend to experience serious problems when things are going *well* and not when things are going *badly*. This can be very confusing but special occasions such as birthdays or family events can often be made "special" for all the wrong reasons. In his mind attending these kinds of events represents threats to his "freedom" as they symbolize an ongoing commitment to the relationship.

The Dynamics Of The Relationship Begin To Change

- Very sure about his intentions during Stage 1 but now you are receiving mixed messages. He may not make contact as frequently and is less attentive. You begin to get the distinct impression he is pulling back from the relationship.

- Had all the time in the world for you during Stage 1 but now he hardly has any time for you at all! It may feel like you have to book an appointment to see him as he is very "busy" all of a sudden. Now he has other things to attend which have a higher priority before he can "fit" you in. The dynamics of the relationship begin to feel disrupted.

- Begins to make excuses that make it clear your priority in his life has been downgraded. These excuses sound reasonable at face value but you suspect he is pulling away from the relationship.

- Makes excuses for excluding you from significant parts of his life that include his family and friends. You begin to get the feeling "something else" is actually going on.

- He begins to find problems with seeing you or finds faults with your personality or something you do. He starts to drop hints or looks for reasons to justify why continuing the relationship is not a good idea.

- Avoids attending any functions or social events that may include your friends or family.

- Becomes difficult to connect with emotionally or to communicate with. You begin to notice he lacks any interest in your emotional or practical requirements.

- Seems resentful if you make any requests or ask too many searching questions. He implies or makes it clear he does not want to be relied upon. Resents any expectations you may have based on what occurred during Stage 1. May be so vague you are unsure about exactly what expectations he is talking about.

- Will praise all of your good qualities like being understanding, loyal, intelligent or kind but these very same qualities now appear to make him uncomfortable. This discomfort is caused by not having a valid reason to reject you or the relationship.

- His sexual pattern changes but you are not sure why. He might become passive in this area, which can subtly turn you into the one who initiates any sexual interaction.

- Fails to keep his promises and this prevents the relationship from progressing in any meaningful way.
- If you express your dissatisfaction with the relationship, he refuses to enter into any discussions.
- Gives the impression he is hiding something or someone might know something about him he doesn't want you to know. He seems to be uncomfortable about something but you're not quite sure what it is.

Mixed Messages & Contradictory Behavior

The conflicting feelings of a Commitment Phobic manifest themselves when he begins to feel a woman is getting too close to him and then his behavior becomes increasingly contradictory. During Stage 1 he wants to get closer and spend quality time with you so it's natural to assume he wants to move the partnership forward. During Stage 2 he can be incredibly attentive and romantic, constantly calling you, sending little love notes via email or texting, making you feel completely loved and cherished; at other times he will suddenly withdraw and stop interacting so intensely or even demand his own "space." You will probably begin wondering if you have done something wrong to cause this change of behavior or start questioning your own judgment.

He may be frequently moody or sullen but will probably try to deflect any questions about what is actually bothering him. At this stage he is probably considering ending the relationship to relieve his anxiety and he may even experience feelings of guilt for misleading you. He probably looks extremely unhappy, distressed, tormented or may behave in strange and bizarre ways at times. In extreme cases a man with severe commitment conflicts can appear to be having some kind of mental meltdown. These behaviors are often caused when a Commitment Phobic struggles to decide what to do or doesn't want to take responsibility for ending the relationship.

Warning Signs

- Emotionally present but at other times is very emotionally unavailable
- Romantic but at other times very distant
- Warm and giving but at other times very cold
- Tender but at other times very hostile
- Accepting but at other times very critical
- Seductive but at other times rejecting
- Affectionate but at other times very withdrawn
- Sexually proactive or provocative but at other times not interested in sex

This behavior can be very confusing as it appears you're involved with two very different men who apparently co-exist in the same body. These fears and inner conflicts can motivate a Commitment Phobic to break relationship bonds very quickly or suddenly withdraw sexually, which often comes as a total surprise.

When it becomes clear he is beginning to withdraw many women who have fallen in love typically respond by:

- Trying desperately to make the relationship work
- Assuming the relationship is falling apart due to something she has done or is doing
- Blaming herself for a problem that has absolutely nothing to do with her

If he decides to end the relationship, the "sympathy card" might be played in the hope you won't make too much of a fuss or demand an explanation for his change of heart. If your partner appears needy or vulnerable you may feel sorry for him, believing he needs your support to get through this "difficult time." The truth is he expects your love and support while rejecting you at the same time. This can be very confusing leading some women to believe their partner wants to maintain a genuine connection and just needs some time to "sort himself out." This approach also gives a woman false hope the relationship can be saved so she may decide a Friends With Benefits arrangement is better than nothing. Being supportive and accepting of his "plight" is usually a huge mistake and deciding to embark on a FWB means you will probably be used. There is usually a high price to pay emotionally if you continue to indulge his behavior during this stage.

Commitment Phobic Tactic: Resurrecting An Ex-Partner

When a Commitment Phobic can't make a decision to end a relationship he may try and provoke his partner into walking away. A classic exit strategy is to use a former lover from his past as an excuse to escape.

Typical Behaviors:

- Leaves subtle or obvious clues suggesting he is seeing another woman. You might confront him, hoping he will deny any allegations.
- Drops hints about the possibility of seeing someone else or may actually admit to having an affair. Often the "other woman" is someone he had a relationship with previously who is unexpectedly "resurrected."
- Admits to seeing another woman but claims she isn't important, saying you're still his "number one." Of course he might also lie about having an affair but the clues or your intuition tell you that he is lying.
- He may cry and promise to change if you issue an ultimatum or say you're leaving the relationship. Despite his promises it's obvious he is seriously conflicted about the relationship.

You may be aware of this woman from his past but considering all the grand promises he made it probably never crossed your mind he could suddenly be interested in someone else. His behavior may have caused small doubts but nothing to give you any serious cause for concern, yet now he begins to imply he has feelings for another woman or suddenly announces he is considering going back to his former partner. Both of these stories could be true but the motivating factor will be for the Commitment Phobic to try to create an escape route by forcing you to make a decision to end the relationship. It's quite possible he doesn't want to be with his ex-partner or another woman any more than he wants to be with you at this stage, but this strategy serves as a way out of the relationship – for now.

In this type of scenario a woman involved with a Commitment Phobic has to know how to read between the lines:

- When he says or implies he is thinking about going back to his former partner or lover, this is letting you know indirectly he's no longer sure about the commitments he made to you.
- If he suggests or states directly he is thinking of or interested in another woman, consider this a serious warning; he is preparing to leave or dramatically change the terms of the relationship.
- If he has been actually seeing his ex-partner for whatever reason, alarm bells should be ringing loud and clear!

It doesn't really matter how another woman is introduced into the situation. It is highly likely she is being used as a tool to let you know all the previous promises of commitment made during Stage 1 of the relationship are now being seriously reconsidered or have been revoked. If you confront him about his change of behavior or the "other woman" don't expect a reasonable explanation or a response that makes complete sense.

By this stage you probably have great hopes and dreams for the relationship and want it to work so your first thought may be to fight off the "competition" or to become sexually aggressive to try to win him over. It's easy to fall into the trap of trying to prove yourself "worthy" when the relationship now seems to be slipping through your fingers.

You might even be tempted to plead for him to stay with you after being told he is thinking of another woman or considering going back to her and your self-esteem will probably feel low. He may even seem like the only person in the world who can help you recover your sense of self-worth; feeling hurt and rejected, it might be tempting to try and persuade him to stay and try to make the relationship work, remembering how he was at the beginning when he was so "into you," loving and attentive. Upset and confused by the revelation he is considering leaving you for another woman can make you abandon your reason and common sense, but this is a time for clear-headed thinking and to consider his behavior objectively.

When a woman has fallen in love she may buckle under the emotional pressure, feeling hurt, wounded or confused, and accept whatever terms he may offer including a Friends With Benefits arrangement. In any relationship there are occasions when it's appropriate to be romantic and at other times pragmatic; tough decisions have to be based on facing the facts and maintaining self-respect. Women I have spoken to have explained this is one of the most difficult stages to get through when dealing with a Commitment Phobic. Even if a relationship from his past has not been used as part of his exit strategy, you will probably be feeling very hurt and emotionally deflated. The revelation that he is having serious doubts can be a brutal shock after all the promises that were made about your future together. He believes the relationship has become "too close" or is moving "too fast" which makes him feel deep anxiety or a sense of becoming "trapped." A healthy relationship cannot survive without trust and by this stage you should know you can't believe him. If you're tempted to make excuses for his behavior, remember your love has been badly betrayed. The relationships of Commitment Phobics often overlap so if he declares feelings for another woman from his past this should always be taken very seriously.

At this stage of a Commitment Phobic cycle a woman should:

- Drastically reduce contact
- Begin to pursue other activities that don't include him
- Accept the reality the relationship is probably going to fail
- Start seriously thinking about being single to allow some time for reflection and healing

The only way to regain control of the situation is to give yourself some time and space to consider his behavior. Backing off from the relationship will also give you a chance to process and understand your own thoughts and feelings.

Stage 3: The End Game

If you are still hanging on trying to make it work at this stage get ready for a very bumpy emotional ride! During this phase of the cycle a Commitment Phobic will not fully commit to the relationship but he won't leave it completely either, especially if you're having sex with him hoping he is going to change his mind. Instead of taking responsibility he will probably try and blame you for the situation, do something unkind or try to provoke you into ending the relationship.

Warning Signs:

- Will not talk about the relationship and will not make any efforts to improve it.
- Becomes unreliable, often changes plans at short notice.
- Demands space and wants you to be "flexible".
- Makes it very obvious he is leaving the relationship due to his change of attitude.
- Usually unavailable and provides no real explanations for his absences.
- Continues to give you very mixed messages which are confusing. For example, he may be loving and sentimental and then switch to rejecting you or finding fault with the relationship.

- Has periods when he is moody or talks very little but doesn't admit his mood is caused by fear. He might say his mood has nothing to do with you and in a sense this is true! His internal conflicts are the source of his intense discomfort.
- Is not very interested in sex but may place the blame for this on being tired, not feeling well or work pressures. The emphasis is placed on you being understanding and not asking too many questions so you do not add to any "stress".
- May provoke arguments.

Someone with deep commitment issues and conflicts will not be interested in discussing and resolving any challenges or problems. In the mind of a Commitment Phobic, making any genuine effort to maintain or improve a relationship is exactly the same thing as making a commitment. If he withdraws sexually it's usually for one of two reasons: he is trying to detach himself emotionally or doesn't want his partner to think the relationship is getting better. Sometimes an excuse is offered that indicates his lack of libido is just a temporary problem, which gives him the option to approach you when he is feeling less conflicted. Your observations or intuition might begin to tell you he is trying to keep you interested in the relationship but is unclear about what he actually wants. During this stage it's wise not to have sex with him until you are sure about his intentions and if you really want to be with him.

The Commitment Phobic is frightened of "forever after" so he may actually make a decision to end the relationship himself as leaving means his anxiety levels decrease. His tense internal conflicts can also compel him to break away very quickly, coldly or cruelly which often comes as a complete surprise. Once he has distanced himself for a while and feels less "threatened" these men often rediscover the feelings they had for their partner. While he's rejecting you he often appears to also want you to be supportive and loving towards him. He may come across as being very needy and vulnerable and you may be drawn into thinking he needs your support to get through this "difficult time." You will probably still receive gifts or compliments – even poetry and love cards and definitely lots of phone calls, emails or texts that are romantic in nature. This is all designed to keep you engaged by pushing all the right buttons to gain a favorable response so you can be manipulated into providing advice and even emotional support. This can all be very confusing and can lead you to believe he is trying to maintain a genuine connection.

During this stage a typical Commitment Phobic still seeks all the perks of a relationship without actually giving very much back. He wants to tell you all of his problems and "pressures" and may even ask for help with some of these "issues" while he's still struggling to make a decision. This strategy is also designed to buy him some time to discover if you will accept him on his new terms, which will not include any real commitment, just meeting up occasionally for consensual Friends With Benefits sex. Staying in contact or continuing to see him leaves you open to being available sexually and emotionally while remaining in relationship limbo! If you allow this to happen it will just prolong the pain and delay your emotional recovery. Assess the quality of the relationship and your attitude towards your partner; ask yourself whether you are being realistic about the relationship and are actually satisfied with the partnership as opposed to fantasizing about its "potential." Having an unrealistic romantic agenda with anyone is just asking for serious heartache later on.

Actions Speak Louder Than Words

Talk is cheap and Commitment Phobics can talk a very good game, especially during Stage 1, so pay attention to his actions. Don't let your feelings entice you into believing his excuses or justifications. Constant affection and caring makes him feel increasingly suffocated and trapped instead of feeling loved and cared for. The harder you try the more he will pull away so it's really a no-win situation. The best strategy you can adopt is concentrating on your own emotional wellbeing and sanity. If you arrive at this stage of the Commitment Phobic relationship cycle, be warned: trying to change his mind or behavior is a waste of your precious time and energy. Stop accepting his explanations, excuses and lies, which are designed to keep you engaged and hanging on, hoping he will actually deliver what he promised during Stage 1. By this stage you should be very wary about believing any promises unless they are supported by a consistent change of behavior over a period of time. Step back and be objective before making any major decisions.

This is the time to employ two powerful strategies:

- Always say less than necessary
- Win through your actions and not through any arguments

When you demonstrate your intentions and do not enter any discussions you show you are serious. Actions speak louder than words and withdrawing at this stage is the very best move you can make.

Stage 4: Toxic Termination

The Commitment Phobic coping mechanisms finally fail so he implements one of the following exit strategies:

- Totally disappears and refuses to call you or even return any of your calls.
- Quickly withdraws so eventually the relationship dies a "natural death".
- Does something unacceptable, outrageous or provokes a major disagreement or argument .

When a Commitment Phobic withdraws gradually or suddenly from the relationship you can be left in a state of total confusion while feeling powerless and emotionally distraught. For some people they are actually paralyzed on an emotional level and cannot function normally for a period of time. You may feel at times you are losing control of your emotions and even your mind. The feelings of betrayal and hurt can be very deep when it dawns on you that you have been badly misled and lied to. Feeling hurt and confused you might start to blame yourself for not paying attention to the warning signs during Stage 2. You might begin to doubt yourself and think it was something about your behavior or personality that drove him away. Reminiscing about the special bond you shared during Stage 1 is common and you may even be in denial about the relationship actually being over. While you're grieving the loss of the relationship you may believe he's the only person who can make you feel better. A healthy relationship cannot survive without trust and by this stage you should know he cannot be trusted to make a real commitment. If you're involved with a Commitment Phobic and get to this stage, it can be very damaging to your self-esteem and emotional wellbeing.

The Sequel: The Commitment Phobic Returns!

Relationships with Commitment Phobics don't always end badly and sometimes they just fade away, but if it was a bad break-up, there will probably be some more drama! After you have started to move on with your life there will probably be a call, text, email, letter or card from the Commitment Phobic trying to re-establish contact. If it's your birthday or a national holiday a few months after the break-up this gives him the perfect excuse to get in touch so expect some type of communication at these times. Alternatively, he may have kept some of your belongings after the break-up like a few CDs, books or clothing as an excuse to make contact once his fears have gone away. What has changed his mind? You no longer represent a commitment threat so his feelings of anxiety have subsided and he misses you! Full of remorse for what happened he might tell you how sad his life has been without you and even sound desperate to rekindle the relationship. He may apologize for his behavior admitting his mistakes, promising to try harder or declaring he can't possibly live without you. Whatever his approach, eventually he will try to convince you to give him another chance.

Before considering taking him back, step back and think about his behavior. Yes, you might still be a bit shaky emotionally and not fully healed; you might even want him back, but it's time to be realistic instead of allowing yourself to be swept away by romantic fantasies. You have to ask yourself some tough questions. He couldn't keep his promises before so has he really changed? It's nice to feel special and wanted, but are you willing to pay such a high price again? Are you being tempted by his offer because you are desperate to settle down and motivated by your own romantic fantasies? It can be very tempting to think you can change him and decide to give the relationship another chance, especially if you still have feelings for him. During the sequel he will try to convince you it's possible for him to be different next time. Before making any decisions to allow him back into your life, remind yourself of the facts about the relationship; think very carefully about the broken promises that hurt you so much. Accepting his offer means jumping on the Commitment Phobic roundabout again, but next time it will just spin faster as you go through the same stages at a quicker pace. If you decide to keep trying to make a relationship work with this type of man expect a very challenging time.

The "No Contact" Rule

The recommended strategy after a failed relationship with a Commitment Phobic is absolutely zero contact for a minimum of at least three months. That means no phone calls, texts or emails. This may seem harsh and can be difficult, especially if you still have feelings for him, but any type of contact will often be painful or confusing and delay your emotional recovery. The connection may still feel very intense in the aftermath of a split and you may still want to believe his promises, which were probably everything you ever wanted to hear, but the truth is it wasn't real. Staying in contact or having sex occasionally means leaving yourself open to being sexually and emotionally available while remaining in some sort of relationship limbo which is always a bad idea. Accepting his behavior in the futile hope he is going to change will just continue to waste your time, energy and love. The more you try to understand, rationalize or romanticize his behavior the greater emotional turmoil there will be, especially if you have prolonged contact during Stages 3 or 4 while sharing social or sexual activities together. Allowing him to operate on his own terms is a very bad idea so cutting him off completely for a period of time is the only sensible option. Make a firm decision to cut all communication. If he contacts you by phone your response should always be very brief and business like.

Commitment Phobic Relationship Failure

Entering a relationship with honest intentions and high hopes only to be badly let down and betrayed can be a very painful emotional experience. When the relationship fails with a Commitment Phobic it's easy to start beating yourself up assuming the failure is your fault. A well-intentioned decision to pursue a relationship with someone who promised to love you has turned into a nightmare, but believing false promises is nothing to be ashamed of and the best way to protect yourself in the future is to be aware of the red flags.

How To Identify A Commitment Phobic

A man with commitment conflicts will often have an unrealistic attitude towards his relationships. These men are not really interested in developing or building a serious partnership but are always in a rush to get things "moving" so their approach is often inappropriate. They create intense sexual, passionate and emotional bonds that appear to be genuine but are actually very superficial. Commitment Phobic relationships usually begin with a rush for intimacy and a strong sexual connection but eventually fail due to his intense inner conflicts.

Commitment Phobic Warning Signs

A Commitment Phobic may not display all of these behaviors but look out for the following:

Unwilling to commit to dates in advance

He will be reluctant to make any plans for the future, including dates, preferring to make same-day plans or commit only a few days in advance. Usually attempts to make last-minute arrangements or plans instead of confirming in advance.

He uses modifiers in his speech

If you pay attention, the Commitment Phobic often uses phrases such as: "probably," "maybe," "probably not," "I might" or "I might not" when discussing any plans or arrangements.

Relationship is undefined

Those in relationships with Commitment Phobics often do not know the status of the relationship. There are unlikely to be any significant conversations about the relationship even if it has been ongoing for years.

Sexually active

Commitment Phobics enjoy intimacy like everyone else but they can find it difficult to have these needs fulfilled so may compensate by being sexually active or promiscuous.

Avoids using the word "love"

Men and women with commitment issues often have difficulties expressing their feelings. They may even be afraid of their own feelings so are unlikely to say "I love you" and mean it.

Unpredictable

Moods and behavior often change so it can be difficult to know what to expect. They can be attentive on one day and then act distant avoiding contact the next without any explanation. The behavior can be surprising and confusing.

Avoids using the terms "Boyfriend," "Girlfriend," "Partner," etc.

For the Commitment Phobic, using any words that even imply a commitment can be difficult. Saying these types of words for them signifies a greater commitment than he/she is capable of making. They simply avoid talking about the status of the relationship or may offer excuses to cover why they find using terms of endearment uncomfortable.

Past relationships have mainly been casual or short-term

If he is over 30 and never had a long-term relationship or been married it is unlikely he is going to commit to a long-term relationship. If he had a few long-term relationships but these did not involve any serious commitment on his part this should also be considered a red flag. Each person's relationship history is the most reliable indicator as to how they are likely to behave now and in the future. A Commitment Phobic's romantic history will usually contain several relationship failures and often the reasons given will not be very convincing.

He might be charming, clever, intelligent and sensitive with many other positive attributes, but someone with commitment issues probably has a certain degree of emotional damage. Becoming involved with this type results in using up a great deal of time and emotional energy trying to get closer to make the relationship work. In the meantime he will be busy creating obstacles and boundaries that impede, and after a period of time you will find yourself on an emotional roundabout that isn't going anywhere except in a very painful circle.

How To Avoid Becoming Involved With A Commitment Phobic

Control the pace

This is essential at the beginning of any relationship. Allowing yourself to be swept off your feet might sound and feel very romantic but is not realistic. A Commitment Phobic always wants a whirlwind romance but begins to feel scared when he feels he's getting in too deep.

Be realistic

Love conquering all and every obstacle is a myth. Pay attention to any warning signs and take appropriate action.

Don't make excuses

When you're strongly attracted to a man or in love with him, it can be easy to make excuses for him – stressful job, had a difficult childhood, still recovering from a bad marriage or relationship are the most common. He may offer similar excuses himself but we all go through difficult experiences and have a responsibility for how we manage ourselves.

Be independent

Maintain your independence and pay attention to any warning signs.

Reserve sympathy

Don't fall into the trap of feeling sorry for him if you suspect he has commitment issues. It's very easy for your maternal instincts to kick in and for you to start to act like his mother, therapist or best friend.

Don't pretend

If you're dating, don't start treating him like your official partner prematurely. Don't fall into the trap of acting as if everything is fine when you have concerns or there are alarm bells ringing. When a Commitment Phobic is pursuing a woman he will often drop hints or even be quite candid about being unsure about being involved in a committed relationship or display other warning signs of ambivalence. Establishing a genuine relationship takes time so if a man you're dating seems to be coming on a bit too strong make sure you maintain your own boundaries. The dating stage will often progress rapidly into a relationship and just as you begin to believe the union is about to progress to the next level your partner will begin to pull back. There is nothing wrong with being romantic as long as you are also pragmatic. If you suspect he has unresolved commitment conflicts and doesn't have an ongoing personal strategy for personal growth he isn't ready for a serious relationship.

The Difference Between The Player, Mr. Romeo And A Commitment Phobic

It's important to understand the difference between a Player and a Commitment Phobic. The Player is mainly motivated by sexual conquests but will use the same tactics and strategies as a Commitment Phobic to maintain his sexual supply from a particular woman. There are Players who are Commitment Phobic but a man who is Commitment Phobic is not necessarily a Player. A Commitment Phobic's behavior is usually compulsive while a Player's behavior is often premeditated. In their book *He's Scared, She's Scared* Steven Carter and Julia Sokol say when a man is genuinely Commitment Phobic his pursuit of women is not purely about sexual conquests. I have noticed Commitment Phobics and Players are generally motivated by different mindsets but their strategies, patterns and behaviors overlap in key areas. For example, both types will use similar strategies to gain a potential partner's attention and trust by claiming or implying they want to pursue a relationship at the earliest opportunity or act in ways that convinces a woman they're serious. Both types will use sex to try and control and dictate when intimacy happens, but for the Commitment Phobic sex is used to initiate and establish intimacy but also to withdraw intimacy to *avoid* becoming too close when they begin to feel "pressured" or trapped.

In her book *Emotional Unavailability* psychologist and author Bryn C. Collins provides an excellent description and a checklist for the type she describes as "The Romeo." This type has Player tendencies but is quite capable of being in a full-time relationship while pursuing other women. It's the "thrill" of the chase and the idea of a new romance that excites the Romeo and provides his initial motivation but he will have sex with another woman if the opportunity arises. They enjoy the romance/chase/conquest cycle but are often incapable of actually making a genuine emotional connection no matter how romantic they may appear to be on the surface. The Player/Romeo type is usually obsessed with romantic fantasies concerning love (as they perceive it) and the "perfect" relationship.

351

Bryn Collins' Romeo Checklist

- Intense interest during early dating stages
- Highly romantic but poor at intimacy
- Frequent unexplained absences or lateness
- Disconnected from emotions
- Insincere and superficial
- Irresponsible
- Secretive
- Poor boundaries
- Good in crisis situations but struggles to maintain relationships

Romance should be a part of any healthy relationship but being romantic is based on a set of behaviors partners display towards each other while being in love is based on a range of emotions partners share. Within that range of feelings is an expectancy of trust and fidelity. Romantic gestures should enhance the love two people share but cannot replace a genuine love, which is what most people want – not a fairytale or counterfeit version. A typical Commitment Phobic often doesn't understand why this inner conflict and confusion is happening but is very aware of his feelings. Once the relationship begins to develop, he suddenly withdraws, often leaving a woman very hurt and confused.

The Way Forward

"We have to recognize that there cannot be relationships unless there is commitment, unless there is loyalty, unless there is love, patience, persistence." – Cornel West, Philosopher, Academic, Activist & Author

A hardcore Commitment Phobic cannot offer you a genuine relationship. Once you have accepted this reality it's time to seriously consider your options. Understanding the Seven Stages of Relationship Grief can help you through the process if the aftermath feels difficult to cope with. This isn't a time to overindulge in self-pity; the best way to achieve closure is to be practical and proactive, not wishful and passive. It might seem easier to stay at home and fantasize about what might have been, but this is not healthy or helpful; isolating yourself socially will not change the situation or his mindset.

- Accept the fact the relationship was an illusion and is over.
- Maintain your no-contact rule.
- Keep yourself active and busy; set goals and make plans.
- Resist the temptation to reminisce about the good times.
- Avoid thinking about how great a relationship with him could be .
- Remind yourself you are wiser for the experience and will not so easily be taken in next time.
- Move on with your dignity and self-respect intact.
- Accept the Commitment Phobic is not going to change.
- Release any blame or resentment.

- Don't blame yourself for what happened because it wasn't your fault!

Take some comfort from the thought you were probably not the first person he has misled and probably won't be the last. Remind yourself that a Commitment Phobic's relationships fail due to their own internal conflicts and not because their partners are deeply flawed, so learn the lessons and prepare to move on to a better and brighter future.

Make plans, set goals and reactivate your social life if any of these activities were neglected during the relationship. Accept invitations to socialize and keep your options open; dating can be challenging, especially if you haven't done it for a while; besides, it's important to be confident you're not on the rebound before becoming involved with someone else. Meet new people and try different things. If he's still contacting you and doesn't like the fact you're moving on, that's his problem, not yours!

Are You A Commitment Phobic? Check Yourself Out!

People with commitment issues often find partners who are not necessarily Commitment Phobic themselves. Sadly men and women with a tendency to become involved with Commitment Phobics often lacked positive relationship role models during their formative years. What they failed to witness as a child, they either try to recreate as an adult or they accept their childhood role models who demonstrated that an uncommitted, unstable relationship is "normal." This can cause them to try and create real-life fantasies about how the "perfect" relationship will be for them. When someone is fantasy-driven they will ignore partners who offer the real possibility of a stable relationship and focus instead on finding or meeting the "perfect match" or soul mate.

When a person's relationship history demonstrates they constantly become involved with partners who avoid commitment it is very likely they are subconsciously running away from a committed relationship themselves. If you have a pattern of being involved with Commitment Phobics, consider your childhood experiences and examine whether your role models were stable or erratic.

A person who is subconsciously avoiding a committed relationship frequently:

- Attracts or is attracted to inappropriate partners
- Responds inappropriately to negative information and clear warning signs
- Ignores reality
- Believes what they're told and falls in love far too quickly
- Makes premature and inappropriate relationship commitments

Unresolved emotional issues could motivate you to unconsciously mislead potential partners by failing to keep your promises. You may also behave in ways that are misleading and have unrealistic expectations of your partner. A classic Commitment Phobic pattern is to express total love and acceptance for a new partner very quickly but within a few months they begin to find fault. Often these "faults" are certain aspects their partner cannot change about themselves, for example, age, height or race, which is very unreasonable. You may suddenly raise these type of "issues" when the anxiety or panic begins to surface and you're looking for a way out. When someone begins a relationship knowing they're ultimately going to reject a partner this is very unfair.

Reality Check!

"Usually adult males who are unable to make emotional connections with the women they choose to be intimate with are frozen in time, unable to allow themselves to love for fear that the loved one will abandon them. If the first woman they passionately loved, the mother, was not true to her bond of love, then how can they trust that their partner will be true to love?" – Bell Hooks, Author

There are many single men with a deep fear of commitment and during your lifetime it's possible you will become involved with one of them. The relationship will often progress quickly until he suddenly begins to pull back, leaving you feeling very confused. When a Commitment Phobic is gripped by fear it can be very difficult to believe it's the same person. Each relationship has its own unique dynamic and not every Commitment Phobic will behave in exactly the same way. If any of these stages, scenarios or behaviors sound familiar it's likely you have been involved with a Commitment Phobic or are currently in a difficult relationship. If you have been with a partner for a reasonable period of time (a maximum of two years) but he is unwilling to take the relationship to the next level, do not ignore this if you want more. I have spoken to women who have been involved with a Commitment Phobic for several years and the majority found themselves repeating Stages 3 and 4 with the same man, enduring years of relationship torment and confusion.

When a deep emotional investment has been made it can be very difficult to just walk away with nothing much to show for your love. Once it becomes clear you are dealing with a Commitment Phobic it's time to be realistic and to give up your romantic dreams with him for good. It does not matter how much you may love him, or how compatible you may be, or if the sex is absolutely mind-blowing. When a person has serious commitment issues they are not going to commit to a relationship. Period. One of the big relationship mistakes many people make is trying to change how their partner thinks and behaves. Attempting to change your partner in a relationship eventually leads to resentment or some kind of conflict. Commitment Phobics are usually resistant to change because they are too scared to look at themselves, are stuck in the pursuit/romance/conquest mindset, or receive certain pay-offs for their behavior. Finding someone with the genuine intention of embarking on a committed relationship can be difficult at the best of times. Very often, as we become older it can be even more difficult to find a compatible and loving partner. I know many women who have wasted a great deal of love, time and energy with Commitment Phobic men. Falling in love with a person with commitment issues can be a relationship nightmare.

Each of us has the potential to change but the essential ingredients required for personal development and growth are a strong desire to be different and a willingness to change. Personal growth can be very challenging and requires certain levels of self-awareness and persistence. Commitment Phobic behavior can be the result of a bad relationship experience but change is possible. I know this is true because I was deeply Commitment Phobic myself for several years but recovered through exploring my own personal self-development and recognizing what had made me scared of allowing a woman to get too close. I understood my feelings and behavior would continue to sabotage my intimate relationships until my issues were addressed and healed. My fears were caused by unresolved Emotional Baggage and I regret the emotional distress and pain I caused to several women who could have been great long-term partners. A Commitment Phobic can change but only if he has a deep desire to do so. Be warned: for a person with deep commitment issues, any genuine transformation can be very difficult and if you decide to adopt the role of mother, therapist or best friend instead of being loved and respected as you should be, expect a very challenging time.

Partner Is Unavailable

"Simply put, relationships with unavailable men are frustrating and unsatisfying, yet too many women try-try-try to stick it out and make things work." – Seth Meyers Ph.D., *Psychology Today.*

In the dating game you're going to meet men who are not available because of their circumstances. Women can deceive themselves into believing a potential relationship can succeed despite clear evidence to the contrary. Pursuing a relationship with a man who is involved elsewhere often ends up as nothing more than a sexual Friends With Benefits arrangement or an "affair."

Unresolved Childhood Emotional Issues And Relationship Choices

Why would a woman willingly accept a man into her life when he is clearly involved in a relationship elsewhere? Men and women with unresolved emotional issues caused during childhood can have a tendency to pursue relationships with people who are unavailable. This type of mindset can be a result of being abandoned as a child either physically or emotionally. The experience of abandonment feels very familiar during adulthood so not having someone permanent or consistent in their life feels quite normal.

Physical or sexual abuse during childhood may cause a pattern of thinking that resists others becoming too close as a form of protection. Subconsciously, a person can repeatedly seek out unavailable partners to protect themselves from being hurt, motivated by a fear of intimacy. Affairs with partners who are not actually available for a committed relationship can be a very effective strategy to avoid genuine intimacy.

A child who grows up in an unstable or dysfunctional environment may grow up believing they are undeserving of an exclusive and loving relationship. Growing up with poor or non-existent role models of what a healthy relationship should look and feel like, adults may then struggle to understand how to create and conduct a healthy relationship themselves. During adulthood their self-esteem can be quite low so even very low levels of "love" or attention can feel quite acceptable and normal. Poor self-esteem can encourage low relationship expectations and even the acceptance of damaging behavior from toxic partners. Subconsciously they recreate behavior and scenarios observed during childhood and feel comfortable with substandard "relationships" or sexual arrangements.

Reality Check!

"Wondering if the man you're dating is emotionally unavailable? Maybe you have a pattern of dating emotionally unavailable men? One telltale sign that a man doesn't have the capabilities to be intimate, considerate, compassionate, honest, loyal and open in a relationship is a lack of empathy in moments when you need him most." – Kristina Marchant, Dating Coach

Women who become involved with unavailable men often have some deep insecurities or self-esteem issues which usually stem from their childhoods. They will pursue a man who is clearly unavailable driven subconsciously to prove they are worthy of his love and commitment. If he makes a commitment this proves she deserves his love and boosts her feelings of self-worth but if he doesn't commit the woman is quite likely to be left with lower self-esteem than before she became involved. These women will have a habit of making excuses for the unavailable man and will give him numerous chances feeling they have invested too much time and effort to walk away. When an adult woman is fantasy-driven, desperate, suffering from low self-esteem or in denial, she can conveniently overlook what the word "available" actually means.

The strict definition of a man who is "available":

- Single
- Not seeing anyone else
- Not dating anyone else
- Not sleeping with anyone else
- Not living with someone else
- Not engaged
- Not married

When you meet a man who is available for a potential relationship this means he is single and free to pursue any romantic possibilities without bringing anyone else into the dating process. He might be dating other women, in which case you have to decide if you want to entertain this or make it clear you expect to be dated exclusively.

In the dating game, meeting an attractive man who is already involved is probably going to happen. This doesn't necessarily mean you won't be together in the future, but it *does* mean you shouldn't be entertaining or encouraging him now. It doesn't matter how attractive or compatible a man may appear to be, he is *not* available when:

- He has recently split up with his ex-partner but is considering returning to the relationship.
- In a relationship but claims to be confused and asks you to hang around anyway while he makes a decision.
- In a relationship but claims he is no longer in love.
- In a relationship but claims to stay with her because of the children.
- In a relationship but claims he plans to leave his partner shortly.
- Living with another woman but claims they no longer have sex.
- Involved with another woman but claims it's just an "open" relationship/marriage or a Friends With Benefits arrangement so it's okay to pursue getting together.

While there can be exceptions where he may be telling the truth the reality is a man who is involved in any of the above relationship scenarios is not available. There are men who will tell a woman their relationship is broken or actually finished but they are still involved sexually or emotionally with their current partner. Even if he is telling the truth about the state of affairs with his partner this behavior indicates a man who may have a cheating mindset.

When a man is prepared to cheat on his current partner it's very likely he will eventually cheat on you later on. If he does leave his current partner (which can be a false promise used to string you along) to be with you, there isn't enough time for him to reflect on and process his emotions regarding the previous relationship failure.

Embarking on an affair with a man who is already in a relationship is a waste of time; he won't be in a position to pursue or maintain a genuine relationship and will be constantly distracted and unable to be fully emotionally, mentally or physically present. When a man is interested in you but already involved with another woman he is probably only available for an arrangement that will be based primarily on sex. You will never be a priority in this type of "relationship" situation and eventually may feel used. Consciously deciding to become involved with a man who is clearly unavailable could mean putting yourself at emotional risk. Accepting a "relationship" or affair with a man who is having sex with another woman means you are disrespecting yourself. Avoid men where their circumstances make them clearly unsuitable to be considered for a serious relationship.

Already Involved

"Well, there were three of us in this marriage, so it was a bit crowded." – Diana, Princess of Wales (1961-1997)

If you're currently having sex with a man who is married, cohabiting or otherwise involved, it's time to find some dignity and self-respect. "Love Triangles" often end in tears and the person who is going to get hurt is probably going to be *you*. When or *if* his circumstances change (he becomes single and available) you can reconsider your options and decide if a genuine relationship is actually viable. Terminate seeing him now to avoid being used and probably very disappointed when his promises fail to materialize.

If you're enduring an unhappy and difficult relationship it can be tempting to seek relief and happiness elsewhere. This can leave you vulnerable to being enticed into situations that are very unhealthy so always conduct your relationships with integrity; affairs often have the potential to become extremely messy and can even be dangerous. Don't make the mistake of becoming involved in a messy Love Triangle with another man due to being in an unhappy relationship yourself.

Rebound Relationships

"My first marriage was totally unsuitable and shouldn't have happened. It was a whirlwind, rebound thing. I was 23 or 24-a baby." – Carol Vorderman, TV Presenter

Being on the rebound is a reaction to feeling vulnerable, sad, upset or rejected due to the failure of a previous relationship. It happens when a person becomes involved too quickly with someone new after an upsetting break-up or divorce. This is often motivated by a need to prove to themselves he or she is still worthy of love and affection, or he or she may miss the comfort and affection of a regular relationship. Acting on the rebound can be based on purely selfish reasons such as attempting to boost feelings of low self-esteem or a distraction from feelings of hurt and/or rejection. It is a substitute or a quick fix after a break-up to try and avoid the pain of the previous relationship failure while seeking to feel good again as quickly as possible. Rebound behavior can also be used to deflect any blame for a break-up and to prove you're still desirable and lovable. The mindset of someone on the rebound may not be rational as they are desperately seeking to confirm someone else besides their ex-partner still finds him or her attractive.

The Rebound Mindset

Instead of taking some time out to recover, men and women can rush into new involvements trying to ease the pain of the break-up or to distract themselves from the feelings of failure and rejection, especially if they have been brutally dumped. Men are frequently conditioned as children to avoid expressing or feeling emotions, so often try to avoid the grieving process following a break-up. Instead of embracing a period of time to assess the previous relationship and deal with their feelings of loss, men can be inclined to try and "man up."

Is He Still In Contact With His Ex-Partner?

There are valid reasons why a man may still be in contact with his ex-partner such as if they shared a long-term relationship and remained friends or have children together. If he has children and contacts his ex-partner regarding their welfare, this is appropriate and acceptable, providing contact with the children is not being used as a cover for alternative dishonest reasons.

If you are dating or already involved:

- Do you feel the contact is inappropriate?
- Has he failed to establish clear boundaries regarding how he interacts with his ex-partner?
- Is it possible he is maintaining regular contact with her to keep his options open?
- Do you think his ex-partner is hoping for reconciliation or that he is "leading her on?"
- Is he hiding his relationship with you from his ex-partner claiming he is trying to protect her feelings?
- Has he made excuses for any delay about telling her the truth regarding his involvement with you?
- Does his contact with the ex-partner interfere with any dating arrangements or the growth of your relationship?

Read the above questions again and consider whether any of them relate to your partner or the man you're currently dating. If you responded with a Yes to *any* of the above statements, your partner is still involved with his ex-partner and on some level has not totally released his attachment to her or the previous relationship. A man who maintains regular contact with an ex-partner claiming to be concerned or worried about her welfare may indicate unresolved issues. He may still feel responsible or guilty which can indicate a failure to recover from his previous relationship and being "on the rebound," becoming involved with you too quickly after his last relationship ended.

If he is constantly in touch with a woman from his past, this situation should not be ignored but approached tactfully. You should try to avoid a confrontation or appearing to compete with his ex-partner; in certain circumstances it might be worth making contact with her but generally this approach has to be considered very carefully. Discuss with him why he believes his previous relationship failed and explore what he thinks he can do differently to make your relationship successful. If you began dating or became involved shortly after his previous relationship ended it's reasonable to allow him a little latitude to adjust to the situation. When you have been dating or in a relationship for two months or more, this type of excessive communication and behavior should not be acceptable. If he continues to stay in contact with his ex-partner despite knowing you're uncomfortable this should be considered a major warning sign. Three people in a relationship isn't healthy and will eventually undermine your self-esteem. When this type of constant communication persists, whether you are in the early stages of dating or in a relationship, this type of interaction is going to cause major problems eventually. You will feel unsure, insecure and lack confidence unless there is a very good reason for him to maintain contact.

Dating or being in a relationship with a man with his ex-partner lurking in the background has the potential to create major problems.

- Pay attention to any warning signs, for example, if his previous relationship ended over three months ago but there is still constant communication without a valid reason.
- Look out for any of the warning signs of inappropriate or excessive contact, especially if he is not sharing parental responsibility or there aren't any children involved.
- If you notice any warning signs indicating there may be "unfinished business," be very cautious about becoming involved.

Three people in a relationship isn't going to work! It disrupts the natural dynamics and growth of a new or established partnership when someone is still emotionally connected to their ex-partner. By definition he cannot give you and your relationship his full attention; this will be true even if he doesn't see her physically but is constantly in contact via phone, text or email. Ignoring any obvious warning signs means you are probably signing up for some drama. Understand this: if you're dating a man who has unresolved emotional issues with his previous partner, the competition with his ex for his attention and emotions will probably start as soon as the relationship begins. Often the struggle for his attention is likely to become intense and if he still has strong feelings for his ex-partner this is a competition you're probably going to lose.

Even if the man you're dating or involved with is on the rebound, regular contact with an ex-partner should not continue for much longer than a month or two at the very most. Proceed with extreme caution!

Obsessive

If he is frequently looking at her photos or always checking her Facebook profile, this indicates a problem. It's likely he hasn't recovered from losing the relationship. Deciding to try and make it work means understanding you will be a part of the grieving process and this isn't always easy. A major part of any healthy relationship is sharing experiences whether they are about work, friends or ex-partners and discussing why a particular relationship failed shouldn't be off-limits. Make it clear you are happy to discuss his previous relationships and your own. This approach could help him to work through his grieving and loss, process his feelings and may even help you to grow closer as a couple. If he continues to obsess about his ex-partner despite your best efforts, it's better to cut your losses and explore other options.

Is He Still Bitter?

If a man constantly speaks about his ex-partner in extremes be very cautious. It takes two people to embark on a relationship so it is unrealistic to totally blame the other person for a break-up. Discuss his role in the relationship to discover if he is prepared to take a reasonable amount of responsibility. If he doesn't talk about his previous relationship(s) this isn't healthy either so ask him why he seems to be avoiding the subject. It's important to examine and discuss the past so we don't repeat the same mistakes in the future.

If the man you're dating or involved with appears to have unfinished emotional business with his ex-partner this doesn't mean your relationship with him is doomed but you should proceed with extreme caution. He might be genuine and just require more time to process and manage his feelings. Discussing your concerns and his feelings openly is very important but if he can't let go of his ex-partner the only sensible course of action is to move on. If you suspect he is in denial about his feelings, encourage him to talk about the positive and negative aspects of his previous relationship as well as the part he played in whatever went wrong. If you started dating him shortly after he finished his previous relationship, he may not be fully recovered and still have some baggage to deal with but this doesn't mean a potential relationship is doomed to fail. What it does indicate is that he still has some work and processing to complete, which he should be willing to share if he is serious about pursuing a relationship with you.

When a person feels bitter about a previous relationship he or she might just need time to evaluate what happened and to understand their role as to why the relationship failed. Healing any wounds is also vital before even thinking about getting involved with someone new. Feelings of anger and resentment will sabotage any efforts to contribute positively to a new relationship and a*ny insults and disparaging remarks he makes about his ex-partner will eventually be directed at you!*

Pursuing a relationship with a man who is emotionally unavailable will eventually leave you feeling confused, disillusioned, used and very bitter when it's all over.

- Becoming involved when his healing process is taking longer than you expected can cause problems. You may become impatient or resentful.
- You partner may feel pressured to "sort himself out" so may also become resentful or even angry.

When you become involved with a man who hasn't healed properly from a previous relationship he is still going through a bereavement process. You will struggle to connect with him in any meaningful way as he tries to navigate through the grieving process. Whatever you may try will not make him happy. If he expresses feelings of sadness and regret regarding his previous relationship failure, he could still be too emotionally fragile to become involved or could be afraid to trust you.

*"What is a rebound? To put it simply, it's basically a distraction to keep a guy or girl from thinking about their recent breakup. If a guy goes into a rebound relationship, he's looking for a quick way to get over his ex by being with someone else. But what he's really doing his projecting his feelings about his ex onto a new girl – in a sense, he's **using** the new girl."* – Jessica Booth, Relationship Coach

It's imperative in the dating game to ask important questions about relationship histories to find out if a man is a suitable candidate and definitely not on the rebound. Find out how he feels about his ex-partners; if there is any unresolved anger, bitterness or resentment regarding a previous relationship this should be considered as a huge red flag. He is very unlikely to be ready for a relationship with you – or anyone else!

Human beings are resilient; a person going through the grieving process after a failed relationship often just needs a period of time to heal and resolve any issues. The healing of emotional wounds is best carried out when a person is on their own. It is possible to heal when you're involved but the relationship can become a distraction; the more time devoted to consciously reflecting and healing, the swifter the emotional recovery is likely to be. Allowing some time helps to create space to sort out the issues and to grieve properly. If he is struggling with the grieving process, professional counseling or therapy may help him to regain a realistic perspective. Becoming involved with a man when his emotions are still feeling raw runs the risk of short-circuiting the healing process and if there is any inherent bitterness or anger you will probably be on the receiving end of it. He will only be ready to move on and attempt to enjoy a positive relationship experience when he has completed the process.

If you meet a suitable candidate but believe he just needs some more time to process his feelings after a recent break-up don't make the mistake of ignoring the warning signs, but you shouldn't necessarily write him off either. You can always keep in touch or meet up occasionally to check out if he has made any real progress with his emotional healing.

You're On The Rebound

A negative rebound mindset can lead to the poor decision to date men who are completely different from your ex-partner. This is a mistake because it can badly distort the criteria of the kind of partner and relationship you should be looking for; instead of dating someone who matches your values, standards and requirements, the dominant motivation becomes finding someone who is the ***total opposite*** of your previous partner.

When you're single and considering what type of relationship you would like, it's quite normal to reflect on the personality traits of your ex-partner that you found irritating, annoying or frustrating and look for a man who is the complete opposite. Believing you can have a successful relationship with a man who is totally different from your ex-partner is a very easy trap to fall into when you start looking for a man who is:

- Independent-minded and likes to "do their own thing" because your previous partner was too needy or dependent (excessive "independence" can indicate emotionally unavailable).

- Very outgoing and completely sexually uninhibited because your previous partner had a reserved personality and was uncomfortable or prudish about his sexuality.
- Irresponsible, wild and generally hedonistic because your previous partner was staid, predictable and boring.
- Carefree, unmotivated and with a relaxed attitude because your previous partner was a workaholic and very materialistic.

The man you're involved with may be very different compared to your previous partner, but he might also be very different to you and this can lead to major conflicts and compatibility issues.

Only considering potential partners motivated by the qualities your ex-partner *lacked* instead of looking for someone who meets your standards, values and requirements usually leads to disappointment. There may be important qualities your previous partner lacked that are desirable in a new partner, but this approach is based on a negative perspective which is very unlikely to have a positive outcome. When you go shopping, you don't make a list of the things you **don't want** or need but make a list of the things you require to make sure you take home **what you want.** When you become involved with someone entirely motivated by what you **don't** want, it's doubtful he will truly have the personal qualities that you **do** want. Looking for someone who is the complete opposite of your previous partner and rebounding into a new relationship too quickly will not help you find the kind of relationship you're looking for. To avoid this mistake you have to be self-aware and emotionally centered. Focus on your personal standards and requirements and the essential qualities you would like in a new partner.

▌Reality Check!

"A rebound relationship is basically one that somebody gets into to fill that void after having split with another person. They cannot be by themselves for a length of time because maybe they lack self-esteem or any other reasons. They may find that they are jumping from one relationship to another never being able to make a commitment." – Melissa Jessie, Relationship Coach

The rebound is a quick fix for emotional pain and makes people feel better about themselves for a while. We are all inclined to bring some Emotional Baggage from a previous relationship into a new one, but rebounding into a sexual or romantic liaison usually ends in disappointment, heartache and pain. The majority of these relationships usually end quite quickly and can be more damaging emotionally than the break-up that sent the person on the rebound in the first place. It's a quick fix that can soothe the pain and help you to recover in the short-term but a distraction for dealing with feelings of loss. When you're on the rebound, lacking self-awareness or suffering from low self-esteem, it's quite possible to find yourself with a man just to try and feel good about yourself. Men and women on the rebound use the other person to try and feel better about themselves although they're seldom prepared to admit this. To be fair, the person on the rebound may not even realize what they're doing but ignorance or lack of self-awareness is not an excuse. The best strategy after a break-up or divorce is to take a period of time to reflect, heal or even rediscover yourself especially if your last relationship was dysfunctional, frustrating or confusing. Looking for a quick fix or a distraction to hide from the pain of losing a relationship can never be a substitute for dealing with any feelings of low self-worth.

Do you have a pattern of becoming involved with men who have unresolved issues from their previous relationships? If you do it is likely there is Emotional Baggage that causes a subconscious fear or resistance to committed relationships. This pattern needs to be identified and healed before you consider playing the dating game or embarking on a new relationship.

Parental Rebellion Mindset

"Rebellion cannot exist without the feeling that somewhere, in some way, you are justified." – Albert Camus, Author, Journalist & Philosopher

Teenagers aren't the only ones who rebel: there are adults who choose partners seeking to rebel against their parents' wishes or because they want to make a statement of personal independence. For some people there can be a deep desire to define themselves as an individual and clearly demonstrate they're the very opposite of their parent(s) as they seek to create a very separate, independent and distinct identity.

For example, my father suffered from a personality disorder and was a very poor parental role model. During my childhood and for many years as an adult, I was resolute in my goal to be nothing like him. My childhood emotional wounds made me desperate to prove to myself I was a better man than my father, and I was determined to take my parental responsibilities seriously.

The desire to be independent and to define yourself as distinct and separate from your parents can be very positive, but when someone is deliberately making relationship choices, seeking to hurt or upset their parents, this is a very unhealthy mindset. Rebellion against parents and your relationship choices can be caused by feelings of deep bitterness, resentment or a perception there was excessive control by one or both of your parents during childhood. When these individuals become teenagers or adults they choose to rebel by ***deliberately*** selecting partners knowing their choices will upset or deeply distress their parents.

Warning Signs of Rebellion Against Parents

- Repeatedly chooses partners who clearly will be "unacceptable" to their parent(s).
- Often remains in unhealthy relationships to prove their parent(s) were "wrong" to disapprove or oppose their choice of partner.

Do you choose partners knowing your parents will be upset by your choices?

For example:

- Your parents are White with very conservative views but the majority of your partners have been Black men or you date exclusively outside your race.
- Your parents are strict religious types but your partners have all been disrespectful regarding religion.
- Your parents believe money and status are important but your partners are usually struggling financially or have strong dissident views.

When this type of Emotional Programming is dictating your choices, appearing to conform to your parents' wishes can represent a capitulation and a loss of "independence." Everyone desires independence and to make their own choices but if you're becoming involved with men using a criteria based on your parents' disapproval, this is a very flawed approach to selecting a partner. Choosing partners to primarily rebel against your parents' wishes or preferences can result in being with a partner for all the wrong reasons. While your relationship choices may appear to be "independent" they will often be compulsive, unhealthy or even toxic. Rebelling against your parents can be self-defeating as you avoid, resist or reject potential partners who could be highly compatible.

Reality Check

"I dug the idea that I was being perceived as the black sheep of my family, but for me, it was like, I was a rebel, and that to me was most important." – Larry Bishop, American Actor

The danger of having a strong parental-rebellion mindset is that it can compel adults to reject a highly compatible partner on the basis of their parents' approval. Relationships between couples from different backgrounds can succeed and many do, but deliberately becoming involved with certain types of men knowing this will deeply upset your parents isn't healthy or sensible. A partner should always be chosen based on genuine attraction, a strong connection or feelings of mutual chemistry and not to prove your independence or as an act of rebellion. Review your relationship history and if you suspect you have a parental-rebellion mindset, explore your attitudes towards your childhood and upbringing. If you find yourself struggling with certain issues seek support from a counselor or therapist. Healing any unresolved emotional issues will empower you to explore relationships with real potential instead of having your choices being compelled by negative patterns of thinking.

Limited Compatibility

"You and I both know that love is for children. We're adults. Compatibility is for adults."
– Maggie Stiefvater, Author of *Sinner*

Becoming involved based on limited or partial compatibility is a trap many men and women fall into. This happens when you focus on being well-matched in one particular area while ignoring the fact there is little or zero compatibility in other key areas. These types of relationships can be very deceptive at the beginning. It can be easy to deceive yourself into believing that a strong mutual interest is going to provide a solid foundation for an enduring partnership.

Scenarios

Workplace Romance

You're assigned a joint work project that requires long hours with a colleague so end up spending a great deal of time together. As time passes, you feel there is a mutual attraction growing which leads to a passionate affair. When the project is finished you begin to feel apprehensive as the easy conversation and rapport previously shared begins to feel strained.

Within a relatively short space of time an affair that was probably passionate and full of apparent promise is over as it becomes clear you're not compatible in other essential areas or don't share similar beliefs or values. The mutual connection that seemed so special is exposed as being merely two people working to complete a project, but the shared interest and working together to achieve a goal deceived you into believing there was a great amount of compatibility and even love.

Additional Risks

Having an affair with a work colleague is frequently a high-risk activity especially if you like to keep your personal life private. Being sexually adventurous at work with a partner can be tempting; furtive kissing or even having foreplay or sex during office hours may add to the excitement of the relationship, but there are also some pretty big disadvantages:

- If the affair is discovered it will become the subject of office gossip. Your other office colleagues will know what's going on and may be curious about other aspects of your personal life.
- If the relationship fails this could turn into a messy break-up, especially if other people at your place of work know some or all of the details. Seeing each other at work could make it harder to get over the relationship/affair and probably feel very awkward for a period of time.
- If you are upset about the break-up you may struggle to contain your feelings at work. Eventually, it is likely your colleagues will hear about the affair and know the details of your personal business.
- Your ex-partner may be hurt about the failure of the relationship and reveal certain personal information to your colleagues you would prefer to remain private.

Many people find power attractive. If you're having sex with a superior this could appear to be an effective way to advance within the company or organization but you are taking a huge risk. While there may be potential and actual benefits given to you within the work environment when the affair is going well, if it breaks down either you or your boss may have to leave. If it's a messy break-up and someone has to leave it will probably be you. Alternatively, if you're a superior and decide to embark on an affair with a subordinate which becomes public knowledge within the workplace, you could lose the respect of your colleagues and if it all goes wrong the ex-partner could tarnish your reputation. Being forced to see an ex-partner after a messy break-up can be emotionally challenging and extremely difficult to manage. Think very carefully before you decide to mix business with pleasure.

Holidays

Holiday romances have spawned countless stories of brief or disastrous love affairs but how these affairs unfold often follows a pattern. We usually go on holiday to relax and have fun. Some people go on vacation in search of casual sex or with the furtive hope they might just meet someone who is "special."

Men and women can totally change their behavior when they're away on vacation for a few weeks. Meeting a man on vacation can be a great deal of fun and vacations are often promoted by selling the dream of fulfilling a fantasy. Holidays are meant to be relaxing so when you meet an attractive man who seems like a lot of fun it can be very tempting to just go for it! Even if you don't indulge in sex with someone new, the vacation mindset and environment can seduce you into pursuing a relationship with him when you return home.

Once you return from vacation and you're both back in the real world fantasy meets with reality and it all looks very different. The meetings after the holiday interaction or affair can turn out to be a huge disappointment as you both discover annoying habits about each other or constantly disagree about almost everything. The enjoyable vacation, which sparked the romance, seems very far away as the stresses of the rat race expose aspects of his character you were previously unaware of. You may even feel deceived when it becomes clear the man you met on vacation isn't quite what he seemed to be. Vacation relationships can be very easy to fall into due to sharing activities in a pleasant, unusual or exotic environment that can often be very seductive. Have fun on vacation but make sure you don't make the mistake of believing a holiday romance can be easily integrated into your real life when you return home. These relationships usually don't last very long and whirlwind holiday romances that lead to rushed marriages are inevitably short-lived.

There are other ways to get involved with someone on the basis of limited compatibility. The following types of relationships often begin quite innocently when you're single and meet a man:

- Discovering you share a mutual interest that you are both very passionate about.
- In circumstances or an environment that requires a mutual focus on an unusual joint project or activity.
- In circumstances that require focusing on or sharing a hobby or interest that you don't indulge in often.
- In a situation or environment that is far removed from your usual routine.
- In circumstances that represent an unusual environment (e.g. on holiday or somewhere you don't usually go as part of your normal routine).

The unusual and seductive environment of a holiday destination, a nightclub or a venue you are unfamiliar with can also entice you into a relationship with limited compatibility.

Reality Check

"My point is, there are a lot of people in the world. No one ever sees everything the same way you do; it just doesn't happen. So when you find one person who gets a couple of things, especially if they're important ones... you might as well hold on to them. You know?" – Sarah Dessen, *Lock and Key*

Sharing interests or pleasant experiences can be very enjoyable but compatibility in just a couple of areas doesn't mean the rest of the relationship is just going to "click" and fall into place. You may be thinking at this point, "That could never happen to me!" but before you dismiss the idea that you could be seduced by partial compatibility consider these scenarios carefully. Falling into the trap of limited compatibility can just be a matter of circumstances combined with a moment of weakness and timing. If you're feeling lonely or even a little desperate, it's quite possible to be enticed into a relationship with a man you have shared an activity with and feel a strong connection to, even if this has happened over a relatively short period of time.

Discovering you share a certain area of compatibility with someone new may create a bond leading you to believe the relationship has real potential, but after a few months you begin to feel disappointed with your choice of partner and yourself. The conflicts and arguments seem to be increasing and you begin to wonder how and why the relationship happened in the first place. This often happens when there is only one strong particular area of mutual compatibility and this was the basis for the connection. Trying to build a relationship on the weak foundation of limited compatibility lacks any real substance or realistic prospects.

To avoid making this type of mistake, you have to be pragmatic or you could end up drifting into a brief affair that usually ends in one of the following ways:

- You realize limited compatibility cannot sustain a long-term relationship and decide to leave, even though he still has feelings for you. Result: He gets hurt.
- He realizes you're the wrong person for him so decides to end it, but by this time you have developed feelings for him. Result: You get hurt.

Be realistic and reflect on how much you actually know about this man besides the fact there is a strong mutual interest in a particular subject or you have enjoyed each other's company in a seductive environment or venue.

Think carefully about your requirements, standards and values and if he actually meets your criteria. Consider the possibilities from a wider perspective rather than just concentrating on the narrow issue of the partial compatibility or perhaps one or two shared interests. Happy endings are very unlikely and embarking on a relationship with limited compatibility is a very risky proposition.

Low Compatibility Relationship = Very High Maintenance!

Infatuation

"Infatuation is not quite the same thing as love; it's more like love's shady second cousin who's always borrowing money and can't hold down a job." – Elizabeth Gilbert, *Committed: A Skeptic Makes Peace with Marriage*

We all know sport stars, musicians and celebrities attract groupies. I had several interesting encounters with women who were very interested in getting to know me very intimately when I worked as a club DJ and freelance radio presenter. Primarily these women were attracted to me due to the kudos of my celebrity status. I was certainly not naive enough to believe they liked me due to my handsome looks or winning personality! What do you find attractive about the opposite sex? Do you become infatuated with one or more features of a person's appearance? Perhaps you're attracted by "dreamy" eyes, a certain physique, or men who have a certain ability or are involved in a particular field, occupation or activity. Hero-worshiping a person or putting someone on a pedestal due to their looks, activities, employment or status is a very superficial approach to finding a partner and can get you involved with some very unsavory characters.

"When you develop an infatuation for someone, you always find a reason to believe that this is exactly the person for you." – The Beach Movie (2000)

It should be obvious external appearances or abilities are not reliable indicators of a person's character. Fascination and infatuation lead people to deceive themselves. Becoming involved with a man due to external infatuation often results in ignoring or dismissing very obvious warning signs. The relationship may last for a while but when it becomes clear you have been seduced by infatuation into a partnership with very low or zero compatibility it can get very messy. To avoid the inevitable disappointment this brings, when you meet a potential partner you find attractive be honest with yourself. Carefully consider why you find a particular aspect so attractive or infatuating in the first place. Ask yourself this: "If he lacked that certain attribute I find so alluring or wasn't involved in the activity I find so fascinating, would I still consider him seriously as a potential partner?" These questions can save you a great deal of heartache and bitter regret.

If you suspect or know you have a tendency to become infatuated with external factors, spend some time during your personal self-development thinking about why there are certain physical characteristics about the opposite sex you find so attractive. If you're attracted to a certain activity, employment or status men in your social circle engage in or find celebrities alluring, think about this carefully. It's possible you may be seeking a man to boost your feelings of low self-esteem to make you feel better about yourself.

Rescue Mission Relationships

"Women rescue men just as much as, if not more than, men rescue women." – Criss Jami, *Killosophy*

Are you a Florence Nightingale type, always rushing to help other people feel better or a sucker for a damsel in distress? During my formative years I suffered emotional damage as a result of witnessing episodes of domestic violence; a distressed woman could subconsciously trigger memories of comforting my mother after one of my father's violent outbursts. This left me vulnerable to cynical manipulation as an adult, which led to several unhealthy relationships.

It's important to understand how misplaced sympathy and being too eager to "fix" problems can subconsciously influence you to become involved with the wrong kind of relationships.

Unresolved Childhood Issues

The Rescue Factor

When a child observes either of their parents or siblings being mistreated, unloved or ignored, they can feel compelled to try and rescue other people as an adult. These adults are attracted to relationships where they provide generous love and support for their partners, motivated subconsciously to recreate childhood scenarios where they failed to rescue or comfort a family member. Childhood emotional issues can create a mindset that believes excessive sympathy and compassion equals love.

The Feeling Superior Factor

If you like to rescue your partners, believing this is the "right" thing to do, perhaps it's time to examine your pattern carefully; on closer inspection, your actions may not appear quite so noble or altruistic. The attraction towards men who are inadequate in some way or whose lives are constantly in disarray can boost your self-esteem because in comparison to your partner, you're the superior and the dominant person in the relationship. This constant rescuing of partners in relationships provides a distraction that prevents the "rescuer" from looking at their own inadequacies.

The Control Factor

Unhealthy dynamics in relationships happen when someone appears to be "helping" while they are covertly controlling their partner; their constant "assistance" is actually a strategy to exert power and control over the relationship.

The Guilt Factor

Guilt can be a powerful factor in this type of relationship, believing you could be hurting your partner terribly by abandoning him in his "hour of need." Feeling guilty can make it very difficult to make a final decision to leave so you end up staying with him knowing the relationship is not going anywhere.

Subconscious emotional issues can mislead you into believing intense feelings of sympathy are really the experience of true love. Feeling empathy or compassion for others is a very admirable quality but those emotions are not love. A healthy relationship dynamic contains mutual respect and pride as well as a mutual sharing of love, consideration and kindness.

In the dating game, you can make the mistake of trying to rescue a potential partner by:

- Frequently having to console, support and encourage him because he feels overwhelmed, helpless, confused or victimized by others.
- Stepping in because he has severe financial, emotional or physical problems.

Attempting to rescue someone from financial, emotional or physical problems or who has difficulties running their own lives is a very bad idea. When you have a tendency to go on "rescue missions" it's quite easy to get involved as soon as your Emotional Programming kicks in but these types of relationships can be very difficult to leave and you can end up staying for all the wrong reasons. The noble intentions of helping out can turn into sympathy or guilt resulting in an unstable and dysfunctional dynamic because the partnership is not based on love or any real compatibility.

Are you currently in a relationship? You could be staying for the wrong reasons if you:

- Feel obligated to stay and take care of your partner because he has been mistreated or badly hurt in the past. You want to stay to make him better.
- Frequently think he would end up alone and unloved if you left the relationship as it is unlikely anybody else would want him.
- Constantly provide advice regarding his problems but feel frustrated when your advice is ignored.
- Assume a parental role with your partner.

- Avoid potential confrontations because you don't want to upset him even when you are quite concerned about something.
- Frequently excuse or tolerate certain behavior you would not accept from other people.
- You often act as a support system but he rarely if ever provides you with this type or level of support.
- Believe your partner would collapse emotionally if you left him.
- Frequently defend him if you are questioned about your motives for being in the relationship. You feel very protective towards your partner.
- Believe you cannot leave the relationship because no one else would love or understand him the way you do.

Read the above statements again and be honest with yourself. If you can identify with **any** of these scenarios it is possible emotional issues are motivating you to save, help or rescue your partner.

Consider your relationship history and ask yourself:

- Do I have a tendency to feel sorry for partners to the point that I am uncomfortable with the situation?
- Do I have a pattern of thinking I am responsible for helping my partners to sort out their lives?

There could be emotional issues where your Emotional Programming motivates you to rescue or fix other people. These types of beliefs indicate a codependent mindset which subconsciously compels you to be drawn into relationships to "help" rather than for reasons of love or compatibility. For example, you may be attracted to men who appear to be uncared for, unloved, wounded or overly fragile and this probably makes you feel like a very decent person. Your partners will almost certainly be grateful for your caring attitude and support as you launch and carry out your "rescue operation."

Reality Check!

"Sometimes the relationship you need to rescue is the one with yourself." – Senora Roy, Poetess

Adults who become caught up in relationships trying to rescue people can be quite task-focused. The problem with this approach is there are no guarantees your input and sacrifice will actually produce any positive outcomes. You can stay in an unhealthy or dead relationship hoping and waiting to see the results of all your hard work and often be waiting in vain. Some women try against all odds to love, comfort and take care of their lovers, hoping to nurture them back to emotional health. If you have a tendency to hang on to needy men in order to "love" them back to health, you need to ask yourself why. A sacrificial relationship might seem like the right thing to do but usually ends in disillusionment.

Single, dating or currently involved, you have to be honest with yourself. A pattern of constantly being involved with partners who have major problems or dramas indicates you are probably "falling in love" for the wrong reasons. If you suspect or know you're currently involved in a "rescue mission" take steps to resolve dysfunctional interaction. Support from family members, close friends or professional counseling/therapy should be seriously considered to help you decide if the relationship is really healthy or viable.

In Love With Potential

"Potential has a shelf life." – Margaret Atwood, Poet & Novelist

Making the mistake of falling in love with potential usually happens when you're attracted to enticing possibilities. You fall in love with a man based on projections of what he may do or become in the future while ignoring what is happening in his life right now. This is similar to the fairy tale where the princess kisses the frog who suddenly transforms into the handsome prince. Becoming involved with a man while relying heavily on his unfulfilled potential means you're probably setting yourself up for frustration and disappointment.

Why You Might Fall In Love With Potential

You may be a child who felt:

- Controlled
- Restricted by your parents or circumstances
- Ignored or a lack of validation

A young child growing up in this environment may create a mindset that seeks to "improve" a partner by acting out the role of the controlling or restrictive parent. When these children become adults there can be an element of wanting to control their relationship, which provides feelings of power and superiority. The control doesn't have to be obvious but the belief a partner hasn't reached their full potential places you in a controlling position by default.

The Frustration Factor

Children who grew up feeling rejected or unloved can become adults who recreate the childhood experience of how they were treated by their parent(s). The unhealed emotional patterns and feelings of frustration of being deprived emotionally as a child are relived in their relationships. These people believe they never received the love they crave so feelings of disappointment and frustration are never far from the surface. Subconscious Emotional Programming compels them to recreate childhood scenarios and seek out partners who are unable or unwilling to provide what they really want in their relationships.

The Procrastination Factor

Falling in love with a partner's potential can be a very effective tactic to avoid dealing with issues in your own life. Constant preoccupation with supporting the "positive change" of your partner and working on his improvements leaves very little time to work on your own personal development. This strategy provides a good excuse for failing to examine your own motives and supports the state of being in denial regarding unresolved issues.

In Love With Potential: Warning Signs

- Believing only you know the "real" person inside and everyone else underestimates or misunderstands him.
- Wanting to believe he lacked love and encouragement during his previous relationships and this prevented his potential from flourishing.
- Wanting to believe he is really "trying" even though you suspect he will not deliver.
- Believing he just needs more time to sort himself out and get his act together.
- Believing your love can change him and if you love him enough he will fulfill his potential.
- Having more faith and belief in him than he actually has in himself.
- Making excuses for any problems while waiting for his potential to manifest into reality.
- Telling yourself if you leave him he will not be able to cope so his potential will be stifled.
- If he has low self-esteem you worry he may suffer "fatal" damage.

Potential Problems

Wasting Time

Waiting for a person's potential to "blossom" can be a very time consuming business!

Feeling Bitter

You could become bitter having wasted so much time on him and the relationship.

Disappointment

When it becomes obvious the dream was nothing more than a fantasy and he fails to deliver you will probably feel very disappointed or even deceived.

Anger

Expectations raised are never realized and this eventually leads to feelings of extreme frustration, seething resentment or anger.

Sexually Turned Off

Constantly treating your partner like an exceptional child full of promise will eventually reduce his sexual attraction. When a woman acts like a parent towards their partner this can often lead to feelings of sexual ambivalence.

Reality Check!

"The person who seeks to change another person in a relationship basically sets the stage for a great deal of conflict." – Wesley Snipes, American Actor

Many people have periods in their lives when they suffer misfortune. They may lose their job, suffer financial hardships or experience a long period of illness which impacts on their personal situation. A potential partner should not be dismissed based solely on their current circumstances but in the dating game consideration of suitable candidates with positive potential and strong compatibility should be a priority. Supporting his personal and professional development is the right thing to do but if he is unemployed or in a poorly paid job pay close attention to his activities. What type of person is he? What type of action is he taking to improve his situation? Observe his actions or activities closely to see if he is taking steps to make his objectives and goals a reality. There is a big difference between having/pursuing realistic plans for the future and just talking and day dreaming about them. Waiting for him to take *action* after he promises to do so will be highly frustrating and you will probably be very tempted to pressure him into changing against his wishes or at a faster pace, which is likely to result in resistance and conflicts. Women who fall in love with potential eventually have to make a decision based on practicalities and not empty promises. Falling in love with potential can be a very risky situation as these types of relationships can become very addictive: the longer you stay with a partner waiting for their potential to blossom the harder it can be to leave. If you're involved with a man with great potential but who fails to deliver on his promises while constantly making excuses or procrastinating this will eventually become very frustrating. In the end you may have to take the painful decision to walk away even if you still love him.

Already Involved

Waiting for a partner to fulfill his undeveloped potential is a very high risk strategy. Women in these types of relationships often stay hoping for some kind of a miraculous transformation in their partner but this doesn't happen very often. When you're in a committed relationship, supporting your partner's personal growth development is appropriate. However, staying in a relationship hoping for your partner to change or "fulfill his potential" when there is no evidence he is actually taking action to fulfill potential by pursuing his goals is probably going to be a great waste of your time.

The fact is people only change when they want to and not before; pressuring him to deliver on his potential whether it is real or imagined will probably result in arguments and conflicts. If you're still in love with your partner and determined to make the relationship work accept him as he is and be realistic regarding your expectations.

The Love Miser

"Withholding distorts reality. It makes the people who do the withholding ugly and small-hearted. It makes the people from whom things are withheld crazy and desperate and incapable of knowing what they actually feel. So release yourself from that. Don't be strategic or coy. Strategic and coy are for jackasses. Be brave. Be authentic. Practice saying the word "love" to the people you love so when it matters the most to say it, you will." – Cheryl Strayed, *Tiny Beautiful Things: Advice on Love and Life from Dear Sugar*

A person who makes their partner work hard and struggle to receive their love and attention is a Love Miser. This is where your partner withholds his love and affection. With this type of man you will spend a great deal of time and energy trying to make it work while your partner is usually very "cool" and doesn't seem very enthusiastic about the relationship. The Love Miser often makes his partner "work" for his love and affection by recreating the opposite roles he observed as a child. They become adults who duplicate the behavior of a parent or caretaker who withheld love from their partner. A person with this mindset may know their partner is deeply in love while also being aware that they don't have the same depth of feeling. Guilt in this type of relationship is possible but usually not enough to change the engrained pattern of withholding love. The Love Miser will often deny withholding love even when they know that's exactly what they're doing; other coping strategies may include denial or trying to convince themselves they love their partner even though they often struggle to show it.

A relationship with a Love Miser causes:

- Frustration when you want more love and affection than your partner is prepared to provide.
- Defensive behavior and conflicts when you accuse him of withholding his love, not loving you equally or not enough.
- Annoyance when you seek more love and affection but he thinks you are being too needy or clingy.
- Distance in the relationship because he feels claustrophobic at times and wants his space, and you are considered "too demanding."

Each relationship has different cycles and dynamics and there will be times when each partner will be more loving and attentive than the other. These fluctuations are quite normal in a healthy relationship but *when your partner makes you work constantly for love and affection, this represents a serious problem.*

Contributing the majority of the emotional and practical effort to maintain a relationship while your partner remains fundamentally ambivalent is totally out of balance and dysfunctional. If you suspect you're involved with a Love Miser talk it over with family or close friends, or seek the support of professional therapy or counseling to help you decide whether it is sensible for you to stay with your partner.

Are You A Love Miser? Check Yourself Out!

Have you been in previous relationships where partners have complained about your coldness towards them or accused you of lacking of affection? The Love Miser mindset isn't gender specific and both men and women with this mindset will display similar attitudes and behaviors. If you believe your parents or caretakers withheld their love or felt criticized or rejected as a child this may subconsciously compel you to treat your partner in a very similar way. This is a "back to the future" role reversal where you play the part of the unloving parent while a partner takes on your role as the child. Recreating your parent's behavior towards you leads to punishing and hurting a partner for the "sins" of your parents by proxy. The men you become involved with are usually considered acceptable but the type you're really not that into while subconsciously or deliberately you "ration out" your love as a type of defense mechanism to protect yourself.

Control

"A good relationship has a pattern like a dance and is built on some of the same rules. The partners do not need to hold on tightly, because they move confidently in the same pattern…they know they are partners moving to the same rhythm, creating a pattern together, and being invisibly nourished by it." – Anne Morrow Lindbergh, *Gift from the Sea*

When someone withholds love and affection in a relationship this will usually make their partner feel vulnerable and insecure. While the person withholding their love wants to feel in control the opposite is usually true; this type of behavior can be motivated by trying to disguise deep feelings of a **lack** of control and power. A child who sees a parent consistently acting cold, distant or aloof towards their partner may believe this is how a "typical" loving couple act towards each other. Consciously or subconsciously a decision is made to adopt the role of the parent or caretaker who did not display any love and affection for their partner as it appeared there was less risk of getting hurt by adopting this approach. Adults who behave like this believe they are protecting themselves, but people who become involved with Love Misers often feel frustrated, annoyed and rejected, which leads to inevitable estrangements, conflicts and relationship failure.

Healthy Partnerships

Research strongly suggests certain attitudes and behaviors support successful relationships. Let's look at some of these.

The Team Mentality

Working as a team and with a willingness to consider things from your partner's perspective is an essential factor for a successful relationship. Empathy is an important part of being able to consider something from someone else's perspective and allows both partners to keep their personal power. A lack of sympathy or empathy can leave both partners feeling frustrated and alienated causing major problems.

Mutual Respect And Cooperation

Each person should value their partner's feelings and opinions but this doesn't mean you shouldn't express or assert yourself; respecting your partner's point of view doesn't necessarily mean you have to agree with him.

Communication

Successful couples have open lines of communication at all times. A healthy relationship cannot survive or even exist without effective communication. Communicating assertively and effectively is important if you want others to know what you're thinking! There is a big difference between being assertive and being aggressive; the key to being assertive is to state your position calmly.

- **Deal with one issue at a time** – Be specific.
- **Do not jump to conclusions** – Listen to the other person.
- **Win-Win** – Look for win-win solutions whenever possible

- **Time Limits** – Try and limit how long the discussion on a particular topic takes (approximately 30 minutes should be sufficient).

There is an important distinction to be made regarding the status of each partner. While there often may be a difference in **status** regarding a variety of aspects (education, income etc.) these are not the primary areas that cause problems. The attitudes of the two people involved will be the crucial factor that determines if the relationship is successful or dysfunctional and unhealthy. When each partner has positive self-esteem and can effectively assert their own sense of self instead of one partner deferring or suppressing their opinions, this creates balanced interaction and dynamics.

The Way Forward

"Take stock of your thoughts and behaviour. Each night ask yourself, when were you negative when you could have been positive? When did you withhold love when you might have given it? When did you play a neurotic game instead of behaving in a powerful way? Use this process to self-correct." – Marianne Williamson, American Author

The Love Miser mindset creates relationship dynamics that are out of balance, dysfunctional and highly toxic. Men and women with any of these styles or patterns of relating have very poor prospects for experiencing a truly meaningful relationship. When you're hiding yourself or withholding love because you have unhealed emotional wounds this makes it virtually impossible to share a genuine connection with another human being. The truth is being "in control" in a relationship doesn't equate to "being happy" no matter how much you may try to convince yourself otherwise. If you suspect you are a Love Miser work on your PSD or attend counselling/therapy to address and heal these issues. A potential partner could be on the receiving end of behavior which can be very damaging and no one deserves to be controlled or manipulated.

Single

Believing a potential partner should be content to receive whatever modest amounts of love and affection you are prepared to offer is self-defeating. Constantly seeking to make your partner "work" or struggle to prove he is worthy to receive your love is very unfair and creates a self-fulfilling prophecy where you expect each relationship to ultimately fail. Suspecting or positively identifying with any of these negative patterns of relating should be a major cause for concern as problems, conflicts or repeated relationship failures are inevitable. Explore your personal self-development with professional support if necessary to resolve any Emotional Baggage that may be sabotaging your relationships.

Already Involved

Punishing someone due to unresolved parental issues from the past is very unfair and emotional honesty is always the best policy. If you suspect you're suffering with Love Miser issues and struggling to relate in healthier ways to your partner, professional therapy or counseling may be able to help you to transform your beliefs. Providing the relationship has not been damaged beyond repair your partner may still have enough love to support you and decide to give you some time to heal any issues.

Excessive Admiration

"Admiration: Our feeling of delight that another person resembles us." – Evan Esar, American Humorist

Adults who believe they were extremely controlled by their parents may be subconsciously attracted to partners who are seen as authority figures or role models. They are often attracted to partners who remind them of their childhood experiences seeking to unconsciously recreate the parent/child dynamic. If you have a pattern of becoming involved with partners due to deep feelings of admiration it's likely you're trying to resolve unfinished childhood issues by looking for someone who can provide a sense of guidance and protection that you felt to be missing during your childhood.

When a child is given an excessive amount of admiration or has been extremely enmeshed emotionally with his or her parents, subconsciously this can create an adult with an "arrested development" mindset. These men and women have been so deeply programmed and conditioned to expect admiration and attention they can become withdrawn, depressed or angry if they are not admired. Alternatively, constantly seeking or demanding excessive admiration can be motivated by the belief a person did not receive enough love or attention during their formative years.

Low Self-Esteem

When a person has low self-esteem in a relationship this creates an unbalanced and unhealthy interaction based on deference or anxiety. Those who suffer from low self-esteem often defer to others who appear to be more assertive, powerful or intelligent. Falling in love with a man you consider your role model sets up an abnormal and unequal relationship dynamic; the partnership might *appear* to be equal but it's unlikely it will ever be truly balanced or fair, especially if you feel dominated by your partner's status. Apparent power and influence can seduce a person with low self-esteem issues into giving away their power by constantly deferring to their partner while failing to express themselves.

Becoming involved with a man believing he is vastly superior to you in some way is a bad idea. Going into a relationship with this type of mindset means the balance of power is unequal before the relationship even begins due to the lofty status given to a new partner. There is also the danger of trying too hard to be like him and losing yourself in the process.

When you enter a relationship believing your partner is superior or some type of role model it will create the following scenarios:

- There will be an imbalance in the relationship that is unequal and unhealthy.
- Consistently putting a man on a pedestal and admiring him excessively indicates you are generally submissive in your relationships.
- Being constantly attracted to partners due to their status means there will usually be underlying emotional issues that require attention and healing.

Constantly admiring, agreeing and deferring to his opinions inevitably results in feeling disempowered and always feeling severely restricted when you want to honestly express yourself.

Warning Signs Of Excessive Admiration

You are likely to:

- Suppress your own opinion
- Wish you had similar "superior" qualities as your partner
- Feel inferior to him in many ways and think you could never equal his achievements
- Wish you were more like your partner
- Find yourself deferring to his "superior" opinion
- Assume he is more knowledgeable than you on all subjects
- Try to impress other people by telling them how intelligent, knowledgeable and impressive he is
- Quote what your partner has said
- Believe your partner has superior intelligence
- Believe you are very fortunate to be in a relationship with him and grateful he chose you as his partner
- Be strongly influenced or dominated by what he says and thinks while dismissing your own opinions and intuition

If you think any of these scenarios describe your current relationship, your partner has to give up the dominant role of mentor or parent to allow the relationship to become more balanced. A dynamic where a partner is highly elevated while the other is operating from a much lower position is a very unhealthy state of affairs. Often the person in the dominant position will be very unlikely to give up their superior position voluntarily so a sensible compromise isn't possible. It's best to accept the fact the relationship isn't viable but clearly dysfunctional and damaging to your emotional wellbeing. A couple who both have healthy self-esteem have a much greater chance of creating a secure, nurturing and fulfilling partnership of mutual respect and love.

When a relationship isn't working or is extremely unhealthy you need to be realistic and seriously consider all of the options available. If your partner is prepared to attend couples counseling or therapy this is a positive step. A refusal to even discuss any issues indicates the relationship has very little chance of survival, at least not as a healthy partnership that is going to make you happy. The belief and acceptance of your partner as the clearly dominant person in the relationship may be a conscious decision or subconsciously motivated but will negatively impact on your attitude and behavior. This type of mindset can make it very difficult to leave a dysfunctional relationship especially when you're suffering from low self-esteem. If you feel helpless or extremely unhappy in your current relationship examine your relationship history. You can do so informally on your own, with family or close friends, or arrange professional therapy/counseling for yourself.

If you're single and suspect you have issues around poor self-esteem ask yourself whether there is a possibility this could be due to having a pattern of becoming involved with partners you believed were superior to you in some way. Understanding how to respect and love yourself is an essential aspect of living a happy, healthy life. The fact is, when you find it difficult to love yourself, you are going to find it hard to love someone else. Learning how to assert yourself effectively and regaining a positive sense of self is absolutely essential prior to considering embarking on a new relationship. Excessively admiring someone due their income, intelligence or professional and social status doesn't make any sense as none of these things are a reliable indicator of character or integrity.

Healthy Relationship Checklist

Consider the following questions carefully and be completely honest with yourself.

Status: Single

- Have you healed and recovered from all of your previous relationships?
- Have you considered and healed any issues from your childhood or any feelings of resentment, bitterness, anger or blame regarding your parent(s)?
- Have any other issues you may have been struggling with healed?
- Have you honestly reviewed your relationship history and identified any negative patterns?
- Are you sure you have dealt with any feelings of resentment, bitterness, anger or blame regarding your previous relationships?
- Have you carried out a thorough Process of Self-Discovery (PSD)?
- Have you attended therapy/counseling for any emotional issues you may be struggling with?
- Do you accept yourself?
- Are you taking steps to work on any areas that may require healing?
- Have you taken the time to cultivate higher levels of self-awareness?
- Are you happy with your levels of self-esteem?
- Are you realistic and not pursuing or believing the major love myths?
- Are you happy being single?
- Have you pursued healthy and empowering activities as a single person?
- Have you reviewed and worked on having sensible personal boundaries?
- Do you have a clear idea regarding your probable attachment style?
- Have you taken the Love Styles Quiz? Do you have a clear idea regarding your probable Love Style?
- Do you feel confident asking a date relevant questions?
- Are you confident you can identify any potential relationship red flags or obvious warning signs?

Status: Dating

- Have you taken the Dating Signals Quiz? Are you sure about the type of signals you may be sending out?

- Are you confident you will be able to follow the Dating Guidelines?
- Have you asked the man you're dating sufficient pertinent questions to be satisfied regarding his character, life goals, intentions and background?
- If you haven't, do you feel confident to ask those questions at the appropriate time?
- Are you confident there are not any compatibility hazards lurking if you become more involved?
- Are you confident you both share good compatibility?
- Are you confident you share good levels of chemistry?
- Are you confident you both share similar core values
- Are you sure he doesn't have any toxic flaws?
- Are you sure you have asked enough pertinent questions?
- Are you confident he has the 7 Essential Character Traits? If he lacks any is it realistic to expect an improvement in any of the weak areas?

In A Nutshell

- Don't rush into a relationship! Take your time and get to know a potential partner before you commit.
- If you've had a bad relationship experience previously don't prejudge someone new. Judge each potential partner on their merits. You are less likely to make this mistake when you have carried out your PSD properly over a period of time.
- Input from your friends and family about a potential partner can provide valuable insights. Whether they are supportive or negative about someone new in your life, pay attention to their views before making your own decisions. It can be very easy to get caught up in a new romance and miss important warning signs.
- When you're dating someone new pay attention to what he says about his previous relationships, how he feels about himself and how he interacts with his family and friends.
- Pay attention to how he expresses and demonstrates his feelings. A person who is open and expresses themselves positively is more likely to be ready for a serious relationship.
- Listen to your intuition and use your common sense. Pay attention to your feelings and any other clues that might indicate there could be major problems if you become involved.

Relationship Mistakes

- Are you sure you're not desperate to be in a relationship?
- Is your intuition trying to warn you about something regarding the man you're dating?
- Are you sure you're not ignoring any potential warning signs?
- Are you sure you're not rushing into a relationship based on strong sexual chemistry or physical attraction?

- Are you sure you're not compromising any important relationship standards, values or requirements?
- Are you sure you are not being seduced by any financial or material status considerations?
- Are you sure you're not falling in lust?

Have you checked how many of the Signs You Should End It may apply to what you're feeling or doing?

- Are you unhappy in your current relationship?
- Have you checked how many of the Signs to End It apply to what you're doing or feeling?
- If you have decided to walk away, what kind of realistic plans and actions do you intend to take?

Relationships Probably Doomed to Fail

Are you:

- Confident your (potential) partner is emotionally and otherwise available?
- Confident you're not on the rebound from a previous relationship?
- Confident your potential/current partner isn't on the rebound?
- Sure you're not attracted to your potential partner for superficial reasons (looks, interests or lifestyle etc.)?
- Confident you and your (potential) partner share good compatibility in all of the important areas?
- Confident you're not on a Rescue Mission Relationship?
- Confident you do not have any co-dependency issues?
- Confident you're not in love with potential?
- Confident your (potential) partner isn't a Love Miser?
- Confident you're not a Love Miser victim?
- Confident you're not excessively admiring your (potential) partner by putting him on a pedestal?
- Confident you're not involved with any of the relationship types probably doomed to fail?

Status: Already Involved

Commitment Phobia

- Are you confident about the status of your relationship?
- If you're having regular sex with someone without a firm relationship commitment, are you sure you're not involved with a Friends With Benefits arrangement by default?

- Are you confident you know how to identify a Commitment Phobic?
- Are you sure you're not involved with a Commitment Phobic?
- Have you checked the warning signs regarding being involved in a Commitment Phobic relationship?
- Are you confident you're not Commitment Phobic yourself?

Compatibility Hazards

- Are you in a long distance relationship?
- Do you spend quality time together?
- Have you made any firm plans to take the relationship forward?
- Have you or your partner made a commitment to move closer or made plans to live together?
- Are you sure your partner doesn't have a toxic ex-partner?
- Have you discussed and resolved any potential issues?
- If your partner is from a different ethnic or social background are you comfortable with the relationship dynamics?
- Have you discussed any potential issues?
- Do you and your partner have different religious or spiritual beliefs?
- Have you discussed these differences and found an amicable compromise?
- Do you and your partner have a significant age difference?
- Have you discussed these differences and agreed on any realistic compromises?
- Does your partner have any children from a previous relationship that are causing problems?
- Do you feel supported by your partner regarding any problems caused by his child/children?
- Have you discussed and resolved those issues to your satisfaction?
- Do you feel supported by your partner regarding any problems caused by his parent(s)?
- Have you discussed and resolved any problems regarding any parental issues to your satisfaction?
- If your parent(s) are causing friction in your relationship, are you supportive and respectful of your partner by setting firm boundaries?

Sexual Compatibility Issues

- Are you happy with your sex life?
- Have you discussed any sexual compatibility issues?
- Are there any sexual dysfunction issues?
- Have you discussed any possible childhood experiences that may be effecting his performance?

- If you have discussed these problems have you considered or taken professional advice?
- Does your partner have any sexual addiction or obsession issues?
- Have you discussed these problems and considered or taken professional advice?

Toxic Flaws

- Are you sure your partner doesn't have any unresolved issues from his childhood?
- Are you happy with your partner's description of his childhood /upbringing?
- Are you confident your partner doesn't have any unresolved issues from his previous relationship(s)?
- Are you happy with your partner's emotional availability?
- Is your partner reliable?
- Is your partner motivated?
- Have you checked your relationship history to check if you attract irresponsible partners?
- Is your partner mature and responsible?
- Are you confident your relationship is healthy?
- Are you sure your relationship isn't abusive or toxic?

Relationship Commitments

- Are you sure you're not desperate to be in a relationship?
- Are you clear about what it really means to make a relationship commitment?
- Are you sure you want to make a commitment to the relationship?
- Are you sure you're not putting commitment before compatibility?
- Do you or your partner have any commitment anxieties?
- Have you discussed any commitment fears or anxieties with your partner?
- If your partner is resisting making a commitment or taking the relationship to the next level, have you discussed this?
- Do you know if your partner is a Commitment Phobic or Love Avoidant, or just experiencing general anxieties?
- If you have discovered any commitment issues, has the matter been resolved to your satisfaction? If not, what action do you intend taking?
- Have you discussed and agreed realistic relationship goals?
- Have you discussed and agreed realistic timescales to take the relationship forward?
- Have you discussed living together or marriage? Are you happy with whatever has been agreed?

Answering the questions that apply to your situation honestly will help you to decide if you:

    A.   Are ready for a relationship.

    B.   Need to do some more work on yourself before getting into the dating game.

C. If you are currently in a relationship, consider if there are any issues that require your attention.

"To ask the 'right' question is far more important than to receive the answer. The solution of a problem lies in the understanding of the problem; the answer is not outside the problem, it is in the problem." – Jiddu Krishnamurti (1895-1986), Author

Final Thoughts

Relationships can be very complicated and one book cannot possibly cover every hazard or the variety of problems that may arise. *How To Avoid Making The Big Relationship Mistakes* should be considered as a best practice guide that you can refer to whenever necessary. If you decide to apply the guidance and strategies suggested you will greatly improve your chances of avoiding the big relationship mistakes that can waste a huge amount of your time or cause a great deal of heartache and emotional distress.

The primary purpose of a romantic union is to share love while providing encouragement and support so each partner can go out in the world and pursue their life goals. Unhealthy relationships eventually drain one or both partners creating drama, heartbreak and disappointment. There are rarely any short cuts or quick fixes when it comes to finding a worthwhile partner for a healthy, loving relationship. When you're single and looking for love, the most important things to know are yourself, the type of partner you're looking for and your deal-breakers: the things you're not prepared to compromise on before you get into the dating game. It's always much easier to avoid the big mistakes if you carry out due diligence during the dating phase to ensure your potential partner is someone who is loving, mature and responsible. Always remember there is nothing wrong with being romantic but it is also sensible be pragmatic when it comes to matters of the heart.

I hope this book helps you to find the kind of love you are looking for. I wish you Love and Light on your journey toward finding the kind of loving relationship you want and deserve.

Nigel

Bibliography

Codependence: The Dance of Wounded Souls-Robert Burney, Joy To You Enterprises, Cambria, California, 1995

In The Meantime-Iyanla Vansant, Simon & Schuster Publishing, USA, 1997

Emotional Unavailability – Bryn C. Collins M.A., L.P. Contemporary Books, Illinois, USA, 1997

Help! I'm In Love With A Narcissist. – Steven Carter/Julia Sokol M. Evans & Company, Inc. Publishing, New York, USA, 2005

He's Scared She's Scared: Understanding The Hidden Fears That Sabotage Your Relationships – Steven Carter & Julia Sokol, Bantam Double Day Publishing Group, New York 10036 USA, 1993

Men Who Can't Love – Steven Carter & Julia Carter E. Evans & Company, New York 10017 USA, 1987

The 7 Habits of Highly Effective People – Stephen R. Covey, Simon & Schuster Publishing, UK, 1992

Body Language – Allen Pease, Sheldon Book Press, 1981

Are You The One For Me? Barbara De Anglis, Harper Collins/Thorsons Publishers, 1993

Loving Yourself, Loving Another: The Importance of Self Esteem for Successful Relationships – Julia Cole, Vermilion Publishing, 2001

Relationship Rescue – Dr. Phil C. McGraw, Ebury Publishing Random House UK Vermilion, 2002

The Book of Tells – Peter Collett, Bantam Books Transworld Publishing, 2004

Games People Play: The Psychology of Human Relationships-Eric Berne, Penquin Books, 1964

10 Bad Choices That Ruin Black Women's Lives – Dr. Grace Cornish, Three Rivers Press, 1998

Intuition & Beyond – Sharon A. Klinger, Random Books London, UK, 2002

Your Sixth Sense: Activating Your Psychic Potential – Belleruth Naparstek, HarperOne, USA, 1997

The Celestine Prophecy: An Experiential Guide – James Redfield & Carol Adrienne, Bantam Books London, UK, 1995

You Can't Afford The Luxury of a Negative thought – John Roger & Peter McWilliams, Prelude Press, Los Angeles, USA, 1986

Happiness Now!-Robert Holden, Hodder & Stoughton, London, UK, 1998

Nasty People - Jay Carter Psy.D., McGraw-Hill, New York, USA, 2003

Acts of Faith - Iyanla Vanzant, Simon & Schuster, New York, 2003

Men Are from Mars, Women Are from Venus: A Practical Guide for Improving Communication and Getting What You Want in Your Relationships – John Gray, Harper Thorsons Publishers, 1992

The Relate Guide To Better Relationships: Practical Ways to Make Your Love Last From the Experts in Marriage Guidance Sarah Litvinoff, Ebury Publishing, 2001

He's Just Not That Into You: The No-Excuses Truth to Understanding Guys - Greg Behrendt & Liz Tuccillo, Publisher Simon Spotlight Entertainment, 2004

Act Like A Lady, Think Like A Man, Steve Harvey, Publisher *Amistad*, 2009

The Relate Guide To Sex In Loving Relationships – Sarah Litvinoff, Vermilion Publishing, 2001

Getting to Commitment – Steven Carter & Julia Sokol M. Evans & Company, Inc. Publishing, New York, USA, 1998

Online Resources & References

Ten Relationship Myths
http://www.drphil.com/articles/article/26

The 3 Biggest Myths About Romantic Relationship by Lynn Marie Lumiere
http://www.yourtango.com/experts/lynn-marie-lumiere/3-biggest-myths-about-romantic-relationship

The Top 10 Myths About Relationships... and the surprising ways each of them goes wrong by Susan Krauss Whitbourne Ph.D.
http://www.psychologytoday.com/blog/fulfillment-any-age/201203/the-top-10-myths-about-relationships

Top 10 Love Myths Busted: Love Myths that Damage Happy Relationships
http://www.theeurekalife.com/top-10-love-myths-busted-love-myths-that-damage-happy-relationships/

7 Common Romantic Relationships Myths to Stop Believing by Janet Zimmerman
http://loveforsuccessfulwomen.com/2014/06/7-common-romantic-relationships-myths-stop-believing/

The 5 Dating Myths That Are Keeping You From Finding Love by Lisa Copeland
http://www.huffingtonpost.com/lisa-copeland/dating-over-50_b_4807786.html

Common Love Myths and How They Affect Your Dating Life by eHarmony Staff
http://www.eharmony.com/dating-advice/dating/common-love-myths-and-how-they-affect-your-dating-life/#.VcescPlVhBc

16 Facts About Dating That Will Change The Way You Think About Love by Kirsten King & Alex Kasprak
http://www.buzzfeed.com/kirstenking/myths-about-love-that-are-totally-false

The 7 Stages of Grieving a Breakup: Understanding your emotional response to breakup can help you feel less alone by Suzanne Lachmann Psy.D.
http://www.psychologytoday.com/blog/me-we/201406/the-7-stages-grieving-breakup

5 Steps Everyone Should Take To Move On After Break Up
http://thelovewhisperer.me/post/20007873238/5-steps-everyone-should-take-to-move-on-after

The 5 Stages of Grieving the End of a Relationship by Jennifer Kromberg PsyD
http://www.psychologytoday.com/blog/inside-out/201309/the-5-stages-grieving-the-end-relationship

The 7 Stages of Grief after the end of a relationship
http://www.psychforums.com/relationship/topic84035.html

Coping with a Breakup or Divorce by Jeanne Segal, Ph.D., Gina Kemp, M.A., and Melinda Smith, M.A
http://www.helpguide.org/articles/family-divorce/coping-with-a-breakup-or-divorce.htm

Dealing With Separation - Breaking Up, Letting Go And How To Move On by Lilly Calandrello
http://www.selfgrowth.com/articles/Dealing_With_Separation_-_Breaking_Up_Letting_Go_And_How_To_Move_On.html

How to Mourn a Breakup to Move Past Grief and Withdrawal by Suzanne Lachmann Psy.D.
http://www.psychologytoday.com/blog/me-we/201306/how-mourn-breakup-move-past-grief-and-withdrawal

10 Ways to Let Go and Open Up to Love Again by Vishnu
http://tinybuddha.com/blog/10-ways-let-go-open-love/

Is Crying Good for You? It Depends. Six Ways to Make Sure Your Tears are Healing by Tina Gilbertson LPC
http://www.psychologytoday.com/blog/constructive-wallowing/201406/is-crying-good-you-it-depends

9 Surprising Benefits of Crying, or Why It's Okay To Have a Good Cry by Daniel Wallen
http://www.lifehack.org/articles/lifestyle/9-surprising-benefits-crying-why-its-okay-have-good-cry.html

The Health Benefits of Crying by Natasha Mann
http://www.netdoctor.co.uk/healthy-living/wellbeing/the-health-benefits-of-crying.htm

The Benefits of Forgiveness by Elizabeth Scott, M.S.
http://stress.about.com/od/relationships/a/forgiveness.htm

The Healing Power of Forgiveness by Johns Hopkins
http://www.hopkinsmedicine.org/news/publications/johns_
hopkins_health/summer_2014/the_healing_power_of_
forgiveness

Finding Purpose Beyond Our Pain
http://purposebeyondpain.com/2010/02/08/10-benefits-of-
forgiveness/

How To Let Go Of Resentments by Dr Judith Orloff
http://www.drjudithorloff.com/_blog/Dr_Judith_Orloff's_
Blog/post/How_To_Let_Go_of_Resentments/

*How to Let Go of a Past Relationship: 10 Steps to Move On
Peacefully by Lori Deschene*
http://tinybuddha.com/blog/how-to-let-go-of-a-past-
relationship-10-steps-to-peacefully-move-on/

8 Effective Ways to Let Go and Move On by Marc Chernoff
http://www.marcandangel.com/2013/04/21/8-effective-ways-
to-let-go-and-move-on/

10 Steps to Move On From a Relationship
http://personalexcellence.co/blog/how-to-move-on

Love Sometimes Requires Letting Go Disengagement
http://www.keen.com/articles/love/love-requires-letting-go

Are You Letting Go or Just Giving Up? by Eddie Corbano
http://lovesagame.com/are-you-letting-go-or-giving-up/

Letting Go of Love by Dr Phil
http://www.drphil.com/articles/article/172

Surviving Your Breakup by Tyler J. Andreula
http://psychcentral.com/lib/surviving-your-breakup/

Co-Parenting with Your Ex by Dr Phil
http://www.drphil.com/articles/article/534

Divorce and Separation
http://www.understandingchildhood.net/posts/divorce-
and-separation-helping-children-and-parents-cope/

*The "Programming" of Self-Sabotage. What's the "logical
illogic" behind self-defeat? By Leon F Seltzer Ph.D*
http://www.psychologytoday.com/blog/evolution-
the-self/201101/the-programming-self-sabotage-pt-3-5

Changing Our Brains, Changing Ourselves by Lea Winerman
http://www.apa.org/monitor/2012/09/brains.aspx

*Parental Alienation is a Pattern of Severe Psychological &
Emotional Child Abuse by Dr. Randy Rand*
http://www.paaousa.org/parental-alienation-is-a-pattern-of-
severe-psychological-and-emotional-child-abuse.html

6 Steps to Help Heal Your Inner Child by Therese J. Borchard
http://psychcentral.com/blog/archives/2012/09/23/6-steps-
to-help-heal-your-inner-child/

*Inner Child Healing: A Path to Freedom, Serenity, and
Empowerment by Robert Burney*
http://www.healyourinnerchild.com/

7 Steps to Heal Your Inner Child by Beyond Blue
http://www.beliefnet.com/columnists/beyondblue/2008/10/7-
steps-to-heal-your-inner-chi.html

Inner Child
https://en.wikipedia.org/wiki/Inner_child

John Bradshaw (author)
https://en.wikipedia.org/wiki/John_Bradshaw_(author)

Inner Child Healing Techniques by Robert Burney
http://joy2meu.com/InnerChild.htm

*Relationships: Unresolved Childhood Issues Can Create Conflict
by Josephine Ferraro, LCSW – NYC Psychotherapist*
http://psychotherapist-nyc.blogspot.co.uk/2010/11/relationships-
unresolved-childhood.html#sthash.8JwiTzyo.dpuf

Emotional Problems? Could It Be Your Inner Child?
http://www.healththroughenergy.co.uk/emotional-problems.aspx

*Inner Child Healing Explained by Lorraine McReight D. Hyp,
MAPHP, MNCH, MNSHP, NLP & TLT Prac, UKCHO, CNHC*
http://www.hypnotherapy-directory.org.uk/hypnotherapist-
articles/inner-child-healing-explained

*Parental Influence on the Emotional Development of Children
by Bethel Moges and Kristi Weber*
https://my.vanderbilt.edu/developmentalpsychologyblog/
2014/05/parental-influence-on-the-emotional-development-
of-children/

*The Perceived Influence of a Father on His Daughter's
Development by Caitlin Goossen*
http://www.kon.org/urc/v8/goossen.html

*How Our Fathers Influence the Partners We Choose by Anna
Maxted*
http://www.telegraph.co.uk/women/womens-life/10895290/
How-our-fathers-influence-the-partners-we-choose.html

*Like Parent, Like Child: The Enduring Influence of Family by
Stanley J. Gross, Ed.D.*
http://psychcentral.com/library/id162.html

Self and Self-Discovery by Bob Edelstein L.M.F.T., M.F.T
www.psychologytoday.com/blog/authentic-engagement/
201207/self-and-self-discovery

Beginning Your Process of Self-Discovery by Felicia Harlow
http://www.campustalkblog.com/beginning-your-process-
of-self-discovery/

A Fearless Self-Discovery
http://www.calmdownmind.com/a-fearless-self-discovery/

Self Discovery Questions by Natalie Verstraelen
https://selfdiscoverylessons.wordpress.com/2008/02/05/
self-discovery-questions/

Experience Personal Growth through Self-Discovery by Dr Bruce J
http://affordablequalitywriting.com/blog/2013/09/experience-
personal-growth-through-self-discovery#.VcfFKflVhBc

Self Criticism
http://psychcentral.com/blog/archives/2014/05/05/3-ways-
to-quiet-self-criticism/

3 Ways to Quiet Self-Criticism by Margarita Tartakovsky
http://psychcentral.com/blog/archives/2014/05/05/3-ways-
to-quiet-self-criticism/

*The Art of Constructive Self-Criticism: How to learn from your
mistakes without beating yourself up by Juliana Breines Ph.D.*
http://www.psychologytoday.com/blog/in-love-and-war/
201310/the-art-constructive-self-criticism

Four Ways to Constructively Criticize Yourself by Juliana Breines
http://greatergood.berkeley.edu/article/item/four_ways_to_
constructively_criticize_yourself

What is the Secret to Reducing Self?
http://www.recovery.org/pro/articles/what-is-the-secret-to-
reducing-self-criticism/ Criticism?

*How to Stop the Self-Criticism and Feel Better About You by
Leslie Becker-Phelps Ph.D.*
http://www.psychologytoday.com/blog/making-change/
201107/how-stop-the-self-criticism-and-feel-better-about-you

How To Love Yourself First by Ken Page L.C.S.W.
www.psychologytoday.com/blog/finding-love/201105/
how-love-yourself-first

9 Ways to Love Yourself by Margaret Paul Ph.D.
http://www.huffingtonpost.com/margaret-paul-phd/love-
yourself_b_4218211.html

*The Path to Unconditional Self-Acceptance by Leon F Seltzer
Ph.D*
www.psychologytoday.com/blog/evolution-the-self/200809/
the-path-unconditional-self-acceptance

Self-Awareness
https://en.wikipedia.org/wiki/Self-awareness

Self-Awareness and Personal Development
http://www.wright.edu/~scott.williams/LeaderLetter/
selfawareness.htm

Developing Self Awareness
http://www.effective-mind-control.com/developing-self-
awareness.html

Emotional Intelligence (EQ): Key Skills for Raising Emotional
Intelligence
http://www.helpguide.org/articles/emotional-health/
emotional-intelligence-eq.htm

How Self-Awareness Leads to Effective Communication by Aldo
Civico Ph.D.
http://www.psychologytoday.com/blog/turning-point/201404/
how-self-awareness-leads-to-effective-communication

Why Self Awareness is Fundamental to Personal Growth (&
How to Cultivate It) by Stephen Cox
http://www.thechangeblog.com/self-awareness/

Self-Awareness vs "Self-Fixingness" by Melissa Kirk
www.psychologytoday.com/blog/test-case/201102/self-
awareness-vs-self-fixingness

Cultivating Self-Awareness by Bradley Foster
http://www.huffingtonpost.com/bradley-foster/self-
awareness_b_3471801.html

Success Starts With Self-Mastery: 7 Effective Strategies by Skip
Pritchard
www.skipprichard.com/success-starts-with-self-
mastery-7-effective-strategies/

Cognitive Dissonance
https://en.wikipedia.org/wiki/Cognitive_dissonance

Fighting Cognitive Dissonance & The Lies We Tell Ourselves by
John M. Grohol, Psy.D.
http://psychcentral.com/blog/archives/2008/10/19/
fighting-cognitive-dissonance-the-lies-we-tell-ourselves/

Cognitive dissonance and the Human Mind by Dan Eden
http://www.viewzone.com/cognitivedissonance.html

6 Tips to Improve Your Self-Esteem by John M. Grohol, Psy.D.
http://psychcentral.com/blog/archives/2011/10/30/
6-tips-to-improve-your-self-esteem/

Building Confidence and Self-Esteem: 17 simple suggestions for
building confidence and self-esteem by Neel Burton M.D.
http://www.psychologytoday.com/blog/hide-and-seek/
201205/building-confidence-and-self-esteem

7 Ways To Boost Your Self Esteem Quickly by Mark Tyrrell
http://www.self-confidence.co.uk/articles/7-ways-to-boost-
your-self-esteem-quickly/

Increasing Self-Esteem and Happiness: 8 Steps to a Fulfilled Life
by Carolina Ordoñez
http://tinybuddha.com/blog/increasing-self-esteem-
happiness-8-steps-fulfilled-life/

Top Ten Facts about Low Self Esteem by Mark Tyrrell
http://www.self-confidence.co.uk/articles/top-ten-facts-
about-low-self-esteem/

Negative Self Esteem
http://www.therapists.com/fundamentals/self-esteem

Signs You are Ready For a Relationship by Ashley Page
http://madamenoire.com/435883/ready-for-a-relationship/

Low Self Esteem - How Psychologically Abusive Relationships
Impact Our Self Perception by Shannon E Cook
http://ezinearticles.com/?Low-Self-Esteem---How-
Psychologically-Abusive-Relationships-Impact-Our-Self-
Perception&id=1773163

Understanding Low Self-Esteem
http://www.overcoming.co.uk/single.htm?ipg=8611

Raising Low Self-Esteem
http://www.nhs.uk/livewell/mentalhealth/pages/
dealingwithlowself-esteem.aspx

10 Ways Low Self-Esteem Affects Women in Relationships by
Suzanne Lachmann Psy.D.
http://www.psychologytoday.com/blog/me-we/201312/10-
ways-low-self-esteem-affects-women-in-relationships

15 Ways Your Low Self-Esteem Is DESTROYING Your
Relationship by Dr. Shirley McNeal, Mrs. Nancy Philpott,
Deborah Roth
http://www.yourtango.com/experts/yourtango-experts/15-ways-
your-self-esteem-can-make-or-break-your-relationship-expert

How Your Self-Esteem Impacts Relationships by Suzanne
Phillips PsyD
http://www.pbs.org/thisemotionallife/blogs/how-your-self-
esteem-impacts-relationships

How Does Low Self-Esteem Negatively Affect You? by Elizabeth
Venzin
http://psychcentral.com/blog/archives/2014/03/01/how-does-
low-self-esteem-negatively-affect-you/

Overcoming Insecurity and Low Self Esteem
http://www.pathwaytohappiness.com/writings-insecurity.htm

How to Build Self-Esteem After a Verbally Abusive Relationship
by Jill Avery-Stoss
www.livestrong.com/article/178484-how-to-build-self-
esteem-after-a-verbally-abusive-relationship/

6 Warning Signs You're In An Abusive Relationship by Zita
Fekete
http://www.yourtango.com/experts/zita-fekete/6-signs-
abusive-relationship

5 Ways To Escape An Abusive Relationship
http://psychcentral.com/blog/archives/2011/09/28/5-ways-to-
escape-an-abusive-relationship/

Fear of Intimacy: Understanding Why People Fear Intimacy
http://www.psychalive.org/fear-of-intimacy/

Low self-esteem and Your Relationship
http://www.heartspiritmind.com/relationships/low-self-
esteem-and-your-relationship/

Fear Of Intimacy Is Wrecking Your Relationship by Barrie
Davenport
http://liveboldandbloom.com/07/relationships/how-fear-
of-intimacy-is-wrecking-your-relationship

Building Self-Esteem by Lynn Ponton, MD
http://psychcentral.com/lib/building-self-esteem/

13 Tips to Building Self Esteem by Jae Song
http://thinksimplenow.com/happiness/the-art-of-building-
self-esteem/

Tips for Building Self Esteem & Self Love!
http://www.spiritwire.com/selfesteemtips.html

Self-Esteem
en.wikipedia.org/wiki/Self-esteem

Emotional Intelligence (EQ) by Jeanne Segal, Ph.D., and
Melinda Smith, M.A.
http://www.helpguide.org/articles/emotional-health/
emotional-intelligence-eq.htm

Emotional Intelligence by Daniel Goleman
http://www.danielgoleman.info/topics/emotional-intelligence/

What's Your EQ?
http://psychology.about.com/library/quiz/bl_eq_quiz.htm

Emotional Intelligence (EQ): Five Key Skills for Raising
Emotional Intelligence
http://www.helpguide.org/articles/emotional-health/
emotional-intelligence-eq.htm

Emotional Intelligence
en.wikipedia.org/wiki/Emotional_intelligence

What Is Emotional Intelligence? Definitions, History, and
Measures of Emotional Intelligence by Kendra Cherry
http://psychology.about.com/od/personalitydevelopment/a/
emotionalintell.htm

What is Emotional Intelligence (EQ)? by Michael Akers & Grover Porter
http://psychcentral.com/lib/what-is-emotional-intelligence-eq/

10 Ways to Enhance Your Emotional Intelligence by Norman Rosenthal M.D.
http://www.psychologytoday.com/blog/your-mind-your-body/201201/10-ways-enhance-your-emotional-intelligence

5 Ways to Boost Your Emotional Intelligence by Harvey Deutschendorf
http://www.fastcompany.com/3026707/work-smart/5-ways-to-boost-your-emotional-intelligence

Emotional Intelligence
http://www.enkivillage.com/emotional-intelligence.html

Tips for Reducing Stress
http://www.webmd.com/balance/stress-management/reducing-stress-tips

5 Quick Tips to Reduce Stress and Stop Anxiety by Jamie Long Psy.D.
http://www.psychologytoday.com/blog/finding-cloud9/201308/5-quick-tips-reduce-stress-and-stop-anxiety

20 Tips to Tame Your Stress by Lynn Ponton, MD
http://psychcentral.com/lib/20-tips-to-tame-your-stress/

8 Proven Ways to Manage Stress: Tips from Mayo Clinic
http://life.gaiam.com/article/8-proven-ways-manage-stress-tips-mayo-clinic

11 Tips to Lower Stress by Remy Melina
http://www.livescience.com/35957-lower-stress-tips.html

10 Practical Ways to Handle Stress by Margarita Tartakovsky, M.S.
http://psychcentral.com/blog/archives/2011/07/11/10-practical-ways-to-handle-stress/

How We Communicate Through Body Language by Leonard Mlodinow
http://www.psychologytoday.com/blog/subliminal/201205/how-we-communicate-through-body-language

Body Language
en.wikipedia.org/wiki/Body_language

Top 10 Nonverbal Communication Tips by Kendra Cherry
http://www.psychology.about.com/od/nonverbalcommunication/tp/nonverbaltips.htm

5 Ways to Improve Your Marriage Without Talking by Dustin
http://www.engagedmarriage.com/communication/5-ways-to-improve-your-marriage-without-talking

Playful Communication in Relationships: The Power of Laughter and Play by Damon Smith
http://damonsmithnow.blogspot.co.uk/2012/09/playful-communication-in-relationships.html

5 Signs Your Emotional Baggage Is Sabotaging Your Relationship by Steph Auteri
http://www.yourtango.com/201075374/5-signs-youre-carrying-emotional-baggage

10 Signs You've Got Too Much Emotional Baggage for a Relationship by Mike Bundrant
http://magazine.foxnews.com/love/10-signs-youve-got-too-much-emotional-baggage-relationship

Losing Your Emotional Baggage
http://www.twoofus.org/educational-content/articles/losing-your-emotional-baggage/index.aspx

5 Steps to Deal with Emotional Baggage So It Doesn't Define You by Cila Warncke
http://tinybuddha.com/blog/5-steps-deal-with-emotional-baggage-so-it-doesnt-define-you/

Releasing emotional baggage to increase well-being
http://www.gwizlearning.wordpress.com/2012/06/03/releasing-emotional-baggage-to-increase-well-being/

Unpack Your Emotional Baggage to Help Your Body Heal
http://psychcentral.com/blog/archives/2013/10/16/unpack-your-emotional-baggage-to-help-your-body-heal/

Emotional Baggage
en.wikipedia.org/wiki/Emotional_baggage

Resolving Emotional Baggage
http://growchangelearn.blogspot.co.uk/2008/04/resolving-emotional-baggage.html

Owning Our Emotional Baggage in Relationships by Robin Hoffman
http://www.huffingtonpost.com/robin-hoffman/emotional-baggage_b_3770558.html

10 Signs You've Got Too Much Emotional Baggage for a Relationship by Mike Bundrant
http://magazine.foxnews.com/love/10-signs-youve-got-too-much-emotional-baggage-relationship

How to Deal With Emotional Baggage from the Past by Bobbi Jankovich, LMFT
http://howtowinamansheart.com/blog/how-to-deal-with-past-emotional-baggage/

Do You Have Too Much Emotional Baggage?
http://www.gettingtotruelove.com/2012/05/02/do-you-have-too-much-emotional-baggage/

Unpack Your Emotional Baggage to Help Your Body Heal
http://psychcentral.com/blog/archives/2013/10/16/unpack-your-emotional-baggage-to-help-your-body-heal/

5 Ways to Unpack and Heal "Emotional Baggage" by Mary Jo Rapini,
http://blog.chron.com/loveandrelationships/2013/10/5-ways-to-unpack-and-heal-emotional-baggage/

Healing Emotional Baggage & Stress 101
http://amybscher.com/healing-emotional-baggage-stress-101/

Try These Easy Emotional Healing Exercises
http://www.gateways-to-inner-peace.com/emotional-healing-exercises.html

How to Deal With Emotional Baggage Effectively by Lesya Li
http://www.havingtime.com/how-to-deal-with-emotional-baggage-effectively/

Releasing Emotional Baggage by Robbie Holz
http://holzwellness.com/releasing-emotional-baggage/

How To Heal Emotional Baggage and Mental Shadows by Nikki
http://theherbalhealingmama.com/2014/12/08/how-to-heal-emotional-baggage-and-mental-shadows/

Is He Emotionally Unavailable? How To Spot Emotionally Unavailable Men by NATALIE
http://www.baggagereclaim.co.uk/how-to-spot-emotionally-unavailable-men/

Write Letters to Heal Pain, Release Anger, Let Go, and Start Living
http://getbusylivingblog.com/write-letters-to-heal-pain-release-anger-let-go-and-start-living/

Inner Child Healing Explained by Lorraine McReight D. Hyp, MAPHP, MNCH, MNSHP, NLP & TLT Prac, UKCHO, CNHC
http://www.hypnotherapy-directory.org.uk/hypnotherapist-articles/inner-child-healing-explained

5 Toxic Personalities and How to Break the Bad Dating Pattern by Dr. Gail Gross (Human Behavior, Parenting, and Education Expert, Speaker, Author.) Ph.D., Ed.D., M.Ed
http://www.huffingtonpost.com/dr-gail-gross/5-toxic-personalities-how_b_4726254.html

5 Keys to Breaking Bad Relationship Patterns
http://gentlelivingonline.com/relationships-3/bad-relationship-patterns/

Is History Repeating Itself in Your Relationships? by Mary Darling Montero, LCSW
http://www.huffingtonpost.com/mary-montero/is-history-repeating-itse_b_672518.html

Six Fundamental Patterns of Cultural Differences by Rubini Chandra Sekharan
http://kissmetouchmeholdme.blogspot.co.uk/2009/09/six-fundamental-patterns-of-cultural.html

How to End Bad Relationship Patterns
http://www.eharmony.com/dating-advice/dating/how-to-end-bad-relationship-patterns/#.Vci5JflVhBc

How to Break a Toxic Love Pattern by Korin Miller
http://www.cosmopolitan.com/sex-love/advice/a3296/break-toxic-love-pattern/

10 Unhealthy Dating Patterns And How To Break Them by Jennifer Garam
http://www.thefrisky.com/photos/10-unhealthy-dating-patterns-and-how-to-break-them/dating-main/

Break Your Bad Dating Pattern by Margaret Ruth
http://www.huffingtonpost.com/margaret-ruth/break-your-bad-dating-pat_b_222806.html

Relationship Insanity: Understanding Why You Feel Tempted To Go Back and Repeat Your Pattern With Your Pain Source BY NATALIE
http://www.baggagereclaim.co.uk/relationship-insanity-understanding-why-you-feel-tempted-to-go-back-and-repeat-your-pattern-with-your-pain-source/

What Attracts Us to Bad Relationships? by Nathan Feiles, LCSW
http://blogs.psychcentral.com/relationships-balance/2012/08/04/what-attracts-us-to-bad-relationships/

Essential Secrets of Psychotherapy: Repetitive Relationship Patterns by Stephen A Diamond Ph.D
http://www.psychologytoday.com/blog/evil-deeds/200806/essential-secrets-psychotherapy-repetitive-relationship-patterns

Why Am I Attracted to Bad Boys (or Bad Girls)? by Larry Schwimmer
http://www.huffingtonpost.com/larry-schwimmer/why-am-i-attracted-to-bad_b_3567407.html

How to Stop Making the Wrong Relationship Choices
http://www.psychalive.org/relationship_advice/

Dating Checklist: Questions to Ask Yourself Before Falling In Love Again by Seth Meyers, Psy.D. in Insight Is 20/20
http://www.psychologytoday.com/blog/insight-is-2020/201207/dating-checklist-questions-ask-yourself-falling-in-love-again

Building Healthy Boundaries by James J. Messina
http://jamesjmessina.com/growingdowninnerchild/healthyboundaries.html

The Importance of Having and Enforcing Boundaries in Relationships: Why You Need to Draw the Line in the Sand by Savannah Grey
http://esteemology.com/the-importance-of-having-and-enforcing-boundaries-in-relationships-why-you-need-to-draw-the-line-in-the-sand/

How To Set Boundaries With A Narcissist: Is There A Way To Do That?
http://www.huffingtonpost.com/karyl-mcbride-phd-lmft/how-to-set-boundaries-with-a-narcissist_b_6833740.html?ncid=tweetlnkushpmg00000067

When Does Flirting Become Cheating? 9 Red Flags by Therese J. Borchard
http://psychcentral.com/blog/archives/2011/07/06/when-does-flirting-become-cheating-9-red-flags/

10 Way to Build and Preserve Better Boundaries by Margarita Tartakovsky, M.S.
http://psychcentral.com/lib/10-way-to-build-and-preserve-better-boundaries/

Setting Healthy Boundaries: Allowing the True Self to Emerge by Carl Benedict
http://serenityonlinetherapy.com/healthyboundaries.htm

7 Ways to Protect Your Energy & Enforce Healthy Boundaries: Strategies to avoid overwhelm and create boundaries that keep you sane by Susan Biali M.D.
http://www.psychologytoday.com/blog/prescriptions-life/201311/7-ways-protect-your-energy-enforce-healthy-boundaries

How to Set Healthy Boundaries in Every Relationship by Jennifer Kass
http://greatist.com/happiness/how-to-set-boundaries-in-relationship

Healthy Personal Boundaries & How to Establish Them by Z. Hereford
http://www.essentiallifeskills.net/personalboundaries.html

Why Healthy Relationships Always Have Boundaries & How to Set Boundaries in Yours by Margarita Tartakovsky, M.S.
http://psychcentral.com/blog/archives/2015/02/25/why-healthy-relationships-always-have-boundaries-how-to-set-boundaries-in-yours/

Setting Boundaries with Difficult People
https://www.ipfw.edu/affiliates/assistance/selfhelp/relationship-settingboundaries.html

How to Create Healthy Boundaries by Terri Cole
http://www.positivelypositive.com/2012/06/29/how-to-create-healthy-boundaries/

The Guide to Strong Boundaries by Mark Manson
http://markmanson.net/boundaries

12 Core Boundaries To Live By in Life, Dating, & Relationships
http://www.baggagereclaim.co.uk/12-core-boundaries-to-live-by-in-life-dating-relationships/

List of HEALTHY Boundaries
https://acoarecovery.wordpress.com/2011/04/07/list-of-healthy-boundaries-part-1/

10 Ways to Establish Personal Boundaries by Barrie Davenport
http://liveboldandbloom.com/08/life-coaching/want-to-boost-your-self-esteem-10-ways-to-establish-personal-boundaries#sthash.oibojEFy.dpuf

Boundaries
http://www.outofthefog.net/CommonNonBehaviors/Boundaries.html

6 Steps To Set Good Boundaries
http://www.mindbodygreen.com/0-13176/6-steps-to-set-good-boundaries.html

The Science of Attraction: Why do we think some people are attractive and others are not? by Susan Weinschenk Ph.D
http://www.psychologytoday.com/blog/brain-wise/201408/the-science-attraction

The Science of Magnetism
http://www.independent.co.uk/life-style/love-sex/attraction/the-science-of-magnetism-926693.html

The Science of Love
http://www.bbc.co.uk/science/hottopics/love/

The Rules of Attraction in the Game of Love by Bjorn Carey
http://www.livescience.com/7023-rules-attraction-game-love.html

9 Facts Worth Knowing About Human Attraction by Christopher Hudspeth
http://www.thoughtcatalog.com/christopher-hudspeth/2013/07/9-facts-worth-knowing-about-human-attraction/

The Biology of Attraction by Helen E. Fisher
http://www.psychologytoday.com/articles/199303/
the-biology-attraction

The Scientific Rules of Attraction
http://www.independent.co.uk/news/science/the-scientific-
rules-of-attraction-2115495.html

The Psychology of Attraction: How To Flirt With Science by
Sam McNerney
http://whywereason.com/2011/08/09/the-psychology-
of-attraction-how-to-flirt-with-science/

What is Love Addiction? by Alexandra Katehakis, MFT, CST,
CSAT
http://psychcentral.com/blog/archives/2013/05/26/
what-is-love-addiction/

How To Break the Pattern of Love Addiction by Ann Smith
http://www.psychologytoday.com/blog/healthy-connections/
201012/how-break-the-pattern-love-addiction

What Is Love Addiction?
http://www.loveaddictiontreatment.com/loveaddiction/

Signs of Love Addiction
http://www.eharmony.com/dating-advice/relationships/signs-
of-love-addiction/#.Vci_ivlVhBc

Sex and Love Addiction
http://gettotheinside.blogspot.co.uk/2009/03/sex-and-love-
addiction-part-2.html

The Process of Love Addiction Withdrawal by Alexandra
Katehakis, MFT, CST, CSAT
http://psychcentral.com/blog/archives/2014/05/28/
the-process-of-love-addiction-withdrawal/

What is Your Attachment Style?
http://www.psychalive.org/what-is-your-attachment-style/

John Bowlby – Attachment Styles
en.wikipedia.org/wiki/John_Bowlby

Your Attachment Style Impacts Your Relationship. What Is
Your Attachment Style? by Lisa Firestone Ph.D.
http://www.psychologytoday.com/blog/compassion-
matters/201307/how-your-attachment-style-impacts-
your-relationship

Relationship Attachment Style Test
http://testyourself.psychtests.com/testid/2859

Mary Ainsworth by Saul McLeod
http://www.simplypsychology.org/mary-ainsworth.html

A Brief Overview of Adult Attachment Theory and Research by
R. Chris Fraley, University of Illinois
http://www.internal.psychology.illinois.edu/~rcfraley/
attachment.htm

Attachment Theory: Explaining Relationship "Styles" by Dr.
Dylan Selterman
http://www.scienceofrelationships.com/home/2011/7/15/
attachment-theory-explaining-relationship-styles.html

What is My Attachment Style
http://www.tarcherbooks.net/wp-content/uploads/2012/02/
Attached.pdf

20 Things That Are More Fun to Do While Single
http://www.meetmindful.com/20-things-that-are-
more-fun-to-do-while-single/

9 Things to Do While You're Still Single
http://www.relevantmagazine.com/life/relationships/9-
things-do-while-you%E2%80%99re-still-single

15 Glorious Things You Can Do Now That You're Single
http://www.self.com/flash/humor-blog/2014/08/15-glorious-
things-can-now-youre-single/

Men in Relationships: 5 Simple Categories by Suzanne
Lachmann Psy.D
http://www.psychologytoday.com/blog/me-we/201308/
men-in-relationships-5-simple-categories

What Men Want in a Relationship by Rinatta Paries
http://powertochange.com/sex-love/menwant/

3 Things Women Need to Know About Men In Relationships by
Shelley Bullard
http://www.mindbodygreen.com/0-10511/3-things-women-
need-to-know-about-men-in-relationships.html

7 Things Men Want In A Relationship by Jordan Gray
http://goodmenproject.com/featured-content/7-things-
men-want-in-a-relationship-jgc/

18 Secrets Guys Wish You Knew
http://www.webmd.com/sex-relationships/ss/slideshow-
secrets-guys-wish-you-knew

10 Things Men Wish Women Knew About Them by Brendan
Tapley
http://www.womansday.com/relationships/dating-marriage/
advice/a1334/10-things-men-wish-women-knew-about-
them-103922/

13 Things Men Think About Women But Never Say by Cody
Delistraty
http://thoughtcatalog.com/cody-delistraty/2013/07/13-
things-men-think-about-women-but-never-say/

50 Characteristics of Healthy Relationships by Alice Boyes Ph.D.
http://www.psychologytoday.com/blog/in-practice/201301/
50-characteristics-healthy-relationships

18 Qualities You Need To Find In A Partner Before You
Commit To Them by Brian Gates
http://www.thoughtcatalog.com/brian-n-gates/2014/01/18-
qualities-you-need-to-find-in-a-partner-before-you-commit-
to-them/

Characteristics of Healthy Relationships
http://bpdfamily.com/bpdresources/nk_a115.htm

Online Dating: 10 Rules to Help Find The Ideal Partner by
Amy Webb
http://www.theguardian.com/lifeandstyle/2014/mar/18/
online-dating-10-rules-partner-profile

ONLINE DATING ADVICE
http://advice.uk.match.com/dating-advice/online-dating-
advice

6 Online Dating Mistakes to Avoid by Adelle Waldman
http://mashable.com/2013/09/04/online-dating-tips/

11 Insider Tips to Finding Love Online by Winnie Yu
http://www.webmd.com/sex-relationships/features/
online-dating-tips

Dos and Don'ts: Best Tips For Online Dating
http://www.huffingtonpost.co.uk/2013/06/20/online-dating-
tips-dos-and-donts_n_3472326.html

Online Dating Tips
http://www.verizonwireless.com/mobile-living/apps/
online-dating/

Safe Online Dating
http://www.getsafeonline.org/social-networking/
online-dating/

Online daters, be warned! 1 in 10 profiles are scams, report
reveals by Christina Farr
http://venturebeat.com/2012/10/30/online-dating-scam/

Beware the online dating scams: Love-sick Britons cheated out
of £37bn by fraudsters
http://www.dailymail.co.uk/femail/article-2122247/Beware-
online-dating-scams-Love-sick-Britons-cheated-37bn-
fraudsters.html

My online date didn't exist... and the scam cost me my £40,000
life savings by Katherine Faulkner
http://www.dailymail.co.uk/news/article-2100719/My-
online-date-didnt-exist--scam-cost-40-000-life-savings.
html#ixzz3iQl7B5v2

How to Avoid Online Dating Scams
http://www.rd.com/advice/relationships/how-to-avoid-online-dating-scams/

Online Dating Scams: How to Tell If You Are Being Baited by a Catfish by Dr Phil
http://www.drphil.com/articles/article/726

Do You Need A Dating Rotation?
http://www.refinery29.com/2014/02/62119/dating-multiple-peoplehttp://drphil.com/articles/article/726

14 Warning Signs Your Prince Charming Is A Total Scammer by Sharon Lynn Wyeth
http://www.yourtango.com/experts/sharon-lynn-wyeth/17-clues-how-avoid-internet-dating-scams

The Indisputable Case For Dating More Than One Guy At A Time by Katarina Phang
http://www.yourtango.com/experts/katarina-phang/why-dating-rotation-actually-heightens-your-attractiveness

Cosmo's Guide to Dating Mucho Men by Michelle Lee
http://www.cosmopolitan.com/sex-love/advice/a1531/muncho-men/

Speed Dating
http://www.bbc.co.uk/insideout/southeast/series2/speed_dating_date_romance_road_raving.shtml

Speed Dating
en.wikipedia.org/wiki/Speed_dating

How Speed Dating Works by Josh Clark
http://people.howstuffworks.com/speed-dating1.htm

6 Tips For A Successful Speed Dating Experience by J. Cameron Gantt
http://www.yourtango.com/experts/j-cameron-gantt/6-tips-making-speed-dating-work-you-expert

18 Signs Your Date Really Likes You on Your First Date
http://www.lovepanky.com/flirting-flings/dating-game/signs-your-date-likes-you

5 body language signals and what they mean by Fran Creffield
http://www.eharmony.co.uk/dating-advice/dating/5-body-language-signals-and-what-they-mean#.VcjWKPlVhBc

Test Your Romantic Dating Personality
http://www.links2love.com/quizzes/romantic_dating_personality_quiz.htm

Courage to Express and Negotiate Your Needs by Megan Raphael
http://www.eharmony.com/dating-advice/about-you/courage-to-express-and-negotiate-your-needs/#.VcjXGflVhBc

How to Improve Your Love Life By Setting Dating and Relationship Rules by Bobbi Palmer
http://datelikeagrownup.com/2013/12/setting-dating-rules/

What is Negotiation?
http://www.skillsyouneed.com/ips/negotiation.html

Going Dutch on a Date: A Good Idea? by Erina Lee, Senior Research Scientist
http://www.eharmony.com/dating-advice/dating-advice-for-you/going-dutch-on-a-date-good-idea/#.VcjY2flVhBc

The REAL price of feminism: Modern men expect women to go Dutch on dates now there's equality in the workplace by Bianca London for MAILONLINE
http://www.dailymail.co.uk/femail/article-2206665/The-REAL-price-feminism-Modern-men-expect-women-Dutch-dates-s-equality-workplace.html

It's 2012. The New Rules for Going Dutch on a Date by Lisa DeCanio
http://bostinno.streetwise.co/2012/06/07/its-2012-the-new-rules-for-who-pays-on-the-first-date/

Why We Need To Stop Going Dutch On Dates by Yan Koh
http://www.thoughtcatalog.com/yan-koh/2014/07/why-we-need-to-stop-going-dutch-on-dates/

Chemistry (Relationship)
en.wikipedia.org/wiki/Chemistry_(relationship)

Compatibility and Chemistry in Relationships by Mark Manson
http://markmanson.net/compatibility-and-chemistry

Relationship Chemistry: Can Science Explain Instant Connections? Why friends and romantic partners click by Kelly Campbell Ph.D.
http://www.psychologytoday.com/blog/more-chemistry/201108/relationship-chemistry-can-science-explain-instant-connections

What Is Chemistry? by Dr Nerdlove
http://www.doctornerdlove.com/2012/07/chemistry-sexual-tension/all/1/

First Dates: Dos and Don'ts To Create Chemistry by Matt Schneiderman
http://www.chemistry.com/datingadvice/DosandDonts

8 Modern Dating Rules Every Single Should Know by Stephanie Castillo
http://www.yourtango.com/201174240/8-modern-dating-rules-every-single-should-know

Dating Do's and Don'ts
http://health.howstuffworks.com/relationships/dating/dating-in-the-new-millennium.htm

6 Tips for Dating Success: What You Both Want Matters by Jeremy Nicholson M.S.W., Ph.D
http://www.psychologytoday.com/blog/the-attraction-doctor/201107/6-tips-dating-success-what-you-both-want-matters

The Successful Woman's Guide To Dating
http://www.eharmony.com/dating-advice/dating/the-successful-womans-guide-to-dating/#.VcjciflVhBc

9 Dating Mistakes Women Make by Vanessa Burka
http://www.wdish.com/life/9-dating-mistakes-women-make

Dating advice: 10 Classic Mistakes Women Make With Men by Olga Kaushan
http://allwomenstalk.com/dating-advice

12 Biggest Mistakes Most Women Make by Sabrina Alexis
http://www.anewmode.com/dating-relationships/12-biggest-relationship-mistakes/

20 Mistakes Women Make with Men by Brad Paul
http://www.solotopia.com/mistakes-women-make-with-men/

The Top 5 Relationship Mistakes You Should Avoid by Carol Allen
http://soulmatestars.com/relationships/top-5-relationship-mistakes

Top 10 Dating Mistakes
http://www.cognitive-therapy-associates.com/articles/top-ten-dating-mistakes/

How To Avoid Making The Same Relationship Mistakes Over And Over Again by Terry Gaspard
http://www.huffingtonpost.com/2014/08/30/relationship-mistakes_n_5726206.html

11 Signs You Are Not Ready to be in a Relationship
http://www.relrules.com/11-signs-you-are-not-ready-to-be-in-a-relationship/

13 Dating Red Flags for Women by Goal Auzeen Saedi Ph.D
http://www.psychologytoday.com/blog/millennial-media/201312/13-dating-red-flags-women

18 Early Signs During Dating of a Potential Abuser or Batterer
http://www.womenaresafe.org/emotional.html

Are You in an Unhealthy Relationship?
http://www.psychalive.org/unhealthy-relationship/

10 Warning Signs A Guy is Bad News by Lyndsie Robinson
http://allwomenstalk.com/10-warning-signs-that-a-guy-is-bad-news

25 Dating Dealbreakers and How to Spot Them
http://ecosalon.com/25-dating-dealbreakers-and-red-flag-271/

What is Commitment Phobia & Relationship Anxiety? by John M. Grohol, Psy.D.
http://psychcentral.com/blog/archives/2015/01/08/what-is-commitment-phobia-relationship-anxiety/

How to spot a man who won't commit (and why women should run a mile!) by Dr Pam Spurr
http://www.dailymail.co.uk/femail/article-2008455/How-spot-man-wont-commit-women-run-mile.html#ixzz3iR3FNjDv

How to Merge Finances When You Get Married (Without Going Crazy) by Karin Price Muelle
http://lifehacker.com/how-to-merge-finances-when-you-get-married-without-goi-1516718128

Getting married? Six steps in financial planning for newlyweds
http://www.csmonitor.com/Business/2011/0713/Getting-married-Six-steps-in-financial-planning-for-newlyweds/Know-your-partner-s-spending-habits

Benefits and drawbacks: Living together before marriage by Kylie Robinson
https://kylierobinson.wordpress.com/2013/08/01/benefits-and-drawbacks-living-together-before-marriage/

Top 10 Advantages of Live in Relationship over Marriage by Grace Cherian
http://listdose.com/top-10-advantages-of-live-in-relationship-over-marriage/

The Marriage Problem: Why Many Are Choosing Cohabitation Instead by Alice G. Walton
http://www.theatlantic.com/health/archive/2012/02/the-marriage-problem-why-many-are-choosing-cohabitation-instead/252505/

Advantages and Disadvantages of Cohabitation
http://www.cotswoldfamilylaw.co.uk/what-we-do/cohabitation-law-rights/advantages-and-disadvantages-of-cohabitation/

Disadvantages of Cohabitation by Katina Davenport
http://davenstan.hubpages.com/hub/Disadvantages-of-Living-Together-Before-Marriage

The Negative Effects of Cohabitation by Linda J. Waite
http://www.gwu.edu/~ccps/rcq/rcq_negativeeffects_waite.html

Relationship Compatibility
http://www.psychalive.org/relationship-compatibility/

The Truth About Compatibility by Hara Estroff Marano & Carlin Flora
http://www.psychologytoday.com/articles/200411/the-truth-about-compatibility

Romantic Relationship Compatibility...Issues that should not be overlooked by Olalekan Ashiru
http://www.selfgrowth.com/articles/Romantic_Relationship_Compatibility_Issues_that_should_not_be_overlooked.html

What Makes For A Happy Marriage? by Mark Dombeck, PH.D.
http://www.mentalhelp.net/articles/what-makes-for-a-happy-marriage/

The Psychology of Relationship Compatibility by Dr Joel Block
http://instantchemistry.com/psychology-of-relationship-compatibility/

Interracial Relationships: A Rundown of Issues by Nadra Kareem Nittle Race Relations Expert
http://racerelations.about.com/od/interracialrelationships/a/InterracialRelationshipsIssues.htm

Interracial Marriage - Difficulties In Interracial Marriages
http://family.jrank.org/pages/930/Interracial-Marriage-Difficulties-in-Interracial-Marriages.html

Interracial Marriage
en.wikipedia.org/wiki/Interracial_marriage

Interracial Marriage in the United States
en.wikipedia.org/wiki/Interracial_marriage_in_the_United_States

Interracial Marriages in the US: Facts and Figures
http://newobserveronline.com/interracial-marriages-in-the-us-facts-and-figures/

Navigating Interracial Relationships by Saleem Rana, Psychotherapist
http://dating.lovetoknow.com/Interracial_Relationships

Benefits of an Interracial Relationship
http://www.fullerton.edu/universityblues/interracial/benefits.htm

Family In Conflict Over an Interracial Relationship? by Dr Phil
http://www.drphil.com/articles/article/327

Study: Interracial Marriage, Acceptance Growing by Ashley Hayes, CNN
http://edition.cnn.com/2012/02/16/us/interracial-marriage/

10 Pitfalls About Interracial Relationships by Rishona Campbell
http://www.rishona.net/2011/12/27/10-pitfalls-about-interracial-relationships/

Intercultural Marriage: Making It Work by Josh Noem, M.Div.
http://www.foryourmarriage.org/intercultural-marriage-making-it-work/

Interracial Marriage, International Encyclopaedia of Marriage and Family
http://www.encyclopedia.com/topic/Interracial_Marriage.aspx

'Is Marriage For White People?': Stanford Law Professor's Views on Black Women, Marriage by Linsey Davis
http://abcnews.go.com/Health/stanford-law-professor-suggests-black-women-find-husbands/story?id=14620932

Black women should look outside their race for a successful man, says Stanford law professor
http://www.dailymail.co.uk/news/article-2051299/Black-women-look-outside-race-successful-man.html#ixzz3iRP1MGt8

Age disparity in sexual relationships
en.wikipedia.org/wiki/Age_disparity_in_sexual_relationships

5 Considerations for Relationships with a Big Age Difference by Zawn Villines
http://www.goodtherapy.org/blog/five-considerations-for-relationships-with-big-age-difference-0910138

Reasons for Dating An Older Man by Dr Ronn Elmore
http://www.dating-help-for-women.com/dating-an-older-man.html

8 Tips to Handle Big Age Gap Relationships by Heather Jensen
http://love.allwomenstalk.com/tips-to-handle-a-major-age-difference-in-a-relationship

Urban Cougar
http://www.urbandictionary.com/define.php?term=Urban+Cougar

How Do You Know if a Woman is a Cougar?
http://www.wikihow.com/Know-if-a-Woman-is-a-Cougar

Sleeping With Cougars
http://uk.askmen.com/dating/player_100/143_love_games.html

The Cougar phenomenon: why older women should choose young lovers by Sarah Knapton
http://www.telegraph.co.uk/news/science/11181138/The-Cougar-phenomenon-why-older-women-should-choose-young-lovers.html

New breed of 'piranha women' who are preying on rich men to get them pregnant, warns lawyer by Larisa Brown
http://www.dailymail.co.uk/news/article-2097019/New-breed-piranha-women-preying-rich-men-pregnant.html

What Role Should a Stepparent Play? by Dr Phil
http://www.drphil.com/articles/article/243

"My Blended Family Won't Blend!" What to Do When Your Stepkids Disrespect You by James Lehman, MSW
http://www.empoweringparents.com/My-Blended-Family-Wont-Blend-Help-PartII-What-to-Do-When-Your-Stepkids-Dont-Respect-You.php

Avoiding the step-parent trap by Flora McEvedy
http://www.telegraph.co.uk/news/health/children/3323813/Avoiding-the-step-parent-trap.html

Step-Parenting and Blended Families: How to Bond with Stepchildren and Deal with Stepfamily Issues
http://www.helpguide.org/articles/family-divorce/step-parenting-blended-families.htm

How Healthy Couples Deal with Their In-Laws by Margarita Tartakovsky, M.S.
http://psychcentral.com/blog/archives/2013/10/08/how-healthy-couples-deal-with-their-in-laws/

How to Handle Your Monster-in-Law Taking on the Beast by Yvonne K. Fulbright Ph.D.
http://www.psychologytoday.com/blog/mate-relate-and-communicate/201311/how-handle-your-monster-in-law

Managing Your In-Laws by Dr Phil
http://drphil.com/articles/article/28

If you have core values issues, you have compatibility issues by NATALIE
http://www.baggagereclaim.co.uk/if-you-have-core-values-issues-you-have-compatability-issues/

Compatibility & Interest Guide
http://www.positive-way.com/compatibility.htm

30 Days to a Better Man Day 1: Define Your Core Values by Brett & Kate McKay
http://www.artofmanliness.com/2009/05/31/30-days-to-a-better-man-day-1-define-your-core-values/

Improving Communication - Developing Effective Communication Skills
http://www.skillsyouneed.com/ips/improving-communication.html

14 Very Effective Communication Skills
http://advancedlifeskills.com/blog/14-very-effective-communication-skills/

Are You Sexually Compatible? by Dr Nerdlove
http://www.doctornerdlove.com/2014/08/are-you-sexually-compatible/

Sexual Compatibility: The Importance to Your Satisfaction by Kristen Mark, Ph.D., M.P.H
http://www.psychologytoday.com/blog/the-power-pleasure/201203/sexual-compatibility-the-importance-your-satisfaction

THIS Is Exactly How Much You SHOULD Be Gettin' It On by Lissa Rankin
http://www.yourtango.com/experts/lissa-rankin/sexual-frequency-how-much-sex-enough

What Is the Right Couple Sexual Style for You? by Barry W McCarthy Ph.D.
http://www.psychologytoday.com/blog/whats-your-sexual-style/200902/what-is-the-right-couple-sexual-style-you

Sexual Dysfunction
en.wikipedia.org/wiki/Sexual_dysfunction

5 Common Causes of Impotence by Rachel Nall, RN, BSN
http://www.healthline.com/health/erectile-dysfunction/common-causes-impotence#Overview1

Erectile Dysfunction
en.wikipedia.org/wiki/Erectile_dysfunction

Possible Causes of Premature Ejaculation
http://www.dred.com/uk/what-causes-premature-ejaculation.html

Premature Ejaculation
en.wikipedia.org/wiki/Premature_ejaculation

Impact of Child Abuse
http://www.asca.org.au/About/Resources/Impact-of-child-abuse.aspx

Internet porn appears to be "sex-negative" for many users
http://www.yourbrainonporn.com/porn-induced-sexual-dysfunction-growing-problem

Fear of Real Intimacy: Why do some people avoid what they want most? by Frances Cohen Praver Ph.D.
http://www.psychologytoday.com/blog/love-doc/200911/fear-real-intimacy

The Fear of Losing Control by Elliot D. Cohen Ph.D.
http://www.psychologytoday.com/blog/what-would-aristotle-do/201105/the-fear-losing-control

Uncovering the Truth: Why Women 'Fake It' by Jennifer Welsh
http://www.livescience.com/14451-fear-intimacy-faking-orgasm.html

Friends with benefits: The relationships where male and female friends have 'no strings' sex... but it's seldom that simple by Diana Appleyard
http://www.dailymail.co.uk/femail/article-2019124/Friends-benefits-Is-strings-sex-really-simple.html#ixzz3iRjLsRxl

Friends with Benefits: Sex is the icing on the cake of friendship by Aaron Ben-Zeév Ph.D.
http://www.psychologytoday.com/blog/in-the-name-love/201109/friends-benefits

How the 'Love Hormone' Works Its Magic by Brenda Goodman
http://www.webmd.com/sex-relationships/news/20131125/how-the-love-hormone-works-its-magic

Oxytocin
en.wikipedia.org/wiki/Oxytocin

Cuddle hormone holds the secret to looking beautiful: Whiff of oxytocin makes men find their partners more attractive
http://www.dailymail.co.uk/sciencetech/article-2513594/Cuddle-hormone-Oxytocin-holds-secret-looking-beautiful.html#ixzz3iRkf612D

Oxytocin: What Is It? What Does It Do?
http://www.medicalnewstoday.com/articles/275795.php

Friends with Benefits by John M. Grohol, Psy.D.
http://psychcentral.com/blog/archives/2008/11/03/friends-with-benefits/

Friends with Benefits: Can Women Handle It? by Marie Hartwell-Walker, Ed.D.
http://psychcentral.com/lib/friends-with-benefits-can-women-handle-it/

Can Sex Ever Be Casual?
http://www.psychologytoday.com/collections/201201/can-sex-ever-be-casual

The 13 Cardinal Rules of Being Friends With Benefits
http://stylecaster.com/friends-with-benefits-rules/#ixzz3iRldC6cn

The 10 Major Mistakes Most Women Make In Relationships
http://elitedaily.com/dating/the-10-major-mistakes-most-women-make-in-relationships/

10 Mistakes Women Make in a Relationship with a Man!
http://women2hire.tumblr.com/post/25920662648/10-mistakes-women-make-in-a-relationship-with-a-man

Material independence and emotional independence in relation to sex, socio economic status, population density, and college student adjustment by Danesh Karunanyake
http://www.researchgate.net/publication/27233042_Material_independence_and_emotional_independence_in_relation_to_sex_socio_economic_status_population_density_and_college_student_adjustment

Why Do Men Lie About Cheating by Marcelina Hardy, MSEd, BCC
http://dating.lovetoknow.com/Why_Do_Men_Lie_About_Cheating

Why men lie about cheating - What's In It For Them? (Updated on October 15, 2009)
http://staceyreece.hubpages.com/hub/why-men-lie-about-cheating

What EVERY woman needs to know about why men cheat... by a man who spent years talking to hundreds of unfaithful husbands
http://www.dailymail.co.uk/femail/article-1288748/What-EVERY-woman-needs-know-men-cheat--man-spent-years-talking-hundreds-unfaithful-husbands.html#ixzz3iRpEXx9J

The 10 Reasons Why Men Cheat: Some are just immature. Others have deeper issues. By Robert Weiss LCSW, CSAT-S on Oct 30, 2013 in Love and Sex
http://www.psychologytoday.com/blog/love-and-sex-in-the-digital-age/201310/the-10-reasons-why-men-cheat

Why men can never forgive a wife's affair... even though they'd expect YOU to forgive them by Keren Smedley
http://www.dailymail.co.uk/femail/article-1236435/Why-men-forgive-wifes-affair--theyd-expect-YOU-forgive-them.html#ixzz3iRq5R8N6

10 Warning Signs That Your Husband Is Cheating by Shelley Skas
http://www.yourtango.com/experts/shelley-skas/10-warning-signs-your-husband-cheating

Cheating Signs: 15 Signs Your Spouse Is About To Cheat
http://www.huffingtonpost.com/2013/08/13/cheating-signs_n_3750894.html

11 Signs That He Might Be Having an Affair by Kristin Koch
http://www.womansday.com/relationships/dating-marriage/advice/a1586/11-signs-that-he-might-be-having-an-affair-107288/

You think he's cheating on you - Is it intuition or insecurity? by Ruth Houston
http://www.examiner.com/article/you-think-he-s-cheating-on-you-is-it-intuition-or-insecurity

Is My Partner Cheating on Me? 7 Red Flags by Rori Raye
http://blog.havetherelationshipyouwant.com/difficult-situations/is-my-partner-cheating-on-me-7-red-flags/

Top 10: Reasons Women Take Back Cheaters by Giulia Simolo
http://uk.askmen.com/top_10/dating/top-10-reasons-women-take-back-cheaters.html

Why Women Stay With Cheating Men? by Laura Trice
http://www.huffingtonpost.com/laura-trice/5-reasons-women-stay-with_b_521936.html

Father Complex
en.wikipedia.org/wiki/Father_complex

Daughter and Father Complex Issues by Francis Hosein
http://www.selfgrowth.com/articles/daughter-and-father-complex-issues

Not Daddy's Little Girl by Sarah Ivens
http://www.marieclaire.com/sex-love/advice/a7189/daddy-issues/

Manipulative People: How to Deal with Them?
http://www.way-of-the-mind.com/manipulative-people.html

Five Things That Keep You Stuck With a Cheater by Chump Lady
http://www.chumplady.com/2012/07/five-things-that-keep-you-stuck-with-a-cheater/

The Dirty Tricks That Cheaters Use by Chris Baker
http://www.howtocatchacheaterguide.com/tricks-cheaters-use/

Typical Behaviors When Cheaters Get Caught by Steve Johnson
http://cheatingforthrillofit.blogspot.co.uk/2012/07/typical-behavior-when-cheaters-get.html

Could having an affair SAVE your marriage? British scientist recommends 'good infidelity' and looking to the French for inspiration on successful relationships by Anna Edwards
http://www.dailymail.co.uk/femail/article-2190860/Could-having-affair-save-marriage-British-scientist-recommends-good-infidelity-looking-French-inspiration-successful-relationships.html

When Partners Cheat: Who Deserves Second Chances? by Stephen A Diamond Ph.D. on Mar 28, 2010
http://www.psychologytoday.com/blog/evil-deeds/201003/when-partners-cheat-who-deserves-second-chances

Advice for Cheaters and Their Partners by Dr Phil
http://www.drphil.com/articles/article/127

Diagnosing A Dead-End Relationship by Jenny Block
http://www.yourtango.com/experts/jenny-block/diagnosing-dead-end-relationship

Dating tips 101 - ten early warning signs of a dead-end relationship by Deborrah Cooper
http://www.examiner.com/article/dating-tips-101-ten-early-warning-signs-of-a-dead-end-relationship

5 signs you're in a dead-end relationship by Anita Naik
http://www.netdoctor.co.uk/healthyliving/fivesigns.htm#ixzz3iVG8cCsP

5 Ways to End a Bad Relationship for Good by Juliana Breines Ph.D.
http://www.psychologytoday.com/blog/in-love-and-war/201303/5-ways-end-bad-relationship-good

Ending a Marriage - Arriving at the Decision
http://www.womansdivorce.com/ending-a-marriage.html

21 Signs Your Relationship Is Doomed by Thomas G Fiffer
http://goodmenproject.com/ethics-values/should-love-really-be-this-hard-21-signs-you-chose-the-wrong-partner-fiff/

10 Signs You're In The Wrong Relationship by Brittany Wong
http://www.huffingtonpost.com/2014/03/06/relationship-problems_n_4856149.html

17 subtle signs that your marriage or relationship is about to end by Ruth Houston
http://www.examiner.com/article/17-subtle-signs-that-your-marriage-or-relationship-is-about-to-end

12 Red Flags That Could Spell Doom For Your Relationship by Taryn Hillin
http://www.huffingtonpost.com/2014/05/15/bad-relationship-_n_5255994.html

Rebound Relationships by Mary C Lamia Ph.D.
http://www.psychologytoday.com/blog/intense-emotions-and-strong-feelings/201309/rebound-relationships

7 Signs You're In A Rebound Relationship by Jessica Booth
http://www.gurl.com/2013/02/22/what-is-a-rebound-relationship/#1

Withholding Emotional Involvement ~ Passive Abuse by Darlene Ouimet
http://emergingfrombroken.com/withholding-emotional-involvement-passive-abuse/#sthash.n53JYbXF.dpuf

50 Characteristics of Healthy Relationships by Alice Boyes Ph.D.
http://www.psychologytoday.com/blog/in-practice/201301/50-characteristics-healthy-relationships

Lightning Source UK Ltd.
Milton Keynes UK
UKOW06f0620280815

257661UK00001B/4/P